ABOUT THE AUTHORS

Nick Redfern is the author of 30 books on UFOs, Bigfoot, lake monsters, the Abominable Snowman, and Hollywood scandals, including *Monster Files, Monster Diary, Memoirs of a Monster Hunter; Celebrity Secrets; There's Something in the Woods; Contactees; Final Events; The Real Men in Black; The NASA Conspiracies; Science Fiction Secrets; On the Trail of the Saucer Spies; Strange Secrets;* and—with fellow Texas-based researcher and author Ken Gerhard—*Monsters of Texas.* He has appeared on more than 70 TV shows, including: Fox News; the BBC's *Out of This World;* the SyFy Channel's *Proof Positive;* the Space Channel's *Fields of Fear;* the History Channel's *Monster Quest, America's Book of Secrets, Ancient Aliens* and *UFO Hunters;* Science's *The Unexplained Files;* the National Geographic Channel's *Paranatural;* and MSNBC's *Countdown with Keith Olbermann.* Originally from the UK, Nick lives on the fringes of Dallas, Texas.

Award-winning writer **Brad Steiger** has devoted himself to exploring and examining unusual, hidden, secret, and otherwise strange occurrences. He has written over 2,000 articles and more than 180 titles with inspirational and paranormal themes, including *Conspiracies and Secret Societies; Real Aliens, Space Beings, and Creatures from Other Worlds; Real Ghosts, Restless Spirits, and Haunted Houses; Real Monsters, Gruesome Critters, and Beasts from the Darkside; Real Vampires, Night Stalkers, and Creatures from the Darkside;* and *Real Zombies, the Living Dead, and Creatures of the Apocalypse.* Brad is a veteran of broadcast news magazines ranging from *Nightline* to *NBC Nightly News.* He is also a regular radio guest on Jeff Rense's *Sightings, The Allan Handelman Show,* and *Coast to Coast with George Noory.* He resides somewhere in Iowa.

ALSO FROM VISIBLE INK PRESS

Alien Mysteries, Conspiracies and Cover-Ups
by Kevin D. Randle
ISBN: 978-1-57859-418-4

Conspiracies and Secret Societies: The Complete Dossier, 2nd edition
by Brad Steiger and Sherry Hansen Steiger
ISBN: 978-1-57859-368-2

The Government UFO Files: The Conspiracy of Cover-Up
by Kevin D. Randle
ISBN: 978-1-57859-477-1

Hidden Realms, Lost Civilizations, and Beings from Other Worlds
by Jerome Clark
ISBN: 978-1-57859-175-6

The Horror Show Guide: The Ultimate Frightfest of Movies
by Mike Mayo
ISBN: 978-1-57859-420-7

Real Aliens, Space Beings, and Creatures from Other Worlds
by Brad Steiger and Sherry Hansen Steiger
ISBN: 978-1-57859-333-0

Real Encounters, Different Dimensions, and Otherworldly Beings
by Brad Steiger and Sherry Hansen Steiger
ISBN: 978-1-57859-455-9

Real Ghosts, Restless Spirits, and Haunted Places, 2nd edition
by Brad Steiger
ISBN: 978-1-57859-401-6

Real Miracles, Divine Intervention, and Feats of Incredible Survival
by Brad Steiger and Sherry Hansen Steiger
ISBN: 978-1-57859-214-2

Real Monsters, Gruesome Critters, and Beasts from the Darkside
by Brad Steiger
ISBN: 978-1-57859-220-3

Real Vampires, Night Stalkers, and Creatures from the Darkside
by Brad Steiger
ISBN: 978-1-57859-255-5

Real Zombies, the Living Dead, and Creatures of the Apocalypse
by Brad Steiger
ISBN: 978-1-57859-296-8

Unexplained! Strange Sightings, Incredible Occurrences, and Puzzling Physical Phenomena, 3rd edition
by Jerome Clark
ISBN: 978-1-57859-344-6

The Vampire Book: The Encyclopedia of the Undead, 3rd edition
by J. Gordon Melton, Ph.D.
ISBN: 978-1-57859-281-4

The Werewolf Book: The Encyclopedia of Shape-shifting Beings, 2nd edition
by Brad Steiger
ISBN: 978-1-57859-367-5

The Witch Book: The Encyclopedia of Witchcraft, Wicca, and Neo-paganism
by Raymond Buckland
ISBN: 978-1-57859-114-5

"Real Nightmares" E-Books by Brad Steiger

Book 1: True and Truly Scary Unexplained Phenomenon

Book 2: The Unexplained Phenomena and Tales of the Unknown

Book 3: Things That Go Bump in the Night

Book 4: Things That Prowl and Growl in the Night

Book 5: Fiends That Want Your Blood

Book 6: Unexpected Visitors and Unwanted Guests

Book 7: Dark and Deadly Demons

Book 8: Phantoms, Apparitions, and Ghosts

Please visit us at visibleinkpress.com.

THE ZOMBIE BOOK

The Encyclopedia of the Living Dead

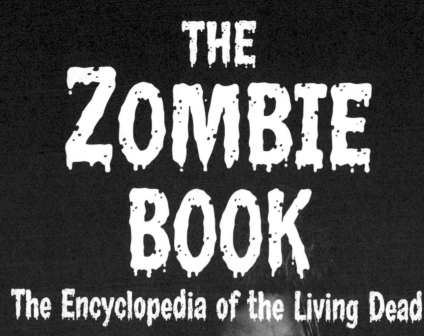

Nick Redfern

with Brad Steiger

VISIBLE
INK
PRESS

DETROIT

THE ZOMBIE BOOK

Visible Ink Press®
43311 Joy Rd., #414
Canton, MI 48187-2075

Visible Ink Press is a registered trademark of Visible Ink Press LLC.

Most Visible Ink Press books are available at special quantity discounts when purchased in bulk by corporations, organizations, or groups. Customized printings, special imprints, messages, and excerpts can be produced to meet your needs. For more information, contact Special Markets Director, Visible Ink Press, www.visibleink.com, or 734-667-3211.

Managing Editor: Kevin S. Hile
Art Director: Mary Claire Krzewinski
Typesetting: Marco DiVita
Proofreaders: Dorothy Smith and Aarti Stephens
Indexer: Shoshana Hurwitz

Cover images: Front cover image: iStock; back cover image: Kobal Collection.

ISBN: 978-1-57859-504-4 (paperback)
ISBN: 978-1-57859-530-3 (pdf ebook)
ISBN: 978-1-57859-532-7 (Kindle ebook)
ISBN: 978-1-57859-531-0 (ePub ebook)

Library of Congress Cataloging-in-Publication Data

Redfern, Nicholas, 1964–
  The zombie book : the encyclopedia of the living dead / by Nick Redfern and Brad Steiger.
    pages cm
  ISBN 978-1-57859-504-4 (paperback)
1. Zombies—Encyclopedias. I. Steiger, Brad. II. Title.
GR581.R43 2014
398.21—dc23   2014013300

Printed in the United States of America

10 9 8 7 6 5 4 3 2 1

CONTENTS

ACKNOWLEDGMENTS

Nick Redfern: I would like to offer my very sincere thanks to my agent, Lisa Hagan, without whose tireless work you would not be reading this book; my co-author, the near-legendary Brad Steiger; and everyone at Visible Ink Press.

Brad Steiger: Some special folks must be thanked for their esoteric skills and knowledge related to Voodoo, Hoodoo, sorcery, necromancy, and the spectres of New Orleans: Lisa Lee Harp Waugh, Laura Lee Mistycah, Aylne Pustanio, Paul Dale Roberts, and Ricardo Pustanio, who also contributed some brilliantly spooky art pieces, as well as portraits of contemporary Voodoo/Hoodoo priests and priestesses. As in every VIP endeavor which I undertake, the project soon becomes a collaborative effort. A grateful thanks to my co-author, Nick Redfern, a man of great talent, wit, and charm; our always helpful and painstakingly precise editor, Kevin Hile; our insightful publisher, Roger Jänecke; Mary Claire Krzewinski, creative art director; Shoshana Hurwitz for indexing; Dorothy Smith and Aarti Stephens, hardworking proofreaders; and my friend and favorite typesetter in the publishing world, Marco Di Vita. I must also thank the brightest light in my life, Sherry, who is always there to pull me out of the shadows when I stray too far into the darkness.

PHOTO CREDITS

INTRODUCTION

The zombie: it is a creature that provokes a wealth of emotional responses: menace, terror, panic, excitement, fascination, and trepidation all share equal, top billing. And it's not just the actions of the zombie that engineer such states of mind. It's the very name, too. Indeed, the "Z word" is one that hits home in near-primal fashion. Just mentioning it strikes a deep, chilling, and malignant chord in our subconscious, even if we're not overly sure why that should be so.

Perhaps it's the image of the rampaging, utterly driven, killing-machine, violently forcing its way into our homes. Maybe, as a result of the fraught, violent, and unpredictable world in which we now live, it's the growing association between the dead-returned and matters of a definitively apocalyptic nature. Or, possibly, it's all due to the sense that the zombie is an unstoppable form of evil; a shambling, marching, or running horror that threatens to overturn society and create a new world in its image, rather than in ours.

In short, the zombie offers us—the human race—one thing and one thing only: extinction. And we know that. As a result, we fear these soulless creatures. Yet, as highly intelligent entities, and ones keenly aware of our own precarious mortality, we find ourselves not just repelled by the zombie, but strangely, and almost hypnotically, drawn to both it and the future it promises of death, decay, and planet-wide devastation. Of course, in today's society, our perceptions of the zombie are primarily driven by the world of entertainment; that is to say, the likes of *The Walking Dead*, *World War Z*, and the *Resident Evil* movies.

But it hasn't always been like that. In fact, there was a time long gone when it was *nothing* like that.

The concept of the zombie has been with us for not just decades or even centuries. It has been an integral part of our myths, legends, folklore, and beliefs for thousands of years. Long before exotic viruses, biological warfare, and sinister military experiments brought the dead back to life in our cinemas and on our television screens, there were the dark spells and incantations of the ancient Egyptians, the Sumerians, and the Babylonians. Their high priests and priestesses sought to restore the dead to some semblance of life and to zombify the still-living. Their goal was to command both categories, to have them do the bidding of their human masters, and to control them—which is very different to the zombies of today that are definitely *out of control*. Within the culture of the Celts and the people of Haiti, Scandinavia, and Africa, belief that the recently deceased could be reanimated, and that the living could be reduced to zombie status and used in almost slave-like fashion, was widespread centuries ago. Today, the zombie serves as entertainment. Back then, it simply served.

In the 1930s and 1940s, the screenwriters, producers and directors of movies of the dead—such as *King of the Zombies, White Zombie,* and *I Walked with a Zombie*—were near-exclusively inspired by Haitian traditions, by Voodoo beliefs, and by sinister spells and incantations. And, invariably, the zombie presence in old-school Hollywood was focused on one locale, such as an isolated island or a creepy old mansion. Zombie hordes devouring the living, the end of the world, and Armageddon-style, worldwide disaster were nowhere in sight. It was not until 1968, when George A. Romero unleashed a certain movie—*Night of the Living Dead*—onto the masses that the zombie largely left the domains of Voodoo and magic behind and entered a new, and far more savage, realm. That realm was, and still is, filled with viruses, bites, infection, and worldwide chaos.

There can be no doubt, however, that the rise of the zombies reached—pardon the pun—epidemic proportions in the first years of the twenty-first century—in fact, post-9-11. When the terrible events of September 11, 2001, occurred, and the United States was faced with its worst nightmare since Pearl Harbor, waves of terror, vulnerability, fear, chaos, distrust, and paranoia swept across the land and quickly infected millions. And something else happened. Perhaps provoked by the shock of assuming it was invulnerable to the types of terrorist attacks that had dominated the Middle East for years, and those that the Irish Republican Army (IRA) unleashed on the British Isles in the 1970s and 1980s, whole swathes of American society became caught up in the idea that the end was near.

There were those who believed that the invasions of Iraq and Afghanistan were not simply modern day equivalents of the Vietnam War or the Korean War. Rather, rabid religious extremists loudly proclaimed and screamed this was a Holy War of literal proportions—that is to say, the beginning of the final battle between good and evil, between God and Satan. Armageddon was on the horizon. Even Hollywood was bitten by the apocalyptic bug. Movies like *The Day After Tomorrow, Contagion, Knowing, 2012,* and *The Road* make that amply clear.

Television was also caught up in such matters. *Life after People,* a History Channel series, aired from 2008 to 2009. It told of what the world of the future would be like if the humans were eradicated. The first episode—which aired in January 2008—was the History Channel's highest-rated show *ever*. Similarly, since 2012 the National Geographic Channel has broadcast a series titled *Doomsday Preppers.* Each episode focuses on different, real-life individuals, or families, preparing for what they believe will be the end of society, whether by an irreversible collapse of the U.S. electrical grid, an economic meltdown, a polar-shift, gigantic solar-flares, or numerous other scenarios. It may not come as a surprise, at this point, to learn that *Doomsday Preppers* is NGC's most successful series since the channel was launched in 1997. And what about the most-watched, basic-cable series of all time, *The Walking Dead?* That series has become far less a TV show and far more a global phenomenon. And it's surely no coincidence that the fascination with zombie-based "end-of-the-world" scenarios has increased as America's obsession with the "End Times" grows.

This has led to an intriguing, but perhaps inevitable, development. Or, rather, to an intriguing suspicion: there are growing numbers of people who now fully accept that a real-life, zombie-driven Armageddon is on the horizon and getting ever closer. Fingers of the paranoid variety are being pointed at "them," and at "the government." Gun-toting loons who live in the woods and sport names like Billy-Bob and Bubba are preparing for the day when they believe the dead really will rise from the grave and overwhelm the rest of us. There is whispered talk of numerous government agencies secretly buying up massive amounts of bullets and guns, all anticipating the day when millions of the living suddenly become the dead, and then, shortly afterwards, turn into the not-quite-so dead, after all. Welcome to the world of the zombie conspiracy-theorists.

Then there are the zombie walks. Definitively social events, they involve thousands of people all agreeing to meet at one particular locale, on a specific time and date, and dressing up to resemble the staggering dead. A good time is had by one and all, living out fantasies of the infected sort. Such is the allure of becoming just about the closest thing to a real zombie as is possible that in October 2012 a stunning 25,000-plus people transformed themselves for a zombie walk in Buenos Aires, Argentina.

What all of this tells us is that the zombie takeover is not just a conspiracy theory, a dream, a nightmare, or a fantasy. It's already a done deal. In the final episode of season two of *The Walking Dead*, the lead-character, Deputy Sheriff Rick Grimes, famously stated: "We're all infected." And we are. We're not infected with a deadly virus that transforms people into homicidal monsters and that leads to the collapse of society, however. Rather, we're infected with *a fascination for the concept* of a deadly virus that transforms people into homicidal monsters and that leads to the collapse of society. And just like the zombie outbreaks of television, movies, graphic novels, video games, and more, the human infection of fascination is growing at what appears to be an unstoppable and incredible rate.

With that all said, it's now time to take a trip into the A-to-Z world of the dead, the bitten, the reanimated, the monsters of the apocalypse, or, as this type of unholy creature is far better known, the zombie.

AIDS

See also: Alien Infection, Alien Virus, Black Death, Creutzfeld-Jacobs Disease, Infection, Spanish Flu

When, in a wholly fictional setting, a zombie outbreak begins, it is usually accompanied by massive amounts of fear and hysteria. In real life, perhaps the closest thing to have ever mirrored that same fictional hysteria and fear came in the 1980s, when the AIDS crisis began. Over-the-top demands, to the effect that the infected should be rounded up and placed in isolation, circulated widely and wildly. Crazed, religious types asserted loudly that AIDS—Acquired Immunodeficiency Syndrome—was God's very own, unique way of punishing homosexuals for their "sins." There was mass confusion—just about everywhere—on how infection could be contained or spread.

These issues and concerns are all remarkably similar to—in fact, almost identical to—those that we have seen in movies, novels, comic-books and television productions of the undead variety. There is another parallel between AIDS and zombies, too: the theory that the virus—whether in reality or in fiction—was created by top secret U.S. government experimentation gone disastrously wrong.

History has shown, however, that with regard to AIDS, the original allegations to this effect surfaced from disinformation spread by experts and psychological-warfare operatives within the heart of the former Soviet Union's KGB. Background data on the KGB's involvement in spreading rumors—to the effect that the U.S. government deliberately engineered HIV (Human Immunodeficiency Virus) as a weapon of biological warfare to wipe out significant numbers of the population—were addressed in a

2005 paper prepared by the U.S. Department of State. Titled *AIDS as a Biological Weapon*, it notes:

"When the AIDS disease was first recognized in the early 1980s, its origins were a mystery. A deadly new disease had suddenly appeared, with no obvious explanation of what had caused it. In such a situation, false rumors and misinformation naturally arose, and Soviet disinformation specialists exploited this situation as well as the musings of conspiracy theorists to help shape their brief but highly effective disinformation campaign on this issue.

"In March, 1992, then-Russian intelligence chief, and later Russian Prime Minister Yevgeni Primakov, admitted that the disinformation service of the Soviet KGB had concocted the false story that the AIDS virus had been created in a U.S. military laboratory as a biological weapon. The Russian newspaper *Izvestia* reported on March 19, 1992:

"'[Primakov] mentioned the well known articles printed a few years ago in our central newspapers about AIDS supposedly originating from secret Pentagon laboratories. According to Yevgeni Primakov, the articles exposing U.S. scientists' 'crafty' plots were fabricated in KGB offices. The Soviets eventually abandoned the AIDS disinformation campaign under pressure from the U.S. government in August 1987."

These particular revelations from the Department of State lead us to an interesting possibility. Currently, there are huge numbers of conspiracy-based stories on the Internet, all telling of a looming, real-life zombie outbreak that will result from top secret medical- and virology-based programs initiated by U.S. authorities. Most people might be inclined to dismiss such scenarios as the work of tinfoil-hat-wearing lunatics. But, maybe that's not the case after all. Perhaps they are the work of hostile forces working to provoke anxiety across a land that is now obsessed with, and by, zombies. After all, if the Soviet Union's KGB could have done it so successfully with the AIDS virus in the 1980s, perhaps shadowy forces in the Age of Terror are doing likewise with the zombie virus.

Aldini, Giovanni

While most people are content to let the dead remain dead—even if they would dearly like to see their loved ones just one last time—that is certainly not always the case. Take, for example, Giovanni Aldini. Although many have seen fit to dismiss him as an outright crank, or as a definitive mad professor-type, this is not the case at all. Born in 1762, Aldini, at the age of thirty-six, achieved the position of a professor of physics at the University of Bologna, in northern Italy. Although much of his work was focused upon issues of a very much down to earth nature—such as coming up with new and novel lights and lamps to illuminate lighthouses—there was a darker, and highly controversial, side to Aldini, too.

It's important to note that Aldini was the nephew of one Luigi Galvani, also of the University of Bologna. Galvani—from whose name the term "galvanism" is direct-

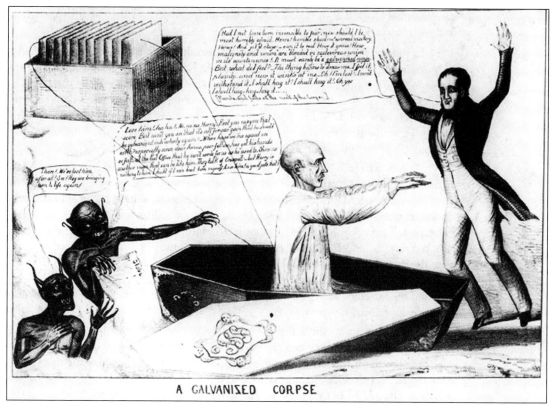

A GALVANISED CORPSE

This cartoon from 1836 shows Giovanni Aldini "raising the dead" by running an electric current through the nervous system of a corpse. It was Giovanni's Uncle Luigi Galvani who discovered what became known as galvinization when he noticed that stimulating the nerves of a dead frog with a scalpel caused its muscles to twitch.

ly derived—was someone who spent a great deal of time experimenting on dead frogs. Galvani came to realize that while it was not possible to breathe new life into the dead creatures, directing an electric current through the spinal cord of the frogs caused the creatures to twitch and move as if they *were* alive—or had been successfully brought back from the other side. Not only was Aldini deeply influenced by the work of his Uncle Luigi, he took matters yet another step further. It was, in fact, just about the most controversial step of them all that anyone could take.

To say that Aldini *literally* reanimated the dead would be incorrect. It would be right on target, however, to say that he animated them. And he did so in a fashion that followed directly in the path of Luigi Galvani. But Aldini's grisly experiments were not undertaken on frogs: his test-subjects were nothing less than the human dead. Such was the scale of the public and media fascination with Aldini's work in the fields of galvanism—that some even perceived as being outright devilish in nature—he traveled the length and breadth of Europe demonstrating how, in an uncanny and disturbing fashion, the dead could be made to appear not quite so dead, after all. As was the case with his Uncle Luigi, Aldini's work was all based around the careful application and use of electric currents.

Certainly, the most memorable and fear-inducing of all Aldini's experiments occurred in 1803, at the London, England-based Royal College of Surgeons. Aldini's test-subject was a man named George Forster, who had been hanged by the neck on January 18, 1803, after being found guilty of murdering—by drowning—both his wife and his youngest child. Aldini wasted no time in securing Forster's fresh corpse for his strange experimentation. The result was uncanny and amazing: only mere hours after his death, Forster was on the move again, so to speak.

As a captivated and spellbound audience looked on in near-hypnotic fashion, Aldini attached two conducting rods to a large battery. The other ends of the rods were affixed, respectively, to Forster's right ear and mouth. When the surge of electricity hit Forster's body with full force, something incredible and obscene occurred: Forster's left-eye opened wide, appearing to stare wildly and malevolently at the shocked crowds, and his jaw began to move and quiver, as if he was about to utter something awful and guttural. If that was not enough to provoke terror in all those in attendance, when the electrified rods were attached to Forster's right arm, his hand rose and his fist clenched. There were audible gasps in the audience and more than a couple even fainted on the spot.

Aldini was not a carnival showman, however. That's to say he did not deceive his audiences into thinking that he had literally raised the dead. Certainly, he was careful to point out that the power of electricity only *appeared* to make the dead come back to life. Nevertheless, in later years, and hardly surprisingly, Aldini became known as a definitive, real-life Dr. Frankenstein, even though he was actually nothing of the sort. Aldini died in 1834, at the age of seventy-two. His reputation as an animator of the dead remains intact two centuries after his death (from which, in case you may be wondering, he did not return).

Alien Abductions

See also: Body Snatchers, Cattle Mutilations

Make mention of the emotive words "alien abduction" and most people will have at least some degree of understanding of the concept, even if they aren't students of the UFO phenomenon. Since the early 1960s, countless individuals—all across the world—have made astonishing claims to the effect that they have been kidnapped and experimented upon in bizarre fashion, by emotionless, dwarfish entities sporting large bald heads and huge, black, insect-like eyes. Those same alleged alien entities have become known as the Grays. Their helpless and terrified victims are the abductees.

A wealth of theories exists to try and explain what may be afoot when darkness sets in and the Grays surface from their hidden lairs. While the skeptics and the debunkers prefer to relegate everything to the realm of nightmarish dreams, sleep disorders, hoaxes, and fantasy, not everyone is quite so sure that is all that is going on. Many UFO researchers believe that the Grays are on a significant and serious evolutionary decline, and that to try and save their waning species, they secretly harvest DNA, blood, cells, eggs, sperm, and much more from the human race. They then use all of this acquired material in sophisticated gene-splicing-style programs to boost their waning bodies and repair their weakened immune systems. There is, however, a much darker theory than that.

Numerous so-called alien abductees—usually when rendered into hypnotic states and regressed to the time of the presumed other-world experience—describe the Grays implanting into their bodies or under the surface of their skin, small, metallic devices. We are talking here about what have become infamously known as "alien implants." If such an astonishing and controversial claim has even a nugget of truth attached to it, then what might be the purpose of these sinister actions? Some flying saucer sleuths have suggested that the implanted devices allow the aliens to secretly track the movements of the abductees throughout their entire lives—thus permitting their extraterrestrial captors to find them, and extract even more cells and DNA, no matter where the people live or to where they might move.

There is a mind-blowing variant on this controversial theory, however. It is one that suggests that implants are put in place to control the minds of the abductees. And here is where things become decidedly sinister and downright zombie-like. Imagine, if you will, millions of people, all across the planet, and all implanted with highly sophisticated devices fashioned in another world. Imagine, too, that the day finally comes when E.T.—a definitively hostile creature very far removed from Steven Spielberg's *E.T.*—decides to take over the planet. But the aliens don't choose to do so via a massive show of force, or by pummeling our cities and landscapes with terrible, futuristic weaponry in *Independence Day*-style. No; instead, they get the abductees to do their dirty work for them.

One day—those researchers who adhere to this particularly controversial theory believe—all of those millions of currently dormant implants will be "switched on." For all intents and purposes, each and every one of the abductees will then suddenly become a mind-controlled, lethal killer. We will wake one morning to frightful scenes of utter carnage on the streets, as the zombified abductees follow their pre-programmed assignments in violent and crazed fashion, which might range from sabotaging missile bases, destroying buildings, and going on wild and rampaging killing sprees. But, it won't be occurring just here or there. It will be on your very doorstep. It will be on all of our doorsteps. It will be *everywhere*. And there will be no stopping it.

The world as we know it will be plunged into utter chaos as the implanted—rather than the infected—do their utmost to wipe out the rest of us for their extraterrestrial masters. And, when the war is finally over and humankind has been decimated and practically destroyed, the aliens will then trigger the release of a deadly virus that currently lies dormant within the implants. In quick time, the implanted will all be dead, too, allowing those hostile invaders from the stars to take over without the need for even a single shot from the average, alien ray-gun or laser-weapon. In view of the above, should you one day encounter someone who claims to be an alien abductee, it might be most wise to follow that one word which so often gets shouted, in fear-filled tones, in just about every zombie movie at some point or another: "Run!"

Alien Infection

See also: AIDS, Alien Virus, Black Death, Creutzfeld-Jacobs Disease, Infection, Spanish Flu

There can be absolutely no doubt at all that one of the most controversial, and some would say outrageous, developments in the field of UFO research surfaced in 1999, when a researcher by the name of Philip Duke, Ph.D., suggested that both cattle mutilations and alien abductions were connected with a nefarious extraterrestrial plot to conquer the Earth by infecting the human population with HIV, and creating a plague-like situation in which the thousands of infected would soon become the millions, then the billions, and, finally, to the point where, as Rick Grimes of *The Walking Dead* so famously and memorably worded it: "We're all infected."

Cattle mutilations, for those who may not be aware of the phenomenon, have gone on for decades. All across the United States, since at least 1967, shocked ranchers have found cows with their organs and bodily fluids extracted via what appears to

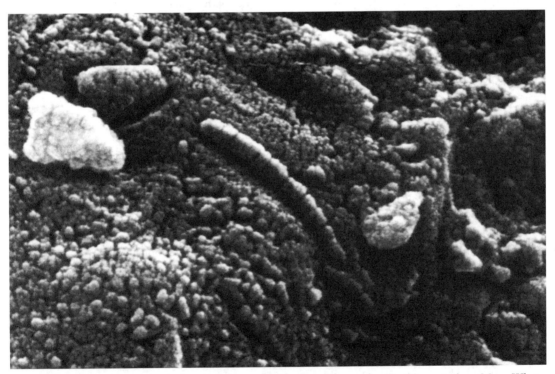

This 1996 photo from NASA shows what many scientists thought were fossilized bacteria from Mars. What if some microorganism like this came to Earth with dire consequences?

be highly skilled means. We are not talking about predators in the slightest. Or, it's more accurate to say that we are not talking about predators as we generally understand the term.

According to Philip Duke's personal hypothesis, so-called cattle mutilations are "logically explainable only as extraterrestrial activities. The mutilation body materials taken, all correspond with sites of HIV transmission or replication (blood) in humans, except for the ear, which may contain a locator device. Circumstantial evidence suggests cattle are mutilated primarily to harvest HIV antibodies and virus from blood in quantity, and to obtain information relating to possible HIV transmission in humans."

And what, exactly, might be the purpose? Hold onto your hats very tightly as we're about to go on a wild ride. Duke adds, on the matter of visiting aliens: "We have a whole new wonderful world, teeming with life, just waiting for them. There is only one thing standing in their way—that is us. Attack us openly, we would retaliate, and they would inherit a radioactive biosphere wasteland. No—the smart thing is to secretly destroy our civilization, and with it our means of organized (atomic) retaliation by employing a Biological Warfare (BW) agent. That agent is HIV. When enough people are sick, dying, and dead from AIDS, then alien colonization will proceed openly."

Is Philip Duke's controversial scenario one of outrageous fantasy and nothing else? Or, incredibly, is it a warning of a dark and dire future that awaits us all, a future dominated by a deadly virus, the apocalypse and the extinction of the entire human race? Time may one day tell. Although, let us all earnestly hope it doesn't.

Alien Virus

See also: AIDS, Alien Infection, Black Death, Creutzfeld-Jacobs Disease, Infection

In the 1968 movie, *Night of the Living Dead*, speculation was raised that the birth of the zombies was possibly triggered by the actions of a U.S. spacecraft. While visiting Venus, the craft, it was surmised, became contaminated by extraterrestrial radiation and, as a result, on its return to Earth let loose that same radiation upon an unsuspecting populace. The outcome: the dead soon walked. And they had no intention of stopping. Is it truly feasible that such a thing could actually occur in the real world?

In a fictional format, at least, a somewhat similar scenario was famously played out in the 1969 book *The Andromeda Strain* (which was written by Michael Crichton of *Jurassic Park* and *Congo* fame), and in the subsequent 1971 movie adaptation of the same name. Although zombies do not appear in either the novel or the film, pretty much everything else does. An American space probe, returning to Earth, unleashes a deadly alien virus that, in its tiny, microbial form, attaches itself to the craft before its reentry into the planet's atmosphere and its crash in the wilds of Arizona. Deaths amount with alarming speed as the U.S. government struggles to find an antidote

James Olson plays a scientist trying to stop a deadly plague from outer space in the 1971 film *The Andromeda Strain*.

before the virus threatens to wipe out the entire human race. While *The Andromeda Strain* is just a highly entertaining, but disturbing and thought provoking story, it does, rather incredibly, have real life counterparts.

As amazing as it may sound, NASA and numerous other worldwide space agencies, military bodies, and governmental agencies have taken serious steps to prevent the human race from falling victim to an extraterrestrial hazard of the viral kind. According to the text of *Article IX* of *The Treaty on Principles Governing the Activities of States in the Exploration and Use of Outer Space, Including the Moon and Other Celestial Bodies*, that was collectively signed at Washington, D.C., London, England, and Moscow, Russia on January 27, 1967, and that was entered into force on October 10 of that year:

"In the exploration and use of outer space, including the Moon and other celestial bodies, States' Parties to the Treaty shall be guided by the principle of cooperation and mutual assistance and shall conduct all their activities in outer space, including the Moon and other celestial bodies, with due regard to the corresponding interests of all other States' Parties to the Treaty."

Most significant of all is the next section of the document: "States' Parties to the Treaty shall pursue studies of outer space, including the Moon and other celestial bodies, and conduct exploration of them so as to avoid their harmful contamination and also adverse changes in the environment of the Earth resulting from the introduction of extraterrestrial matter and, where necessary, shall adopt appropriate measures for this purpose."

It must be stressed that the main concern described in the document revolved around the fear that a deadly virus would be mistakenly released into the Earth's atmosphere, a worldwide pandemic would begin, and an unstoppable plague would escalate, ultimately killing each and every one of us. But what if that same pandemic didn't just kill us, but soon thereafter brought us back from the grave, in the forms of billions of terrifying, violent killers, all intent on preying on human flesh and nothing else?

It might sound just like the hypothesis outlined in *Night of the Living Dead*, until the realization hits home that the plans to cope with the outbreak of an alien virus were discussed, and planned for, by the highest echelons of NASA, the space programs of the former Soviet Union and the United Kingdom, and the governments of numerous other nations—and decades ago, too. Preparing for the sudden surfacing of an alien-originated pandemic may not mean that government officials are also secretly anticipating that a zombie apocalypse will be far behind. On the other hand, there's nothing to suggest they *aren't* secretly planning for just such a possibility.

Andes Cannibals

There can surely be very few people who do not find the notion of cannibalism to be wholly abhorrent. It is one of the world's major, long lasting taboos—unless, that is, you happen to be one of the undead, in which case it is practically *de rigueur* to chow down on the human race. It must be said, however, that none of us can say with complete and utter certainty that, when faced with a grim death by starvation, we would not resort to devouring the newly deceased. In all likelihood we would not do so eagerly, but, as a necessity, it might not be out of the question. Just such a situation occurred in 1972, high in the mountains of the Andes, when, after a plane crash, the survivors were forced to do the unthinkable and feed on the dead.

The date was October 13, 1972, and a Montevideo, Uruguay-based rugby team—the Old Christians Club—was flying to Chile, where they were to play an opposing team. The game, however, was destined never to take place. The crew of the aircraft, a Fairchild FH227D, made a fatal error during their descent towards the city of Curico, Chile. Powerful headwinds slowed the plane to a significant degree, leading the crew to become completely confused as to their exact location. Coupled with the fact that, at the time, the vast Andes was covered by dense clouds, the crew became further disoriented and began their descent while still travelling through the mountains, rather than after they had exited the huge range. The result was just about as disastrous as conceivably possible: the plane clipped two peaks, both wings were violently severed, an entire section of the remaining fuselage was torn open, and the remains of the plane slammed into a peak now called the Glacier of Tears.

Carnage, chaos, and death reigned supreme: five people lost their lives when they were sucked out of the gaping hole as the plane made its tumultuous descent. Four died in the crash itself. Three failed to last the first night. One passed away the following day. Another one lingered on for about a week before finally dying. Seven were tragically killed during a powerful avalanche. And three more died as the weeks progressed. Incredibly, however, sixteen managed to survive against the harshness of Mother Nature and the effects of the impact.

There were, however, two major problems facing those that were still clinging on to life. First, since the crew had become severely confused concerning their location prior to the crash, there was major uncertainty on the part of search and rescue teams regarding the actual location of the impact site. As a result, the search was abandoned after eleven days. The survivors were now all alone. And second, there was even worse news: since the flight was not a long one, provisions on the plane had been kept to an absolute minimum. A few snacks and candy bars aside, there was nothing to eat. Fortunately, snow could easily be converted into water, which prevented death from dehydration. It wasn't very long, however, before the survivors of the crash weren't just hungry—they were *starving*. There was only one possible way for them to keep going, if they chose to take it, that is. It involved breaking that aforementioned taboo.

One of the survivors, Nando Parrado, commented later that even though the hunger of those still alive grew to voracious levels, they did all they could to stave off the near-inevitable, such as even contemplating eating the cushioning material contained in the seats of the aircraft. It was all to no avail, however. Finally, the decision that nobody wanted to take *was* taken: since the cold weather, the ice, and the snow combined had prevented decomposition from setting in, the dead would serve as food. Like it or not, there was no choice if the group was to survive longer than a few more days. It was a decidedly grim task, since most of the dead had been very good friends of the survivors. Resorting to cannibalism worked very well, however: by feeding on the meat of the dead, the sixteen that were still alive managed to keep starvation at bay until they were finally rescued on December 23, some two months after the terrible accident that led man to devour man, high on the Andes.

Ants

While the human race has yet to experience a zombie outbreak of the type that decimates society to a massive degree, such a thing has most assuredly already occurred in other species. Take, for example, the ant. Ants are particularly susceptible to a particular kind of fungus that has the startling ability to control their mental faculties and use and manipulate them in what is very much a zombie-like state. It's a fungus called *Ophiocordyceps unilateralis*. As to how and why this particular fungus works so well, one only has to take a look at the movie version of *World War Z*, which was based on Max Brooks' novel of the same name.

One of the main reasons why the movie was given a "13" certificate, rather than a "Restricted" rating, was because it one hundred percent lacked the graphic slaughtering and devouring of the uninfected that are staple parts of *The Walking Dead*, *Night of the Living Dead*, and *Day of the Dead*. Certainly, in Brooks' novel, the zombies act like the typical reanimated cannibals we have all come to know and love: there is lots of blood, gore, and the living torn to pieces.

The movie, however, makes two very drastic changes from the approach of the book: (a) the infected are of the fast-running kind, rather than of the slow and steady variety; and (b) those affected by the virus are not driven to kill and eat people—in the slightest. In fact, quite the opposite is the case: the sole goal of the mutated monsters is to spread the virus by infecting as many unfortunate souls as possible. After the infected bite down hard on their victims, they simply move onto the next person, and the next, and the next. Eating the attacked in bloody fashion isn't even a part of the equation, hence the "13" certificate. Those who unfortunately fall victim to a bite transform within a matter of seconds, or minutes, and are equally driven to spread the infection. And this all brings us back to *Ophiocordyceps unilateralis* and the ant population.

In the same way that in the *World War Z* movie, the spreading of the virus is the *only* goal of the zombies, *Ophiocordyceps unilateralis* acts in an extremely similar fashion: it's all about survival and absolutely nothing else. The whole process eerily mirrors the average zombie movie. *Ophiocordyceps unilateralis* is what is known as a parasitoid. In essence, the virus relies upon a host to allow it to live and thrive. The zombies of the *World War Z* movie chose us. *Ophiocordyceps unilateralis* chooses ants, specifically one kind: *Camponotus leonardi*, the carpenter ant.

The deadliest part of a zombie is not the creature itself, but its mouth, which, via a savage bite, spreads the undead virus, usually in mere seconds. It is very much the same with *Ophiocordyceps unilateralis* too: it's not so much the fungus itself that the ants have to be wary and worried of, but its spores. As soon as the spores enter an ant's body, it's already a case of game over. And that is when another zombie parallel occurs: the brain of the ant becomes

Ants can be infected with fungi that modify their behavior, turning them into insect zombies.

significantly affected, to the point where its behavior becomes erratic in the extreme. Also mirroring the average zombie outbreak and the actions of the survivors, the uninfected ants are able to recognize those that have turned and they quickly remove them from the colony in an effort to prevent the beginning and escalation of an ant apocalypse.

Certainly, removing the infected is the only option available, since there is no cure for the fungal infection. Those ants affected by the spores are destined for short, horrific and very strange lives. In an acutely weird fashion, the zombie ants effectively become mind-controlled by the fungus and are driven to find a nearby tree, to climb it, and to bite down hard on one of its leaves. That's right: just like their human equivalents, the ants of the dead deliver savage bites. This is not done as a means to devour or infect the plant, however. Rather, the purpose is to provide a stable surface for the parasitoid to thrive on: when the teeth clamp down, they never let go. Very appropriately, and when also addressing the zombie parallels, this action is termed the "death grip."

At that point, and now completely done with controlling the mind of the ant, *Ophiocordyceps unilateralis* invades, to a massive degree, the body of its host. The ant is not digested, however. Rather, the fungus has the remarkable ability to actually strengthen the body of the ant and turns its skeleton into nothing less than a form of highly effective armor. There is a very good reason for this: this particular parasitoid is reliant upon a heavily protected host in which it can thrive without being threatened by outside forces, such as other fungus, as well as insects, birds, or small animals that may try and eat the ant. With the jaws of the ant still clamped on the leaf—even in death—and its body turned into a toughened shell, there is very little chance of the fungus, growing deep inside the body of the ant, being adversely affected. To further ensure that the ant remains firmly affixed to the leaf, the fungus not only grows within its host, but it also starts to spread outwards. Tough threads, known as mycelium, break through the surface skin of the ant and affix themselves to the leaf, thereby allowing for additional support.

Finally, the sporocarp, on which the spores of *Ophiocordyceps unilateralis* develop, tears its way through the neck of the ant and stands tall in stalk-like fashion. Roughly a week or so later, the spores are released and the process of infection, of yet more and more ants, begins again. And again. And again. To the average human, a zombie-like ant apocalypse might not sound like a big deal. But try telling that to the ants.

Apocalypse

See also: Armageddon, End Times, Megiddo, Norwegian Armageddon

In the Jewish tradition, apocalyptic thought presupposes a universal history in which the Divine Author of that history will manifest His secrets in a dramatic End-Time that, with finality, will establish the God of Israel as the one true God. The end of days (*Acharit Hayamin*) is bound up with the coming of the Messiah, but before he arrives, governments will become increasingly corrupt, religious schools will become heretical, the wisdom of the scribes and teachers will become blasphemous, young people will shame their elders, and members of families will turn upon one another. Then, just prior to the arrival of the Messiah, the righteous of Israel shall defeat the armies of evil and monsters that have gathered under the banner of Gog and Magog, and the exiles shall return to the Holy Land.

The advent of the Messiah promises a great Day of Judgment in which the dead shall rise from their graves to begin a new life. During the period known as the World to Come (*Olam Haba*), the righteous will join the Messiah in partaking of a great banquet in which all foods, even those previously judged impure, shall be declared kosher. All the many nations of the world will communicate in one language, the Angel of Death will be slain by God, trees and crops will produce fresh harvests each month, the warmth of the sun shall heal the sick, and the righteous will be nourished forever by the radiance of God.

To most orthodox Christians, the profound meaning of the New Testament is that Jesus Christ will one day return in the Last Days and his Second Coming will prompt the resurrection of the dead and the Final Judgment. The heart of the gospels is eschatological, end-oriented. The essential theme of Jesus and the apostles is that the last stage of history, the End-Time, was being entered into with his appearance.

But John the Revelator does present monsters in Revelation, the last book in the New Testament, and he provides a guidebook for the Christian on what to expect during the time of Tribulation. Specifically, the book was written for the members of the churches of Ephesus, Smyrna, Pergamum, Thyatira, Sardis, Philadelphia, and Laodicea in order to prepare them for what John the Revelator believed to be a fast-approaching time of persecution and the return of Jesus Christ.

The first terrible beings arrive when the Seven Seals are opened (Revelation 6:12) by the Lamb (Christ). This action discloses a conquering king astride a white horse, the first of the Four Horsemen of the Apocalypse. Some believe this to be Jesus, but since no good comes of his arrival, more contemporary scholars maintain that this is the Antichrist in disguise.

The Second Seal (6:34) reveals the red horse, representing civil war; the third, the black horse, symbolizing famine (6:56); the fourth, the pale horse, representing the suffering that follows war and famine. The Fifth Seal to be opened by the Lamb yields a vision of the persecution of the Church throughout history and during the Last Days.

When the Sixth Seal is revealed, it displays the coming signs of a great Day of Wrath when there will be earthly upheavals, a darkened sun, stars falling from the heavens, mountains and islands removed, and more strife and revolution throughout the nations.

The Seventh and final Seal releases seven trumpets that sound the triumphant blast signaling the approach of the final and everlasting victory of Christ over the Kingdoms of the World.

Rising out of the abyss to block Christ's triumph at Armageddon is a monstrous army of demons, some resembling locusts and scorpions, others a repulsive mixture of human, horse, and lion. This motley crew of hideous demons is soon joined by 200,000 serpentine-leonine horsemen capable of belching fire, smoke, and brimstone. Led

The Four Horsement of the Apocalypse is a fifteenth-century engraving by German artist Albrecht Dürer. The horsemen symbolize the Conquest, War, Famine, and Death that will come with the Apocalypse.

by Satan, the once-trusted angel who led the rebellion against God in Heaven, the Prince of the World sets his legions upon the faithful to make their lives as miserable as possible in the End-Time.

To make matters even more complex for those who serve God, the greatest monster of all time, the Antichrist, appears on the scene pretending to be the Lamb, the Messiah. John the Revelator is told that this man, this Beast in lamb's clothing, can be recognized by a name, the letters of which, when regarded as numbers, total 666.

Although the term Antichrist is frequently used by those Christians who adhere to the New Testament book of Revelation as a literal guide to the time of the End of Days, which they feel is upon us, the word is nowhere to be found within its text. It is, however, very likely from the apostle John that we first learn of the Antichrist. In 1 John 2:18, he declares that the enemy of Christ has manifested and that many false teachers have infiltrated the Christian ranks, and in 2 John, verse 7 he declares that there are many deceivers already at work among the faithful.

At last Christ and his angelic armies of light destroy the forces of darkness at Armageddon in the final battle of good versus evil. Babylon, the False Prophet, and the Beast (the Antichrist) are dispatched to their doom, and Satan, the Dragon, is bound in a pit for a thousand years. With Satan imprisoned and chained, the millennium, the Thousand Years of peace and harmony, begins.

Although Christ's Second Coming is said to be mentioned over 300 times in the New Testament, the only references to the millennium are found in Revelation 20:27. Christian scholars disagree whether or not there will be an initial resurrection of the dead just at the advent of the millennium and a second one a thousand years later, immediately prior to the Final Day of Judgment.

For some rather incomprehensible reason, Satan is released from the pit at the conclusion of the millennium; and true to his nature, he makes a furious attempt to regain his earthly kingdom. His former allies, The Beast (the Antichrist), the False Prophet, and the hordes of Babylon, were destroyed at Armageddon, but there were some demons who escaped annihilation at the great battle who stand ready to serve their master. In addition to these evil creatures, Satan summons Gog and his armies of the Magog nations to join them in attacking the saints and the righteous followers of God. Although the vast multitude of vile and wicked servants of evil and grotesque monsters quickly surrounds the godly men and women, God's patience with the rebellious angel has come to an end. Fire blasts down from Heaven, engulfing and destroying the satanic legions and the armies of Gog and Magog. Satan himself is sent to spend the rest of eternity in a lake of fire.

Armageddon

See also: Apocalypse, End Times, Megiddo, Norwegian Armageddon

When a fictional zombie outbreak occurs, there is always at least one character that believes the rise of the dead is the work of an angry God, one that decides to punish the living by raising the dead. In other words, the war against the zombies becomes a confrontation of definitively religious proportions. Rather interestingly, over the course of the last decade or so, the Pentagon has quietly and carefully promoted the idea that the War on Terror is not just a battle against bearded maniacs from the Middle East, but a confrontation of biblical proportions, one that is a fight between good and evil, God and Satan. Of course, the reality is that the War on Terror is simply the latest conflict of many that have always plagued the human race and, in all likelihood, always will plague us. But, that has not stopped Uncle Sam from seeding meme-like messages to the effect that this war is very different from all previous wars.

In January 2010, a great deal of press and television coverage was given to a very strange development in the War on Terror: the U.S. Marine Corps signed a contract with a company called Trijicon—based out of Wixom, Michigan—which provided rifle sights containing inscribed quotes from the Bible. And we're not talking about a handful of sights: it was in excess of three quarters of a million of them, which netted Trijicon a nice sum of $650 million.

Despite the fact that many might see this as a positive thing, official regulations exist specifically, and quite rightly, banning the promotion of any and all religious belief in both Afghanistan and Iraq, specifically to prevent claims being made that the War on Terror is a religious one. Inscribing the following onto the sights was hardly perceived in many quarters as keeping the hostilities deity-free: "For God, who commanded the light to shine out of darkness, hath shined in our hearts, to give the light of the knowledge of the glory of God in the face of Jesus Christ." Significantly, additional quotes came from the *Book of Revelation*—a book that perhaps far more than a few people might turn their attentions to if the dead really do rise from the grimy soil below.

It was this development that got Michael Weinstein, of the Military Religious Freedom Foundation (MRFF), in a state of rage. He said: "It's literally pushing fundamentalist Christianity at the point of a gun against the people that we're fighting. We're emboldening an enemy." He had a point: senior military personnel were referring to the weapons equipped with the saintly sights as a "spiritually transformed firearm of Jesus Christ." Such was the

The Death and Conflagration by Albert Chmielowski is a circa 1870 oil painting that was part of the triptych *Disaster* that captures the mood of Armageddon quite poignantly.

furor that all of this provoked, Trijicon took two new steps: (a) they had the messages removed from those sights still in their factory; and (b) they provided what were described as modification kits to allow for the removal of the references from the already deployed optical sights.

"We must ensure that incidents like these are not repeated, so as not to give the impression that our country is involved in a religious crusade, which hurts America's image abroad and puts our soldiers in harm's way," said Haris Tarin, Director of the Washington, D.C. office of the Muslim Public Affairs Council.

Armando

Voodoo is not a religion with a commonly held dogma or creed. There are many styles of Voodoo being practiced in contemporary New Orleans. Among them is the Cult of the Chicken Man that was originally created by the late Prince Ke'eyma. The Prince is said, by some authorities on Voodoo, to have founded one of the largest secret societies since the one created by the legendary Voodoo Queen Marie Laveau. The

RICARDO PUSTANIO 2009

Armando the Voodoo King is the successor to Prince Ke'eyman. (*Art by Ricardo Pustanio*).

RICARDO PUSTANIO 2009

Voodoo's Prince Ke'eyma created the Cult of the Chicken Man in New Orleans. (*Art by Ricardo Pustanio*).

Cult of the Chicken Man survives today, according to many, because of the devotion of Prince Ke'eyma's devotee, Armando.

Armando begins his day with a Voodoo grave ritual at the tomb of Marie Laveau. His apartment on the edge of the French Quarter is dominated by a large portrait of Prince Ke'eyman, who took the Cuban orphan under his wing and taught him the ways of Voodoo. Armando is proud to have received the power of Chicken Man's legacy as his chosen priest, but also to have ceded him the right to become the guiding force of the secret sosyete. Although Chicken Man died just a few days before Christmas in 1998, a full Voodoo Burial and New Orleans Jazz funeral was held for him in January 1999. His ashes are kept in Priestess Miriam's Temple on Rampart Street.

Armando does not believe in permitting those not practicing Voodoo to observe performances of the rituals. His detractors argue that Armando is against public demonstrations of Voodoo because he does not wish anyone to share the special rites taught to him by the Chicken Man.

Many individuals have reported seeing the spirit of Chicken Man all over the city of New Orleans, and Armando is upset about those who create fabrications about the True King of Voodoo. However, he is secure in the knowledge that Prince Keeyama's followers know that his Voodoo was the real thing and that it will stand the test of time.

Asclepius

Within ancient Greek teachings and lore, Asclepius was the Olympian god of medicine and the offspring of the mighty Apollo and his lover, Coronis. But Asclepius was far more than that: he possessed the supernatural ability to raise the dead from the grave. Perhaps somewhat appropriately, his birth was itself dominated by death. When an enraged Apollo learned that Coronis had committed adultery, he had her killed—immediately after which she was sliced open. At the very last moment, however, Asclepius was rescued from the clutches of the Grim Reaper. The tiny, premature baby was duly raised by Chiron, a legendary centaur and the son of Cronus, one of the mighty Titans that dominate ancient Greek mythology.

Skilled in the mysteries of medicine—to the extent that he learned the ancient secrets of literal reanimation—Asclepius soon became adept at ensuring the dead didn't always remain where they should. That, as we all know, is in the ground. There was, however, a steep price to be paid for guaranteeing reanimation and a second chance to live. In return for breathing new life into the dead, a significant amount of gold had to be handed over by the loved ones of those destined to be brought back. Asclepius' biggest, and ultimately fatal, mistake was in resurrecting Hippolytus, the stepson of one Phaedra, who was the wife of Theseus, the king of Athens.

When Hippolytus declined Phaedra's offer to take their relationship in a direction that no stepson and stepmother should ever contemplate taking it, Phaedra—angered at being coldly spurned—told Theseus that Hippolytus had raped her, which was nothing but a rage-induced lie. Theseus, unfortunately, fell for the ruse and placed a curse on his son that resulted in a terrible end for Hippolytus: he was dragged to a horrible, bloody death by his very own horses.

When Asclepius elected to return Hippolytus to the world of the living, his actions did not sit well with Zeus, the all-powerful leader of the Olympians, who viewed the idea of resurrecting the dead abhorrent and against the natural order of life and death. As the god of thunder, Zeus unleashed a powerful thunderbolt that took the life of Asclepius in just

A circa 1860 drawing based on a statue of Asclepius at the Louvre museum in Paris, France.

seconds. There was, however, another reason for Zeus' actions. Such was the sheer extent of Asclepius' dead-raising activities, none other than Hades himself—the Greek god of the dreaded Underworld—became furious that, thanks to Asclepius' life-returning powers, Hades' dark domain would soon become bereft of the souls of the dead. And, as Zeus and Hades were brothers—and brothers with a mutual interest in seeing Asclepius dead and gone—the outcome was pretty much inevitable. As the old legend demonstrates, there are very good reasons for letting the dead stay dead, lest you soon become one of them yourself, which is *exactly* what happened to Asclepius.

Aswang

Within the mythology of the Philippines there exists a deadly and diabolical creature known as the Aswang. Also referred to as the Sok-Sok and the Tik-Tik—as a result of the strange and menacing vocalizations it makes—the Aswang is said to predominantly dwell in Mindanao, which is the second largest island in the Philippines, and in the Visayas Islands, chiefly on the islands of Bohol and Negros.

For many Filipinos, however, the Aswang is not just a monster of legend: it is also one of cold, grim, reality, and has been so for centuries, too. Since the Aswang is said to suck vast amounts of blood out of its human victims, it has become definitively, and inextricably, linked to vampire lore and legend. There are, however, a number of characteristics attributed to the Aswang that suggest it is far more zombie-like in nature and appearance than it is vampiric.

Usually, although not exclusively, female in appearance, the Aswangs are very often described as resembling normal human beings, but with several key characteristics that reveal their true identities, and which also provoke zombie-style imagery. They are, for example, thin to the point of near-emaciation, they are often described as being dressed in dirty and ragged fashion, they are able to run with astonishing speed, and they have gaunt, pale faces, and malevolent-looking eyes. And it's not just blood they feed on. The Aswangs are full-on carnivores with a love of meat of the human variety. Could there be a better description of a zombie? Certainly, we would be very hard-pressed to find one, no matter how hard we looked.

Horrifically, the personal, favorite delicacies of the Aswangs are newly born human babies and young children. The reasons are as simple as they are horrific: the young are easy to catch, kill, and savagely devour. Aswangs are known for their particular, voracious love of human organs, particularly the heart and the liver, which are considered to be particularly prized delicacies. And, on occasion, they will even devour the bodies of the recently deceased. Further emphasizing the zombie links, when a person is bitten—but not outright killed—by an Aswang, widespread infection very soon sets in and spreads. Inevitably, the infected soul soon begins to take on not just the appearance of the dreaded monster, but also its near-maniacal lust and need for human flesh, bodily organs, and blood.

The Aswang is also said to have the ability to shape-shift into certain other creatures, such as a monstrous hound, a werewolf-like beast, and a giant, marauding hog. It does so to ensure a swift and decisive kill while stalking its prey, after which it returns to humanoid form to devour the fresh kill.

August

For traditional Chinese in many countries, August is known as the Month of the Hungry Ghosts. In the Chinese calendar (a lunisolar calendar), a special Ghost Festival is held on the fifteenth night of the seventh lunar month. In Chinese tradition, the thirteenth day of the seventh month in the lunar calendar is called Ghost Day, and the seventh month in general is regarded as the Ghost Month, in which ghosts and spirits, including those of deceased ancestors, come out from the lower realm. During

Spirits are offered food at a Chinese temple during the Ghost Festival.

the Qingming Festival, the living descendants pay homage to their ancestors and on Ghost Day, the deceased visit the living.

On the thirteenth day, the three realms of Heaven, Hell, and the realm of the living are open, and both Taoists and Buddhists perform rituals to transmute and absolve the sufferings of the deceased. Intrinsic to the Ghost Month is ancestor worship, where traditional filial piety of descendants extends to their ancestors even after their deaths. Activities during the month would include preparing ritualistic food offerings, burning incense, and burning joss paper, a papier-mâché form of material items such as clothes, gold and other fine goods for the visiting spirits of the ancestors. Elaborate meals would be served with empty seats for each of the deceased in the family. The deceased were treated as if they are still living.

Ancestor worship is what distinguishes Qingming Festival from the Ghost Festival because the former includes paying respects to all deceased, including the same and younger generations, while the latter only includes older generations. Other festivities may include releasing miniature paper boats and lanterns on water, which signifies giving directions to the lost ghosts and spirits of the ancestors and other deities.

The Ghost Festival shares some similarities with the predominantly Mexican observance of El Da de los Muertos. Due to its theme of ghosts and spirits, the festival is sometimes known as the Chinese Halloween, though many have debated the difference between the two.

Baron Samedi and Maman Brigitte

Voodoo deities, or loas, are among the most feared divine beings in the world. Wild, short-tempered, and immensely powerful, these spirits communicate with humans by possessing those attending Voodoo rituals. Those who obey the loa are granted their wishes and good health, but those who do not can meet a terrifying fate at the hands of their gods.

Baron Samedi is the most famous and the most frightening of the loa spirits. The Baron is the infamous master of the dead who escorts souls from the graveyard to the underworld. However, the Baron does not concern himself with only the dead; he can enter the realm of the living and force people to do his terrible bidding.

Baron Samedi (Baron Saturday, also Bawon Samedi, or Bawon Sanmdi) is one of the loa of Haitian Vodou. Samedi is usually depicted with a white top hat, black tuxedo, dark glasses, and cotton plugs in the nostrils, as if to resemble a corpse dressed and prepared for burial in the Haitian style. He has a white, frequently skull-like face (or actually has a skull for a face). He is the head of the Gud (also Ghede; pronounced GAY-day) family of loa, those gods concerned with death and resurrection.

Many call Baron Samedi the ruling loa or god of New Orleans. He and his bride, the Great Maman Brigitte, are sometimes referred to as the king and queen of the Zombies. Voodooists believe that only through his power can a soul be forced from a living body and placed between life and death.

On Halloween night, Baron Samedi stands at the Crossroads, where the souls of dead humans pass on their way to the gate to Guinee, the astral counterpart of the ancient homeland in Africa. Samedi is a sexual loa, frequently represented by phallic symbols, and he is also noted for disruption, obscenity, debauchery, and has a particular fondness for tobacco and rum. As he is the loa of sex and resurrection, he is often called upon for healing by those near or approaching death. It is only the Baron who can accept an individual into the realm of the dead. Samedi is considered a wise judge and a powerful magician.

He, as well as Ghede, the most benevolent loa of the dead, often possesses individuals whether they are practicing Voodoo-Hoodoos or not. Many have documented and experienced such possession.

As well as being master of the dead, Baron Samedi is also a giver of life. He can cure any mortal of any disease or wound if he thinks it is worth his time to do so. His powers are especially great when it comes to Voodoo curses and black magic. Even if somebody has been inflicted by a hex which brings them to the verge of death, they will not die if the Baron refuses to dig their grave. So long as this mighty spirit keeps them out of the ground they are safe. What he demands in return depends on his mood. Sometimes he is content with his followers wearing black, white, or purple clothes, and offering a small gift of cigars, rum, black coffee, grilled peanuts, or bread. On other occasions, the Baron will ask for a Voodoo ceremony in his honor. If he is in a bad mood, he may dig the grave of his supplicant, bury him alive, or bring him back as a mindless zombie.

The spiritual children of Baron and Maman Brigitte are the Ghede loa, the protectors of the dead. A New World loa, Maman Brigitte is probably traceable back to the Irish Saint Brigid. The Ghedes are powerful, and will prophesy the future, heal the sick, give advice, or perform magic of all descriptions. They also exert control over those who become zombies.

At Voodoo ceremonies, the Ghede possess the Voodooists and dance the banda, which is a wildly suggestive dance miming sexual intercourse. And in the midst of all this winding and grinding, these loa keep perfectly straight faces. They have reached such a deep trance state that it is as if they are cadavers and feel nothing.

Papa Legba (also Papa Ghede) is considered the counterpart to Baron Samedi. If a child is dying, it is Papa Legba to whom the parents pray. It is believed that he will not take a life before its time, and that he will protect the little ones.

Papa Ghede is supposed to be the corpse of the first man who ever died. He is recognized as a short,

Baren Samedi is one of the loa of Haitian Voodoo. He is often depicted as looking like a well-dressed corpse awaiting burial. (*Art by Ricardo Pustanio.*)

dark man with a high hat on his head, a cigar in his mouth, and an apple in his left hand. Papa Ghede is a psychopomp who waits at the crossroads to take souls into the afterlife.

Although he was one of the most revered loa in Haitian Voudun, Papa Ghede was eventually transformed into the figure of a gentle and loving old man, who stands as the Guardian of the Centerpost, the Opener of the Gates, to any who communicate with the loa.

Ghede Nibo is a psychopomp, an intermediary between the living and the dead. He gives voice to the dead spirits that have not been reclaimed from below the waters.

Ghede Masaka assists Ghede Nibo. He is an androgynous male or transgendered gravedigger, and spirit of the dead, recognized by his black shirt, white jacket, and white head scarf.

November 2, All Souls Day, is also The Feast of the Ancestors, commonly called Fet Ghede. New Orleans Catholics attend mass in the morning, then go to the cemetery, where they pray at family grave sites, and make repairs to family tombs. The majority of New Orleans Catholics are also said to be Vodouisants, and vice versa, so on the way to the cemetery many people change clothes from the white they wore to church to the purple and black of the loa Ghede, the spirits of the departed ancestors.

Fet Ghede is considered the end of the old year and the beginning of the new, much as in the European Wiccan tradition. Any debts to Baron Samedi, Maman Brigitte, or Ghede must be paid at this time.

Berwyn Mountains Zombie Dogs

See also: Black Dogs, Chupacabras, Zombie Dogs of Texas

Deep in the heart of North Wales is a stretch of mountains collectively called the Berwyns. They are huge, daunting, and picturesque. And they are saturated with tales of paranormal phenomena.

T. Gwynn Jones was an investigative author who penned a classic book on the legends and mythology of Wales. It was titled *Welsh Folklore and Welsh Folk-custom*, and suggested the name "Berwyns" was derived from two words: "bre," which is an old Welsh term for "hill," and "Gwynn," a word that paid homage to a legendary member of Welsh royalty, Gwun ap Nudd. Notably, the mighty king oversaw humans who were not normal, but nothing less than a race of magical and diminutive fairy folk. Known as the Tylwyth teg, they lived in the heart of a supernatural realm known as Annwn. It was a place where time was non-existent and the fairies stayed forever youthful. As bright and positive as all of that sounds, however, there is a distinctly dark side to the Berwyn Mountains: they are said to be the home of an infernal pack of what can most accurately be termed zombie hounds.

Before the word of the Christian God reached the United Kingdom, it was told in hushed tones on the Berwyns that Odin, the legendary overlord of the ancient and

The Berwyn Mountains in Wales are known as a magical place where fairy folk dwell ... and also zombies.

mighty Norse gods, travelled the night skies of the old Welsh mountains with nothing less than a pack of supernatural and deadly hounds at his side. Considered as either dogs of the undead kind or deceased people returned in animalistic form, they were driven by one thing and one thing only: to be seen. Anyone unfortunate enough to lock eyes with the deadly dogs would be whisked away by the terrifying pack and torn apart and eagerly devoured by their savage jaws—in a fashion not unlike the zombie dogs of *I Am Legend* and the *Resident Evil* movies. Thus was born the Wild Hunt in which monsters hunted man, purely out of a need to feed.

Bhangarh

When a fictional, on-screen zombie apocalypse erupts big time, one of the very first things that happens is that the cities quickly collapse and fall. As the numbers of the marauding dead increase near-exponentially, and as the cities become overrun by the hungry and deranged dead, those who have managed to avoid getting infected are invariably forced to leave for far more isolated, out of the way areas. But cities from which the living have fled are not just found in the domain of fiction. One such real world example is located in the heart of India: it's the city of Bhangarh. That the city may be bereft of people because of a deadly virus will surely make all fans of the living dead sit up and take careful notice.

Bhangarh Palace in India was a thriving center of activity for centuries until a bizarre plague struck the area in the 1800s, and the disease spread to the human residents.

Located in the Indian state of Rajasthan, Bhangarh has origins that go back to the early 1500s when, thanks to the vision of the Maharaja Bhagwant Das, plans for the creation of the huge, sprawling city were first made. In no time at all, Bhangarh was a veritable hive of activity filled with more than ten thousand homes, a huge market place, and a spacious palace for its rulers. By the early 1600s, Bhangarh became significantly fortified, chiefly to deal with threats posed by the hostile hordes of opposing kingdoms. It was thanks to this careful fortification—combined with the fact that it was surrounded by a number of large hills and hard to penetrate forestland—that Bhangarh remained free of attack for decade upon decade. That life of bliss and relaxation all changed, however, in the latter part of the eighteenth century when the city became a definitive ghost town.

While the circumstances that provoked the sudden evacuation of Bhangarh are steeped in mystery, one story that persists has more than slightly zombie-themed aspects attached to it. Reportedly, the local animals, which the residents of Bhangarh used as their primary source of food, became the victims of a mysterious virus that killed them with frightening speed. Shades of something akin to so-called mad cow disease, perhaps? Not surprisingly, when the virus reportedly, and suddenly, jumped from animal to human, complete and utter chaos broke out, and the entire population quickly left for new homes—ones just about as far away from Bhangarh as was conceivably possible.

THE ZOMBIE BOOK: THE ENCYCLOPEDIA OF THE LIVING DEAD

The dark memories of that long gone exodus still dominate the minds of the people around Bhangarh to this very day. As astonishing as it may sound, in the almost two and a half centuries that have now passed since Bhangarh became a city of the dead, there has not been even a single, solitary attempt to breathe new life into the abandoned city: Bhangarh remains just as dead today as it was back in the eighteenth century.

Biochip Implants

In the 1950s and 1960s, a large number of experiments in behavior modification were conducted in the United States, and it is well known that electrical implants were inserted into the brains of animals and humans. Later, when new techniques in influencing brain functions became a priority to military and intelligence services, secret experiments were conducted with such unwilling guinea pigs as inmates of prisons, soldiers, mental patients, handicapped children, the elderly, and any group of people considered expendable.

Rauni-Leena Luukanen-Kilde, M.D., Former Chief Medical Officer of Finland, has stated that mysterious brain implants, the size of one centimeter, began showing up in X-rays in the 1980s. In a few years, implants were found the size of a grain of rice. Dr. Luukanen-Kilde stated that the implants were made of silicon, later of gallium arsenide. Today such implants are small enough that it is nearly impossible to detect or remove them. They can easily be inserted into the neck or back during surgical operations, with or without the consent of the subject.

It has been stated that within a few years all Americans will be forced to receive a programmable biochip implant somewhere in their body. The biochip is most likely to be implanted on the back of the right or the left hand so it will be easy to scan at stores. The biochip implant will also be used as a universal type of identification card. A number will be assigned at birth and will follow that person throughout life. Eventually, every newborn will be injected with a microchip, which will identify the person for the rest of his or her life.

Initially, people will be informed that the biochip will be used largely for purposes of identification. The reality is that the implant will be linked to a massive supercomputer system that will make it possible for government agencies to maintain a surveillance of all citizens by ground sensors and satellites. Today's microchips operate by means of low-frequency radio waves that target them. With the help of satellites, the implanted person can be followed anywhere. Their brain functions may be remotely monitored by supercomputers and even altered through the changing of frequencies. Even worse, say the alarmists, once the surveillance system is in place, the biochips will be implemented to transform every man, woman, and child into a controlled slave, for these devices will make it possible for outside intelligences to influence a person's brain cell conversations and to talk directly with the individual's brain neurons. Through cybernetic biochip brain implants, people may be forced to think and to act exactly as government intelligence agencies have preprogrammed them to think and behave.

The technology exists right now to create a New World Order served by the zombie-like masses. Secret government agencies could easily utilize covert neurological communication systems in order to subvert independent thinking and to control social and political activity.

The National Security Agency's (NSA) electronic surveillance system can simultaneously follow the unique bioelectrical resonance brain frequency of millions of people. NSAs Signals Intelligence group can remotely monitor information from human brains by decoding the evoked potentials (3.50 hertz, 5 milliwatts) emitted by the brain. Electromagnetic frequency (EMF) brain stimulation signals can be sent to the brains of specific individuals, causing the desired effects to be experienced by the target.

A U.S. Naval research laboratory, funded by intelligence agencies, has achieved the incredible breakthrough of uniting living brain cells with microchips. When such a chip is injected into a man's or a woman's brain, he or she instantly becomes a living vegetable and a subservient slave. And once this device is perfected, the biochip implant could easily be converted by the Defense Department into an army of killer zombies.

Tiny microchips can be implanted in people's bodies. It's possible that in the future all Americans will be required to have implanted biochips.

Experts have said that a micromillimeter microchip may be placed into the optical nerve of the eye and draw neuro-impulses from the brain which embody the experiences, smells, sights, and voice of the implanted subject. These neuro-impulses may be stored in a computer and may be projected back to the person's brain via the microchip to be re-experienced. A computer operator can send electromagnetic messages to the target's nervous system, thereby inducing hallucinations.

Beyond all science-fiction scenarios, we could become a nation of zombies.

Black Death

See also: AIDS, Alien Infection, Alien Virus, Creutzfeld-Jacobs Disease, Infection, Spanish Flu

There can be absolutely no doubt at all that the most lethal part of the zombie is its head. Aside from the fact that the head just happens to be home to a zombie's vicious mouth—from which an infectious, and usually fatal, bite is invariably delivered—the head has the ability to keep on living and snapping even if, or when, it is severed from its decaying body. The only surefire way to ensure that a zombie stays down forever is to penetrate its brain—either with a bullet or two or a sharp and deadly object.

Few people realize, however, that centuries before the fictional zombies of television and cinema infected the imaginations of people here, there, and pretty much everywhere, the severed heads of the dead were spreading deadly disease in the real world. It was the ruthless and deadly Mongol Empire—which rose to prominence under the rule of the maniacal Genghis Khan—that came up with a novel, and admittedly horrific, way to defeat and kill their sworn enemies. And it was a method most famously put to outstandingly good use way back in 1347.

At the time in question, the Mongols were engaged in a violent confrontation with the people of Caffa, an ancient city located in the Ukraine. It transpired that this was the very same timeframe in which a dreaded plague that became known as the Black Death had taken a decisive and deadly grip on the landscape. It was a plague that went on to kill around 200 million Europeans between 1348 and 1350, and took its name from the hideous blackening of the skin that was caused by massive and

Peter Breughel's painting *The Triumph of Death* captures the horrors of a Europe caught in the grip of the bubonic plague.

unstoppable hemorrhaging. Always on the lookout for new and novel ways to exterminate the enemy, the Mongols had a sudden (no pun intended) brainwave.

Carefully protecting themselves from the risk of infection as best they could, the Mongols sought out the corpses of the infected dead, and then quickly and decisively severed head from body. The decapitated heads were then placed into huge catapults and shot across the sky, over the surrounding walls of the city, and right into the heart of bustling Caffa. Even in death, history has graphically demonstrated that the Black Death could still be quickly spread. And, indeed, in no time at all, the heads of the infected ensured that the people of Caffa—the arch-enemies of the Mongols—soon became victims of the deadly virus.

For those who think that the only hazardous head of the dead kind is to be found on-screen or in the pages of a novel or comic book, it's time to think again.

Black Dogs

See also: Berwyn Mountains Zombie Dogs, Chupacabras, Zombie Dogs of Texas

In the 2007 movie *I Am Legend*, Will Smith's character—Lieutenant Colonel Robert Neville—comes under attack from a vicious pack of zombified dogs. While Neville survives the onslaught unscathed, his own dog, a German Shepherd named Samantha, does not. With shocking speed, she transforms into one of the crazed, barking dead. Similar hounds of the dead appear in the *Resident Evil* series, too. Of course, zombie dogs are just the stuff of horror fantasy, aren't they? Just maybe, they are not.

Within British folklore and culture of centuries past, one of the most feared of all supernatural beasts was the so-called phantom black dog. Typically the size of a small pony and with a pair of blazing eyes—often described as looking like red hot coals—the creepy canine was feared all across the land. The names of these infernal beasts varied widely and wildly according to locale, and include Padfoot, Black Shuck (which takes its name from an old English word, "scucca," meaning "demon"), Skriker, and the Girt Dog.

According to some of the ancient traditions, the black dogs were the reincarnated, supernatural forms of recently deceased people. And, if someone was to encounter a black dog on a lonely and isolated stretch of road, late on the proverbial dark and stormy night, it meant only one terrible thing: the fiendish hound would soon be coming for the soul of the witness or that of a family member or close friend. So, what you may ask, does this all have to do with zombies? Well, consider the lore and traditions surrounding the phantom black dogs. A person dies, then very soon thereafter returns from the grave in monstrous form and fashion, and has only one goal on its mind: to take the lives of the living. Sound familiar? It should!

Black Sheep

Making a highly watchable zombie movie that combines chills with laughs is not always the easiest thing in the world to successfully achieve. *Shaun of the Dead* was right on target, as was *Zombieland*. A further movie that falls into this particular category is *Black Sheep*, a 2006 production that was shot in the green and pleasant pastures of New Zealand. Or, rather, they are green and pleasant for a while. They soon become very *unpleasant* pastures, however, ones that are soaked and saturated in pint upon pint of human blood.

Transforming a healthy looking person into a violent, killer zombie is not a difficult task: make-up, ragged clothes, and near-endless amounts of fake blood work absolute wonders when placed in the right hands. In *Black Sheep*, however, the zombies are not people. They are, as you may have surmised from the title of the movie, sheep. Nevertheless, the company that handled the special-effects, Weta Workshop—one that also played a major role in the production of *The Lord of the Rings* movie-series and the television series *Xena: Warrior Princess*—did a fine job of turning the usually meek and mild animals into crazed, four-legged killers.

As is so very often the case in zombie movies, the cause of all the death and destruction is bizarre, and fringe-based, medical experimentation, coupled with reckless, mad scientist-style genetic tinkering. In short, the sheep find that blissfully munching on the lush grass of New Zealand just doesn't cut it for them anymore. With their bodies, DNA, and make-up wildly altered, the woolly ones develop a distinct taste for human flesh.

Just as is the case when a person is bitten by a human zombie, after being chomped on by a savage and infected sheep, it's best to be put out of one's misery before the unstoppable mutation into a killer corpse begins. The main reason being that not only does the victim become zombified, they also transform into a bizarre creature that is, in essence, half-human and half-sheep. Sheebies, rather than zombies, as one might perhaps be inclined to call the infected abominations. Or maybe we should call them Baaaabies.

As *Black Sheep* progresses, we are treated to a great deal of dark hilarity, horror, and death as the cast, one by one, succumbs to the bleat of the dead. We also learn that the deranged soul who is responsible for all of the death and tragedy has a personal interest in sheep that goes a little too far than most of us would consider appropriate, if you see what I mean. The psychotic sheep, showing that they are not just the relatively simple numbskulls that most of us assume them to be, don't just take out their rage on people. A sheepdog, one that has made their lives a living hell by constantly herding them back and forth from field to farm, also becomes a victim of the whitest, fluffiest zombies of all time. We know this, as in the final moments of the movie the dog utters not a typical bark but a definitive and ominous bleat.

The sheep apocalypse: coming soon to a field near you. Maybe.

Body Snatchers

See also: Alien Abductions

In 1954, a writer named Jack Finney penned a story that became a classic in the field of science-fiction. It went by the title of *The Body Snatchers* and was published in serialized form in *Collier's*—a magazine that began in the late 1800s and which closed down three years after Finney's article appeared. It was, however, relaunched in 2012. Such was the success of the story, one year later—in 1955—it surfaced as a full-length book. And, in no time at all, Hollywood came knocking on Jack Finney's door. Just twelve months after the book hit the stores, a big-bucks movie version of *The Body Snatchers* appeared in cinemas all across the world. Its famous reworked title was *Invasion of the Body Snatchers* and starred Kevin McCarthy as Dr. Miles Bennell, the first man to stumble upon the terrible truth of the alien invaders in our midst.

The 1956 movie production of Finney's story is the definitive one, filled with chills and thrills, and shot in moody black and white. The 1978 version, with Donald

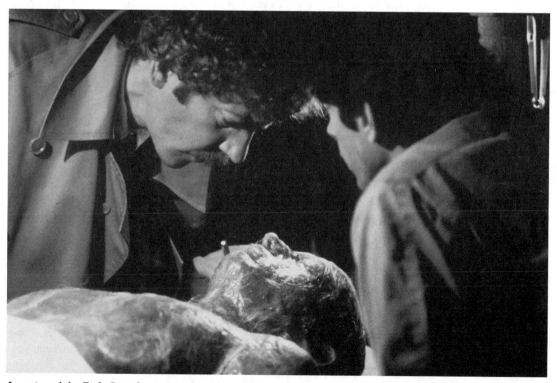

Invasion of the Body Snatchers was released in 1958 and had a remake in 1978 (shown here, featuring Donald Sutherland). In both, space pods arrive on Earth and form replicants that replace human beings one by one.

Sutherland taking the lead, is very good also. *Body Snatchers*, of 1993, is not a bad film. *The Invasion*, of 2007, which saw Nicole Kidman taking the primary role, is undeniably terrible and should be missed at all costs.

The story is as original as it is creepy. Most of us assume that if aliens are going to invade, then they will likely do it in *Independence Day*-style, with gigantic spacecraft, awesome weapons of frightening power, and armies of hostile aliens. *Body Snatchers* (and the movie versions) took a very different approach to a planetary takeover by extraterrestrials.

There are no aliens to be seen, no gigantic flying saucers, no laser guns—in fact, there is nothing whatsoever to even suggest an alien invasion is in the cards. That is, until strange flowers start popping up here, there, and everywhere. They are flowers to be avoided at all costs. Why? Because they have the ability to duplicate and replace people with identical, lifelike equivalents, that's why. Well, they are *physically* identical, but as far as their personalities are concerned, they are very much akin to the mind-controlled undead of the likes of such movies as *I Walked with a Zombie*, *White Zombie*, and *King of the Zombies*.

This brings us to a big, important, and controversial question: was Jack Finney's creation only fiction? Is it feasible that high-tech experimentation has been undertaken—and even perfected—to create cloned, lifelike equivalents of people, ones that look like their originals, but which are truly old-school zombie-like in their actions and manner? It couldn't really happen, could it? Some say that it already has. In the latter part of the 1990s, a very strange story circulated amongst UFO researchers, newsletters, and magazines in the United Kingdom. It was a story that, incredibly and in hair-raising fashion, suggested Jack Finney was right on the money.

Although the story didn't surface until 1997, the events it told supposedly occurred in the early 1990s, possibly either 1991 or 1992. The location was a highly secure facility in the south of England called Porton Down, which is located in the county of Wiltshire. The county itself is typified by rolling green fields, enchanting old villages, and beautiful countryside. There is nothing beautiful or enchanting about Porton Down, however. It's an installation where the British government undertakes its most secret research into such domains as lethal viruses, chemical weapons, and biological warfare. Should zombies ever walk the streets of Britain, the likelihood is that they will be shown to have had their origins in some fortified lab far below the secret facility.

As for the story in question, it went like this: given that Porton Down's staff are known to have undertaken controversial experimentation on animals, on one occasion—late at night, or in the early hours of the morning—a team of animal-rights activists broke into the base, with the specific intent of releasing into the countryside just about as many of those same animals as possible. While the team failed to find any such animals, they came across something else: a room that contained dozens of curious-looking containers, all around eight or nine feet in length, and all containing nothing less than duplicates of well-known British politicians of that particular era. Not surprisingly, the terrified activists fled.

Today, the story is still told in those places where UFO fanatics hang out. It's a story that remains as intriguing and amazing as it was when it was first told. But it remains something else, too: completely unverified. To date, the animal-rights activists have not been identified and officialdom is saying nothing, one way or the other. True or not, the story of Britain's zombie-like politicians lives on. And a word of caution: should you, one day, find yourself in the vicinity of Porton Down and you stumble upon some strange looking, colorful flowers, whatever you do, don't touch them or pick them: just run!

Bourbon Street Devil Baby

The most popular version of the Bourbon Street Devil Baby legend began in the early 1800s, when a young Creole woman married a plantation owner, a very wealthy man who wanted a male heir to continue the Louisiana family name he had established. He already had three daughters from his first wife, so the new wife was kept continually pregnant. After bearing six healthy female children, she was dismayed to find herself pregnant with her seventh child. She knew this child had better be a boy, or she would be likely to find herself abandoned and a new wife would be selected to bear a male heir. The anxious mother-to-be is said to have gone to a Voodoo-Hoodoo Queen and asked her to use her powers to help her deliver a boy child.

Unbeknownst to the desperate mother-to-be, the Voodoo Queen hated the plantation owner because of his past actions against her, so under the guise of manifesting a healthy male heir for the woman to deliver to her husband, the Voodoo Queen cursed the unborn child, making certain that the woman would bear Satan's son. The Voodoo Queen's magic was strong, for the boy child was delivered from the womb with horns, red eyes, cloven hooves, claws, and a tail. The Devil Baby's birthday was said to be on a Mardi Gras Day.

The horrific newborn proceeded to eat the neighbors' children, bare its teeth at its terrified siblings, and was locked away in the attic garret room. It was here that his parents held him captive before he escaped to begin his reign of terror on New Orleans' citizens.

The legend of a Devil Baby invites a number of accounts of its origin. Rather than the desperate wife of a plantation owner insistent upon the birth of a male heir, certain versions of the lore have the monster born of a slave girl who was raped by a plantation owner. Still others state that the horrid

The Devil Baby of Bourbon Street is said to look like a small, bald-headed child with hooves and a ratlike tail. (Art by Ricardo Pustanio).

abomination was born of a French aristocrat's daughter who was addicted to absinthe. As the lurid story goes, she was drunk to the very hour that she gave birth, and that she abandoned the grotesque infant in Pirates Alley. His demonic cries are said to have disturbed the Ash Wednesday Mass.

St. Anthony's Garden, sometimes called the Devil Baby's Playpen or simply the Devil's Garden, is said by some to be the place where the Devil Baby hides at night to attack unsuspecting passersby. The garden is thought by some locals to be one of the very seven gates of Hell.

Another old New Orleans oral tradition tells that the Devil Baby was born in that very garden. According to this version of the creature's birth, its mother took refuge here in the late hours of her labor just before dawn on a Mardi Gras Day. As dawn approached and the long early morning hours turned to day, some churchgoers at early Mass later testified that they had seen a bloodied young woman staggering from the garden, just as a scream from Hell could be heard coming from the low hedges. The woman managed to walk toward the church and leave the newborn devil infant on the back door steps before she died.

The large open garden behind the eighteenth century St. Louis Cathedral is said to be the best spot to sight the Devil Baby today. A history of duels fought and much bloodshed on the grounds is said to be the reason that he haunts the spot.

Bowery at Midnight

Some movies of the undead are very good. Others are extremely bad. Many are downright mediocre. Then there are those which are just plain weird. One of those that most definitely falls into the latter category is *Bowery at Midnight*, a movie whose name gives away absolutely nothing at all about its odd plotline. Despite the fact that the production, made in 1942, starred Hollywood horror legend and crowd puller Bela Lugosi, it has long since vanished into much welcome obscurity.

To say that the story is a strange one is an understatement of mammoth proportions. Lugosi takes on no less than two roles: by day he is Professor Frederick Brenner, a noted expert in the field of psychology who is employed at the University of New York. By night, however, Brenner has not just a different trade but an entirely different name, too: that of Karl Wagner. Lugosi, in his Wagner guise, is presented to the viewer as a kindly character, one who helps the needy, the broke, the homeless, and the sick, by giving them much needed shelter and food. Wagner even has his nurse, Judy, dishing out medicine to help those that need it. It is, however, all a big sham. Behind the scenes, Wagner has major, controversial plans in store for the growing numbers of the needy.

The dark reality of the situation is that, unbeknownst to Judy, Wagner and another of his associates are using mind-altering drugs to render the dregs of society into zombified states, and near identical conditions to those undead of Haitian lore. Or are they actually *Night of the Living Dead*-style zombies, after all? Confusingly, we never really know the truth. Neither, it seems, do the writer, director, and producer, since the movie is hardly easy to follow, as it meanders along its curious way. Wagner then uses his gang of dead or alive controlled characters to go robbing here and there, after which they take their dutiful steps into the cellar of the building in which he, Wagner, works, and where they remain until the next job looms on the horizon.

Judy's boyfriend, Richard, just happens to be a student of Professor Brenner and views him as something of an inspiration—in terms of his dedication to the realm of psychology. So, one night Richard decides to visit the professor and Judy, chiefly because he, Richard, hopes that speaking with Brenner at a personal and private level will help his grades at school. It does not. Instead, Brenner—in his Wagner guise—drugs unfortunate Richard, turning him, too, into a walking and thieving automaton of the night.

Judy finally realizes the gravity of the situation, however—particularly so when Richard first vanishes then transforms—and the police are soon on the scene. Richard miraculously (and, for the viewer, confusingly) comes out of his undead state, while Brenner/Wagner meets a gruesome end at the hands of his zombie slaves. He does so deep in an old cellar: shades of a certain, memorable scene in George A. Romero's 1968 production of *Night of the Living Dead* when young Karyn Cooper, perhaps *the* definitive zombie child of all time, kills her parents, Harry and Helen, in the basement of the farmhouse in which they are hiding.

That, however, is where the *Night of the Living Dead* parallels end. Of Romero quality *Bowery at Midnight* is most definitely not. Arguably, it's not of *any* quality, except mediocre.

Brain Eaters of Ancient Kenya

See also: Brains

When it comes to the matter of eating brains, our ancient ancestors had a deep understanding of just how tasty and nourishing the average brain could really be. Millions of years ago, early man was engaging in the sorts of actions that, today, are chiefly relegated to the world of on-screen horror.

In May 2013 a series of amazing and controversial discoveries were made at a place called Kanjera South in Kenya, which is located in East Africa. Archaeologists discovered, to their amazement, evidence of widespread hunting and scavenging of animals by primitive man—better known as *Homo erectus*—up to around three million years ago, and possibly even earlier than that. But there was something very special, and almost unique, about the particular type of hunting and scavenging that was afoot on the plains of Kenya. The fossilized remains of numerous animals our ancestors secured for food revealed that one specific part of the slaughtered beasts were being targeted for food: no less than the heads.

Securing the heads of dead animals would actually not have been a difficult task, as it's a fact that the big cats that roamed the plains of Africa millions of years ago were very partial to antelope and wildebeest flesh—as are their descendents to this day. Such big cats are, however, far less partial to the heads, which are very often the only remaining telltale sign of a big cat attack. Thus, it was speculated, the ancient Kenyans followed stealthily in the tracks of the huge cats and then patiently and silently waited until the latter had finished feasting, after which they quickly moved in to secure the heads of any and all dead antelopes and wildebeest they could get their paw-like hands on. But what was it, specifically, about the heads that made them so special? Well, it was what was contained within the heads that really mattered: the brains.

Demonstrating that the average zombie might not be quite so brain-dead after all, the average antelope and wildebeest brain provides a great deal of tissue that is high in fat. In combined format the organs would have provided the average brain-eater with a significant percentage of the energy they would have required to live, survive, and thrive on the harsh, hot plains of Kenya. This raises an interesting possibility: when a voraciously hungry zombie sinks its wretched teeth into the head of its unfortunate victim, there may be a very good reason why it so often focuses on that one, particular part of the human anatomy: not only is the brain a source of food, it's also a source of much-needed nutrients.

Brain Experiments

On April 13, 1953, CIA chief Allen Dulles ordered the creation of a program of mind control known as MK-ULTRA to be conducted by Dr. Sidney Gottlieb. Rumors and half-truths about new mind-control techniques being used by Soviet, Chinese, and North Korean interrogators on U.S. prisoners of war had panicked the CIA into a search for its own sure-fire method of questioning captives.

In April 1961, Dr. Gottlieb decided the animal experiments, which he had been conducting with electrode implants in their brains, were successful and that it was time to experiment with human brains. Information has leaked out concerning experiments with three Viet-Cong (VC) prisoners in July 1968.

A team of behaviorists flew into Saigon and traveled to the hospital at Bien Hoa where the prisoners were being confined. The agents from Subproject 94 set up their equipment in an enclosed compound, and the team's neurosurgeon and neurologist inserted miniscule electrodes into the brains of the three VC prisoners.

After a brief recovery period, the prisoners were armed with knives and direct electrical stimulation was applied to their brains. The goal of the experiment was to determine if individuals with such electrodes implanted in their brains could be incited to attack and to kill one another. Once again, the Agency was seeking a perfect sleeper assassin, a true Manchurian Candidate, who could be electronically directed to kill a subject.

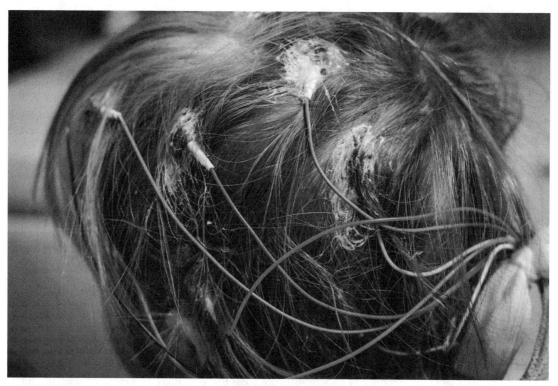

The CIA has experimented with behavior modification using electrodes as part of the MK-ULTRA mind-control program.

After a week of enduring electrical shocks to their brains, the prisoners still refused to attack one another. They were summarily executed and their bodies burned.

Brains

See also: Brain Eaters of Ancient Kenya

It was the 1985 film *The Return of the Living Dead* that initially introduced horror movie fans to the concept of zombies having a particular taste for brains over other parts of the human anatomy. Most people view zombies as largely brain*less* creatures, ones that are solely driven by a need to devour just about as much human flesh, bone, blood, and organs as is conceivably possible. The intriguing fact, however, is that when it comes to munching down on a brain, or several, there is a distinct method in the seeming madness of the killer zombie. It may sound wholly repugnant to the vast majority of people, but brains—or, at least *certain* brains, and most definitely healthy, disease-free brains—can offer a great deal of nutrition to the average hunter of heads.

Maghaz, for example, is a firm, favorite dish for the people of Bangladesh, India, and Pakistan. It is a mixture of the brains of sheep, goats, and cows (except in India, where cows are sacred). And to give it a bit of extra flavor, it is topped off with a sprinkling of crushed pistachios and brown gravy. Much loved in Borneo, Malaysia, Java, and Sumatra, Gulai is very much curry-like in its taste, texture and appearance. One of its staple ingredients is the brain of a cow. In the western part of Central Africa, and specifically in the Republic of Cameroon, for centuries it was a much revered tradition for a newly crowned tribal chief to devour the entire brain of a freshly slaughtered adult gorilla. Going way back in time, tens of thousands of years ago, much of what is today Europe was dominated by Neanderthal man. Evidence and fossilized remains suggest that not only were the Neanderthals cannibals, but they were also keen connoisseurs of the brains of their fellow, dead tribes-people.

It is hardly surprising that, today, the vast majority of the population turns its collective nose up at the very thought of eating brains—quite possibly because it provokes latent, subconscious thoughts of cannibalism. Nevertheless, there is a real advantage to eating the occasional brain, now and again. DHA, or docosahexaenoic acid, is a form of omega-3 fatty acid that is vital to the sustainment of human health. And to give you an idea of just how beneficial a brain can be to a person (or even to a zombie), the daily recommended intake of DHA for an average adult male and female is four grams. The typical cow's brain provides a full twenty percent of that figure.

It should be stressed, however, that as well as the advantages to eating brains, there are distinct disadvantages, too. Brains are, for example, very high in cholesterol, which is typically not good for people. For those who are already dead, but reanimated, however, worries about cholesterol levels matter very little in the larger scheme of things. The biggest concern when it comes to dining—and dining regularly—on brains is the very real, and deeply serious risk of developing variant Creutzfeldt-Jacob disease (vCJD), which is the currently incurable, human equivalent of bovine spongiform encephalopathy, which is far better known as Mad Cow Disease.

All in all, then, while eating the occasional brain might not be the worst thing you could do in life, and which could actually prove to be welcomingly nutritious, it's perhaps best to err on the side of caution. That means leaving the brain-eating to those that do it best: the risen dead.

Brides

According to legend, the Devil himself taught the great Voodoo Master Dr. John over one hundred rituals that could immediately transform a living or dead person into a zombie. Dr. John took immediate advantage of this newly acquired mastery to seize lovely young women and turn them into the living dead.

Zombie brides were the most sought-after creatures throughout the South after the American Civil War. Creole zombie brides were considered the most beautiful;

and after men saw Little Sister Sally on Dr. John's arm, every rich man in the city wanted to have a zombie bride of his own to show off at the next major social event.

Of all the women who gained Dr. John's special attention, his favorite may have been a very young Voodoo Queen of great beauty. He called her Little Sister Sally just because he liked that name, and the way it rolled off his tongue. Sally, whose real name was Alice Slowe Jefferson, was the youngest Voodoo Queen ordained, and she was personally taught by Dr. John, who also zombified her alive.

Though he was advanced in age and she was a mere girl of twelve when he took her into his fold, some believe that it was Little Sister Sally who took possession of Dr. John's dark book of all the hundred-plus spells on how to zombify someone. Even today, members of the Secret Society of Dr. John believe that Sister Sally is the only complete Zombie Queen who ever existed. Through some dark, mysterious spell that Dr. John perfected in St. Louis Cemetery Number One, the exotic Creole beauty, the daughter of a rich plantation owner, remains alone as the world's most perfect youthful living Zombie Queen. Zombified on her seventeenth birthday, Little Sister Sally has never had to fear the passage of time.

Would the perfect bride be a zombie who would submit to your every command? After the American Civil War, such zombie brides were reportedly quite popular in the South.

Bullets

It was a very odd story that got the zombie faithful in states of foaming at the mouth excitement when it first appeared. In 2012, and to the amazement and puzzlement of many, it was revealed that none other than the United States' Social Security Administration (SSA) had secretly, and then recently, purchased almost a quarter of a million rounds of ammunition. Was the SSA fearful of being overwhelmed by hordes of angry grannies, all demanding increases to their benefit payments? No, it was possibly much worse than such a scenario could ever be.

When the story broke, the SSA was quick to play the whole thing down as a matter of little consequence at all. Some conspiracy-minded figures suggested the agency was perhaps just a bit *too* quick to lay matters to rest. It may come as a surprise to the majority of people to learn that the SSA actually has its very own, independent police force. So the SSA assured everyone that the bullets were simply bought for target-practice, as a means to train its personnel on all the latest tactics and trends in the world of law enforcement. Uh-huh. Of course, what else? Well, maybe, quite a lot else.

Not everyone, unsurprisingly, was buying into the SSA's version of events. In fact, it's correct to say that hardly *anyone* bought into it. Certainly, the news provoked understandable suggestions that the SSA—possibly alongside many other agencies of the U.S. government—was preparing for a near-future period of nationwide civil uprising, possibly from the effects of a collapse of the entire U.S. economy, or maybe, as a result of an outbreak of a nationwide zombie infestation.

In those online domains where the conspiratorial and the paranoid like to hang out, even bleaker rumors were quickly taking shape. One of the most controversial theories presented suggested that, to avoid complete economic collapse, plans were afoot to secretly, and drastically, lower the population level of the United States. This, we were told, would be achieved by switching on a dormant virus that was deliberately been inserted into the flu vaccine.

All of those tens of millions of people who regularly get flu jabs would suddenly mutate into murderous maniacs. In the days after the outbreak, the government would then step in and wipe out the infected—using not just the regular police and the military, but also agencies such as the SSA, that in 2012, as we have seen, very conveniently decided to arm itself to the absolute teeth. With millions upon millions dead and the population significantly reduced in number, the economic strain would be gone, or at the very least, be significantly lifted.

Of course, it's all paranoid nonsense and couldn't really happen. Could it? Maybe we won't know the answer to that question until it's way too late to do anything about it—aside from not getting a flu-shot, perhaps.

Burial Traditions

See also: *Cemeteries and Tombs, Cremation, Funerals, Mummies, Mummification*

The coffin has taken many shapes and forms in its evolution as a final resting place for the deceased. Many authorities attribute the presence of trees in the church-yard or cemetery to ancient notions concerning a hollowed out tree as a dwelling place for the spirits of the dead. In Babylonia, great boxes of clay were baked to form a kind of coffin in which the dead were buried.

The first actual coffins, as we know them today, probably originated in ancient Egypt where the people believed that the body of the deceased must be kept safe until a future time of resurrection. The Egyptian word for coffin is from Kas, which means to bury. Another form of the word became Kast, indicating the receptacle into which the body is placed, the coffin.

A Hindu ceremony is seen here in Kathmandu, Nepal, at the Pashupatinath Temple. The departed one's body is cremated and the remains sent on their way down the holy Bagmati River.

In the Hindu faith, the deceased are given a ceremonial washing, then the body is wrapped in a burial cloth and placed on an open casket. If at all possible, within one day of death, the body is to be carried to a place of cremation by six male relatives. The body is placed on a stack of wood and covered with flowers. Melted butter is poured over the body to help it to burn, and the eldest son or nearest male relative of the deceased lights the funeral pyre.

Traditionally, the cremation takes place outdoors and the ashes are collected and scattered in the waters of a holy river, such as the Ganges. In other countries, Hindu dead are taken to a crematorium. Followers of the Hindu religion believe that the soul, the Atman of each individual, is reborn many times in a cycle of spiritual evolution before it can become one with God.

Those who follow the path of Judaism bury their dead in a plain coffin after the body has been washed and dressed. If possible, the funeral takes place on the day after the death has occurred. The coffin containing the deceased is taken first to the synagogue and then to the place of burial.

At the gravesite, the rabbi says a few words of remembrance about the deceased, and the coffin is placed in the grave. The closest male relative of the deceased says a prayer called the Kaddish to help the soul travel to the Olam Haba, the world to come, and the family of the dead person fills in the grave with earth.

Muslims prefer not to use coffins for their dead unless they are residing in a country that requires such containment for the deceased. If it is possible to do so, the dead are buried on the day following their death. The deceased is washed, perfumed, and wrapped in three cotton burial cloths.

Those who follow the religion of Islam believe that the soul of the deceased is guarded by the angel of death in a place called Barzakh until the Day of Judgment. If at all possible, friends and relatives gather around a dying person and read verses from the Quran. With his or her last breath, the dying person always tries to say the Shahadah: There is no God but Allah, and Muhammad is his messenger.

Large graves and headstones are not permitted to mark a Muslim burial site, but the grave itself is to be raised above ground level. As the body is being taken to the burial ground, the Salatul Janazah, a prayer for the deceased is read. The body is buried facing Mecca, the sacred city toward which all Muslims turn when they pray.

Carp, Canada, Conspiracies

In early November 1989, a very strange, and highly controversial document was circulated among various prominent individuals in the field of UFO research. One of those individuals was Leonard Stringfield, a former intelligence officer with the United States Air Force. The document told the sensational story of an incident involving nothing less than a UFO that supposedly crashed to Earth in the large swamps of Carp, a community in the Canadian city of Ottawa. According to the anonymous writer of the document: "On November 4, 1989, at 20:00 hrs., Canadian Defense Department radars picked up a globe shaped object travelling at a phenomenal speed over Carp, Ontario. The UFO abruptly stopped, and dropped like a stone."

The source of the story claimed that both Canadian and American military personnel were involved in a secret operation to retrieve the fallen UFO, which was allegedly taken to a secret facility in Kanata, Ontario. Stringfield was told that a number of alien bodies had been recovered from within the UFO, and were described as being reptilian, fetus-headed beings. One presumes they weren't locals.

Matters became even more controversial when the alleged whistleblower claimed that after the craft from another world was carefully examined, evidence was found that shocked the investigation team to its absolute core. That evidence was in the form of small metallic devices that, analysis suggested, were being implanted into the bodies of people, with one goal in mind: to give the aliens complete mental and physical control over the implanted unfortunates.

Stringfield was told that: "All individuals implanted by the aliens are classified as zombies. The zombies have been programmed to help overthrow mankind in the near future. When China finishes with Israel, it will invade Europe. At the same time, Chinese space-based bacteriological weapons will be launched at the Arctic. The winds will carry the diseases into Russia and North America. In days, hundreds of millions will be dead; the survivors will have to deal with the Chinese, the aliens, and the zombies. The aliens want an all-out war so that human resistance would be minimal."

It turns out, however, that the aliens were not quite so alien after all. Stringfield's informant explained: "Data aboard the sphere explained why the aliens are so comfortable in our world. They preceded man on the evolutionary scale by millions of years—created with the dinosaurs. Some sixty-five million years ago, an inter-dimensional war destroyed most of their civilization, and forced them to leave the Earth. Now, they have chosen to reclaim what was once theirs."

Well, that's quite a story. It seems very likely, however, that it was nothing stranger than a bizarre hoax, since the alleged insider maintained that "the alien forces with their Chinese and Arab allies will attack within the next five years." That would have placed any such attack no later than 1994. Clearly, no such attempt to wipe out the human race occurred between 1989 and 1994, suggesting that the whole thing was someone's idea of a tasteless joke. Unless, that is, the aliens decided to put their plans on-hold for a couple of decades. And let's face it: fraught Middle Eastern issues, the growing power and influence of China, the fear of bacteriological weapons, and, of course, zombies, are all staple parts of twenty-first-century civilization. Maybe Leonard Stringfield's source was not so wide off the mark after all. The time frame might have been off-target, but perhaps the future we face is not.

Carradine, John

The well-known Hollywood actor Ving Rhames has starred in no less than three zombie-themed movies: the 2004 remake of George A. Romero's *Dawn of the Dead*, 2008's *Day of the Dead* (which was also a Romero remake), and the downright terrible *Zombie Apocalypse* (2011). In terms of starring roles in zombie movies, however, Rhames has nothing on horror legend John Carradine, who appeared in numerous undead-based productions, including *Revenge of the Zombies, Voodoo Man, Face of Marble, Invisible Invaders, Dr. Terror's Gallery of Horrors, The Astro-Zombies, Blood of Ghastly Horror, The House of Seven Corpses,* and *Shock Waves.*

It is most unfortunate that, at best, all of Carradine's forays into the world of the zombie ranged from what can only be described as awful to mediocre, since he was actually a highly skilled actor. Born in 1906 in Manhattan, New York City, Carradine broke into the movie industry in 1930, in *Bright Lights*. It is ironic that Carradine should be so associated with horror-movies, since his very first credited role in the field of acting was a comedy-musical of no particular, longstanding merit. Nevertheless, Carradine, like all actors, had to start somewhere.

Dramas and westerns soon followed (although Carradine did have un-credited roles in both *The Invisible Man* of 1933 and the 1935 movie, *The Bride of Frankenstein*), as did the 1939 version of Sir Arthur Conan Doyle's classic novel, *The Hound of the Baskervilles*. It was a film in which Carradine took on the significant role of Barryman, the sinister butler of Baskerville Hall. Interestingly, in the original novel, Barryman is named Barrymore, but Twentieth Century Fox chose to make the change to prevent viewers from thinking there might be a connection to the actors John Barrymore and Lionel Barrymore, both of whom were big draws for cinema-goers in the 1930s.

While zombie fanatics may wish to check out each and every one of Carradine's movies of a reanimated and undead fashion, very few are worthy of comment. *Revenge of the Zombies* (1943) is somewhat notable, as it was the sequel to *King of the Zombies*, which was made two years earlier. *Voodoo Man* (1944) starred Bela Lugosi in the lead, which made it a crowd-puller with the viewers, but it can hardly be regarded as a classic.

Certainly, the most interesting of all of Carradine's zombie movies is a 1959 production, *Invisible Invaders*. It focuses on a hostile alien force that plans on enslaving the people of Earth by inhabiting the corpses of the recently deceased, and using the newly animated bodies as vessels to attack and kill the living while simultaneously causing chaos all across the planet. Not quite *Night of the Living Dead*, but most definitely ahead of its time in terms of its concept—although sadly not in terms of its less than impressive special-effects and less than great acting.

Although Carradine worked alongside such famous actors as Spencer Tracy, Basil Rathbone, and Charlton Heston, made more than 200 movies on a wide and varied body of subjects, and spent extensive time working in the world of theater, it is for the incredibly huge number of horror movies that he made for which Carradine is most remembered and loved. He was still active right up until the time of his death, in Milan, Italy, in 1988. Carradine did not, by the way, subsequently "come back."

Cats of the CIA

Pre-George A. Romero era, pretty much each and every scenario involving zombies revolved around not the literal dead, but mind-controlled individuals behaving in a distinctly undead, emotionless state. Such movies as *I Walked with a Zombie* and *White Zombie* make that abundantly clear, as does Wade Davis' book, *The Serpent and the Rainbow*. It may very well be the case that none other than the CIA took deep note of some of those old black and white zombie movies of the 1930s and 1940s. Such a theory is born out by the fact that in the 1960s, scientists of the CIA tried to create an army of loyal and obedient zombie cats.

It was an operation that covertly received funding, not in the tens or even hundreds of thousands of dollars, but in the *millions*. The idea was to transform regular, everyday cats into something hideous, something akin to the *Terminator* or *Robocop*. CIA boffins came up with the ingeniously odd idea of implanting transmitting devices and listening gadgets into the bodies (and even the tails) of cats, and then have them

Believe it or not, the CIA was also involved in a plan to create zombie cats that were obedient to commands. The result was, to say the least, unsuccessful.

wander around the grounds and—if the CIA got *really* lucky—the interior of the Soviet Embassy in Washington, D.C. Anything the cats might have picked up, conversation-wise, was deemed that it could have had a major bearing on national security.

Demonstrating that the CIA's finest knew more than a bit about how to place a cat into a zombified condition, not only did they slice the poor animals open and fill them with wires and metal: they also tinkered with the brains of the cats. Doing so placed the cats into a kind of lobotomized, subservient state, one in which their natural instincts and wild urges were reigned-in, thus allowing the CIA to keep their zombie-spies under control at all times. Unfortunately for those involved in the operation, and particularly so the first cat that was designated for zombification, it didn't work out so well. And that's putting it mildly.

One of those that had an awareness of the program (which went by the amusing, but admittedly appropriate title of *Acoustic Kitty*), was Victor L. Marchetti, Jr., formerly a special assistant to the Deputy Director. Marchetti says that when the controlled cat in question was ready for its very first mission, CIA agents carefully released it close to the Soviet Embassy and prompted the animal to make its way to the building, where, hopefully, it would pick up a few juicy nuggets of information. What the 007-like zombie cat actually did was to get squashed under the wheels of a speeding taxi. The undead cat was now well and truly dead.

The CIA, having decided that the program was not going to work as well in the real world as it did on paper, quickly closed it down and gave it the proverbial bullet to the head. So far as we know, the project has never since been reanimated—so to speak.

Cattle Mutilations

See also: Foot-and-Mouth Disease, Mad Cow Disease

Since at least 1967, just about the entire United States of America has been beset by a disturbing phenomenon. It has infamously become known as cattle mutilations. Exactly who, or indeed what, is responsible for the widespread killing of cattle under very bizarre circumstances is far from clear or understood. On many occasions, farmers, police officers, and veterinarians throughout North America have come across cases where cattle have been subjected to unusual surgical procedures, such as having organs expertly removed and being completely drained of blood—and also in the exact locations where both UFO and black, unmarked helicopter activity is highly prevalent, too.

This has inevitably led to suspicions that extraterrestrials are engaged in a covert, and possibly sinister, program that may relate to the attempted introduction of a lethal virus of truly cosmic origins into the human food chain. Adherents of such theories suggest that the destruction of the human species in a *War of the Worlds*-style scenario may not be the only way to systematically wipe us out.

On the other hand, there's not necessarily a need to bring aliens into the mix at all. A report from the files of the Federal Bureau of Investigation, dated February 2, 1979, and which has been released under the terms of the Freedom of Information Act, lends significant credence to the possibility that the helicopters of unknown origin are implicated in the cattle mutilation mystery to some degree. The report also suggests that the mutilators may have a far more down to earth point of origin, and may very possibly be utilizing the UFO mystery as a highly convenient cover for clandestine bacteriological and biological warfare activities. A significant section of the FBI document at issue states:

"Officer Gabe Valdez, New Mexico State Police, has been handling investigations of these mutilations within New Mexico. Information furnished to this office by Officer Valdez indicates that the animals are being shot with some type of paralyzing drug and the blood is being drawn from the animal after an injection of an anti-coagulant. Officer Valdez is very adamant in his opinion that these mutilations are the work of the U.S. government, and that it is some clandestine operation either by the CIA or the Department of Energy, and in all probability is connected with some type of research into biological warfare."

A terrifying theory for the mutilations, one that has nothing whatsoever to do with bio-war or UFOs, has been carefully developed by Colm Kelleher, Ph.D., formerly of the Ontario Cancer Institute. In 1979, statistics from the U.S. Center for Disease Control show that, by that time, 653 people had officially died of Alzheimer's in the United States. By 1991, the figure had reached 13,768. Eleven years later, it was 58,785. That is an increase of astonishing proportions in a little less than a quarter of a century. As of 2013, more than *five million* Americans are estimated to have Alzheimer's. According to the Alzheimer's Association, an American develops the disease once every sixty-eight seconds of every minute of every day. By 2050, it will be once every thirty-three seconds. It's perhaps not even wise to muse upon what the figure might be by the turn of the twenty-second century, lest you wish to spend your nights sleeplessly tossing and turning in your bed.

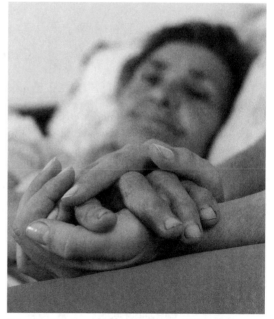

The debilitating, eventually deadly Alzheimer's disease may be escallating in America because of a rise in mad cow disease in the nation's meat supply.

Colm Kelleher believes that this massive increase is not due to Alzheimer's, after all. Instead, he believes that the U.S. food-chain—with the emphasis on the cattle herd—is overwhelmingly infected with bovine spongiform encephalopathy: BSE, or mad cow disease, which can lead to variant Creutzfeldt-Jacob disease (vCJD) in people. In this particular scenario, countless Americans are being disastrously misdiagnosed with Alzheimer's, when the real cause is vCJD, or a further mutant variant.

Kelleher believes that the cattle-mutilators are stealthily trying to prevent public panic, and are secretly monitoring the food-chain to determine how serious the spread of disease is and how fast it is growing. Whether the mutilators work for an agency of government, such as the Centers for Disease Control (CDC) or the Federal Emergency Management Agency (FEMA), or if they are private organizations, secretly contracted by officialdom, is a matter very much unknown.

Given that both vCJD and BSE provoke erratic and, at times, distinctly violent behavior, will we see—in, perhaps just a few more decades from now—an entire nation held in the vice-like grip of a devastating virus that provokes major changes in human personality? The zombie apocalypse of the future may not involve the infected feeding voraciously on the uninfected. Instead, we may see a landscape filled with millions upon millions of shuffling, scarred souls whose minds are descending into nothingness, and all as a tragic and catastrophic result of a love for burgers and steaks.

Cemeteries and Tombs

See also: Burial Traditions, Cremation, Funerals, Mummies

The marking of graves goes back into remote antiquity. The ancient Hebrews buried their dead and used stone pillars to mark the graves. The Greeks often placed gravestones and various kinds of ornate sculpture on their burial sites.

The Assyrians (c. 750–612 B.C.E.) dug huge excavations which sometimes reached a depth of sixty feet into which they cast the bodies of their dead, one upon the other. Even when they began to place their dead in coffins, the Assyrians continued to pile one above the other in great excavations.

The Iberians, the original people who inhabited the peninsula where modern day Portugal and Spain exist, buried their leaders with great pomp and ceremony in chambers made of huge stones, covered over with earth. The bodies were placed in these megalithic chambers in a sitting posture. The Aryans, an Indo-European people, burned their dead and placed the ashes in urns shaped like rounded huts with thatched roofs.

Decorating graves with flowers and wreaths is an old custom which appears to date back to the earliest human burial observances. Wreaths made of thin gold have been found in Athenian graves during archaeological excavations. The Egyptians adorned their mummies with flowers, and paintings on the walls of tombs that depict the mourners carrying flowers in their hands.

Not everyone who died in ancient Egypt was buried in a tomb. Although the Egyptians believed firmly in an afterlife, they were also of the opinion that only the powerful and important in the earthly life would have any notable status in the world to come. According to rank and wealth, those who were great in Egypt, and therefore likely to be important in the next life, were laid to rest in magnificent tombs with treasure, servants, food, and weapons to accompany them; the ordinary people were buried in rude stone compartments.

The rulers of the ancient city of Thebes, once the capital of upper-Egypt (1580–1085 B.C.E.) and their subjects never constructed massive pyramids to house their coffins, but cut their tombs from rock. As soon as a pharaoh would ascend the throne, his loyal subjects began the preparation of their tombs. Excavation went on uninterrupted, year by year, until death ended the king's reign and simultaneously the work on his tomb which also became a kind of an index revealing the length of his reign. These tombs, cut from the rock in the mountains in Upper Egypt, are still to be seen.

In sixteenth century Europe, it was customary to make wreaths of flowers from ribbon and paper and give them to the church in memory of the deceased. These artificial wreaths of long ago evolved into the contemporary mourning wreath of living flowers, usually brought by friends or relatives of the deceased and placed upon the grave.

Centers for Disease Control

In the event that a real-life zombie uprising really does occur, there is one agency of government—more than any other—that will likely play a major, leading role in trying to quickly find an antidote for the virus that brings back the dead in horrific, murderous form. Its name is the Centers for Disease Control, or the CDC. In a strictly fictional format, this has already happened. In "Wildfire," the fifth episode of the first season of AMC's phenomenally popular show, *The Walking Dead*, group-leader Rick Grimes leads his band of starving, exhausted survivors to the headquarters of the CDC in Atlanta, Georgia. After begging to be let in, they are met by the mysterious and cautious Edwin Jenner. He is the very last survivor of the installation and someone who seems to be, suspiciously, highly informed about the zombie virus, as well as its origins, nature, and history. As the episode comes to a climactic close, Jenner quietly tells Grimes something terrible. In a later episode, the group finally learns the awful secret.

Rick Grimes explains to his shocked comrades exactly what Jenner confided in him: "We're all infected." And we are. At some point before the apocalypse exploded all across the planet, Jenner revealed, every single person was *already* unknowingly infected by the zombie virus. Yes, a bite from the walking dead will kill you and bring you back. But, death under *any* and *all* circumstances—a fatal accident, old age, sui-

The headquarters of the Centers for Disease Control are located in Atlanta, Georgia.

cide, or a terminal disease—will bring you back, too. Jenner did not reveal how, or under what circumstances, the virus spread—or, perhaps, was *allowed* to spread—but that made very little difference to Rick Grimes and his friends, who now knew that even if they successfully avoided a deadly zombie bite for all of their lives, they would still, one day, ultimately transform into something hideous.

So much for the world of television fiction, but what is the actual nature of the CDC? Would it take a leading role in combating an outbreak of marauding zombies? Certainly, without doubt, the answer is: yes, absolutely. The real world CDC is at the forefront of helping to lessen, and ultimately stop, any and all threats posed by deadly viruses. "Category A" viruses, for the CDC, are considered to be the most serious ones of all.

They are those specific viruses that, says the CDC, "can be easily spread or transmitted from person to person," that "result in high death rates and have the potential for major public health impact," that "might cause panic and social disruption,", and that would "require special action for public health preparedness." It practically goes without saying that all four of those criteria which fall into the CDC's "Category A" could more than easily apply to the outbreak of a virus that returns the dead to some psychotic semblance of life.

Moreover, and by the CDC's very own admission, its work is "a critical component of overall U.S. national security." The U.S. government most assuredly recognizes the profound importance of the CDC from that very same national security perspective. Currently, the CDC receives yearly funding of around $1.3 billion to "build and strengthen national preparedness for public health emergencies caused by natural, accidental, or intentional events." It also works closely with the Department of Homeland Security, and with FEMA, the Federal Emergency Management Agency.

If, one day, the dead do return to cause chaos and carnage, our best hopes for survival may very well be wholly dependent upon the finest minds of the CDC.

It may sound like the ultimate April Fools' Day joke, or a tall tale with which to terrify children on the spookiest night of the year: Halloween. Incredibly, however, it is not. The U.S. government's Centers for Disease Control has a section of its website devoted to nothing less than how to deal with a zombie outbreak. Yes, we are talking about a *real* zombie outbreak. Not only that: much of the online data at the site was provided by Rear Admiral Ali S. Khan, who, in August 2010, was assigned to lead the work of the CDC's Office of Public Health Preparedness and Response. Rear Admiral Khan is also the Deputy Director of the National Center for Emerging and Zoonotic Infectious Diseases. He is, therefore, a prestigious and highly regarded figure.

In a May 2011 article for the CDC's website, Khan gave a brief history of zombie lore. It encompassed Haitian beliefs on the subject, its links with Voodoo rites and rituals, and its place in the field of movies, such as *Night of the Living Dead*. Khan noted: "The rise of zombies in pop culture has given credence to the idea that a zombie apocalypse could happen. In such a scenario, zombies would take over entire countries, roaming city streets eating anything living that got in their way."

More intriguing were Rear Admiral Khan's words on what direct action the CDC might have to take in the event that a real world scenario befitting *The Walking Dead* one day comes to pass. "Technical assistance," stated Khan, would be provided at a city, state, and even international level when, or if, a "zombie infestation" began. Control of the spread of infection would be achieved by quickly placing those affected into quarantine and isolation. Attempts to find a cure for the zombie virus would be paramount, explained the admiral. He also revealed that much time would be spent on determining how the outbreak began, what caused it, and how best to combat the "cycle of transmission" that led to the situation in which zombies were overrunning the landscape. Clearly, then, the CDC has given a great deal of thought to what might happen when the zombies attack and the world is in turmoil and upheaval.

It must be noted that the CDC's zombie-themed material is presented in slightly tongue in cheek fashion: it even has a non-profit partner called the CDC Foundation that sells "Zombie Task Force" t-shirts. The profits go toward disaster-relief programs. Despite the curious and undeniably surreal humor in all of this, one is inevitably forced to muse upon a potentially alarming possibility: does the CDC secretly know something that the rest of us *don't* know? Is its staff aware that, one day, possibly in the very near future, a genuine zombie outbreak may very well occur? If so, is the CDC trying to subtly warn us to be prepared, maybe in a fashion that does not overly alarm us? At least, it won't alarm us until the dead rise up and start attacking the living.

If, one day, the recently deceased really *do* surface from the grave and go on a virus-spreading, homicidal killing spree, you would be wise to check out the location of your nearest CDC center. It may very well prove to be the best place in which to hide out when the lights go off, the electricity shuts down, and the news suddenly stops broadcasting.

Chamani, Miriam

Priestess Miriam Chamani gives Consultations and African Bone Readings both in person and via the telephone. She specializes in Voodoo Weddings, Damballah for Healing, and Erzulie for Love. Priestess Miriam designs Voodoo Dolls and Kits tailored to each person's needs and desires.

Priestess Miriam was born and raised in Mississippi, where she experienced the power of mysterious spiritual forces beginning in early childhood. Around 1975, the power of the spirit called strongly to Priestess Miriam, leading her to many spiritual orders and ultimately to a seat at the Angel All Nations Spiritual Church. There she increased her knowledge of spirit and explored metaphysical concepts and teachings.

In 1990, Priestess Miriam and her late husband, Oswan Chamani, settled in New Orleans, where they founded the Voodoo Spiritual Temple, the only temple of its kind in the city at that time. The Temple is located next to Congo Square, and its rituals are directly connected to those performed on Congo Square by Marie Laveau and Doctor John. It is the only formally established Spiritual Temple with a focus on traditional West African spiritual and herbal healing practices currently existing in New Orleans.

Upon the death of her husband, Voodoo Priest Oswan Chamani, on March 6, 1995, Miriam Chamani continued her husband's Belizan Vodou and herbalism traditions in addition to her own spiritualist practices, and she pursues many of the inclusive trends of Black Christian Spiritualism, seeking to serve all peoples, regardless of race or belief.

Visit Priestess Miriam Chamani's website at http://www.Voodoospiritualtemple.org/

Chinese Zombies

If you think that the concept of the jerky, slow-moving dead is a relatively modern one, then it is very much a case of time to think again. Within Chinese culture and folklore, tales of such abominations date back centuries. In China, the zombie is known as the jiang-shi. And it is just about as deadly and terrifying as its Haitian and western counterparts. Jiang-shi translates into English as "stiff corpse." And there is a very good reason for that: the movements and gait of the Chinese undead are not at all dissimilar to the zombies of George A. Romero's *Night of the Living Dead*.

In China, the jiang-shi is a creature with a seemingly never-ending case of rigor mortis. Most people are familiar with the concept of this post-death condition: when a person dies, the body significantly stiffens. This is due to a now-permanent lack of oxygen, which prevents the body from producing adenosine triphosphate, a molecule significantly involved in the regulation of the human metabolism. As the metabolic system finally comes to an irreversible halt, the process of rigor mortis quickly begins.

Many people, however, are unaware that rigor mortis is not a permanent condition. While it typically sets in just a few hours after death, within a day or so, its effects have completely vanished and the body is as supple in death as it was in life. For the jiang-shi, however, rigor mortis never, ever goes away, something which ensures the creature retains a stiff, robotic gait at all times, just like Romero's infamous ghouls.

Notably, the jiang-shi has another zombie parallel: like its cinematic counterpart, the jiang-shi feeds on humans. Whereas the walking and running undead need human flesh to fuel their bodies, the jiang-shi is fuelled by the very essence of what makes us human: the soul. Chinese tradition tells of the soul being the container of a powerful energy, one that the average jiang-shi craves, and that is known as Qi. The average zombie may be quite content to eat its prey while they are still alive and fighting for their lives, but the jiang-shi is first required to slaughter its victim before the act of Qi-devouring can begin in earnest.

In the same way that there are two kinds of zombies—the Haitian, mind-controlled type and the rabid, infected kind most often seen in movies—so too there are two groups of jiang-shi. One is a freshly dead person who reanimates extremely quickly, perhaps even within mere minutes of death. The other is an individual who rises from the grave months, or even years after they have passed away, but who displays no inward or outward evidence of decomposition.

As for how and why a person may become a jiang-shi, the reasons are as many as they are varied: being buried prematurely, dabbling in the black arts, and, rather interestingly, getting hit by lightning can all result in transformation from a regular human to a jiang-shi. On this latter point of lightning, electricity has played a significant role in the resurrection of the dead in the world of fiction, and most notably in Mary Shelley's classic novel of 1818, *Frankenstein*. There is another way of transforming into a jiang-shi, too, one which zombie aficionados will definitely be able to relate to: when a person is killed and their Qi is taken, the victim also becomes a jiang-shi. What this demonstrates is that the jiang-shi's act of stealing energy is very much the equivalent of the zombie delivering an infectious bite.

And, just like most zombies of movies, novels, and television shows, most jiang-shis don't look good in the slightest. Although the jiang-shi typically appears relatively normal when it first reanimates—in the sense that decomposition is not in evidence—things soon change, and not for the better. The walking, jerky corpse of the jiang-shi begins to degrade significantly, the rank odor of the dead becomes all-dominating, and the flesh begins to hang, turning an unhealthy-looking lime color as it does so.

Killing a jiang-shi can be just as difficult as putting down a cinematic zombie. A bullet to the body of a zombie may briefly slow it down. But only a head-shot is going to guarantee the monster stays down permanently. It's very much the same with the jiang-shi: the trick is in knowing what actually works best. The jiang-shi cannot abide vinegar, which acts as the equivalent of a deadly poison. While actually managing to pour significant amounts of vinegar into the mouth of a ferocious jiang-shi may prove to be far more than tricky, it is said to work at a rapid rate. Smearing the skin of a jiang-shi with the blood of a recently dead dog will also put a jiang-shi to rest, although exactly why is a very different matter. Mind you, providing it worked, would you even care why? No, you probably would not. You would simply be glad to be alive!

Chupacabras

See also: Berwyn Mountains Zombie Dogs, Black Dogs, Zombie Dogs of Texas

Since at least the mid 1990s, the island of Puerto Rico has been the home of a terrifying, marauding animal that reportedly sucks the blood out of farm animals, chiefly goats and chickens. Its name is the Chupacabras, a Spanish term meaning—very appropriately—Goat-Sucker. Whatever the true nature of the monster, it's clearly as unique as it is hideous. It sports fiery red eyes, a row of sharp spikes running from the back of its head to the middle part of its spine, pointed fangs, razor-like claws, and brings nothing but death and disaster to whomever or whatever it crosses paths with.

While the answers are few and far between concerning the true nature of the Chupacabras, the theories are many. For some, the Chupacabras is a giant bat. For others, it's an extraterrestrial entity. Then there is the theory it's something infernal and paranormal-based, something that was conjured up by occultists; but from where, exactly, remains unknown. There is, however, an explanation that is acutely different to all of those above, one which, in many ways, is even more disturbing. It's also one that the average zombie aficionado can likely relate to and appreciate.

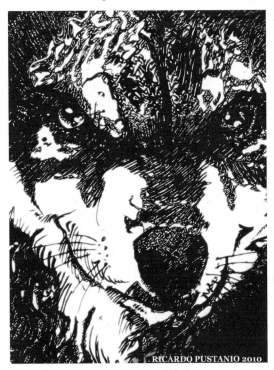

The Chupacabras, or Goat-Sucker, is sometimes described as a giant bat or extraterrestrial, but more often it is seen as a creature resembling an ugly canine.

Situated on Puerto Rico, and established back in the 1930s, is a facility called the Caribbean Primate Research Center. By its own admission, the work of the CPRC is focused upon "the study and use of non-human primates as models for studies of social and biological interactions and for the discovery of methods of prevention, diagnosis and treatment of diseases that afflict humans." And its work is very well-respected: both the U.S. National Institutes of Health and the National Center for Research Resources provide significant funding for the center.

One of the most controversial aspects of the work of the Caribbean Primate Research Center is that devoted to the study of SIV, which is the monkey equivalent of HIV, the virus that leads to AIDS. Such work is undertaken by staff in the CPRC's Virology Laboratory. There are longstanding rumors on Puerto Rico that the Virology Laboratory has been engaged in something else, too; something profoundly disturbing. According to the locals, back in the 1990s, highly secret research was undertaken at the CPRC that revolved around the deliberate infection of monkeys—specifically Rhesus Monkeys—with a real-life equivalent of the "Rage Virus" of *28 Days Later* and *28 Weeks Later* infamy.

The story continues that not long after the experimentation began, some of those same Rhesus Monkeys escaped from the CPRC—or were deliberately released from it—and made new homes deep in Puerto Rico's El Yunque rain-forest. Savage, violent, and deadly, they were avoided at all costs by the staff of the CPRC, who knew only too well of their marauding, zombie-like behavior. To cover its tracks, however, the CPRC did something ingenious: it carefully spread stories that the monkeys were, in fact, Chupacabras—and lots of them, too. Circulating fear-filled tales of monsters would hopefully achieve three things: (a) it would keep people out of the area; (b) it would prevent people from becoming bitten and infected by the rage-inducing virus; and (c) it would ensure the CPRC received no backlash for its fringe-research into dangerous viruses. If the story is true, then the ruse worked very well, indeed. Belief in the Chupacabras quickly became widespread on Puerto Rico, and pretty much everyone forgot about the CPRC and its weird experimentation.

Civil War Zombies

According to the research of historians at Haunted America Tours (http://hauntedamericatours.com), many Voodoo and Hoodoo Kings and Queens became wealthy during the Civil War in the 1860s by reanimating fallen Confederate and Union soldiers and selling them as zombie slaves. The sorcerers mixed up dead things in a big black stew pot. They ground up corpses and zombie fingers and toes to make special Zombie Brand powders that only the very rich could afford and only the very evil would want to employ.

For some, this was the Golden Era of Zombies. Half white/half black Creole queens and kings plied their special dark swamp medicines, amulets, charms, and zombified wares from coast to coast after Ulysses S. Grant became president.

Experts on the history of Voodoo, such as Lisa Lee Harp Waugh, Karen Beals, and the noted New Orleans artist Ricardo Pustanio, have observed that the deep dark secrets of a Voodoo-Hoodoo person at the time was always well accepted. These special Creole people were never more sought after and revered than those of the Great White Mambas whose names are still remembered and honored today.

The old red-bricked, crumbling, white-washed tomb of Marie Laveau is the spot where many say the eternal Voodoo queen still grants wishes from beyond the grave. However, some say she will grant your wish only if you promise to come back to the tomb no later than one year and a day. If you do not show at the allotted time then you might just find that you have lost all you gained. Even worse, is the curse that the one you love most will become a real zombie when he or she dies.

Many researchers in certain Voodoo-Hoodoo circles believe that real zombification came to America through the teachings of Marie Laveau, the Voodoo Queen of

New Orleans. Others believe it was her teacher and mentor Dr. John who first taught Marie. Still others claim that the Great Texan Voodoo Queen Black Cat Mama Couteaux was the ultimate zombifier.

Black Cat Mama Couteaux, according to Lisa Lee, was the ultimate Voodoo-Hoodoo Queen in Marshall, Texas. The stories of her in the state are often told as far away as Abilene and Fort Worth. They say she even rode out the Great Storm of 1900 in a row boat. The woman was said to have been married to her zombie lover. The dead Mamba husband zombie is said to still be around, guarding the treasures she amassed.

Texan Lisa Lee Harp Waugh states that the old spells that they speak of in her part of the United States seem to have originated from Black Cat Mama Couteaux. But if you listen to most of the old stories, Waugh notes, they suggest that she was actually taught by a great Voodoo-Hoodoo king from New Orleans who had a secret circle of Voodoo-Hoodoo Queens that gave him all their personal attentions as they sat at his knee begging him to teach them more. That great King would, of course, be Dr. John.

Coffins

See also: Burial Traditions, Cemeteries and Tombs, Cremation, Funerals, Mummies

If there is one thing that can be said with certainty about the human race, it's that each and every one of us is on a time limit. Not to be gloomy about it, but sooner or later—and hopefully the latter—we will all shuffle off of this mortal coil. And, when we finally do go, there are two primary options available when it comes to the type of send off we receive. One is cremation and the other is burial in a coffin. But have you ever wondered why coffins have locks on them? Is it, perhaps, due to age-old superstitions and fears that the dead might actually awaken and try to rise from the grave? After all, locking a corpse inside a coffin that is six feet or so underground makes no sense at all. Or, does it? It just might, if there is a fear that the very same corpse may try and force its way to the surface.

Traditions of showing respect to the dead, by doing something beyond simply dumping their bodies for wild animals to feed upon, date back thousands of years. In ancient Egypt, for example, the elite, the rich, and the powerful were carefully wrapped in cloth and placed in a sarcophagus. In Europe, even when civilization was in its infancy, there was an understanding that death was something to honor. Lacking the skills of the Egyptians, the tribes of Europe—and particularly so the Celts—wrapped the average dead person in a sheet of cloth and buried them in the ground. Revered warriors, warlords and kings were placed in coffin-like creations comprised of carefully positioned rocks and stones. In the United States, the coffin industry very much—and very understandably—came to the fore at the height of the American Civil War of 1861 to 1865, in which no less than 600,000 people lost their lives during the carnage of battle.

As for the matter of why, exactly, today's coffins are firmly sealed on the outside, while the idea that it is done to prevent the zombified dead from digging their way out is an engaging and thought-provoking one, that is not actually the case. In centuries past, such practices were done to prevent grave robbing—which was rife in the United Kingdom, and particularly so in the 1800s. Take, for example, the so-called London Burkers. They were a team of London-based body-snatchers that stole dozens of fresh corpses from graves throughout the nation's capital during the nineteenth century.

Have you ever wondered why coffins are firmly sealed? There is, after all, a logical explanation that does not have to do with a fear of zombies.

A further, and equally understandable reason for keeping the lid on a coffin is to ensure that if, in a worst-case scenario, the coffin is dropped on its way to burial, the corpse does not tumble out in front of shocked, grieving mourners. And, finally, contrary to popular belief, the coffin is not actually locked. It is simply sealed with what is termed a gasket. Securely fastening the gasket helps prevent water from entering the coffin after it has been placed in the ground. The coffin, therefore, is all about respect for the dead, rather than being based upon age-old fears that the dead might rise from the grave and devour the living. Of course, in the event that a real-life zombie pandemic *does* one day occur, many will surely sigh with relief that they chose to have their loved ones placed inside a sealed coffin!

Cold War

If, one day, the zombie virus becomes not just an issue of fiction but one of stark, terrifying fact, the possibility cannot be denied that it may fall into the hands of terrorists, ones that may wish to see it used to target specific nations and wipe them out in apocalyptic style. It might sound outrageous, but official files that have surfaced under the terms of the U.S. government's Freedom of Information Act show that, back in the 1940s, there were significant fears on the part of officialdom that a hostile nation—or a rogue body of terrorists—might infect the American cattle herd with a deadly virus, one which could quickly spread to the human population and utterly decimate it.

Prepared by the Committee on Biological Warfare at the request of the U.S. government's elite Research and Development Board, the fifty-page file in question dates from March 1947 through the latter part of 1948 and makes for disturbing and grim reading.

In a Top Secret paper from March 28, 1947, it was stated that: "A memorandum from the Secretaries of War and Navy dated February 21, 1947, Subject: International Aspects of Biological Warfare, regarding biological warfare in relation to United

Nations negotiations for regulation of armaments was referred by the Board to Committee 'X' for consideration and recommendations."

Seven months later, the Research and Development Board prepared an in-depth report (also classified at Top Secret level) that outlined its worries concerning biowar. The Board stated: "Preparations for biological warfare can be hidden under a variety of guises. The agents of biological warfare are being studied in every country of the world because they are also the agents of diseases of man, domestic animals, and crop plants. The techniques used in developing biological warfare agents are essentially similar to the techniques used in routine bacteriological studies and in the production of vaccines, toxoids, and other beneficial materials."

In its report, the Board continued: "... the Committee feels that although it may be possible to control atomic research and insure that it be devoted to peaceful purposes, it is impracticable to control research on biological agents because of the close similarity between such research and legitimate investigations of a medical, agricultural, or veterinary nature."

What of the possibility that biological warfare could have been utilized as a weapon of mass destruction and the cause of extreme devastation, via the spreading of a deadly virus? In March 1947, the Board had its doubts that biological warfare could be considered a tool of destruction on par with atomic weapons; however, seven months later that view had changed radically.

With respect to this matter, in October 1947, the Board recorded that: "On the basis of present knowledge the Committee feels that biological weapons cannot be compared in their effect with such so-called weapons of mass destruction as, for example, the atomic bomb. It is doubtless true that if a self-sustaining epidemic of a fatal disease could be established in a human population, indiscriminate destruction of life on a great scale might result. However, as has been pointed out earlier in this discussion, the Committee knows of no epidemic agent that could presently be used with confidence in its significant epidemic-producing property.

"The spread of epidemics depends upon a number of complex inter-related factors, many of which are poorly understood or perhaps even unknown. Furthermore, it is believed that the chances of discovering an unusually virulent epidemic-producing biological agent is highly improbable and cannot be anticipated at any time in the predictable future."

So much for the Committee's beliefs with respect to biological warfare and the human race.

The Colonized

In a world in which all things of a zombie nature are becoming ever more dominating, the biggest challenge facing filmmakers, Hollywood studios, script-writers, and authors is not so much just to come up with ideas, but to create and weave storylines that are actually fresh, rather than yawn-inspiring. Certainly, one only has to take a mere glimpse at the large amount of both literary and on-screen productions of the undead variety to realize that tedious repetition, overwhelming sterility, and far less than inspiring scripts are, today, the definitive name of the game. We have seen it all, and we have heard it all, time and time again. Fortunately, however, that is not always the case. Take for example, Chris Ryall and Drew Moss' graphic-novel series *The Colonized*.

For Ryall and Moss, your average zombie apocalypse-style scenario is simply not nearly good enough—and although that may not be such a positive thing for the characters who are fighting for their very lives, for the readers it is very good news. While it is one thing to have to face a full-on maniacal assault from hordes of flesh-devouring recently deceased, it is an entirely different matter to insert nothing less than visiting aliens from a faraway world into the story, too. But, this is exactly what our intrepid duo of Ryall and Moss does—and in a fashion that works very well, it must be stressed. Add to the undead and the extraterrestrials a cast of survivalist fruitcakes, gun-toting, small town gangs, and a slightly sinister government agent lurking in the shadows, and you have a great story unfolding before your very eyes.

It is most refreshing, too, to see a high degree of thinking outside the box taking place. There is a nice touch about how the aliens themselves—or their unearthly biology, at least—have an impact on the nature and effects of the zombie virus. Sly and wry humor abounds. And we even get treated to the freakishly fun sight of not just human zombies, but the animals of the undead, too. Of course, the fact that *Colonized* is set in small-town USA means we are talking farm animals. Or, perhaps, *Barn of the Dead* would be far more apt. Have you ever seen a pig, a chicken, or a horse wildly racing and raging around like the fast-running infected of *28 Days Later*? To be sure, it's not a pretty sight, to say the very least. But it *is* highly entertaining.

As is always the case when fiction and zombies cross paths, things finally reach their bloody finale, and it all too quickly becomes a case of do or die—and that goes for the humans and the aliens alike. Even the dead do all they can to avoid death—for a second time, naturally. In finality, *Colonized* is a decidedly surreal, alternative, and fun take on a topic that brings something very welcome and important to the table of the reanimated and the cannibalistic: it is called originality.

The Colony

Made in 2013, *The Colony* is a Canadian movie that, when all is said and done, is pretty good. The film stars Lawrence Fishburne (Briggs), Bill Paxton (Mason), and Kevin Zegers (Sam). The latter took on the role of Terry, a security guard, in the 2004 remake of George A. Romero's *Dawn of the Dead*. Whereas in *Dawn of the Dead* the flesh-eating monsters are literally dead, in *The Colony* they are the starving survivors of a worldwide apocalypse that have descended into primitive, cannibalistic states.

The storyline is an interesting one: *The Colony* is set midway through the twenty-first century, at a time when weather-modification technology has brought the human race to its knees. In the decades leading up to disaster, such technology was used to try and combat the effects of ever-increasing global warming. As the planet gets hotter, the machines try to combat things by lowering the temperature. They do so, but in catastrophic fashion. Not only does the planet cool, but it starts to snow—*everywhere*. And the snow does not stop. *Ever*. As a result, and years later, the earth is now in the grip of a modern day ice-age.

The landscape of the whole planet resembles the North and South Pole. Cities are buried under tons of ice and snow, and civilization is no more. Those that have managed to survive the worldwide freezing do so in huge underground installations where life is bleak, food is scarce, and a deadly form of flu is on the loose. Everyday is a fight for survival and things are getting grimmer by the hour.

The Colony begins in what is termed Colony 7, where Briggs, Mason, and Sam live—the latter with his girlfriend, Kai, played by actress Charlotte Sullivan. After the group receives a distress call from another group of survivors—also deep underground, at what is termed Colony 5—Briggs decides that someone must go and check out what's afoot and why Colony 5 is now not just in trouble, but has subsequently gone completely silent, too. When Briggs asks for volunteers to accompany him, Sam and a teenage boy named Graydon (actor Atticus Dean Mitchell) are quick to accept the challenge. Mason, meanwhile, plots behind the scenes to try and take control over Colony 7.

After an arduous and hazardous trek through arctic weather and a ruined, snow-covered city, the three finally make it to Colony 5 and descend into its underground depths. Not only is the colony quiet, it's downright *too* quiet. And when the trio finally stumbles upon a solitary, terrified colonist, they know something bad has gone down. Exactly how bad, soon becomes apparent. Colony 5 has been invaded by a band of psychotic cannibals. Whereas those that live underground have retained their humanity, those who still live topside have descended into states of definitive savagery. To the horror of Briggs, Sam, and Graydon, the colonists have been killed. The three find this out in graphic fashion when they stumble on the flesh-eaters slicing up body upon body, all being prepared for dinner.

Although the cannibals are not of the dead kind, they're not just regular, but desperate people, either. Their teeth are like fangs and they scream, howl, and roar rather than talk. In many respects they come across not unlike a combination of the infected of *28 Days Later* and the animalistic vampires of the 2007 movie, *30 Days of Night*—which, incidentally, is also set around a snowbound background. The three men make a run for it, with the hungry hordes in hot pursuit. Unfortunately, Graydon doesn't make it. There's equally bad luck too: Briggs sacrifices himself to prevent the cannibals from finding out where he and Sam live, namely Colony 7. It's to no avail, however. The people-eaters manage to follow Sam's footprints and, in no time, break in to the colony, where a life or death battle begins—one which culminates in a fiery explosion as Mason kills himself and countless invaders. And it's finally up to Sam to take on the leader of the cannibals—something that ends triumphantly for the dwindling band.

The Colony ends on a positive note when Sam, Kai, and the few who are left head for new pastures, a place where, reportedly, the icy environment has been reversed and blue skies and green terrain are once again the norm. The end of the human race just might not be in the cards, after all.

Columbia, Space Shuttle

When the space shuttle *Columbia* was catastrophically torn to pieces during its reentry on February 1, 2003, in addition to the astronauts who died in the explosion, nearly ninety on-board science experiments were lost as what was left of *Columbia* plummeted to the ground. Three weeks later, however, it was revealed that Texas State University-San Marcos biologist Robert McLean had managed to save something completely unanticipated from the widely spread debris: namely, a strain of slow-growing bacteria that had survived the crash. It was a discovery that may have significant implications for the concept of panspermia, which is the scenario of life—perhaps even viruses—"hitchhiking" on rocks ejected from meteorite impacts on one world, and that could travel through space and seed other worlds with life under favorable conditions.

Notably, found within the wreckage of *Columbia* was a bacteria called Microbispora: a slow-growing organism, normally found in soil, that McLean determined had probably contaminated the experiment prior to launch. "This organism appears to have survived an atmospheric passage, with the heat and the force of impact," McLean said. "That's only about a fifth of the speed that something on a real meteorite would have to survive, but it is at least five or six times faster than what's been tested before. This is important for panspermia, because if something survives space travel, it eventually has to get down to the Earth and survive passage through the atmosphere and impact. This doesn't prove anything; it just contributes evidence to the plausibility of panspermia."

It also demonstrates that when we head into outer space, we may bring back something terrifying, something viral, something that may lead to a real-life dawning of the dead. Or, a case of: one small step for man, one giant leap for zombiekind.

Examination of the debris from the space shuttle *Columbia* disaster showed that bacteria could survive being in space and even the high-temperature process of reentry into the atmosphere.

Congo Conspiracies

In August 1964, a very strange yet fascinating document was secretly prepared for senior personnel in the U.S. Army and the Pentagon. A copy even reached none other than the White House. Its title was *Witchcraft, Sorcery, Magic, and Other Psychological Phenomena and Their Implications on Military and Paramilitary Operations in the Congo*. It was a document written by James Price and Paul Juredini, both of whom worked for the Special Operations Research Office, SORO, which was an agency that undertook top secret contract work for the military.

The document, now in the public domain under the terms of the Freedom of Information Act, is a fascinating one, in the sense that it focuses on how beliefs in paranormal phenomena can be successfully used and manipulated to defeat a potential enemy. The bigger the belief in the world of the supernatural, note Price and Juredini, the greater the chance that a particularly superstitious foe could be terrorized and manipulated by spreading faked stories of paranormal creatures on the loose, of demons in their midst, and of ghostly, terrible things with violent slaughter on their monstrous minds.

Interestingly, one portion of the document deals with a classic aspect of the zombie of the modern era: its terrifying ability to keep on coming, even when its body is riddled with bullet upon bullet. In the example, the authors reported that: "Rebel tribesmen are said to have been persuaded that they can be made magically impervious to Congolese army firepower. Their fear of the government has thus been diminished and, conversely, fear of the rebels has grown within army ranks."

That was not all: rumors quickly spread within the army to the effect that the reason why the rebels were allegedly so immune to bullets was because they had been definitively zombified. Not in Romero-style, but by good old, tried and tested Voodoo techniques. The rebels, entire swathes of army personnel came to fully believe—and very quickly, too—had literally been rendered indestructible as a result of dark and malignant spells and incantations. On top of that, the minds of the rebels, controlled by a Voodoo master, had been magically distilled, to the point where they were driven by a need to kill and nothing else. Or so it was widely accepted by the Congolese military.

It transpired, as one might guess, that the stories were actually wholly fictional ones. They were ingeniously created and spread by none other than the rebels themselves, and with just one purpose in mind: to have the army utterly convinced that the rebels were unbeatable and indestructible. Such was the ingrained fear that infected the army, the brilliant piece of disinformation was accepted as full-blown fact—as was the belief that fearless, and fear-inducing, zombies were roaming the landscape and who were impervious to bullets. The result: the rebels delivered the army a powerful blow of a terrifyingly psychological kind. While the bullet-proof zombies of the Congo never really existed, for all of the stark fear and mayhem they provoked, they just might as well have been the real thing.

The Crazies

When you think of George A. Romero, several things immediately, and inevitably, spring to mind: death, chaos, a deadly virus, societal collapse, people running for their lives, and—last, but most assuredly not least—zombies. Well, in Romero's 1973 film, *The Crazies*, you have all of those ingredients, except for one: the shambling dead. A Romero film, but one specifically without walking corpses: can it be true? Yes, it *is* true. But, instead of the dead, the cast of *The Crazies* are forced to do battle with something just as fearsome; hordes of *living* people who have been driven to homicidal levels of madness after being exposed to a military-created biological weapon.

Like most of Romero's zombie movies, *The Crazies*—also released under the far less fearsome title of *Code Name: Trixie*—makes the viewer ponder deeply on how fragile society really is, and the speed with which it can fragment and collapse when death, disaster, and terror become overwhelming. It's also a film from which the production teams of the likes of *28 Days Later* and *28 Weeks Later* likely took a great deal of inspiration.

The scary humans in 1973's *The Crazies* are not zombified undead, but rather people ill with a disease that turns them into homicidal maniacs.

Evans City, Pennsylvania is where all of the carnage and homicidal behavior occurs. As it does so, we follow the plight of a trio of people trying to comprehend, and survive, the anarchy exploding all around them. They are David and Judy—a fireman and a nurse who also happen to be boyfriend and girlfriend—and Clank, also a fireman. When violent behavior quickly turns Evans City into a living hell, a large military contingent quickly arrives to take control of the alarming situation. Each and every one of them is decked out in protective gear of the type generally seen in chemical- and biological-warfare outbreaks, and are led by a Major Ryder.

Taking control basically means killing anyone and everyone who is living—whether they are infected or not. So, as is often the case when Romero is behind the lens, the stars of *The Crazies* are not just in danger of losing their lives to those with the virus, but to their normal, fellow people, too. As the film progresses, the death rate rises, the deranged infected become even more deranged, two of the characters fail to survive the onslaught, and the military starts to lose control of the situation. Zombie fans that have not seen *The Crazies* will be satisfied by its bleak ending: the Army is forced to retreat from what is now, for all intents and purposes, a city transformed into an outdoor asylum. Word reaches Major Ryder that *another* city is showing signs of infection. The end is becoming ever more nigh.

The Crazies was not a big hit with cinema-goers in 1973 or, indeed, ever since. In fact, it wasn't even a small hit. In short, it bombed, big time. It has, however, and quite rightly, become a cult-classic among those that have a love for the crazed, the infected, and Romero. It also inspired a remake, in 2010, starring Timothy Olyphant of such movies as *Hitman* and *Live Free or Die Hard*. The budget was a big one, and the profits were impressive. Audience reactions, however, were mixed. Even though Romero himself acted as the executive producer and the co-writer on the new incarnation, many preferred the 1973 original to the special-effects-driven version of nearly forty years later. In short, not everyone was, ahem, crazy about bringing back *The Crazies*.

Cremation

*See also: **Burial Traditions, Cemeteries and Tombs, Funerals, Mummies***

Because early humankind so feared the evil spirits that caused death and believed that these entities continued to dwell in the corpse of their beloved, awaiting new victims, it is not surprising that cremation, the burning of the body, became one of the earliest methods of disposing of the dead. Cremation appears to have been practiced widely in the ancient world, except in Egypt, in China, and among the Hebrews.

In ancient Greece only suicides, infants who had not yet grown teeth, and persons who had been struck by lightning were denied the privilege of cremation and were buried instead. When cremation was conducted, the ceremonies were elaborate and solemn and the ashes of the deceased were placed in urns of burned clay and buried. Later, when burial became the custom in Greece, the bodies were enclosed in elaborate stone caskets, similar to the Roman sarcophagus.

In the Danish colony of Greenland, the Vikings who settled on its shores believed that there was danger of pollution from the evil spirits that lurked around the corpse until the smell of death had passed away. They burned the dead body before it became cold and tried to avoid inhaling any of the fumes from the fire. They also burned every object in the dead person's house.

The Zulu tribe of Africa always burns the property of the dead to prevent evil spirits from remaining in the person's home. Many Native American tribes followed the same custom of burning the possessions of the deceased, and it is not uncommon to hear of contemporary men and women who, after the funeral of a relative, superstitiously burn the individual's clothes and other belongings.

Buddhists, Hindus, and Sikhs employ cremation as a standard method of disposing of the dead. In India the body is cremated on a funeral pyre whenever possible, and in ancient times widows were sacrificed alive on the burning pyres with their husbands.

Creutzfeldt-Jacob Disease

See also: AIDS, Alien Infection, Alien Virus, Black Death, Infection, Mad Cow Disease, Spanish Flu

In 1986, the initial signs of a frightening new disease began to quietly surface in the United Kingdom. It was given the name of bovine spongiform encephalopathy (BSE). It has since become far better known as mad cow disease. For the farmers whose animals were affected, identifying a BSE-infected cow quickly became a very easy task: quite simply, they moved, and acted, like zombies.

The way in which the cows walked noticeably altered: as the effects of BSE increased nearly day by day, walking became shuffling. Their manner changed from docile to erratic and, at times, to dangerously belligerent and violent. And it was all due to the fact that cows were secretly being fed the remains of other cows. The infected were, in effect, cannibals, and just about the closest thing one could imagine to real-life animals of the zombie variety.

When the scale of the disaster became apparent, huge concerns dominated the minds of just about everyone in the United Kingdom: did the virus have the ability to jump from species to species? Could eating the meat of an infected cow cause the development of BSE-like symptoms in people? And, if so, what about sex or kissing: could bodily fluids spread the disease? As the outbreak grew on a near-daily basis, the answers to those controversial questions became the stuff of nightmares. And a stark realization hit home all across the land: *Britain was infected.*

When matters were at their absolute height, sensational rumors were rife in the media that millions upon millions of British people were very likely *already* affected and, when the symptoms started to manifest, the nation would quickly be plunged into unrelenting chaos. People would be split into two camps: those free of infection and those irreversibly affected by it. Fortunately, such a cataclysmic situation failed to come to pass. It did not, however, prevent a significant number of people falling victims to the deadly human version of BSE: Creutzfeldt-Jacob disease, or CJD.

While there are several categories of CJD, the one which caused so much panic across the United Kingdom was vCJD, which is better known as variant Creutzfeldt-Jacob disease, and that is specifically caused by eating BSE-tainted beef. Official figures in the United Kingdom suggest that around two hundred people died from vCJD which, like its animal form, provokes distressing, strange and violent behavior of both a physical and psychological nature. Although, in a nation of around sixty million people, two hundred may not sound like many, it is important to note one disturbing factor: vCJD can, it is believed, take decades to develop. That is to say, it's not out of the question that millions of British people—who unknowingly ate BSE-infected beef products back in the 1980s—might, in just a few years from now, start to develop the classic symptoms of vCJD. The rise of the infected could, one day, be coming to the United Kingdom yet again.

Crosse, Andrew

See also: Frankenstein, Mary Shelley

Born to Richard Crosse and Susannah Porter on June 17, 1784, at Fyne Court, Broomfield, Somerset, England, Andrew Crosse was a definitively self-made amateur scientist and an early pioneer in the field of electricity. He was also someone who, ultimately, was likened to a real-life equivalent of Dr. Victor Frankenstein, of Mary Shelley's much-revered 1818 novel, *Frankenstein*. It's a book that tells the story of a crazed scientist who procures various human body-parts and stitches them together. Then, via electricity, he animates the terrible, obscene creation, which goes on a violent killing spree. But how, and under what particular circumstances, did Andrew Crosse become so linked to Mary Shelley's fictional mad-scientist?

In 1800, when Crosse was still just in his mid-teens, his father passed away. Five years later, his mother did likewise. As a result, at the age of just twenty-one, Crosse took on the running of the family estate. And, with a significant inheritance in-hand, Crosse was free to pursue his passions of alternative science and electricity. Such was the strange nature of many of Crosse's early experiments—which were conducted in a laboratory of the type in which Dr. Victor Frankenstein would have been right at home—that, amongst the locals in the village of Broomfield, Somerset, Crosse quickly became known as "the thunder and lightning man."

By the 1830s, Crosse's research had reached epic and impressive proportions: his lab was packed with advanced and unusual machines; powerful batteries dominated the room, and rumors flew around Broomfield that Crosse was up to no good. Then, in 1836, something remarkable happened: Crosse found in his lab what he described as "the perfect insect, standing erect on a few bristles which formed its tail." In the days that followed, yet more curious, little insects appeared. Very soon, Crosse's laboratory was teeming with them. It appeared to Crosse that they had spontaneously manifested during an electro-crystallization experiment that he had performed.

The local media soon got wind of the story and Crosse found himself deep in controversy. The reason why was simple: dark tales started surfacing to the effect that Crosse had found a way to both create and animate new life. Anonymously sent threats reached his mailbox. There were accusations that he was engaged in Witchcraft and the black-arts, and Crosse was even blamed, by irate farmers, for a crop-failure in the area.

To this very day, there is still a great deal of debate on the nature of Crosse's bizarre experiments and the apparently spontaneous manifestation of unusual insects in the lab. The most obvious explanation is that the experiments were unknowingly contaminated from the beginning, and the insects hatched in wholly normal fashion. There are, however, suggestions that Crosse may have succeeded in animating life—even if he, himself, was unsure how such a phenomenon was astonishingly achieved. Crosse's fringe science research continued until May 1855, when he died from the effects of a devastating stroke. Nevertheless, the legend of "the thunder and lightning man" lives on.

As mentioned above, one person who has very often been described as a definitive real-life Dr. Frankenstein, and someone on whom Mary Shelley may very well have based the lead character in her novel, is Andrew Crosse. And the significant fact that much of Crosse's lifework was undertaken in complete and utter solitude and behind the firmly closed doors of a futuristic-looking laboratory dominated by bangs and crashes, flashes of lightning, and bolts of electricity, only succeeds in adding to the eerie *Frankenstein* parallels. There is, however, one particular flaw in this argument: Mary Shelley's classic novel was written almost twenty years *before* Crosse's most controversial and strange research of all, even began. But, that does not mean that Crosse did not play at least some sort of role in the nurturing and creation of *Frankenstein*. The evidence strongly suggests that he did exactly that.

Meet the real Dr. Frankenstein: Andrew Crosse.

Rather interestingly, Mary Shelley actually met Crosse, albeit a significant time before his wildest research began. Mary, and her husband, Percy Shelley, were introduced to Crosse by a mutual friend: a poet named Robert Southey. Moreover, both husband and wife attended one of Crosse's lectures on the nature of life and death in London in 1814. It was a lecture in which Crosse expanded at great length on his then-burgeoning research into the domain of electricity and how it might conceivably revive the dead. And twenty-two years later, in 1836, Edward W. Cox, a writer for the England's *Taunton Courier* newspaper, interviewed Crosse and learned that both Mary and Percy had visited the Crosse residence on several occasions, specifically prior to Mary having written *Frankenstein*.

We can—and, indeed, are forced to—speculate on what might have been discussed between Mary Shelley and Andrew Crosse while behind the closed doors of the latter's bizarre lab. But of one thing we can be sure: Mary Shelley, the brains behind the world's most infamous patchwork zombie of all time, had a connection to a man who earnestly believed he had uncovered something significant about life, death, and animation.

The matter of the full extent to which the character and work of Crosse inspired Shelley is something that, two centuries later, is unlikely to ever be resolved to the satisfaction of students of both Shelley's *Frankenstein* and Crosse's work. Without any shadow of doubt, however, Andrew Crosse—the man, the visionary, and the self-made alternative scientist—was a character that, one way or another, will forever remain tied to Mary Shelley and to her diabolical zombie-like creation: Victor Frankenstein's terrifying but tragic monster.

In late 1836, and in the wake of the publicity given to Andrew Crosse's controversial experimentation, a journalist, Edward W. Cox, had an article published in England's *Taunton Courier* newspaper that served to deeply reinforce the growing whispers that Crosse was a real-life maker—or reanimator—of monsters. It was an article prompted by the fact that, as part of an effort to have the public and the media view him in a favorable light, Crosse invited Cox to his Broomfield, Somerset home. It was an action that proved to be very costly for Crosse.

If Cox thought, prior to visiting the Crosse residence, that the Frankenstein parallels were uncalled for, his views soon changed. In his article, Cox wrote that on entering the old mansion he was confronted by "the philosophical room, which is about sixty feet in length and upwards of twenty feet in height, with an arched roof—it was built originally as a music hall—and what wonderful things you will see: a great many rows of gallipots and jars, with some bits of metal, and wires passing from them into saucers containing dirty-looking crystals."

Adding even more to the legend of Crosse, Cox expanded that, while in the creepy house "you are startled in the midst of your observations, by the smart crackling sound that attends the passage of the electrical spark; you hear also the rumbling of distant thunder." And the Frankenstein-like comparisons continued to flow forth from Cox in fine style: "Your host is in high glee, for a battery of electricity is about to come within his reach a thousand-fold more powerful than all those in the room strung together. You follow his hasty steps to the organ gallery, and curiously approach the spot from where the noise proceeds that has attracted your notice. You see at the window a huge brass conductor, with a discharging rod near it passing into the floor, and from the one knob to the other, sparks are leaping with increasing rapidity and noise."

If that wasn't enough to convince many of the *Courier's* readers that Crosse was a definitive mad scientist, there is the following from Cox, who said of his host:

"Armed with his insulated rod, he plays with the mighty power; he directs it where he will; he sends it into his batteries: having charged them thus, he shows you how wire is melted, dissipated in a moment by its passage; how metals—silver, gold, and tin—are inflamed, and burn like paper, only with the most brilliant hues."

While Cox's article was not a damning one, it most certainly helped to reinforce the unease that the villagers of Broomfield had about Crosse. And, in addition to that, Cox's amusing and entertaining piece helped to solidly cement the Frankenstein parallels that still exist to this very day.

Cypress, Texas, Mummy

Paranormal authority Brad Steiger notes: "Perhaps of all the classic monsters that have terrified theater audiences and groups gathered around campfires, the two most likely to be confused with one another are the mummy and the zombie. One thinks of curses and spells associated with both of these beings. Of course, the principle difference is that the mummies pronounce curses upon those who disturb their elegant tombs, while zombies lie for a time in crude graves because a curse has been placed upon them."

Steiger is not wrong when he refers to mummies and zombies causing confusion due to the somewhat similar territory they inhabit. His words are made all the more significant by the fact that in 2011 startling rumors began to circulate that a zombified mummy was roaming around the Texas town of Cypress, which is located northwest of the city of Houston. The quickly escalating atmosphere of terror and menace led Houston's KPRC news to home-in on the controversy. In semi-comic tones, they reported on how whole swathes of the population of Cypress were "living in fear," as a result of the bandaged nightmare said to be walking the streets, specifically in the town's Fairfield area.

While jokes and comments were made about a looming zombie apocalypse, not everyone was laughing. In fact, in Cypress itself, hardly anyone saw the joke. "It's scary not knowing what this man is up to or what he wants," said one of the town's residents, Jon Hill, who saw the creature moving around in his front yard. Another of the townsfolk, Steven Scheiffele, added: "It's creepy, especially since he's here in the neighborhood with the kids and stuff."

Harris County police officers tried their very best to diffuse the anxiety by asserting that it was all the work of a prankster—albeit a slightly warped one—that enjoyed scaring the living daylights out of people, and nothing else. Others were not quite so sure, however, and noted that the person responsible might well suffer severely, given that Texas is very well known for its "shoot first and ask questions later" attitude towards dealing with potentially violent individuals. In view of that, would someone really have been so stupid as to invade private land in the Lone Star State, while swathed in bandages, staggering around like the living dead, and all without thinking

Dancing Devil of San Antonio

One of the strangest stories to come out of the Texan city of San Antonio is that which revolves around a terrifying character referred to locally as the Dancing Devil, and who surfaced briefly in 1975. According to many eyewitnesses, as well as newspaper articles from the time, a dashing, handsome, young man dressed entirely in white entered the *El Camaroncito* night club on Old Highway 90 late one night, around the time of Halloween, 1975.

According to all of those who were present, the man was a fabulous dancer and impressed and captivated many of the ladies who were in attendance that evening. As the night progressed, however, things took a horrific turn when one of the man's dancing partners happened to glance down at his feet. The woman screamed out in terror, broke free of the man's grip and immediately began pointing downward. It was then, amidst a flurry of gasps and shrieks that the patrons noticed the man's shoes had transformed into creepy, clawed, chicken's feet!

In some versions of the story, his feet had become something akin to the hooves of a goat. Either way, it was certainly a bad sign to be sure, as the night club attendees were now quite certain they were in the presence of none other than the Devil himself. After a couple of seconds of uncomfortable silence, the man dashed, or perhaps waddled or galloped, towards the men's room, where he vanished out of an open window. In his wake remained a cloud of smoke, which was permeated with a strong, sulfuric smell—surely a classic calling card of the horned and forked-tailed one himself.

But that's not all: for weeks afterwards, stories circulated that the Dancing Devil had been seen performing late-night, Voodoo-style rituals in a certain area of San

Antonio woodland, where he and his disciples secretly sought to create a slave-like army of definitive *I Walked with a Zombie* style. Since, as history has clearly shown, the city did not become overrun by mind-controlled dead(ish) slaves, we can conclude one of two things: (a) the rumors were without merit; or (b) the Dancing Devil failed in his attempt to plunge San Antonio into apocalyptic chaos. Either way, it was very good news for the people that called the city their home.

Darklings

Since the late 1800s, strange creatures that the great Voodoo Queen Marie Laveau described as "the evil thoughts that good church people have, but do not act upon" have prowled the streets of New Orleans, seeking innocents whom they may possess. These beings, aptly called The Darklings, will take possession of people and make them act like someone they are not. In extreme cases, those who are possessed by a darkling have been known to kill or to hurt their family members.

Some believe that a darkling enters an individual through his or her mouth. The victim is like a zombified demon. Marie Laveau is said to have used ground-up monkey and cock statue powder, red brick, and a secret ingredient to chase them off.

Dawn of the Dead (1978)

Although George A. Romero's *Night of the Living Dead* movie hit the big-screen in 1968, and proved to be a huge hit with audiences, it took Romero pretty much a full decade before a follow-up appeared in cinemas. Granted, Romero's *The Crazies* surfaced in 1973, but the infected of that particular movie were not of the undead kind. Rather, they were still living, albeit highly dangerous, all the same. In that sense, they were very much the inspiration for the infected of the likes of *28 Days Later* and *28 Weeks Later* that act like zombies but actually aren't in the slightest. But, in the same way that it's very hard to stop a zombie, it was equally hard for Romero to stay away from the gory genre—which was very good news for fans of the flesh-eating ghouls everywhere.

The location of the filming of *Dawn of the Dead* has become almost as famous as the movie itself. It was the Monroeville Mall in Monroeville, Pennsylvania, where shooting was chiefly undertaken, at night, from October 1977 to January 1978. There was, however, a break for Christmas, since mall staff had adorned the complex with seasonal decorations that, to say the very least, would have looked decidedly out of place at the height of a zombie-based Armageddon!

Dawn of the Dead certainly follows on from Romero's first foray into zombie-world, but it's definitely not a direct sequel to *Night of the Living Dead* since the characters are completely different, as is the time-frame. In *Night*, the zombie outbreak has just begun. In *Dawn*, it is weeks later, and the United States of America is quickly becoming the United States of Anarchy. As is the case in so many zombie productions, the best places to try and survive are the rural parts of the nation. In the cities, the infected are swarming like flies. And there's another aspect to the movie that has become a staple part of just about all zombie productions. As the chaos, carnage, and death all increase, and as food and shelter become more and more important to the uninfected, those who have yet to fall victim to the undead turn upon each other. Survival is not just about avoiding the dead: it's also about being very wary of the living.

Just like *Night of the Living Dead*, *Dawn of the Dead* is set in Pennsylvania, specifically in the city of Philadelphia which, like the rest of the country, is now under martial law. Not that such a law is doing any good at all, however. Those who have successfully managed to avoid infection are very much taking the law into their own hands, regardless. The authorities, meanwhile, take a decidedly dim view of such things and summarily execute those that don't abide by the emergency laws. Or, they take a dim view of such things until even the military and the police become overwhelmed by the ever-increasing number of walking corpses. Then it becomes a case of every man for himself—soldier, cop, or member of the public alike.

In *Dawn of the Dead* the zombie infection is already in full swing when the movie starts, and director George A. Romero explores how the living begin to compete not only with zombies but also each other.

Dawn of the Dead chiefly revolves around four characters: Stephen (who works for a local television channel), Francine (who is Stephen's pregnant girlfriend) and two SWAT men, Roger and Peter, who astutely realize that trying to enforce martial law is likely to get them killed very quickly. When Philadelphia becomes more and more overrun by bone-crunching cannibals, and it's clear that the battle to beat the dead has taken a severe turn for the worse, the four flee, by helicopter, to the Monroeville Mall.

Thanks to a bit of nifty fortification, they are able to keep the undead hordes out of the mall—for a while, at least. Unfortunately, during the process of getting the mall in lock-down mode, Roger falls foul of a wandering zombie and receives a bite that decides his fate before the movie is over. Or, rather, Peter decides his fate: a bullet to the head—what else should we expect? As the movie comes to its climax, the mall is invaded by a gang of bikers, whose door-opening actions allow the dead to make their presence known, and in the hundreds. There is only one thing for Stephen, Francine and Peter to do: make a run for it to the helicopter. Unfortunately, Stephen isn't so lucky: he soon becomes zombified himself. Only Peter and Francine survive unscathed, taking to the skies and heading for destinations unknown, as the movie closes.

Romero was back, right where the fans wanted him: deep in the heart of the domain of the dead. And those same fans lapped up the movie like the dead enjoy lapping up the living. As evidence, *Dawn of the Dead*, which cost less than $1 million to make, has earned close to $60 million.

And there is one final matter that must be mentioned: *Dawn of the Dead* saw one of the world's leading special-effects and make-up artists come to the fore: Tom Savini, who also happened to play the role of biker, Blades, in *Dawn of the Dead*. Savini's zombie credentials do not end there: he went on to direct the 1990 remake of Romero's *Night of the Living Dead*, appeared in 2001's *Children of the Dead*, surfaced in *Zombiegeddon* two years later, had a role as a sheriff in the 2004 version of *Dawn of the Dead*, played a zombie in *Land of the Dead* of 2005, and took on a starring role in the 2007 zombie-themed movie *Planet Terror*.

Dawn of the Dead (2004)

In the early 2000's, many George Romero purists were completely appalled by the news that the man's 1978 movie, *Dawn of the Dead*, was going to be remade in new, lavish style. Worse, the traditional slow-walking killers, for which Romero has become justifiably famous, were going to be replaced by *28 Days Later*-style, super-fast infected. Tensions ran high as the March 2004 release date got closer and closer. But, there was no real cause for concern, after all. Under the directorship of Zack Snyder, the 2004 remake of *Dawn of the Dead* was a superb, nerve-jangling, non-stop descent into a world turned on its head, overnight. That Snyder brought accomplished actors to the production—including Sarah Polley, Jake Weber, Mekhi Phifer, and Michael Kelly— was a great plus, too. *Dawn of the Dead* also marked the first of three zombie-themed movies in which Ving Rhames has starred, the others being 2008's *Day of the Dead* and

Zombie Apocalypse of 2011. While the plotline of the 2008 version of *Dawn of the Dead* contains some considerable differences from Romero's original story, it does, nevertheless, follow a largely similar path.

Filmed in Ontario, Canada—with a predominantly Canadian cast—*Dawn of the Dead* first introduces us to Ana, a nurse from Milwaukee who, when the end of the world begins, is on her way home from work. As Ana switches frequencies on her car-radio, we hear snippets of news stories, suggesting something strange and unsettling is going down big-time. Somewhat amusingly, Ana elects to ignore the news and, instead, listens to *Have a Nice Day*, a 2001 song from Welsh band the Stereophonics. As time progresses, the day becomes anything but nice. Less than twenty-four hours later, Ana does violent battle with her husband, Luis, and with Vivian, a little girl who lives down the street. Both have become infected with the zombie virus (the former after getting bitten by the latter), and both are after one thing, and one thing only, human flesh.

Just about making it out of the house in one piece, Ana races for her car—with homicidal Luis hot on her tail—and floors the accelerator for a journey to destinations unknown. The roads are in chaos; zombies are here, there, and everywhere. After crashing her car, Ana teams up with Rhames' character (a cop named Kenneth), Michael (played by Weber), and Andre and Luda (a couple portrayed by Phifer and Inna Korobkina). They soon decide that, to survive, there is only one option: they head to the nearest mall.

As *Dawn of the Dead* progresses, various other characters appear on the scene, all of who think that it's a very good idea to hole up in a secure shopping mall. Well, it is, for a while. Divisions in the group, violent altercations, growing panic, and a deep sense of claustrophobia soon set in, however, and the survivors—finally realizing that the only way to stay alive is to put aside petty differences and work together—decide to make a run for it. Or, rather, make a drive for it, in a pair of buses stored in the mall's garage. They try their very best, but fail, to bring along another uninfected soul, Andy, an expert shot who spends most of his time on the roof of his gun store—that is, until he, too, finally succumbs to a deadly bite. Those who manage to get out of the mall in one piece, head to a marina where there is a key to survival: a boat. It is owned by one of the group, Steve, the villain of the movie, who gets a much-deserved bullet in the head from Ana, after he too, is zombified.

Ana, Michael, Kenneth, and Terry and Nicole—the latter being a young couple thrust together during the crisis—manage to escape the zombie hordes. As Kenneth prepares to get Steve's boat moving, Michael reveals he was bitten during the race to reach the marina. Ana says her tearful goodbyes to Michael, before he blows his brains out and the now-four exhausted survivors head for an isolated island in the distance. Isolation means safety. Well, sometimes it does. In this case, however, it does not. *Dawn of the Dead* reaches its knuckle-clenching conclusion with the four finally reaching the island and disembarking from the boat. As they do so, savage growling, and shadowy, fast-running figures can be seen in the wooded land ahead. Infection has reached the island. As the dead loom into view, Kenneth warns the other three to stay behind him and he lets loose with a salvo of bullets. As the zombie hordes race towards Steve's boat, the screen goes black. It's game over and adios amigos.

Day of the Dead (1985)

If, as a zombie apocalypse grows, the sheer number of undead staggering around the streets makes it impossible to wipe them all out, there is one final alternative, when all others have been exhausted: teach the murderous hordes to behave like civilized undead. In essence, that was the central theme of George A. Romero's third zombie production, *Day of the Dead*. Made in 1985, the movie provided a refreshing departure from what usually passes for standard zombie fare and lore.

The story follows *Dawn of the Dead*, and at this point civilization is in complete tatters, cities are little more than eerily silent ghost towns, and the human race is rapidly spiraling down to extinction. In terms of numbers, the zombies are growing as fast as the survivors are shrinking. As for the government and the military, they have taken the cowardly approach of heading deep underground, leaving the rest of humanity to its own devices. "Underground" essentially means secure and fortified U.S. Army bunkers. It's deep inside the bowels of one of these well-fortified installations that groundbreaking research is taking place.

Located in the Florida Everglades, the facility is home to a brilliant but eccentric scientist, Dr. Matthew Logan, and a band of soldiers led by the certifiably psychotic Captain Henry Rhodes. It's the job of Rhodes' team to provide Logan with zombies for his strange experiments. Dubbed "Frankenstein" by the soldiers, Logan believes that it's actually possible to control the zombies by means of training them to obey commands, for which they will receive rewards in the form of food. Unbeknownst to the troops, the "food" that Logan supplies secretly comes in the form of Rhodes' comrades, who died in earlier, violent confrontation with the zombies.

There is soon another addition to the underground survivors: Dr. Sarah Bowman, pilots Bill McDermott, and John, whose last name we never learn, and a soldier, Miguel Salazar. Things do not go well for the new arrivals. In fact, they have sought refuge at just about the worst time possible. The fraught situation, the daily fight to stay alive, and the fact that Rhodes' men are constantly risking their lives to provide Dr. Logan with new specimens, are all now taking their physical and psychological toll. As so often happens when large-scale disaster strikes, people start to split into factions, and hostilities break out. The troops stick firmly together, preferring their own company and no one else's; Bowman and her friends do likewise, increasingly fearful of Rhodes and the soldiers; and a crazed Logan continues to do his own dark and solitary thing behind closed doors.

Integral to the story told in *Day of the Dead* is the character of Bud, a zombie who retains some of his human faculties and memories. Logan comes to believe that, with enough training and conditioning, Bud—and all those now like him—can be taught to reel in their deadly streaks and, essentially, behave like subservient cattle to their human masters. It doesn't quite work out like that, unfortunately. The troops soon learn that Logan has been feeding their dead comrades to the zombies, while Sarah and her group realize that Captain Rhodes has descended into an even more dangerous state of mind, and, as a result, poses as much a threat to them as do the zombies. In fact, he and his men may be *more* of a hazard than the dead. Things quickly begin to unravel.

Logan is soon thereafter killed by Rhodes, who is outraged by the doctor having used his men as nourishment for the dead. Miguel, in a deranged state after getting bitten, opens the huge doors to the underground realm, which allows hordes of stinking, rotting zombies to pour in. The soldiers fall victim to the infected. Death is everywhere. In a particularly amusing and satisfying scene, mad Rhodes is shot by half-trained Bud, who still recognizes a gun when he sees one. Unable to escape due to the effects of his bullet wounds, Rhodes is torn apart by the starving dead, who proceed to devour his intestines. "Choke on 'em! Choke on 'em!" screams Rhodes, in his final few seconds. Only Sarah, Bill, and John escape to a deserted island, where Sarah ponders on how, and even if, humankind can ever be saved and resurrected.

Any Romero movie is, of course, going to be filled with zombies. *Day of the Dead*, however, and perhaps more than any other Romero film of this genre, shows us something else, too. When society disintegrates it's very often each other—not the risen enemy—that we have to fear the most. *Day of the Dead* makes us realize that in a zombie outbreak, and when battle lines are drawn, the guy who works

A chained zombie awaits the experiments of Dr. Matthew Logan and his quest for a cure in *Day of the Dead.*

at the gas station, your next door neighbor, or your kid's math teacher might be as much a threat as the infected, near-unstoppable dead.

Day of the Dead (2008)

Based on George A. Romero's 1985 movie of the same name, Steve Miner's *Day of the Dead* of 2008, has very little in common with the acclaimed original. Yes, it has a heavy U.S. Army presence, Bud has a starring role (albeit in a significantly different fashion), and there are a number of key scenes shot in an underground military facility. But that's about it. Despite the differences, *Day of the Dead* is not a bad film at all. In fact, it's pretty good. And its cast was not comprised of a bunch of nobodies. It starred Mena Suvari (of the *American Pie* movies) and Ving Rhames, noted for having appeared in no less than two additional zombie movies: *Dawn of the Dead* (2004) and

Actor Ving Rhames has appeared in such zombie films as *Dawn of the Dead* and *Zombie Apocalypse*.

Zombie Apocalypse (2011). *Day of the Dead* had a budget of $18 million and its special effects are impressive. Nevertheless, it's a movie that many were not happy with. So, what was the problem?

More than a few zombie enthusiasts were deeply displeased that the 2008 version of *Day of the Dead* veered dramatically away from the plot in Romero's film. It should be noted, however, that it was never specifically billed or even intended as a direct, faithful remake. Steve Miner openly stated that his version would be a stand-alone movie, one that would have a fresh, new approach. But even aware that there would be changes, it must be said that sizeable numbers of fans of Romero's work were far from impressed with the finished result. One of the biggest problems that the Romero devotees had with *Day of the Dead* was the nature of the army of zombies with which the stars do battle in ravaged Leadville, Colorado.

The reanimated dead of the Romero movies provoked so much fear because of the very fact that their slow, menacing, and unrelenting style was exactly that: slow, menacing, and unrelenting. Likewise, the fast-running, killing machines of *28 Days Later* and the 2004 version of *Dawn of the Dead* kept audiences on the edges of their seats as a result of their manic, high-speed attacks. The big issue that many had with the infected of *Day of the Dead* is that they weren't just remarkable: they were just *too* remarkable. Not only are the zombies of *Day of the Dead* the decaying equivalents of Olympic runners, but they can also walk on ceilings—Spiderman-style—and leap huge distances, also in comic books—superhero fashion. For zombie aficionados, and particularly those that saw Romero's work as being wholly untouchable, this was all way beyond the pale. That collective, negative attitude was, however, most unfortunate and short sighted. Yes, the 2008 version of *Day of the Dead* was very different from the 1985 original, as was the nature of the infected. But change can be a good thing. And, in the case of Steve Miner's *Day of the Dead*, it was.

The Dead and The Dead 2

In 2009, brothers Howard and Jon Ford—both writers and directors—put together an excellent zombie movie set in a place far removed from most productions of the undead kind: Africa. It surfaced one year later, in 2010, and was titled simply, *The Dead*. There's nothing wrong with getting straight to the point, and the title did exactly that.

The story is very much based around the life of one man, Lieutenant Brian Murphy (actor Rob Freeman) of the U.S. Air Force. When Murphy's aircraft crashes in the scalding hot plains of West Africa, not only is he forced to try and survive the pummeling temperatures and a distinct lack of food and water, he also finds himself confronted with ever-growing numbers of zombies. Eventually, Murphy encounters someone that hasn't yet turned: Daniel, a member of the African military who, having recognized that civilization is in the process of crashing big time, does his utmost to reach his son, who is holed up at a military installation somewhere to the north.

When Daniel becomes zombified, it's up to Murphy to keep the promise he makes to dying Daniel that he will do his utmost to find the boy. As the movie nears its end, Murphy reaches the army base in question and learns—via radio-contact—that the United States has pretty much already fallen to the virus. The chances of combatting and beating the reanimated, it becomes quickly clear, are slim in the extreme. Amid all of the chaos, as crowds of the dead close in, Daniel's son and Murphy finally cross paths. Is a happy ending guaranteed? Not at all: man and boy are suddenly confronted by swarms of hungry monsters, at which point the credits roll.

In a strange bit of irony—although most definitely not a welcome bit of irony—during the course of the production of *The Dead*, Rob Freeman became a victim of malaria. Having fainted on the set, Freeman was rushed to a nearby hospital, where after a week or so of treatment, he finally recovered, demonstrating that zombies are not the only near-lethal dangers on the plains of West Africa.

Then, in 2013, there came the much anticipated sequel to *The Dead*. Its title was *The Dead 2: India*. Fans of the first production were very pleased to see the Ford brothers once again at the helm. The scene of all the carnage and death that soon strikes is the Indian state of Rajasthan. At the start of the movie, the place is free of infection—as is the rest of India. Unfortunately for anyone that calls Rajasthan their home, infection-free it does not stay for very long.

The cause of the outbreak of the zombie virus in India is an infected man who, having just arrived from zombie-ravaged Somalia, Africa, is solely, and wholly, responsible for the rise of the dead that quickly develops. The action soon becomes focused on Nicholas Burton (an American engineer played by Joseph Millson) and his beloved (and pregnant) girlfriend, Ishani Sharma (portrayed by Meenu Mishra).

Unfortunately, for both Nicholas and Ishani, when the zombie virus starts to spread at a terrifyingly fast rate throughout Rajasthan and beyond, the lovers are hundreds of miles apart. So, it is left to Nicholas to make, and fight, his way to Ishani, to save both her and their unborn baby from the crazed dead. High on tension and gore, *The Dead 2: India* aims to please zombie fanatics and in doing so hits its target solidly and decisively.

Death Definition

One of the most confounding things about zombies is how, after death, they are able to retain at least a few of their basic functions, even though they are technically dead. But what, exactly, is death? While that may sound like a strange question, it is not. For the most part, death is defined as the period when, collectively, brain activity has ceased, the damage caused by a lack of oxygen to the brain has irreversibly destroyed what is termed consciousness (that which defines us as unique entities possessing self-awareness), and respiration has come to a complete halt. But, it's not quite as simple as that.

"Brain death" is described as occurring when the brain is starved of oxygen, which then leads to the necrosis, or the destruction, of the billions of neurons in the brain. A person who is brain dead, however, may still exhibit a functioning heart and lungs and can be kept alive via artificial means. Then there is the matter of "clinical death," which is when the individual exhibits a complete lack of respiration and blood circulation. Problematic, here, is the fact that the clinically dead can be kept from the clutches of the Grim Reaper via a respirator. On top of that, under carefully controlled circumstances, the human blood-supply can be brought to a complete halt in those parts of the body, specifically below the heart for around half an hour—with little sign of appreciable damage occurring.

Since neurons play vital roles in the function of the human sensory organs—those responsible for our ability to speak, hear, touch, smell, and taste—how is it that the reanimated dead are able to make use of their senses if brain death, and a lack of

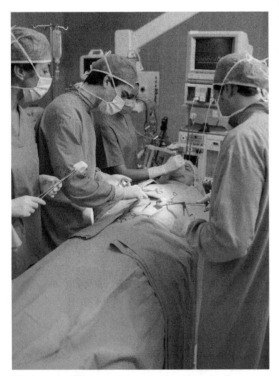

Flatlining while in surgery or elsewhere in the hospital means only that the heart has stopped. The body can still live for a while and be revived, but brain death is a different matter.

oxygen to the neurons, destroyed them when death took them in their original, human form? Granted, the average zombie does not speak, but it does growl or grunt. And the creature certainly exhibits the ability to smell, hear, touch, and taste.

This gives rise to an important question: since, in most zombie-themed scenarios, the infected person dies and reanimates relatively quickly, should we consider them to be literally dead? Perhaps, instead, the dead are actually returning from a very deep, but brief, state that is not literal death, but one that only mimics the *appearance* of death. That would be a far more likely scenario in the real world. There is some evidence that suggests we should look at the zombie in a new light.

In September, 2013, it was revealed that doctors in Romania had discovered something remarkable: on occasion, when a patient flat-lined and both clinical death and brain death were declared, a small amount of what is termed electroencephalogram—or EEG—activity in the brain could still be detected. The patient was, for all intents and purposes, gone; yet, in both the hippocampus and the upper-cortical areas *something was still going on*. Interestingly, the hippocampus plays a significant role in memory. Perhaps, when the infected die—or descend into a brief, death-like state—a portion of the hippocampus survives, albeit in a somewhat damaged state, but which allows for just about the most basic memories to survive—namely, those which are based around self-preservation. After all, no one can say that the zombie does not do all it can to preserve its "life." More intriguingly, scientific tests have demonstrated that people whose hippocampus are damaged display clear signs of hyperactivity—a state into which each and every zombie descends when it spots a tasty human meal on the horizon.

Finally, there is a near-consensus that the hippocampus performs a significant function in the development of what are termed "cognitive maps." Essentially, and in simple terminology, a cognitive map allows us to store data to recognize, and to remember our immediate locale. And what does this have to do with the undead? Very often, the zombie, while searching for food, will continue to roam around its own, original neighborhood, rather than venturing far and wide. A classic example is the situation in the 2004 remake of *Dawn of the Dead*, in which hordes of the infected head for the local mall—a place they would have been deeply familiar with in their previous lives. In view of the above, perhaps we should rename the dead as the "almost dead."

Death Line

Deep below the city of London, England, there lurks something almost as unimaginable as it is unbelievable: a colony of devolved humans that kill and feed on those who travel on the London Underground subway-system by night. It sounds like the perfect plot for a horror movie or television series. In fact, it has served as both, and on far more than a few occasions.

Such examples include (a) the 1967 production of *Quatermass and the Pit*, in which bizarre, mutated and diminutive cave men—who were the subject of advanced genetic experiments, undertaken millions of years earlier, by visiting Martians— appear in the London Underground of the 1960s in the form of spectral, manifested, inherited memories; (b) *The Web of Fear*—a *Dr. Who* adventure that surfaced in the following year, 1968, that saw the doctor and his comrades doing battle with robotic Yetis on the Underground; (c) *An American Werewolf in London*—a 1981 film in which the beast of the title feasted on a doomed, late night rail traveler; and (d) *Reign of Fire*, a 2002 production starring Christian Bale and Matthew McConaughey, that revolves around literal fire-breathing dragons burst forth from the old tunnels of the Underground and which decimate Britain, and, eventually, the rest of the planet, too.

Without any doubt, however, the definitive story of monsters on the London Underground—ones of a modern day, zombie-like persuasion—is *Death Line*. A British production released in 1972 (and retitled for the American market as *Raw Meat*), it starred Christopher Lee and Donald Pleasance and told a story of skin-crawling proportions. In the late 1800s, a team of workers becomes trapped in the old tunnels of the Underground when the ceiling and walls of the new platform they are building collapses. Attempts to free the workers—comprised of men and women—fail and, when the construction company goes broke, everything is quietly and conveniently forgotten. The hope is that the workers all died and the story will do likewise.

No one realizes, however, that against all odds, death did not claim the workers, after all. Trapped hundreds of feet below ground, they manage to survive by living on rats, mice, and whatever other animals might cross their paths. Over the course of several generations, however, the people have become something more—or something less: savage, brutish cannibals that creep around the tunnels of the London Underground by night, killing unwary travelers and feasting on their body-parts deep below London.

Death Line is a highly entertaining movie that inevitably makes the viewer ponder upon the possibility that, just maybe, it's not fiction. Certainly, hundreds of people vanish from London every year. Granted, many may simply be people who want to start new lives, under new guises. But, maybe some of them have fallen victim to what have become known as the "London Subterraneans," alleged, real-life equivalents of the flesh-eating monstrosities of *Death Line*. If you ever take a trip on the London Underground, take great care: you never know what might be lurking in the shadows of those old tunnels, ready and waiting to pounce, kill, and devour.

Decapitation and Reattachment

Practically no fan of all things zombie needs to be warned just how dangerous and deadly the heads of the walking or running dead are. Not only is the zombie capable of inflicting a devastating, infectious bite when its head is attached to its body, it can also do likewise after decapitation. While penetrating the brain of a zombie will put it down permanently, just removing the head from the body will not reduce—at all—the ability of the creature, or what is left of it, to bite down hard on its victim. Such a scenario was put to very good and graphic use in *The Walking Dead* and in the 2004 remake of George A. Romero's *Dawn of the Dead*. But, is it really feasible that a head could be removed from its body and still continue to not only exist, but to even retain some of its faculties? Incredibly, the answer is: Yes.

In December 1959, news surfaced to the effect that Chinese medical experts had succeeded in achieving something as incredible as it was horrendous: they removed the heads from no less than two living dogs and then attached them to the decapitated bodies of two additional dogs. Undertaking the decapitations at high speed, reattaching them with equal speed, and taking care that all of the relevant nerves and veins remained intact, reportedly ensured that the surgeries were complete successes. Although there was a degree of skepticism at the time, specifically exhibited by factions of the Western media and scientific communities, the operations were ultimately shown to have worked just as the Chinese had claimed. And there was more to come. But it didn't come from China: it came right out of the heart of the United States.

The location was Case Western Reserve University, which is situated in Cleveland, Ohio. The mastermind behind the experimentation was Dr. Robert White. The

Decapitation would seem like a good way to get rid of a zombie, but if an ordinary dog could survive such treatment, as a Chinese study showed, then likely a zombie could, too.

date when history was made was March 14, 1970. Rather than taking the Chinese approach of using dogs, Wood's guinea pig was a monkey. Aside from the not so insignificant fact that because the spinal cord of the monkey had to be severed to allow its head to be detached and reattached, it was paralyzed from the neck down, the head and brain acted in relatively normal fashion.

Rather chillingly, however—and eerily prompting zombie-style visuals—one of the first things the monkey attempted to do upon recovering was to deliver a vicious bite to one of the medical team. The animal may not have been infected with rage, as per *28 Days Later*, but it was most certainly not happy. Intriguingly, tests undertaken by White's team showed that the monkey's primary senses of smell, sight, hearing, and taste remained intact. Inevitably, this has given rise to a controversial question: will we, one day, see the transplant of a human head? Quite possibly, yes. In fact, it's pretty much destined to happen one day.

Dr. Sergio Canavero, an Italian neuroscientist, believes that human head transplants are not out of the question. By significantly cooling the head, removing it from the body with a very sharp blade, and then reattaching it with a donated spinal cord—

to ensure paralysis does not occur—may be feasible at some point during this century. As the doctor notes, however: "The problem is not really technical but is completely ethical." Or, conversely, it's unethical.

DeDe, Sanite

The first Voodoo Queen in New Orleans, of whom there is any record, was Sanite DeDe, a young woman from Santo Domingo, who may have arrived as a slave sometime in the early 1800s. Once in New Orleans, she bought her freedom through the power of her secret hexes and Hoodoo Voodoo.

By around 1815, she was holding rituals in her brick-lined courtyard on Dumaine and Chartres Streets, just walking distance from the St. Louis Cathedral. The rhythmic beat of the drums could be heard inside the great church during mass, and it was because of this that the Church brought pressure upon city government to forbid any religion that was not Roman Catholic to be practiced within city limits. It was at that time that Congo Square, now known as Armstrong Park, became the location where the early Voodoo worshippers would hold their rituals, which the *Times Picayune* described as serpent worship amidst uncontrolled orgies (February 1932).

Defining Zombies

Brad Steiger's book, *Real Zombies, the Living Dead, and Creatures of the Apocalypse* posits that a real zombie is not the victim of biological warfare, a blast of radiation from a space vehicle, or an unknown virus that escaped a secret laboratory. A real zombie is a reanimated corpse that has most often been brought back to life to serve as slave labor. Originating in West Africa as the worship of the python deity, Voodoo was brought to Haiti and the southern United States, particularly the New Orleans area. Voodoo holds that a supernatural power or essence may enter into and reanimate a dead body.

Steiger says: "As my friend Lisa Lee Harp Waugh, a noted necromancer and writer, put it: A Zombie is a soulless human corpse, still dead, but taken from the grave and endowed by sorcery with a mechanical semblance of life. It is a dead body, which is made to walk and act and move as if it were alive."

Voodoo lore actually has two types of zombies: the undead and those who died by violence. Those who adhere to the Afro-Caribbean spiritual belief of Vodun, popularized as Voodoo, are very cautious in their approach to a cemetery, for it is there that one is most likely to encounter the unfortunate wraiths who died violently and without adequate time for a proper ritual.

There is a third spirit that may be classified as a zombie—that of a woman who died a virgin. A terrible fate awaits her at the hands of the lustful Baron Samedi, Master of the Netherworld.

For those who embrace the teachings of Voodoo, the zombie, the living dead, are to be feared as very real instruments of a priestess or priest who has yielded to the seduction of evil and allowed themselves to be possessed by negative forces and become practitioners of dark side sorcery.

Waugh said that some Southern zombie-making rituals consist of digging up a fresh corpse from its tomb or deep grave: The body is then fed strange potions and whispered to in strange chants, she explained. Many individuals who have witnessed the evil, dark deed say that it is disturbing to view. You stand frozen in the shadows as a voyeur to some devil dark secret spell. You see a recently dead man being made into a zombie before your eyes.

Allowing that disturbing scene to linger a moment in one's mind, Waugh came up with an image much worse: Picture the image of a beautiful Voodoo Queen riding a rotting corpse like a wild banshee, having dark magical sex in a graveyard. Certainly this would be a sight that you will never forget. Imagine the strange image as candles flare,

Artist Jean-Noël Lafargue portrayed a Haitian zombie in a sugar cane plantation.

and mosquitoes bite hard into your skin. Then the spell comes to a conclusion as the zombie corpse comes to life. At that moment the Voodoo Queen takes him into what seems to be a deep kiss and bites off his tongue to make him her eternal slave.

Most contemporary experts on New Orleans Voodoo and zombies agree that the legendary Dr. John, believed to be a zombified Voodoo master, created the perfect zombie juices and powders to make a living, breathing zombie that will not die or age and be truly immortal.

Waugh commented that the most dangerous zombies are those that stay infants.

Voodoo midwives often play this cruel trick on unsuspecting mothers who are about to give birth, she said. The Voodoo Queens sit between the legs of the soon-to-be mother, as any midwife would, but they are chanting a secret spell.

When the child is emerging from the womb, they will snatch them up at the second of birth. The cunning midwife Queen will then break the child's neck and bite off the tip of its tongue as its soul hangs between the point of living and dead, thus making the enfant diabolic as they were called.

According to Voodoo lore, zombie children taken straight from the womb never age as mere mortals do. They may take over thirty years to grow into a beautiful girl or a handsome boy in their teens. Many Voodoo cultists insist that Marie Laveau, the queen of New Orleans Voodoo, never grew old because she was of zombie birth. Dr. John himself had performed her zombification at birth.

Zombie gumbo is a concoction that some people say Black Cat Mama Couteaux, a Voodoo Queen from Marshall, Texas, made to feed her zombie army each month. It usually consisted of dead animals found on the side of the road, onion peelings, and scraps her dogs would not eat.

Marie Laveau fed her zombies a fine gumbo made with fish heads and scales and bones and anything except banana peels, which tend to constipate a zombie.

Some historians of Voodoo suggest that the origin of the word zombie may have come from jumbie, the West Indian term for a ghost. Other scholars favor the Kongo word nzambi, the spirit that has resided in the body and is now freed as filtering down through the ages as zombie. Although the practice of Voodoo and the creation of zombies was familiar to the residents of Louisiana before 1871, a number of etymologists believe that it is about this time that the word "zombi" entered the English language. The word that was originally used by the Haitian Creole people, these scholars main-

Damballah is the snake god worshipped by practitioners of Voodoo. Damballah is a creation god who made the skies, hills, and valleys. (*Art by Bill Oliver*).

tain, was "zonbi," a Bantu word for a corpse returned to life without speech or free will. There are others who argue quite convincingly that Zombi is another name for Damballah Wedo, the snake god so important to Voodoo. In other words, a zombie would be a servant of Damballah Wedo. A common ritual that creates a zombie requires a sorcerer to unearth a chosen corpse and waft under its nose a bottle containing the deceased's soul. Then, as if he were fanning a tiny spark of fire in dry tinder, the sorcerer nurtures the spark of life in the corpse until he has fashioned a zombie.

In Haiti the deceased are often buried face downward by considerate relatives so the corpse cannot hear the summons of the sorcerer. Some even take the precaution of providing their dearly departed with a weapon, such as a machete, with which to ward off the evil sorcerer.

There are many terrible tales of the zombie. There are accounts from those who have discovered friends or relatives, supposedly long dead, laboring in the fields of some sorcerer. One story that made the rounds a few years back had the zombified corpse of a former government administrator, officially dead for fifteen years, as having been recognized toiling for a sorcerer in the fields near a remote village in the hills.

The connotations of evil, fear, and the supernatural that are associated with Vodun (also Voudou and, popularly, Voodoo) originated primarily from white plantation owners' fear of slave revolts. The white masters and their overseers were often outnumbered sixteen to one by the slaves they worked unmercifully in the broiling Haitian sun, and the sounds of Voudou drums pounding in the night made them very nervous.

Vodun or Voudou means spirit in the language of the West African Yoruba people. Vodun as a religion observes elements from an African tribal cosmology that may go back 10,000 years and then it disguises these ancient beliefs with the teachings, saints, and rituals of Roman Catholicism. Early slaves who were abducted from their homes and families on Africa's West Coast brought their gods and religious practices with them to Haiti and other West Indian islands. Plantation owners were compelled, by order of the French colonial authorities, to baptize their slaves in the Catholic religion. The slaves suffered no conflict of theology. They accepted the white man's water and quickly adopted Catholic saints into the older African family of nature gods and goddesses.

When Voudun came to the city of New Orleans in the United States, it became suffused with a whole new energy and a most remarkable new hierarchy of priests and priestesses developed, including the eternally mysterious Marie Laveau. And, of course, with Voodoo came the chilling accounts of zombies.

Some Voodoo traditions maintain that the only way that people can protect themselves from a zombie is to feed it some salt.

Lisa Lee Harp Waugh said that the story of not feeding salt to a zombie is actually overrated. Yes, it can destroy a zombie, she said, but if given to them in moderation, it tends to keep a zombie frozen for a few years until its services are once again needed. A full dose of pure white salt—about a full teaspoon—would put an end to animated corpse in a minute or less. They usually fall to the ground with violent convulsions and all the fluid drains from their bodies.

Devil's Chair of New Orleans

Legend has it that each of the twenty-three cemeteries of old New Orleans has a Devil's Chair placed among its gravestones and crypts. There is, however, only one cemetery that has a Devil's Throne where the Voodoo folk, the witches, and all those seeking to make a pact with the Master of Darkness go to meet with him eye to eye. That awesome throne is located in St. Louis Cemetery Number 1.

Old Voodoo tales relate that Marie Laveau, the Queen of New Orleans Voodoo, learned the powerful secret of the chair from her immortal, zombified Voodoo master and mentor, Dr. John. Laveau's many followers tell how Dr. John would sit on the throne on nights when the moon was covered by clouds and converse with the Devil about the secrets of zombification, the power to turn someone into a zombie. According to some accounts, the Devil taught Dr. John more than a hundred rituals or hexes that would almost immediately transform a living or dead man into a real zombie.

The Devil's Throne in St. Louis Cemetery Number 1 is often called the Zombie Making Chair, because, according to Voodoo lore, it was while Dr. John was sitting on the Devil's Throne that his satanic majesty turned him into the first living, immortal zombie to walk the earth. Only the Devil himself would be able to bestow such powers upon a mortal.

Voodoo practitioners believe that if you sit on the Zombie Making Chair on a dark, moonless night and ask the Devil to transform you into a living zombie, you will live a healthy, immortal life, and will not age, die, or be able to be hurt or maimed. The catch to the bargain is that when Judgment Day comes and Satan is thrown into the dark, bottomless pit, it is you upon whom he will sit for one thousand years.

Diary of the Dead

Diary of the Dead, which hit the screens in 2008, was George A. Romero's fifth, fierce foray into the world of the zombie. One would imagine that after the success of the previous Romero production—2005's *Land of the Dead*—*Diary of the Dead* would have had the same big budget as its predecessor. Maybe even a bigger budget, given that Universal Studios had footed the bill for *Land of the Dead*, which reaped in excess of $40 million. Not so. In fact, the exact opposite was the case. *Diary ...* was an independent piece of work, produced at a cost of barely $2 million by Romero-Grunwald Productions. Low bucks did not mean low production values, however. Nor did it mean a lack of thrills, chills, and spilled blood.

One of the reasons why cost was not the critical issue that it was on *Land of the Dead* is because, for this movie, Romero radically changed his production methods and approach. Rather like with *Paranormal Activity* and *The Blair Witch Project*, most of the action in *Diary of the Dead* is shown through the lenses of the jerky, hand-held cameras of the cast. Thus, instead of being exposed to lavish sets, crowds of characters, and high-tech special-effects of the type that dominated *Land of the Dead*, the audience is treated to something very different, and something that was much cheaper to put together.

As is typically the case in most zombie-based productions, *Diary of the Dead* focuses the bulk of its attention on one particular group of characters, doing all that they can to stay alive. In this particular case, they are students from the University of Pittsburgh, who happen to be film-makers, rather ironically engaged in putting together nothing less than a horror movie when disaster strikes. News broadcasts suddenly start reporting on savage deaths. Widespread chaos erupts. There is mayhem on the streets. The end has officially begun.

It scarcely needs mentioning that the cast, one by one, fall foul of the dead—this is, after all, a Romero movie, and we should expect nothing less. In fact, we demand it! What does need mentioning, however, is how the refreshing approach to *Diary of the Dead* did the zombie genre, and Romero himself, a great favor. Viewing the action through the lenses of the students' cameras immediately created deep senses of claustrophobia and vulnerability. In a wide-screen shot of a ruined city, filled with hundreds of reanimated and contaminated monsters, and as typified in the likes of 2004's *Dawn of the Dead*, at least you can see what's coming your way. In complete contrast, the shadowy and size-restricted images recorded by the characters in *Diary of the Dead* dramatically increased the foreboding feelings that one of the dead might suddenly loom into view, stage left, without warning and violently tear into skin and muscle. Time and again, such feelings prove to be correct.

When a filmmaker produces movie after movie in one particular genre, the key to continuing success is ensuring that diversity and originality are all-dominating. Granted, there's only so much diversity and originality that can go into a production about what happens when the dead become restless and hungry. But, *Diary of the Dead* is diverse and it *is* original. And it's to Romero's credit that he didn't follow up *Land of the Dead* with a big-budget, blood-splattered sequel. Instead, he went low-key, but high on suspense and, in the process, scored another home run.

Doctor John

Dr. John ruled New Orleans with Sanite DeDe until he began to mentor a captivating young woman named Marie Laveau, who supported herself as a hairdresser while gaining a widespread reputation as a Voodoo practitioner.

Marie Laveau succeeded Sanite DeDe as the ruling Voodoo Queen of New Orleans around 1830. No one in the hierarchy of Voodoo priests and priestesses disputed Laveau's assuming the position of authority, for it had become known among her peers, as well as both the common folk and the aristocracy of New Orleans, that she was extraordinarily gifted with powers of sorcery.

Marie Laveau and Dr. John have been mentioned numerous times in this book. Many of the claims made about the two remarkable figures have lifted them to the realm of supernatural figures who still maintain a powerful hold on the city of New Orleans. Although the feats of Dr. John have elevated to the near-status of a Voodoo god, the fame of Marie Laveau has surpassed that of her mentor, and hers is the name most associated with Voodoo in the entire world.

In her ordinary human incarnation, Marie married Christopher Glapion, a freeman of color, who worked as a cabinet maker while she styled the hair of her clients, some of the wealthiest women in New Orleans. It is recorded that the couple had fifteen children and that one of their daughters, also named Marie, would assume her mother's throne as Marie Laveau II, the Voodoo Queen of New Orleans, in 1869. Most authorities agree that Marie I died in 1891.

The mysterious Dr. John has blended so completely with his legend that it is difficult at times to determine if he was a real flesh-and-blood person or some other dimensional entity that visited New Orleans only to create zombies and initiate Voodoo Queens. According to certain recorded accounts of the day, he was a true Voodoo King of enormous power who had been a Prince in Senegal before coming to New Orleans. Others state that Dr. John's full name was John Montenet and that he was a freeman of color who wielded great influence in the city. It is said that he owned extensive property, was married to several beautiful wives, kept a harem of lovely mistresses, and fathered as many as sixty children.

Whether or not he was a Prince from an African nation, Dr. John was unquestionably an accomplished African priest who became the most famous Voodoo Doctor in New Orleans in the period from about 1810 to 1840. Dr. John was said to be able to predict the future, cure illnesses, cast spells, and create zombies to serve him as laborers and sex slaves. Even more incredible, Dr. John was rumored to have the power to zombify instantly those unfortunate individuals who angered him or who appealed to his sexual desires.

Dog of the Dead

In January 1955, one of the most graphically unsettling creatures of all time was paraded for display at the Surgical Society of Moscow, in the former Soviet Union. That creature was a large white dog, happily wagging its lengthy tail, and not at all concerned or intimidated by the large and eager crowd. But, this was no normal dog. Protruding from its right-hand side was the head of a second dog. It belonged to a small, brown-haired puppy and had been sliced off its original body and reattached to the seemingly quite happy hound now on public display. But how had such an abomination come to be?

It was all due to the work, and decidedly fringe research, of a Dr. Vladimir Petrovich Demikhov, who, at the time, ran the Soviet Academy of Medical Sciences' organ-transplanting facility. Demikhov's research—as the events of January 1955 made clear—did not begin and end with the likes of hearts, kidneys and livers, however. He was fascinated by the idea of head removal and reattachment. Despite having effectively been killed by decapitation, the head was quickly scooped up and immediately thereafter affixed to the body of its new host. Things did not go what one might term smoothly, however.

Post-death, and after reanimation, the newly attached head of the puppy did not act like those of most puppies—that's to say in happy fashion. Rather, it exhibited definitive zombie-like behavior. The reanimated dead of zombie lore generally only attack the life forms they once were—namely, human beings. That, apparently, goes for dogs, too. Without warning, the zombified puppy suddenly lashed out at the dog to which it was now permanently tied. It did so violently, and on one occasion succeeded in chomping down hard on the ear of the unfortunate animal. The team hastily tried to calm the rage-filled pup, particularly given the fact that their shocked audience was looking on with growing horror and unease.

As for what this particular experiment achieved, it demonstrated that it was feasible to essentially kill a living creature by decapitation—a procedure that, for all intents and purposes, results in death every time—but then to breathe life into it again via a somewhat symbiotic process of the most unwise kind. Those who believe that only the head of a fictional zombie can remain active, violent, and crazed after it is removed from its body might now very well want to reassess that particular stance.

Donner Party

Imagine the scene: it was the cold, harsh winter of 1846 and a group of more than eighty pioneers were making their weary way, via wagon-trains, from Springfield, Illinois to California. The group was primarily comprised of two families: the Donners and the Reeds. The former was headed by a man named George Donner, whose background was in the farming industry. The Reeds, meanwhile, were led by James F. Reed. He was an Irishman who, as a child, moved to the United States in the early 1800s with his mother, and who later made his mark in the fields of real estate and mining.

The biggest challenge for what became known as the "Donner party" was the route: since the journey was clearly going to be a long and arduous one, and one that spanned several states, the two families decided to follow the recommendations of one Lansford Hastings. He was the author of a book entitled *The Emigrants' Guide to Oregon and California*, and someone who suggested taking a shortcut through an area of Utah that now bears his name: the Hastings Cutoff. For the Donners and the Reeds, trimming down the time frame for the mammoth trip was not just welcome: it was absolutely vital, given the harsh, winter weather that loomed large on the horizon. No one could have guessed exactly just how catastrophic the weather would turn out to be for both families.

Disaster upon disaster descended on the Donner party as they made their way to California: dwindling food supplies, widespread malnutrition, violent attacks by Native American tribes, and deaths from both disease and accident piled on one another. And

A statue honoring the Donner party stands near Truckee, California, in Donner Memorial State Park.

it all came to a head at a place called Freemont Pass, which has since been renamed Donner Pass. Located on the 400-mile-long Sierra Nevada Mountains that span parts of both Nevada and California, it is here that the group, as a result of the terrible weather conditions, became well and truly stranded. It was also at Freemont Pass that a true nightmare unfolded.

As the scarcity of food eventually became a complete *lack* of food, the weak and malnourished families had to resort to catching rats, mice, and rabbits to try and sustain themselves. Such small creatures were simply not enough, however, and the group then turned on the faithful horses that had hauled the wagons across so many miles. Then, when the horses were gone, the family dogs were next on the list. And, finally, when just about all other avenues were exhausted, the Donner party became nothing less than living zombies: they devoured the bodies of their comrades and relatives that had finally succumbed to the calamitous conditions.

In later years, those that survived the events on the Sierra Nevada, and who declined to dine on their loved ones, recalled a shocking situation at the camp: cooked and half-eaten limbs, heads with a significant amount of flesh gnawed off, tufts of hair, and bones stripped of flesh and marrow, were strewn around the site. There was even a story of a newborn baby devoured *raw*. Rather like a zombie apocalypse in reverse, the living fed maniacally on the dead. To this day, the saga of Donner Pass remains one of the most notorious examples of what may happen when the need for food reaches the most critical of all levels.

Draugr

See also: **Grettis Saga**

Long before both the apocalyptic zombies of today and those zombified unfortunates of Haitian lore were on the scene, there was a breed of undead that was arguably far more frightening and fierce than both of the aforementioned combined. Its name was the Draugr and it struck deep terror in the hearts of the people of Denmark, Iceland, Sweden, and Norway more than 1,000 years ago. Its alternative name, the Aptrgangr, translates into English as nothing less than "one who walks after death." Could there be a better description of a zombie? No, there probably could not.

Centuries-old Scandinavian lore tells of a belief that to ensure the dead would never rise from the grave, it was vital that the newly deceased be laid to rest in horizontal fashion. Any attempt to bury a body at an angle or—worse still—in an upright position, was inviting just about the worst trouble imaginable. Although the Draugrs retained their original, human forms after death, as well as some of their more primal instincts and memories, they were noted for having distinct supernatural qualities, too.

The Draugr could, for example, transform into a form of mist that allowed it to rapidly and easily pass through the soil—and, indeed, through any solid object—thus giving it the ability to move around in practically unhindered fashion. The Draugrs—particularly those that had been Viking warriors before death—were obsessive hoarders of priceless treasures and artifacts, many of which had been brutally plundered by the Vikings, as their influence and power spread across Europe, and which the Draugrs obsessively buried and guarded in their graves.

Related to the Draugr is the Haugbui. Unlike the Draugr and the cinematic zombies of today, the Haugbui did not roam the land in search of prey to feast upon. Rather, they preferred to spend most of their time in their burial mounds, only making their presence known when an unfortunate soul might pass by—by which time the person's fate would already be sealed.

As for the means by which these menacing creatures ensured their survival, it was in classic zombie style: both the Draugr and the Haugbui dined on human flesh. Typically, they ensnared their unfortunate victims in a decidedly strange fashion: the creatures could significantly alter their height, weight, and muscle power via magical means—effectively ensuring that no mere mortal would ever be able to defend itself against such huge, violent monsters. There were other zombie similarities too: Norse mythology told of the Draugr emitting a powerful stench that was part-rotting meat and part-soil.

Also paralleling the zombie lore of today was the belief that, according to legend, it was incredibly difficult to permanently put down a person who had reanimated in the form of a flesh-eating Draugr. Piercing the body of a Draugr with a rod, or a blade of iron was said to lessen its strength, but would not ultimately disable or kill it. There was really only one way to ensure that a Draugr's reign of terror was firmly ended. It also happens to be the best way to ensure that a zombie remains down today: the head had to be removed from the body. As the old saying goes, there is nothing new under the Sun.

In centuries past, and to ensure that the newly deceased did not return as deadly and predatory Draugrs, the people of Scandinavia—whose world was steeped in dark superstition and legend—performed a series of complex rites and rituals. Typically, these rites and rituals occurred before burial, in the confines of the family home, and while the body of the deceased was on open display to allow friends and relatives to pay their last respects. Failing to follow the age-old traditions would very likely, and very quickly, provoke just about the worst outcome possible: the hideous rise and rampage of a Draugr.

The first step in the process was to carefully position a pair of scissors on the chest of the corpse. The scissors had to be fully open, however, for the ritual to work properly. Then, small amounts of straw were placed on the body in "X"-style patterns. Rather ingeniously, the families of the dead tightly tied together the big toes of the deceased, primarily to ensure that if the person did transform into a Draugr they would be unable to walk or run—thus lessening the threat they posed to the living. And just for good measure, needles were pushed into the soles of the feet, the idea being that this, too, would prevent the Draugr from roaming the land in search of sustenance of the human kind. The final touch, as far as the body was concerned, was to cover it—from head to toe—in a shroud.

The coffin of the dead individual was also the subject of stringent rituals. When the coffin was ready to be removed from the family home, those carrying it had to perform a very important action: specifically in the open doorway to the home, the coffin had to be lifted and lowered three times, and in different directions, to denote the sign of the cross. Then when the coffin was removed from the premises, any and all pots, pans, and both glass and stone jars had to be turned upside down—as did the chairs or tables upon which the coffin had previously stood.

The Draugr are the undead of Scandinavian legend. Not only are they undead, they also seek blood like vampires do and possess magical abilities.

There was one alternative to taking the body to its place of burial via the front-door and while making the sign of the cross. Scandinavian lore taught that if a Draugr returned to the home it dwelled in during its human life, it could only enter via the door through which its coffin had originally exited the house. Since it was not feasible to have the main door to the home continually barricaded, another route was taken.

Many families fashioned small cat-flap-style openings into the walls of their homes—openings that were just about tall enough, and wide enough, to slide a corpse or a coffin through. Then when the body was fully outside of the house, the hole would be quickly bricked-up, thereby preventing the Draugr from having any way to force its way into the building in its hunger-filled, zombie state.

Although the ritualistic actions described above reportedly prevented the dead from returning from their grimy graves as ruthless *Walking Dead*-style Draugrs, there were times when—chiefly as a result of unforeseen circumstances—it was simply not possible or feasible to perform the necessary rites. One classic example, and particularly so in relation to the seafaring Vikings, was when the person in question was drowned at sea—whether as a result of an accident or during violent combat—and when their body remained unrecovered. In such very common cases, the first indication that a person who died in the waters had reanimated was when they rose from those very same watery depths, took to the land, and began their wild slaughtering and feasting.

The water-born Draugr differed from its land-based counterpart in several significant ways. First, it lacked a head. Or, rather, it's more correct to say that it lacked a human head. In its place, however, was a hideous and terrifying facsimile of a human face, one of which horror maestro H. P. Lovecraft would likely have mightily approved. It was one comprised of wet and glistening seaweed, through which cold, evil, and malevolence-filled eyes stared forth. Its original attire was magically replaced after death by nothing but a coat made of oilskins. And, whereas the Draugr roamed the Scandinavian landscape exclusively on foot, the sea-born incarnation hunted on both land and water. For the latter, the Draugrs constructed large wooden boats, in which they sailed the coastal waters off of Norway, Denmark, Sweden, and Iceland, mercilessly seeking out any and all unwary sailors on whom they could dine in deadly style.

The Draugr of the deep was also a master of camouflage. It could radically alter its appearance to resemble a large, seaweed-covered rock—via the age-old tradition of shape-shifting, which is most often associated with the legendary werewolf. Invariably, the Draugr masked itself on stretches of sandy beach—usually a beach situated near to a town or a village—thus increasing the likelihood that an unfortunate local would soon pass by the "rock," at which point the Draugr would reveal its true colors and lunge at, and voraciously devour, the now-doomed individual.

Notably, in specifically Norwegian lore, it was believed that it was possible to call upon the souls of the dead—namely those who had moved on to the realm of the afterlife—and pray for them to do battle with the Draugrs. Nordic mythology tells of violent altercations between the spectral dead and the walking dead. They were encounters that, invariably, the deceased of the ghostly variety won.

Drug Dealers and Voodoo

See also: Hoodoo, Vodun: Mambo and Houngan, Voodoo, Voodoo and the CIA

In 1996, seeking to prove that Voodoo may be used for good, High Priestess Sallie Ann Glassman called upon the gods of Voodoo to help rid their New Orleans neighborhood of drug dealers and crime. Sallie Ann and her business partner Shane Norris, both practitioners of Voodoo, had enough of the soaring crime rate when they were robbed and attacked.

About a hundred people gathered outside their store one night and they led a procession to the nearest street corner. They set up an altar in the middle of the street, using a sewer cap as its base. Against the background of beating drums and flaming torches, Sallie Ann performed a ritual to dispel any evil intent. Then she knelt before the altar and made an offering of rum, cigars, and bullets to Ogoun La Flambeau, the Voodoo god of war, fire, and metal.

Within a very short period of time, the Voodoo ritual had worked wonders. The crime rate dropped from seventy burglaries per month to about six. Before the ceremony, crack could be bought at seven houses. After the ritual, only one crack house remained.

Captain Lonnie Smith of the New Orleans police department, who witnessed the Voodoo rite, agreed that something seemed to have worked. And as long as they were getting positive results from Voodoo, he was all for it.

Dugway Proving Ground

Located approximately eighty-five miles outside of Salt Lake City, the huge Dugway Proving Ground (DPG) sits squarely within Utah's Great Salt Lake Desert, and is shielded and protected via a huge expanse of mountains that dominate the surrounding landscape. The highly classified work of the DPG falls under the control of the U.S. Army, and its role is to research chemical and biological weaponry from a defensive perspective.

Late on the afternoon of January 27, 2011, the super-secret DPG went into a definitive lockdown mode. If you were inside at the time the doors closed, then you stayed there. And if you were outside, there was no chance of getting in—at all. For the better part of a day, the situation did not change. Despite the tight security, word leaked outside that something of a disastrous nature had occurred, possibly even the mistaken release of a deadly pathogen, one that if it had escaped from the sterile confines of Dugway just might have started spreading all across the planet. Was it really

A view of Dugway Proving Ground almost a hundred miles outside of Salt Lake City, Utah, where secret government experiments purportedly led to the accidental release of a deadly pathogen.

that serious? Well, it very much depends on who you ask: the locals, the staff of Dugway, or nosey journalists.

Whistleblowers from Dugway claimed that, *yes*, it actually *was* that serious. When an everyday stocktaking of certain dangerous items was undertaken on the 27th, it was found, to the complete and utter consternation of just about everyone on base, that one particular vial wasn't where it should have been. In fact, it wasn't *anywhere*: it had vanished. Well, what was one little vial in the bigger scheme of things? Actually, one little vial could have been quite a lot.

The vial contained nothing less than a deadly chemical warfare agent called VX, which has significant and horrific effects on the human body and not unlike those that set in when one receives a vicious bite from one of the undead. Nausea and sweating are just the start. Bizarre twitching follows, as does uncontrollable vomiting. Then there is an accompanying fever, the victim's nose runs uncontrollably, and breathing becomes labored. Left untreated, the infected are in for quick and horrible deaths.

We are assured, however, that when further checks were made, it was discovered to the joy and relief of everyone that the deadly vial hadn't vanished after all. It had simply been mislabeled and placed on the wrong shelf. Problem solved! True or not, we are fortunate that the apocalypse did not begin and millions of people did not turn into staggering, twitchy nightmares.

In addition to missing vials of deadly agents, there's also the not-exactly insignificant matter of the Dugway Proving Ground's secret connections to the world of the zombie. And, no, we are not talking about within the realm of fiction.

Clairvius Narcisse was a resident of Haiti, and a man who claimed that, in 1962, he was zombified and forced to work in his undead-like state, on a Haitian plantation owned by his brother. Research undertaken after Narcisse's story came to light, and specifically that done by Wade Davis for his excellent book, *The Serpent and the Rainbow*, strongly suggested that Narcisse was rendered into such a bizarre condition after being given a powerful combination of two particular agents: (a) bufotoxin, which is found in, and extracted from, the paratoid glands of toads; and (b) tetrodotoxin, which can majorly affect the human nervous system. Combined, however, they can render an individual into a death-like state, in which both pulse and blood pressure plummet dramatically.

Additional research suggested strongly that Narcisse was then awakened from his "dead" state via Datura Stramonium, which is a form of herbal medicine that can provoke hallucinogenic experiences and amnesia. As a result of this mind-bending cocktail, Narcissse was led to believe by his brother that he, Narcisse, was a literal zombie who had been brought back from the dead. The outcome was that Narcisse began to act like a zombie—for no less than eighteen years. So, what does this have to do with the top secret world of the Dugway Proving Ground?

When, in late January 2011, there was that aforementioned mishandling of a highly toxic nerve-agent at the DPG, persistent digging by the media revealed that both bufotoxin and tetrodotoxin had been the subjects of highly classified studies at the secret installation. And what might be the reason for the DPG researching a controversial cocktail that can render a human being into a definitively zombie-style state? That is a question that no one in officialdom—and, certainly, least of all the staff of the Dugway Proving Ground—wants to answer. Is someone at Dugway planning on creating a zombie-like slave society? If it happens, remember that you read it here first.

E-F

End Times

See also: Apocalypse, Armageddon, Megiddo, Norwegian Armageddon

Currently, the most watched basic-cable television series—*ever*—is *The Walking Dead*. Not only is it a show that instantly attracted the zombie faithful, but it also turned millions of people, all across the globe, into fans of all things undead, even though they had previously never given the subject much thought. And, almost certainly, there is hardly a single fan of the show who has not at least once pondered on an important question: how would *I* survive a real-life version of *The Walking Dead*? The answer is a stark but simple one: with great difficulty and probably not at all. And here is the reason why:

In the likes of *Dawn of the Dead*, *Day of the Dead*, *Shaun of the Dead*, *Land of the Dead*, and *Diary of the Dead* (in fact, in just about everything of an … *of the Dead* nature), infection, death, resurrection, and mutation are all solely dependent upon one thing: being bitten by one of the undead. In *The Walking Dead*, however, matters are very different: everyone on the planet somehow became mysteriously infected with the zombie virus *prior* to the beginning of Armageddon. So, yes, getting bitten by a member of the walking dead club will almost certainly ensure you will quickly die and return in hideous form. But, here's the really bad news: on *The Walking Dead*—given that everyone is *already* infected—should you die from, for example, a heart-attack, cancer, suicide, murder, or even old age, the virus swarming around your body will ensure that you will return in an undead, rabid state. And that's where the big problem starts when it comes to surviving an apocalypse of *The Walking Dead* kind.

A Halloween zombie parade in Moscow, Russia, was just for fun, but such throngs of the walking dead could be much more sinister in the End Times.

In today's world, the causes of death are many and varied: heart-disease, cancer, strokes, respiratory conditions, age, obesity, murder, suicide, accidents, and more. As astonishing as it may sound, the average daily death toll, all across the globe, is around *150,000 people per day*, of *every* day, of *every* year. And here's the problem that would face the survivors in a real-world scenario of *The Walking Dead* kind: on "Day 1" of the apocalypse, those 150,000 who die on a daily basis would, within seconds, minutes, or hours, reanimate. On "Day 2" there would be 300,000 zombies. By the end of "Day 3" 450,000 undead would be walking the streets. By the end of the first week alone, the figure would be in excess of one million. At the end of the first month, four million zombies would be on the loose. By the close of the first year, the statistics would be around fifty million. After a decade, we are talking about *half a billion*. And, so the mind-numbing number grows and grows and grows. And that doesn't even begin to take into account those millions that will become zombified as a result of a bite: this is just the number who will die (and turn) each day as a result of the normal rigors of life.

In *The Walking Dead*, Sheriff Rick Grimes and his band of buddies have done an admirably successful job at thwarting the undead, time and time again. But that's because they seldom have to deal with more than a dozen or so zombies per episode. If *The Walking Dead* one day becomes reality, however, and as Grimes notes, "we're all infected," then the chances of defeating an army of the dead that is increasing by a minimum of 150,000 every twenty-four hours will not just be unlikely. It will be nigh on impossible.

Evil Twins

The contemporary cultural fixation on the zombie has made him become our evil twin. The zombie is the Other Self that we choose to treat with disdain and contempt—the mindless, subservient Self, that one day rises up and takes its revenge on our carefully ordered vision of our mores, our morality, and our dream of immortality. We have met the zombies in our fears, and we will soon join them in their graves.

The vampire is an evil being whose supernatural powers allow it to look like a human for the length of time it requires to drink our blood. But a zombie is one of us, rendered mindless by a clever sorcerer.

The werewolf is a shape-shifter, seized by a horrible hunger for human flesh and possessed of a strength that permits it to savagely slash and devour its victims. But a zombie is one of us unwillingly enslaved and exploited by a cruel master or stricken by a deadly virus.

The Gaia Hypothesis, named after the ancient Greek Goddess of the Earth, became popular in the 1960s and thousands upon thousands of people warmed to the idea that the Earth is not simply a planet that supports life, it is itself alive. Gaia continually improves the conditions for life through a series of biological and biochemical feedback systems that maintain the best possibility habitability of the planet.

However, in his article in *New Scientist* (June 20, 2009), Peter Ward argues that our planet may not be a nurturing mother of life like Gaia, but perhaps a more murderous mother like Medea, the sorceress and princess who killed her own children. Ward, a professor of biology at the University of Washington in Seattle, sees that life on Earth is ultimately self-destructive. Gaia's evil twin is its Medean tendency to pursue its own demise, moving Earth ever closer to the day it returns to being sterile.

In his book from Princeton University Press, *The Medea Hypothesis: Is Life on Earth Ultimately Self-Destructive?* Ward states that two lines of research are especially damning to the Gaia Hypothesis: One comes from the study of ancient rocks and the other from models of the future. Both suggest that life on Earth has repeatedly endured Medean events (drastic drops in biodiversity and abundance driven by life itself) and will do so again in the future.

An 1875 painting by Anselm Feuerbach portrays the great goddess Gaia. The Gaia Hypothesis proposes that our entire planet is a living being.

If Ward is correct in suggesting that our planet pursues its own demise and that one day in the future Gaia's Evil Twin will usher in the mass extinction of Earth as we know it, we may wonder if the sudden great popularity of the zombie is a precursor in the human mass consciousness that will permit those who heed its warning to begin to craft a new science of survival for our species?

Extraterrestrial

See also: Alien Infection, Alien Virus, Outer Space

Writer Leslie Mullen tells a story of potentially catastrophic proportions: "When diseases like SARS, Mad Cow Disease, and Monkey-pox cross the species barrier and infect humans, they dominate news headlines. Just imagine, then, the reaction if potentially infectious pathogens were found in rock samples from Mars. As we look toward exploring other worlds, and perhaps even bringing samples back to Earth for testing, astrobiologists have to wonder: could alien pathogens cross the 'planet' barrier and wreak havoc on our world? Even though there is no proof of bacterial or viral pathogens anywhere except Earth, there is already a worried advocacy group called the *International Committee Against Martian Sample Return*, and science fiction novels like *The Andromeda Strain* depict nightmare alien infection scenarios."

In similar fashion, "Sample Return Missions Scare Some Researchers" was the title of an article that surfaced on www.space.com in April 2000. "Researchers, environmentalists and policymakers want NASA to consider carefully its plans to visit and bring back samples from Mars, Europa, and other solar system bodies," it was reported. According to Norine Noonan, director of the Environmental Protection Agency's research arm, who also had recently chaired a NASA-sponsored panel on planetary protection: "This is a very serious issue, and there are clearly many concerns."

It was added: "NASA's longstanding policy is to both protect the Earth and preserve planetary conditions for future biological and organic constituent exploration … In recent years, NASA has commissioned the National Research Council to conduct several studies on the potential for contaminating other worlds. Now that the space agency also is considering a variety of sample return missions, researchers are becoming increasingly aware that they must put clear standards in place to protect against the highly unlikely but possible introduction—and escape—of extraterrestrial life to Earth. While minimal, the risk level 'is not zero,' warns one NRC study."

Science writer Robert Roy Britt noted, also in 2000: "A group of scientists says it has collected an alien bacterium ten miles above Earth, plus signatures of other extraterrestrial microbes even higher in the atmosphere. … The bacterium was collected at that altitude by a balloon operated by the Indian Space Research Organization. Chandra Wickramasinghe, who leads a study into the results, called the microbe a previously unknown strain of bacteria and said it likely came from a comet. Wickramasinghe and a colleague, Fred Hoyle, say the findings support an idea they pioneered, called panspermia, which holds that the seeds of life are everywhere in space and are the source for life on Earth."

Three years later, *National Geographic News* reported "In a letter to the British medical journal *The Lancet*, Chandra Wickramasinghe, from Cardiff University in Wales, and other scientists, propose that SARS may have originated in outer space then fallen down to Earth and landed in China, where the outbreak began. It sounds like a headline from a supermarket tabloid, but the idea may not be as outlandish as it first appears. One hundred tons (90 metric tons) of space debris fall on Earth every day; some scientists believe as much as one ton (0.9 metric ton) of bacteria from space is part of that daily deposit. Particles carrying the SARS virus could have come from a comet, the researchers say, and released into the debris trail of the comet's tail. The Earth's passage through the stream would have led to the entry of the culprit particles. 'We're not saying this is definitely what happened,' said Wickramasinghe, who is also the director of the Cardiff Center for Astrobiology, a research effort that seeks evidence of extraterrestrial life. 'But the theory should not be ruled out.'"

A zombie apocalypse provoked by something deadly and from outside of our own world? It happened in precisely that very fashion in George A. Romero's *Night of the Living Dead* movie of 1968. Why not in the real world, too?

FEMA: The Federal Emergency Management Agency

Should the unthinkable ever really occur, and the dead suddenly begin to roam our cities and towns, one agency of the U.S. government that will be at the forefront of trying to contain the explosive situation is FEMA, otherwise known as the Federal Emergency Management Agency. Established in 1978 and fully operational by April 1979, it is FEMA's role to provide relief and support in the event of large scale disasters that occur within the United States. There is, however, one key and important stipulation: a state of emergency has to be officially declared before FEMA can officially act; something which a state governor or the president has the power to declare.

When formally created, FEMA took on the responsibility of running the entire nation's civil defense programs, which were previously overseen by the Department of Defense. In the wake of the terrible events of September 11, 2001, however, FEMA was radically reorganized and integrated into the newly created Department of Homeland Security (DHS), which came into being in November 2002.

Since becoming an integral part of the DHS, FEMA, which has an annual budget in excess of $10 billion, has played leading roles in managing many high profile disasters, including Hurricane Katrina, which, in 2005, pummelled New Orleans; the Buffalo, New York snowstorm of 2006; and the raging fires that devastated much of southern California in 2007. There is—allegedly, anyway—a darker side to FEMA. It

A FEMA employee makes preparations for Hurricane Awareness Day in a Mobile Emergency Response Support (MERS) vehicle. Now part of the Department of Homeland Security, FEMA is supposed to help victims of disasters in the United States, but some suspect it could also be used to help enforce martial law.

is one which may have a significant bearing upon the role the agency might play if and when the dead awaken and attack.

Within the field of conspiracy theories and cover-ups, much attention has been given to the subject of what have become known as "FEMA camps." Supposedly, according to the theorists that hold to such beliefs, the camps are being secretly created for the day when the people of the United States will be placed under martial law, and any and all individuals the government considers to be undesirables will be rounded up and placed in such detention camps for indefinite periods—perhaps even for the rest of their lives.

At the extreme end of this particularly controversial area of conspiracy research, there are those who suspect that Nazi-style concentration camps are also being built in stealth, where thousands upon thousands of people who the government views as troublesome and a threat to national security—such as agitators, activists, and demonstrators—will be put to death at a time of nationwide crisis. What, you may wonder, does this have to do with zombies? Simple: the undeniable rise in the interest in, as well as the fascination for, zombies since the earliest years of the twenty-first century has put a whole new spin on the "FEMA camp" controversy, as we shall now see.

Conspiracy theorists believe that not only is an apocalypse of the dead and decaying kind just waiting in the wings, but that anyone and everyone infected by the zombie virus will be quickly arrested and transferred to the nearest FEMA camp, where they will be exterminated. As the nation descends into escalating chaos and anarchy, even the uninfected will be taken into custody, and held against their will behind the secure doors of these massive FEMA camps, as the government struggles—but probably fails—to keep control of what is going on outside.

It may all sound like tinfoil hat style paranoia, but the fact is that FEMA and zombies are becoming more and more interconnected. On May 19, 2011, FEMA decided to "share a blog post from our friends at the Centers for Disease Control." That shared blog post was none other than the controversy-filled 2011 article on zombie-preparedness penned by Rear Admiral Ali S. Khan, who, in August 2010, was assigned to lead the work of the CDC's Office of Public Health Preparedness and Response.

Then, in 2012, Danta Randazzo, of FEMA's Individual and Community Preparedness Division, said that: "Zombie-preparedness messages and activities have proven to be an effective way of engaging new audiences, particularly young people who are not familiar with what to do before, during or after a disaster. It's also a great way to grab attention and increase interest in general."

While Randazzo's words were intended to demonstrate that introducing zombies into disaster-preparedness programs was an ideal way to increase awareness in the young on the matter of surviving a large scale event of catastrophic proportions, more than a few conspiracy theorists concluded it was something very different: namely, a subtle hint that people should start thinking carefully and closely about real world zombies and FEMA's attitude to the soon to be dead, the infected, and the straggling survivors.

The strangest story of all, however, surfaced in March 2013. It was revealed by David Lory VanDerBeek, the Governor of Nevada, that FEMA had plans to stage a training-style "drill" for its staff involving nothing less than a fictional zombie outbreak provoked by a crashed UFO event in Moscow, Latah County, Idaho. Rather notably, when word got out, FEMA suddenly removed the relevant information from its website and hastily scrapped the drill—but not before VanDerBeek was astute enough to secure screenshots of the relevant pages, thus confirming the reality of the secretly planned operation.

It should be stressed that none of this means that top secret camps are being prepared by FEMA as part of a classified program to deal with a zombie infestation. On the other hand, it doesn't mean such camps *aren't* being secretly planned and constructed.

Flight of the Living Dead

It's a movie that is very much underappreciated, but which is actually quite a good one. It's *Flight of the Living Dead*—a title that hammers home the theme of the movie far more than its originally planned moniker of *Plane Dead* did. Made in 2007, the movie suffered from one thing when it came to making it a big success: it failed to make it into cinemas. Very often, a good movie can become swept up with the garbage when it goes straight to DVD and sits buried amongst cheap and awful productions in the local grocery store discount bin. Worse still, when such a movie then hits the television, it's invariably shredded to pieces and trimmed to give it a lower rating, one that is guaranteed to ensure a larger audience.

Despite the fact that *Flight of the Living Dead* didn't entertain cinema-goers by the millions, that doesn't mean it should be avoided. Quite the opposite: it fares very well against much of what passes for quality zombie fodder. There is tension, horror, graphic attacks on the living, and, getting to the theme of the movie, a pretty much unique setting: a Boeing 747 *Jumbo Jet* aircraft.

In most zombie movies, the survivors have at least some chance of combating the horrific hordes. They usually do so by staying on the move or finding somewhere to hunker down in that is fortified to such a degree that the dead stand little chance of breaking in. Such scenarios have been played out well in both cinematic versions of *Dawn of the Dead* and in AMC's *The Walking Dead*. It is, however, not quite as easy to avoid getting bitten when you are trapped within the confines of a 747! Nevertheless, our cast of characters does its best to avoid becoming infected. Not all of them succeed. But, do they ever?

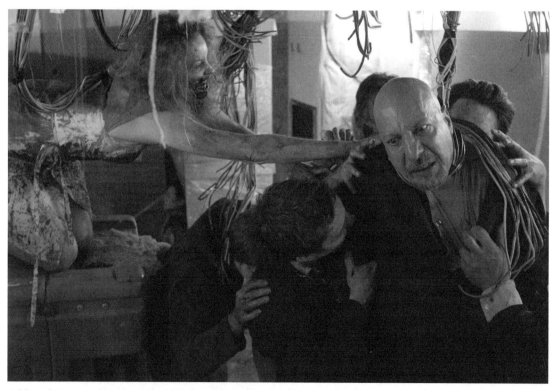

Although it went direct to video, *Flight of the Living Dead* is a worthy addition to the zombie film genre.

The storyline is nothing new, but is still handled in good fashion. What starts out as a regular flight—in this case a transatlantic journey from the United States to France—rapidly becomes a nightmare. Unknown to the passengers, amongst the suitcases and various other checked-in items in the 747's hold is a secure container hiding something nightmarish: a virus designed to ensure that when U.S. soldiers are shot and killed on the battlefield, they won't stay dead, but will rise up again and continue to attack the enemy. Guns, ammo, and grenades won't be their weapons of choice anymore, though. The virus will ensure that the troops of the dead will *eat* the enemy—a novel approach indeed.

One doesn't have to be an Einstein to realize that when the plane is hit by violent turbulence at the height of a huge storm, it won't be long at all before the virus escapes from its confines, and the passengers and crew start to turn. The production team does a good job of emphasizing the claustrophobic atmosphere on-board as more and more people—including the pilot, co-pilot and various flight-attendants—are mutated into savage killers. But it's not just the dead with who the survivors have to contend: the military decides to take the drastic approach of blasting the 747 out of the sky, as a means to hopefully kill all the zombies and have the virus obliterated in the heat of the fiery furnace.

At the last minute, however, two of those that have avoided the plague succeed in making it to the cockpit, and do their utmost to land the plane. The pilot of the military fighter plane that is tasked with bringing down the 747 is alerted to what is going on. Unfortunately, he has already launched the missile that will destroy the huge aircraft while it's still at a high altitude. While the pilot scrambles to abort the missile—and actually succeeds in doing so—it's too late. The missile explodes close enough to the plane that it causes catastrophic damage to its fuselage and the aircraft crash-lands in the deserts of Nevada, not all that far from Las Vegas.

In satisfyingly bleak fashion, *Flight of the Living Dead* ends with the infected making their way towards Sin City itself. The implication is that, in no time at all, Armageddon will begin in Nevada.

Flying Zombies

Back in 1969, the U.S. government and military were deeply embroiled in the Vietnam War, one that was filled with carnage and death. It was also a war in which nothing less than a flying zombie put in an appearance—as bizarre as it undeniably sounds. The story comes from one Earl Morrison who, at the time, was attached to the Marine Corps. The location was an area dominated by hills and forests near the Han River. According to Morrison, when the spooky encounter occurred, it was night-time: the sun had set, the landscape was dark, and something horrific surfaced out of the shadows and into the skies. As Morrison and two colleagues scanned the skies for evidence of North Vietnamese aircraft, something vile loomed into view: a flying humanoid.

Morrison said: We saw what looked like wings, like a bat's; only it was gigantic compared to what a regular bat would be. After it got close enough so we could see what it was, it looked like a woman, a naked woman." The strange yet striking woman sailed by at a perilously low level, both amazing and terrifying Morrison and his comrades. They could only look on in dumbstruck fashion as the woman—practically a female equivalent of the winged beast of the *Jeepers Creepers* horror movies—was lost in the distance and the darkness.

As for the zombie connection: the day after the flying woman was seen, the bodies of eleven North Vietnamese troops were found dead, right around the area where the winged woman was lost from sight. The bodies of the soldiers—stumbled on by a U.S. Army detachment—had been ferociously torn apart and partially devoured. Whatever had attacked the unit did so in fast and furious fashion. Perhaps, the dead don't just walk; maybe they fly, too.

Foot-and-Mouth Disease

See also: Cattle Mutilations, Creutzfeld-Jacobs Disease, Mad Cow Disease

On the issue of the animal kingdom, the U.S. Committee on Biological Warfare noted: "As far as non-epidemic producing agents are concerned, the committee feels that the use of these as weapons would cause no more indiscriminate destruction of life than would, for example, use of incendiary munitions. Also, destruction of property would be practically nil with biological agents, whereas it is considerable with conventional incendiary or explosive munitions. While it is granted that innocent civilians would be affected by all biological agents, the same can be said for any type of explosive munitions. Furthermore, since non-epidemic agents do not spread rapidly from one individual to another, an attack with these agents would be as indiscriminate and probably as localized as would an attack with incendiary bombs or high explosive munitions."

In conclusion, it was stated that:

As a matter of fact, predictions of effectiveness of biological agents against a human population must be taken with reservations. No experimental animal is available that can be used to measure the effectiveness of these weapons against man. For these reasons the Committee feels that at present biological warfare cannot be correctly classed as a means of mass destruction of human beings. The use of most biological agents might be more humane and less objectionable than the use of conventional weapons for two reasons. In the first place, property is not destroyed in biological warfare and production facilities of a defeated nation may recover more quickly than if large amounts of property were destroyed. In the second place, destruction of life may be less with biological warfare if debilitating but non-fatal agents are used. For example, the use of the agent causing undulant fever as an offensive weapon might be expected to cause large numbers of casualties and thus greatly aid the war effort of the attacking nation, but most of the casualties would recover after a period of illness and could resume active lives.

With that, the committee chair, Vannevar Bush, prepared a confidential memorandum for the Joint Chiefs of Staff that summarized the Committee's findings and recommendations with respect to biological warfare from a defensive perspective.

By the latter part of 1948, as will now become apparent, biological warfare was seen as a major threat to the United States by the Research and Development Board. Moreover, the fear that a hostile nation would attempt to ravage the American food-supply by deliberately infecting its cattle herd with diseases and viruses was running high in official circles.

According to the 1948 documents at issue, biological warfare "lends itself especially well to undercover operations, particularly because of the difficulty in detecting such operations and because of the versatility possible by the proper selection of biological warfare agents."

The Committee expanded: "Within the last few years there have been several outbreaks of exotic diseases and insect pests which are believed to have been introduced accidentally, but which could have been introduced intentionally had someone wished to do so. The use of epizootic agents against our animal population by sabotage is a very real and immediate danger. Foot-and-mouth disease and rinderpest are among those which would spread rapidly, and unless effective countermeasures were immediately applied, would seriously affect the food supply of animal origin."

Worse still is the following extract: "Since foot-and-mouth is now present in Mexico, it would be relatively easy for saboteurs to introduce the disease into the United States and have this introduction appear as naturally spread from Mexico. Since rinderpest and foot-and-mouth disease are not present in the United States, our animal population is extremely vulnerable to these diseases."

Alarmingly, the papers reveal, the United States was (and logic dictates, *still is*) in no position to prevent a large-scale biological attack on the animal population had it indeed occurred: "The United States is particularly vulnerable to this type of attack. It is generally believed that espionage agents of foreign countries, which are potential enemies of the United States, are already present in this country. There appears to be no great barrier to prevent additional espionage agents from becoming established here, and there is no control over the movements of people within the United States."

The authors of the document note further: "North America is an isolated land mass and, hence, specific areas therein present feasible biological warfare targets for an extra continental enemy since fear of backfiring is minimized."

Most disturbing, however, was the potential outlook for the United States in the event of a country-wide biological warfare on the nation's cattle herd: "The food supply of the nation could be depleted to an extent which materially would reduce the nation's capacity to defend itself and to wage war. Serious outbreaks of disease of man, animals, or plants would also result in profound psychological disturbances."

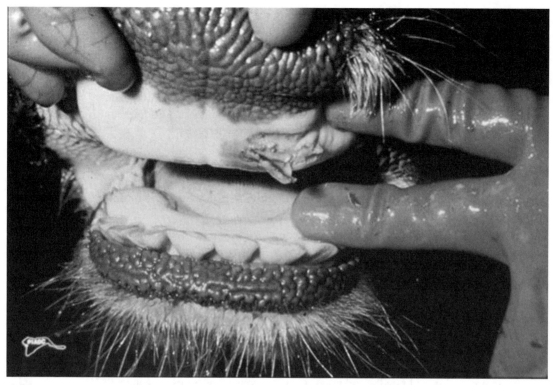

A farmer examines a mouth sore on a cow, a symptom of foot-and-mouth disease.

But how would a covert introduction of foot-and-mouth disease in the United States' food chain be undertaken? The Committee had a number of ideas: via "water contamination;" "fodder and food;" "infected bait;" "contamination of soil;" "Biological Warfare aerosols;" and deliberate "contamination of veterinary pharmaceuticals and equipment."

Realizing the potentially grave implications that such a scenario presented, the government carefully and quietly began to initiate a number of plans to try and combat any possible attack on the continental United States that might have occurred. Recommending that a special unit should be established to deal with the situation, the committee asserted that ventilation shafts, subway systems, and water supplies throughout the country should be carefully monitored. Similarly, the Committee stated, steps should be taken to determine "the extent to which contamination of stamps, envelopes, money, cosmetics, food, and beverages as a means of subversively disseminating biological agents is possible."

In addition to preparing for the worst from a defensive perspective, however, authorities were not above planning their own biological warfare operations from an offensive perspective. "Major goals and objectives of a research and development program in the field of offensive special biological warfare operations include: (1) Development of new agents suitable for special operations; (2) development of methods of dissemination for special BW operations; (3) determination of effectiveness and feasibility of methods of dissemination; and (4) estimation of approximate dosages required for specific special BW operations."

But it was in the conclusions of the Committee's report on the use of foot-and-mouth disease and other diseases as a biological weapon that the utter lack of defense against such an attack was spelled out: "It is concluded that: (1) biological agents would appear to be well adapted to subversive use. (2) The United States is particularly susceptible to attack by special BW operations. (3) The subversive use of biological agents by a potential enemy prior to a declaration of war presents a grave danger to the United States. (4) The biological warfare research and development program is not now authorized to meet the requirements necessary to prepare defensive measures against special BW operations."

Fort Detrick

The year 1941 was a devastating year for the United States: on December 7, 1941, the U.S. Naval Base of Pearl Harbor, on the island of Oahu, Hawaii was attacked by Japanese forces. More than two thousand Americans lost their lives. It was a terrible event that led the United States to enter World War II, which had been raging across Europe since September 1, 1939. There are good indications, however, that pre-Pearl Harbor, the U.S. government already realized it would only be a matter of time before it got dragged into the conflict. The events of December 1941 only ensured that was the case.

One of the reasons we know there was mounting American concern regarding World War II is because—also in 1941, but months earlier—the president of the day, Franklin D. Roosevelt, signed off on new legislation to create what became known as the U.S. Biological Warfare Program (BWP). Since it was known that both the Japanese and the Nazis were working to perfect devastating weapons of war, ones of a viral and biological nature, the United States needed an official body that could assess the threat and then fully counter it. The job fell to the BWP. Its headquarters were housed at Camp Detrick, Maryland, which, today, is officially titled Fort Detrick. Its mandate remains very much the same: to help protect the nation from the threat of biological warfare, plagues, and viruses. And then we have the zombie connection to the base.

Rather amazingly, Fort Detrick and zombies are not what could be termed uncommon bedfellows. In 2012 a "Run Zombie Run" obstacle course was organized by staff at the facility, which was described as being "not only a race against time, but also a race from bloodthirsty zombies. Navigate the course, conquer the obstacles, and cross the finish line with at least one health flag, and you will have made it without becoming one of the undead."

This is made all the more thought provoking by the fact that within the domain of conspiracy research, rumors circulate to the effect that scientists at Fort Detrick have secretly perfected a monstrous combination of rabies and the flu virus, which has

The U.S. Biological Warfare Laboratory at Fort Detrick in Maryland, circa 1940s.

the ability to instill violent, zombie-like rage in people. Worse still, is the rumor that becoming infected is not just dependent on getting bitten. The virus is said to be one that has the ability to spread wildly in airborne fashion. The virus will not turn people into literal zombies—those that have died and returned to a hideous form of life—but it *will* mutate them into insane, frightening, aggressive killers whose minds will be reduced to the most primal of all levels possible.

Think it couldn't happen? You might want to reassess your stance. Consider the following words of Samita Andreansky, a virologist at the Florida-based University of Miami's School of Medicine, who says: "I could imagine a situation where you mix rabies with a flu virus to get airborne transmission, a measles virus to get personality changes, the encephalitis virus to cook your brain with fever, and throw in the Ebola virus to cause you to bleed from your guts. Combine all these things and you'll [get] something like a zombie virus."

Frankenstein

See also: Andrew Crosse, Mary Shelley

One of the most intriguing issues relative to Mary Shelley's classic and acclaimed novel of the reanimated dead, *Frankenstein*, is how, and under what specific circumstances, did she come up with the memorable title? The official story, which surfaced directly from the author herself, is that during the writing process, Shelley had a dream-like vision in which the name came to her in almost magical, supernatural fashion. While that may perhaps have been the case, the fact of the matter is that it's not quite as straightforward as that.

Frankenstein, despite what many might conclude, is not a fictional name. In fact, it's actually far more than quite common in certain parts of Germany. As evidence, there is a town called Frankenstein located in the region of Palatinate, southwest Germany. Similarly, and prior to 1946, the Polish town of Zabkowice Slaskie also shared that infamous and monstrous moniker. It was a name that, for the town at least, dated back to the thirteenth century when the area was invaded and decisively conquered by the Mongols. It is entirely possible that Shelley, who travelled quite extensively across Europe during the process of planning and writing her book, encountered the name during the course of her journeying. Perhaps she then forgot about it until, late one night, it surfaced from within the depths of her buried memories and subconscious. There is, however, a far more interesting possibility on the matter of how Shelley decided upon Frankenstein as the name of the book and of her chief character in its dark pages.

In his book, *In Search of Frankenstein*, author Radu Florescu suggested that, while en-route to Switzerland, both Mary and her husband, the acclaimed poet Percy Shelley, visited a very real Castle Frankenstein; one situated near the city of Darmstadt, along the Rhine, and which was home to a highly notorious alchemist, one Konrad Dippel. Significantly, it is said that Dippel performed diabolical experiments on human corpses, with the goal of trying to bring them back to some form of life—a zombie, one might be very inclined to suggest. Florescu also suggested—and in a fashion that makes a great deal of sense—that Mary Shelley chose to deny the Dippel connection as a means to convince people that her novel, *Frankenstein*, was a wholly original one, when in reality it may well have taken deep inspiration from both Dippel and his notoriously named castle of the undead.

In the same way that Dr. Frankenstein's monster was a mixture of numerous body parts taken from numerous people, perhaps Mary Shelley's novel took inspiration from just about as many sources.

Mary Shelley completed the writing of her novel, *Frankenstein*, in May 1817. The first historic edition of the book appeared in London stores on New Year's Day, 1818, thanks to the publishing house of Harding, Mavor & Jones, that released it after several other publishers—including John Murray and Charles Ollier—rejected it outright. Notably, and curiously, the very first edition of the book did not even include Mary's name on the front-cover. Instead, the novel was simply prefaced by Mary's husband, the poet Percy Shelley. Despite the fact that, today, sales of *Frankenstein* are in the millions, the first print-run was a mere and measly 500 copies. Needless to say, today, those originals are near invaluable.

Very ironically, and particularly so for a book that is now so well acclaimed, *Frankenstein* was overwhelmingly slammed by critics upon its release. In part, this was provoked by the lack of guts on the part of Harding, Mavor & Jones to actually reveal the name of their author. As evidence of the less than favorable reviews that directly followed the publication of the book, *Quarterly Review* wrote that *Frankenstein* was "a tissue of horrible and disgusting absurdity." Nevertheless, Mary Shelley did have some fans in high, distinguished, and influential places. One of them was the acclaimed writer, Sir Walter Scott (perhaps most famous for *Ivanhoe* and *Rob Roy*) who said of Shelley's novel that it "impresses us with a high idea of the author's original genius and happy power of expression."

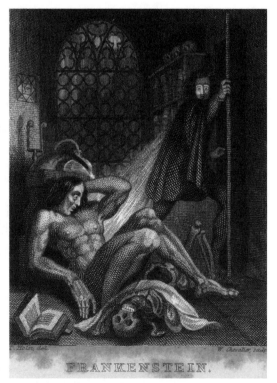

FRANKENSTEIN.

An illustration from the 1831 edition of Mary Shelley's *Frankenstein* features the reanimated man created by the title scientist.

Fortunately, the general public chose to ignore the many less than flattering reviews and made up their own minds about the book. They loved it. *Frankenstein* became, appropriately, a monster-sized hit. And not just in the United Kingdom, either. Overseas editions quickly appeared, too. On top of that, in 1823, a theater production of the novel was staged by dramatist Richard Brinsley Peake and titled *The Fate of Frankenstein*, a production that Mary Shelley herself watched and eagerly enjoyed. Then, on Halloween 1831, the definitive version of *Frankenstein* was published by Richard Bentley and Henry Colburn. It was a version for which Mary Shelley made substantial edits and revisions, and that is the most widely read version available today—even though the original is still in great demand, too.

Things didn't come to an end with the domains of book publishing and the stage, however. Thanks to the likes of Universal Studios and the United Kingdom's Hammer Film Productions, the zombified monster struck fear into the hearts of cinema-goers from the 1930s to the 1970s. Then, in 1994, a big budget movie version of the novel hit the screens, with Robert De Niro and Kenneth Branagh taking the lead roles of monster and mad scientist, respectively. And, in 2014, *Bruce vs. Frankenstein* (starring Bruce Campbell of *The Evil Dead*) is slated for release. Just like the walking dead of today, there is practically no stopping Frankenstein's monster.

Funerals

See also: Burial Traditions, Cemeteries and Tombs, Coffins, Mummies

For those Buddhists who believe in reincarnation, funerals are happy occasions. Death in the present life frees the soul from Dukkha (worldly existence) and returns it to the path that leads to Nirvana, where all misery and karma cease. The coffin of one who has died in the Buddhist belief system is taken to the funeral hall in a brightly decorated carriage. The coffin is carried three times around the Buddhist temple or funeral hall and then brought inside, where it is set down in the midst of the flowers and gifts which friends and family of the deceased have placed around it.

A Buddhist monk leads the people in a prayer known as the Three Jewels that helps the soul find refuge in the Buddha, the Dharma (the true way of life that a devout Buddhist seeks to lead), and the Sangha (the unified faith of the Buddhist monks). Together with the people in the funeral hall, the monk recites the Five Precepts, the rules by which Buddhist strive to live.

Throughout the ceremony, food is served and music is played. There are few tears of mourning, for the family and friends are reminded by the monk that the soul will be reborn many times in many bodies. After the service, the body is cremated, and the ashes are buried or kept in the temple in a small urn.

The followers of Tao envision the soul of the deceased crossing a bridge to the next life. Ten courts of judgment await the new soul, and if it passes this series of trials, it may continue on the path to heaven. If it fails because of bad deeds during the person's lifetime, the soul must be punished before it is allowed to go to a better place.

The family and friends of the deceased place the body in a wooden coffin and carry it to the graveyard. They pound drums, clang cymbals, and shoot off fireworks to frighten away any evils spirits that might attempt to catch the soul even before it reaches the ten courts of judgment. Beside the grave as the coffin is being lowered into the ground, paper representations of houses, money, and other material objects are burned, symbolically providing the soul of the deceased with property which to pay the judges who await the spirit in the afterlife.

After ten years have passed, the coffin is dug up, and the remains are cleaned and placed in an urn, which is then sealed. A Taoist priest assesses the home of the person's immediate family and decides the most harmonious spot for the urn of bones to be placed. It is of utmost importance that the priest finds a place where the spirit of the deceased will be happy among its surviving family members, or the spirit may return to punish those it deems disrespectful of its physical remains.

A first century C.E. carving of the Buddha's foot shows the Triratna (Three Jewels) symbol.

Gargoyles in Texas

Situated not too far from the Texas–New Mexico border is the small Texas town of Littlefield, which is just a short drive from the city of Lubbock. It's a quiet, pleasant place; one which is surrounded by endless fields of cotton, and through which an abundance of tumbleweeds regularly roll. Back in the 1940s, however, Littlefield was plunged into a state of terror. Nothing less than a pair of flesh-eating gargoyles was on the loose. Real-life equivalents of the monsters made famous in the likes of the movies *The Mothman Prophecies*, *Jeepers Creepers*, and *Max Payne*? Just possibly, yes.

The year was 1946—just twelve months after World War II finally came to an end. Situated on the fringes of Littlefield at the time was an old, tall house, one not at all unlike that in which crazy Norman Bates lived in Alfred Hitchcock's acclaimed thriller of 1960, *Psycho*. Given that the house had long been abandoned, it became an ideal place for the children of Littlefield to play in, scaring themselves stupid with tales of ghostly goings-on in its cobwebbed, decaying rooms. Maybe at least some of those tales were something far more.

Local legend tells of how, late one night in 1946, several young teenagers were walking towards the old house—to have a few secret smokes and drinks—when they were stopped dead in their tracks by something terrifying: a pair of large, human-like creatures that crawled out of the outside entrance point to the building's cellar. They were easily seven and a half feet tall, maybe even taller than that. They were not, however, human. That much was made clear by the large, bat-like wings that protruded from their muscular, oily black backs. And if that wasn't enough, there were the glowing red eyes that both creatures sported.

Gargoyle statues adorn many churches in Europe as a way of protecting the buidling from evil forces; could real-life equivalents be plaguing Texas?

When both man-beasts stared directly at the kids, the latter did the wisest thing possible: they ran. The creatures were last seen soaring high into the clear, star filled night skies of west Texas. The tale is not quite over, however. Wild and controversial stories swept across town suggesting that the local police had gotten wind of what was afoot and, to their horror, found more than twenty partially devoured human bodies in the cellar.

In an attempt to get to the bottom of the story, I spent much time in Littlefield in 2001, spoke with some of the elderly locals that lived there back in the 1940s, checked newspaper archives, and even chatted with the local police. Although a couple of people remembered the old house, and the rumors that it was haunted, vindication for the bodies in the cellar angle did not surface. Was the whole thing down to nothing more than a teenage prank? Might the authorities have stamped on the story and warned all those in the know to keep their mouths firmly shut? Whatever the answer, it might be wise to keep a careful eye on the sky if you ever find yourself driving through Littlefield, Texas.

Gay Bomb

It sounds like just about the most bizarre bit of fakery that you could possibly ever imagine. In reality, however, it's deranged reality. In the early 1990s, the U.S. Air Force came up with a decidedly unusual, and wildly alternative, way to defeat enemy troops on the battlefield. It was a way that would have avoided the use of any form of lethal weaponry at all, as incredible as that may sound. The ingeniously weird plan was to alter the mindset of the enemy, and to render them completely incapable of fighting, albeit in a very strange fashion.

In the words of senior Air Force personnel, extracted from the official, top secret files that are now in the public domain, it was suggested that "a bomb be developed containing a chemical that would cause soldiers to become gay, and to have their units break down because all their soldiers became irresistibly attractive to one another." No, it's really not April 1. Project Gay Bomb was the real deal—at a theoretical level, at least.

The story tumbled out into the public domain in 2007, when a public organization called the Sunshine Project—which scrutinizes how, and on precisely what, the military spends its vast budgets—secured files on the program under the terms of the

U.S. government's Freedom of Information Act. The files showed that recommendations had secretly been made to have the project housed at Brooks Air Force Base, Texas, and that initial funding for the operation was planned to run to around a fairly impressive $7 million.

When contacted by numerous media outlets, all probing to get to the bottom of things—so to speak—the Pentagon assured the world's news that, yes, the program was real, but that it was just one of many proposals that was looked at and ultimately discarded as being simply too weird, and lacking in solid science, to work successfully. Nevertheless, despite the undeniable humor in all of this, there is an important and disturbing issue worth noting. The program was designed to use a chemical—to be released in aerosol form—that would radically alter and affect the minds of the enemy, and cause them to suddenly engage in wild, sexual behavior.

But what if a very different chemical agent was secretly and successfully developed that instilled not feelings of a sexual nature, but thoughts and actions of a decidedly violent nature? Conspiracy researchers claim knowledge of the existence of the exact opposite of the "Love Bomb." Its name is the "Rage Bomb." In this scenario, the airborne, mood-altering spray, would cause enemy troops to turn on each other—not in loving fashion, but in violent, murderous style. It would be nothing less than a real life, carnage filled equivalent of *28 Days Later*, but, on the battlefield, rather than in the streets of London, England. What happens, however, when the airborne nightmare spreads from the zone of battle and reaches major areas of population? Could we see something akin to a genuine dawning of the infected? Many might be inclined to suggest that such a theory is just far too ridiculous for words. But, remember this: the bomb of love was an all too real idea, and it was an idea given very serious and top secret consideration by the highest echelons of the American military. In view of that, why not a bomb of rage, too?

Germ Warfare

Germ warfare, also known as biological warfare, is not a new concept. In the Middle Ages, opposing armies would catapult diseased animal and human corpses into their foes encampments or over their city walls. When the Black Death, the bubonic plague, nearly decimated Europe's population in the fourteenth century, attacking armies flung excrement and bits of diseased corpses over castle walls.

Use of biological weapons was outlawed by the Geneva Protocol of 1925, but reports of the uses the Japanese Imperial Army made of such weapons on Chinese soldiers and civilians began to filter out of Asia to Great Britain and the United States. During the war years of 1937 to 1945, the infamous Japanese Unit 731 conducted gruesome experiments that resulted in the deaths of an estimated 580,000 victims.

In 1941, in response to the bio-weapons that were developed in Japan and Nazi Germany in the late 1930s, the United States, the United Kingdom, and Canada established their own biological warfare program and produced anthrax, brucellosis, and botulinum toxin that could be used in war. In 1942, British tests with anthrax spores contaminated Gruinard Island, Scotland to such an extent that it was rendered unusable for forty-eight years.

In 1972, the Biological and Toxin Weapons Convention reinforced the prohibition of all chemical and biological weapons. The international ban pertains to nearly all production, storage, and transport of such biological agents; however, numerous researchers believe that the secret production of such weapons actually increased.

In 1986, a report to Congress stated that the new generation of biological agents includes modified viruses, naturally occurring toxins, and agents that are altered through genetic engineering to prevent treatment by all existing vaccines.

The Department of Defense admitted in 1987 that regardless of treaties banning research and development of biological agents, it operates 127 research facilities throughout the nation.

The U.S. military was frequently accused of using various biological and chemical weapons in the Gulf War in 1991. Often mentioned was the charge that BZ, a hallucinogen, was sprayed over Iraq, causing its citizens to surrender as totally passive, drooling, troops with vacant stares.

In 1994, it was revealed that many returning Desert Storm veterans are infected with an altered strain of Mycoplasma incognitus, a microbe commonly used in the production of biological weapons.

In 1996, the Department of Defense admitted knowledge that Desert Storm soldiers were exposed to chemical agents.

In 2004, dangerous super bugs were popping up out of nowhere. Suddenly there were cases of flesh-eating bacteria, fatal pneumonia, and life-threatening heart infections seemingly all caused by mutating strains of *Staphylococcus aureus* that shrugged off penicillin as a duck shakes off rain.

Japan's Unit 731 was the site of gruesome experiments that resulted in the deaths of an estimated 580,000 victims during World War II.

With the advent of genetic manipulation, deadly designer viruses can be created. Through recombinant engineering, the highly contagious influenza virus could be spliced with botulism or the toxin from plague.

The smallpox virus is said to be particularly amenable to genetic engineering. The deadliest natural smallpox virus is known as *Variola major*, and it would be especially deadly now because the disease was eradicated from the planet in 1977. The smallpox vaccine dissipates after ten to twenty years, so unless someone has had a reason to be vaccinated against the disease, no one today is immune.

Three years after an endemic outbreak of smallpox in Somalia occurred in 1977, on May 8, 1980, the World Health Assembly declared the dreaded disease of smallpox to be eradicated. In 2001 a diagnosis of smallpox in Florida had the CDC in full alarm until the "smallpox" turned out to be false diagnoses of three cases of shingles. The only legal stocks of the smallpox virus are kept in two repositories at the Centers for Disease Control in Atlanta, Georgia, and the Vector Research Center in Koltsovo, Siberia.

While it seems a smallpox outbreak is unlikely in today's vaccinated world, no one can guess how many canisters of the lethal virus reside in laboratories awaiting deadly use in biological warfare. American intelligence reports that the virus is in repositories controlled by the North Korean bioweapons program, as well as the secret Russian military laboratory at Sergiyev Posad. If that's not enough to produce bad dreams, many intelligence sources believe that Iran, China, India, Syria, and Israel have ample stocks of the virus. An educated estimate is that if smallpox were used in an attack about one infected person in three would die.

Some researchers name the Ebola virus as the ideal biological weapon, because it has the potential of killing 90 percent of infected humans within three weeks of contact. The virus first emerged in three European vaccine production laboratories virtually simultaneously in 1967. Leonard G. Horowitz says that the virus was named the Marburg virus, after one of the vaccine-makers home in Marburg, Germany. Scientific consensus has it that this virus arrived in Europe in a shipment of nearly five hundred African monkeys from Kitum Cave near the West Nile region of Central Africa.

In April 2005, the World Health Organization reported an Ebola-like virus spreading rapidly through seven of Angola's eighteen provinces. The initial outbreak appeared to have spread from a pediatric ward about 180 miles north of Luanda. Most of the victims of the virus were children. Over a dozen health care workers had died from the disease, and those who remained were deserting hospitals and clinics. In one village, terrified people had attacked members of the World Health Organization out of fear of catching the disease.

In the fall of 2009, we faced the yet-unknown force of the H1N1 virus. If this should be discovered to be yet another designer drug, then we might wonder if a zombie-type virus, a pandemic that would steal the free will and minds of the masses might not be far behind.

Ghoul

The ghoul is often linked with the vampire and the werewolf in traditional folklore, but there are a number of obvious reasons why the entity has never attained the popularity achieved by the Frankenstein monsters, Draculas, and Wolfmen of the horror films. First and foremost is the nauseating fact that the ghoul is a disgusting creature that subsists on corpses, invading the graves of the newly buried and feasting on the flesh of the deceased. The very concept is revolting and offensive to modern sensibilities.

Ghouls are similar to zombies in many ways, being repulsive creatures that feast off the dead, usually invading graveyards to do so.

There are a number of different entities that are included in the category of ghoul. There is the ghoul that, like the vampire, is a member of the family of the undead, continually on the nocturnal prowl for new victims. Unlike the vampire, however, this ghoul feasts upon the flesh of the deceased, tearing their corpses from cemeteries and morgues. The ghoul more common to the waking world is that of the mentally unbalanced individual who engages in the disgusting aberration of necrophagia, eating or otherwise desecrating the flesh of deceased humans. Yet a third type of ghoul would be those denizens of Arabic folklore, the ghul (male) and ghulah (female), demonic jinns that haunt burial grounds and sustain themselves on human flesh stolen from graves.

Sgt. Bertrand, the infamous so-called werewolf of Paris was really a ghoul, for rather than ripping and slashing the living, he suffered from the necrophilic perversion of mutilating the dead.

It is not difficult to envision how the legends of the ghoul and vampire began in ancient times, when graves were shallow and very often subject to the disturbances of wild animals seeking carrion. Later, as funeral customs became more elaborate and men and women were buried with their jewelry and other personal treasures, the lure of easy wealth superseded any superstitious or ecclesiastical admonitions that might have otherwise kept grave robbers away from cemeteries and from desecrating a corpse's final rest.

Then, in the late 1820s, surgeons and doctors began to discover the value of dissection. The infant science of surgery was progressing rapidly, but advancement required cadavers and the more cadavers that were supplied, the more the doctors realized how little they actually knew about the anatomy and interior workings of the human body, and thus the more cadavers they needed. As a result, societies of grave robbers were formed called the resurrectionists. These men made certain that the corpses finding their way to the dissection tables were as fresh as possible. And, of course, digging was easier in unsettled dirt. The great irony was that advancement in medical science helped to perpetuate the legend of the ghoul.

Goat Man

Situated in the heart of the Texas town of Denton—just north of the city of Dallas—is an 1884-built structure known amongst the locals as the Old Alton Bridge. According to an enduring legend, many years ago, wannabe devil-worshippers in the area inadvertently opened up a portal to some hellish realm that allowed a vile beast open access to our world. It became known as the Goat Man, as a result of its humanoid body but goatish head. And now, today, and as a direct result of that reckless action, the Goat Man has no intention, at all, of returning to the unearthly zone from which he appeared; hence his deep desire to forever haunt the old steel and wood bridge at Denton.

An even weirder story maintains that the Denton Goat Man's origins can be traced back to a resident of the town who, decades ago, slaughtered and voraciously devoured his entire family, and was quickly hanged as a punishment for his terrible crime. As the local legend tells it, at the moment he was hung, the man's head was torn from his body by the weight of his blubbery form. For the average zombie, losing one's head is a major problem, as the head still retains its ferocious faculties but—quite obviously—has no means to move around and catch and devour new prey. But it wasn't a problem for the Old Alton Bridge's flesh-eater, however: he took the easy approach of simply finding himself a new head.

It was the head of an innocent goat that had the great misfortune to be in the area at the time. And so, the Goat Man of Denton was born. Was this merely a tall tale? Well, yes, of course, it was! But that does not take away the fact that local folks, on many occasions, have reported seeing the nightmarish, goat-like killer roaming around the woods behind the bridge. In other words, whatever the real origins of Denton's Goat Man, there does appear to be a significant amount of substance to what many merely perceive to be an entertaining piece of local, headless hokum.

Golem

The Golem is the Frankenstein monster of Jewish tradition. It is, in fact, in the eyes of many literary scholars, one of the principal inspirations for Mary Shelley's *Frankenstein: The Modern Prometheus*. The Golem, however, is not patched together from the body parts of cadavers robbed from their graves, but it is created from virgin soil and pure spring water. It is also summoned, more than created, by those who purify themselves spiritually and physically, rather than by heretical scientists in foreboding castle laboratories who bring down electricity from the sky to animate their patchwork human.

The word Golem appears only once in the Bible (Psalms 139:16). In Hebrew the word means shapeless mass. The Talmudic teachings define the Golem as an entity unformed or imperfect. The Talmud states that for the first twelve hours after his creation, Adam himself was a Golem, a body without a soul.

According to certain traditions, the creation of a Golem may only be accomplished when one has attained one of the advanced stages of development for serious practitioners of Kabbalah and alchemy. The Sefer Yezirah (Book of Creation or Formation), a guidebook of magic attributed to Rabbi Eliezar Rokeach in the tenth century, instructs those who would fashion a Golem to shape the collected soil into a figure resembling a man. Once the sculpting has been completed, the magicians were to use God's name, He who is the ultimate creator, to bring the Golem to life.

A Jewish rabbi brings a golem to life from a mixture of virgin soil and water.

Other instructions in the ancient text advise the magician to dance around the creature fashioned of soil, reciting a combination of letters from the Hebrew alphabet and singing the secret name of God. Once the Golem has completed its assigned tasks or mission, it may be destroyed by walking or dancing around it in the opposite direction and reciting the letters and the words backwards.

The Kabbalah gives instruction that once the Golem had been formed, it was given life by the Kabbalist placing under its tongue a piece of paper with the Tetragrammaton (the four-letter name of God) written on it. Other traditions state that one must write the Hebrew letters aleph, mem, tav on the forehead of the Golem. The letters represent emet (truth), and once the characters have been inscribed on the Golem's forehead, it comes alive. When it has completed the work assigned to him, the magician erases the aleph, leaving mem and tav, which is met (death).

In his modern adaptation of the ancient text, Rabbi Aryeh Kaplan stresses that the initiate should never attempt to make a Golem alone, but should always be accompanied by one or two learned colleagues. Extreme care must be taken by its creators, for the Golem can become a monster and wreak havoc. When such a mistake occurs, the divine name must somehow be removed from the creature's tongue and it will then be allowed to revert to dust.

The most famous Golem is the creature created by Judah Loew Ben Bezalel (1525–1609) to help protect the Jews of Prague from the libel that the blood of a Christian child was used during the Passover Seder. There are many accounts of how Yossele saved innocent Jews from reprisals directed against them by those citizens who had been incited by the anti-Semitic libel.

Once the Golem had served its purpose, the rabbi locked it in the attic of Prague's Old-New Synagogue, where it is widely believed that the creature rests to this day. The synagogue survived the widespread destruction directed against Jewish places of worship by the Nazis, and it is said that the Gestapo did not even enter the attic. A statue of Yossele, the Golem of Prague, still stands at the entrance to the city's Jewish sector.

Gregg Family

Bideford is an ancient town which is situated in the English county of Devon, where Sir Arthur Conan Doyle set his classic Sherlock Holmes novel of 1902, *The*

Hound of the Baskervilles. It's a place filled with bleak and ominous moorland, old stone circles, foggy landscapes, and picturesque and sleepy villages that have remained relatively unchanged for centuries. Devon has also played host to nothing less than savage, terrifying, and in-bred cannibals—possibly the closest thing you could ever imagine to real zombies.

The dark and turbulent story of the Gregg family of the Devon village of Clovelly can be found in an old manuscript housed in a collection of centuries-old books in the aforementioned Bideford. From the heart of a huge, dark cave on the coastal part of the moors, the Greggs held terrifying sway over the area for more than a quarter of a century, robbing, murdering, and eating just about anyone and everyone that had the misfortune to cross their path. Indeed, they appear to have become distinctly zombified as time, locale, and circumstances all took their toll.

According to the ancient papers held at Bideford, in excess of one thousand unfortunates became breakfast, lunch, and dinner for the hideous Gregg clan. Eventually, however, enough was seen as being well and truly enough: a posse of four hundred local men stormed the huge and labyrinthine cave to finally put an end to the reign of fear. When the men arrived, however, they got far more than even they had bargained for. The old records state that deep in the cave were found, "such a multitude of arms, legs, thighs, hands, and feet, of men, women, and children hung up in rows, like dried beef and a great many lying in pickle."

Outraged and horrified by the shocking scene before them, the men hauled the entire Gregg family out of the cave—which amounted to around fifty people, most of who were the result of endless incest, which had ensured they were physically deformed and mentally subnormal—and brought them before magistrates in the Devon city of Exeter. On the following day, without benefit of a trial, they were all hung by the neck until they breathed no more. They did not reanimate, for those that may be wondering.

It must be noted that A. D. Hippisley-Coxe, who, in 1981, penned a book titled *The Cannibals of Clovelly: Fact or Fiction?*, suggested that the story of the diabolical Gregg family had its roots in folklore, rather than reality—a piece of folklore deliberately spread by local smugglers and designed to keep terrified locals away from the areas where the smugglers operated. In this scenario, then, the flesh-eating subhumans were merely a myth brought to life. Nevertheless, not everyone is quite so sure that is all there is to the mystery.

A near-identical story to that of the Greggs of Devon can be found in *The Legend of Sawney Beane*, which was the work of Daniel Defoe, the acclaimed genius behind *Gulliver's Travels*. Defoe, however, suggested that the story of the Gregg family had its origins not in Devon, but hundreds of miles north, in Galloway, Scotland. And, said Defoe, John Gregg was not the leader of the infernal pack, after all. It was one Sawny Beane who ruled the roost. Whatever the real truth of the matter, it has failed to put paid to rumors that in some of the wilder parts of Devon, even more devolved, cannibalistic descendents of the Gregg family still lurk in the old caves that pepper Dartmoor, and who just may be responsible for the hundreds of people that go missing in the United Kingdom every year.

Grettis Saga

See also: **Draugr**

Written across the thirteenth and fourteenth centuries, the *Grettis Saga* tells of the wild life, and the even more wild exploits, of an infamous Icelandic outlaw named Grettir Asmundarson. Arson, murder, and pillaging were just a few of his many and varied crimes. Some scholars and historians, however, see Asmundarson's actions as not being definitively evil in nature, but simply the result of unfortunate circumstances provoked by the wild, violent, and turbulent world of the late ninth and early tenth centuries in which he lived. Although Asmundarson was not a Viking, he had the trademark, long, red locks, and the hair-trigger temper of the Celts of old. Not only that, he was a powerful and mighty figure, and could boast of being a relative to King Olaf Tryggvason of Norway, who ruled over the land from 995 to 1,000 C.E.

Notably, the *Grettis Saga* tells of Asmundarson's very own, terrifying, and almost fatal encounter with a Draugr. It occurred when the famous anti-hero decided—somewhat unwisely, but ultimately triumphantly—to plunder the grave of the creature and steal its well-guarded treasures. As the old book notes, in its very earliest English-language translation:

> "Grettir broke open the grave, and worked with all his might, never stopping until he came to wood, by which time the day was already spent. He tore away the woodwork; Audun implored him not to go down, but Grettir bade him attend to the rope, saying that he meant to find out what it was that dwelt there. Then he descended into the howe. It was very dark and the odor was not pleasant."

It was then that the malignant man-eating monster loomed into view: "Grettir took all the treasure and went back towards the rope, but on his way he felt himself seized by a strong hand. He left the treasure to close with his aggressor and the two engaged in a merciless struggle. Everything about them was smashed. The howedweller (an old term meaning 'mound dweller') made a ferocious onslaught. Grettir for some time gave way, but found that no holding back was possible. They did

A seventeenth-century illustration from an Icelandic manuscript depicts the outlaw Grettir Asmundarson, who fought against the Draugr.

not spare each other. At last it ended in the howedweller falling backwards with a horrible crash, whereupon Audun above bolted from the rope, thinking that Grettir was killed."

Asmundarson knew there was only one way to end this battle. It was by decapitation: "Grettir then drew his sword Jokulsnaut, cut off the head of the howedweller and laid it between his thighs. Then he went with the treasure to the rope, but finding Audun gone he had to swarm up the rope with his hands. First he tied the treasure to the lower end of the rope, so that he could haul it up after him. He was very stiff from his struggle with Kárr, but he turned his steps towards Thorfinn's house, carrying the treasure along with him."

Not even a terrible Draugr, with all its strength and supernatural abilities, could triumph over Grettir Asmundarson's head-severing approach.

Halloween

Today, it is, beyond any shadow of doubt, the spookiest and most chillingly atmospheric night of the year. It is Halloween. It's the one night of the year when kids, all across the world, dress up as ghosts, skeletons, witches, and zombies, and knock on the doors of their neighbors in search of plentiful amounts of candy. And it's all done in good fun and humor. In centuries past, however, Halloween was far from being a night on which to hit the streets and have a good time. In fact, the exact opposite was the case. Long before Halloween existed, as we know it today, there was All Hallows' Eve, which was inextricably linked to the surfacing of the dead. It was hardly a time for laughs and jokes of the supernatural variety. As for candy, there was none in sight, none at all.

All Hallows' Eve was terminology first employed in the early part of the sixteenth century. Its direct association with All Saints Day (celebrated on November 1, the day after Halloween) has led to an understandable assumption that Halloween has its roots firmly in the domain of Christianity and its teachings. It is an assumption which is wrong, however. Christianity most certainly did help to model Halloween and make it what it is today. The reality, however, is that the origins of the event date back to much earlier times. They were times when paganism ruled on high.

While some aspects of the earliest years of Halloween are lost to the inevitable fog of time, there is very little doubt that the Gaelic festival of Samhain played a large role in its development. As far back as at least the tenth century, Samhain was celebrated by the people of Wales, Ireland, Scotland, and Brittany. Commencing on October 31 and lasting for twenty-four hours, Samhain marked the beginning of the darker months ahead and the looming, ice-cold winter. Samhain was also perceived as the one night of the year when the dead walked the landscape.

The concept of the dead rising from the grave as Samhain struck was somewhat different to that portrayed in the average zombie movie, however. For the Gaels, Samhain was actually a time to invite the souls of the dead to join them for a hearty feast. This was done as much out of fear as it was a desire to see deceased loved ones again. Of course, in spirit form, there was little—if anything at all—upon which the dead could literally dine. The invite, therefore, was more of a welcoming symbol than anything else. There is, however, another matter that bears mention. While the Samhain invite was open to friendly spirits, Gaelic teachings and folklore made it very clear that some of those souls of the dead were hardly what one might term friendly in nature.

To make sure that one or more of the malignant dead would not recognize a living person when they saw one, many Gaels elected to wear costumes as a cunning means of disguise on October 31. Camouflaging themselves as the very ghouls, ghosts, and strange creatures that were hunting them down helped the Gaels to avoid detection by the predatory souls of the departed.

Interestingly, taking on the guise of a zombie to ensure that one can move amongst them—at least for a while, if nothing else—is something that was put to good use on several occasions, in *The Walking Dead*, on *Shaun of the Dead*, and in the movie version of Max Brooks' *World War Z*, too. In *The Walking Dead*, Rick Grimes and his band of survivors smeared the blood of the dead on their clothes to mask their human odor. In *Shaun of the Dead*, matters were played strictly for laughs: Shaun and his own group of survivors staggered drunkenly around the streets, hoping they wouldn't get recognized by the dead. Their hopes were decisively dashed; they were recognized by the astute zombies in mere seconds. And, in *World War Z*, the zombie onslaught is finally contained when a viral cocktail is created that effectively camouflages the living and the healthy from detection by the dead.

Thus, we see uncanny similarities when it comes to Halloween, the ancient beliefs of Samhain, the rise of the dead in centuries long gone, and the world of the zombie.

Heaven's Gate

Life is something that we experience until we no longer do so. Depending on your personal beliefs, death is either a state of never-ending lights-out or the start of a new and endless adventure. But, what about the central themes of this book: reanimation, resurrection, and an undead state? It's fair and accurate to say that no one really knows what (if, indeed, anything at all!) goes through the mind of the average zombie.

But, someone who was convinced that dying and coming back—in some form, at least—would be a wholly positive experience was a certifiable lunatic named Marshall Herff Applewhite, Jr. A native of Texas, Applewhite gained infamy in 1997 when he convinced thirty-eight of his followers in the so-called Heaven's Gate cult to take their own lives—chiefly because doing so would see them return in reanimated, immortal form. But before we get to death, reanimation, and immortality, let's see what it was that led to that terrible tragedy.

From a very young age Applewhite's life was dominated by religious teachings: his father was a minister who lectured to, and thundered at, his meek followers. It was made clear to Applewhite that he was expected to do likewise. Exhibiting a high degree of youthful rebellion, however, Applewhite did not. Instead he joined the U.S. Army. After leaving the military (which involved him spending a lot of time at the White Sands Proving Ground, New Mexico), Applewhite's life went in a very different direction: he became a music teacher. He could not, however, shake off altogether that religious programming he received as a child and took a job with Houston, Texas' St. Mark's Episcopal Church. But, demonstrating that he was not quite so saintly after all, in 1974, he was arrested for credit card fraud. It was also in the 1970s that Applewhite met the love of his life: Bonnie Nettles.

From then on, the devoted pair began to delve into the world of cultish, crackpot activity: they established the Total Overcomers Anonymous (TOA) group that assured its followers that benevolent aliens were out there, ready and willing to help all those that pledged allegiance to the TOA. And many did exactly that. It was a group that eventually mutated into the infamous Heaven's Gate cult. All of which brings us up to March 1997.

Three weeks into the month, Applewhite started brainwashing his duped clan into believing that if they killed themselves they would reanimate in some angelic dimension that was far away from, and far different from, our earthly realm. Since the comet Hale-Bopp was just around the corner, so to speak, Applewhite even weaved that into his story. There was, he said, a huge UFO flying right behind the comet, and when death came for the group it would transfer them to that same UFO and new and undead lives elsewhere. His loyal followers eagerly swallowed every word. To their eternal cost, they eagerly swallowed something else, too: highly potent amounts of Phenobarbital and vodka. In no time at all, almost forty people were dead, all thanks to the words of a crazed, old lunatic.

Aliens did not call upon the members of the Heaven's Gate group. No UFO was ever detected behind Hale-Bopp. And the dead did not rise from the floor of the Heaven's Gate abode, which was situated at Rancho Santa Fe, California, and where one and all took their lives. Their bodies stayed exactly where they were until the authorities took them to the morgue for autopsy. There is a major lesson to be learned here: don't base your life around the claims of a man who tells you that knocking back large amounts of Phenobarbital and vodka will ensure your reanimation and immortality. It won't.

Hitler, Adolf

See also: *Nazis, World War II*

Although Brad Steiger was only nine years old during the closing days of World War II, he can clearly remember stories of the desperate struggle of the Wehrmacht to

Adolf Hitler's regime of terror over Germany in World War II included, some say, turning some Nazis into the walking dead.

defend the last stronghold of their Fuhrer in his underground bunker. He also has clear memories of the newsreels of the Allied victory that we cheered in our little small town theater.

Often he heard eerie stories about both veteran German soldiers and members of the Hitler Youth who were hit by machine gun or rifle fire who just kept marching toward the overwhelming tide of Allied soldiers. Some said that the men had been so indoctrinated by the Nazi propaganda of the majestic Third Reich that would dawn under Hitler's leadership that they sustained bullet after bullet ripping through them, ignoring the pain to reach their own special Valhalla.

Some who were there said that not only were the German soldiers marching to their death as if they were zombies, some G.I.s swore that the men, especially those in the S.S. and the Hitler Youth, were zombies. Some of the charging troops, it was said, revealed faces that had been half-blown away in earlier conflicts. Some of the zombie-like troops had a number of old, unclosed or unhealed bullet wounds that had left gaping wounds before they were finally struck down for the final count.

While some of their buddies laughed at the wild war stories and stated that the Nazi troops were fanatics and bore terrible wounds to fight on for their Fuhrer, others would insist that Hitler's scientists had begun to produce an army of zombies.

One veteran of such an encounter told Steiger that when he searched for a fallen German's identification papers, he was repelled by the stench of death. "People were dying all around us," he said, "but some of these SS guys smelled like they had been dead for days and decomposition was setting in."

Holodomor

When George A. Romero's *Land of the Dead* was released in 2005, fans of the acclaimed zombie visionary were overjoyed. Not everyone was happy with the movie, however. In fact, in certain quarters, *Land of the Dead* provoked a very different response to that of moviegoers. Particularly appalled and worried by the movie was the Ukrainian government's Culture Ministry, but not for reasons that one might imagine. It wasn't so much that the Culture Ministry had anything against graphic horror films in general, or Romero, as a person or as a director, in particular. Instead, it was something very different, something which officialdom concluded and feared threatened to reignite terrible memories of an all too real story; one which was of shocking proportions.

In the concerned minds of government officials, *Land of the Dead*, if shown in Ukrainian cinemas, might very possibly have caused the nation's viewers to dwell on a truly nightmarish event that affected both Ukrainians and Russian Cossacks from 1932 and 1933. It became known as the Holodomor, or, in English, "Extermination by hunger." As the populations of both the Ukrainians and the Cossacks grew in significant numbers in the late 1920s and early 1930s, the Soviet government struggled to meet rapidly escalating demands for food. Widespread famine was very soon the calamitous result. Over the two year period, more than three million people died of starvation. But it wasn't just a lack of food that killed so many Ukrainians.

As the supply of food dwindled to perilously low levels, and finally to just about nothing at all, Ukrainians, by now crazed by the need to feed, soon turned savagely upon each other and resorted to nothing less than the ultimate no-no: full-blown cannibalism. To say that chaotic and haunting events, chillingly similar to those portrayed in *Land of the Dead*, occurred during the Holodomor is not an exaggeration in the slightest. Nearly three thousand people were convicted of devouring their fellow humans during the turbulent period of carnage and famine; and that is just the ones that were identified and caught. No one really knows how many additional terrible atrocities went by ignored, unnoticed, and unpunished. In terms of the closest thing one can currently imagine to a real zombie-dominated disaster, the Holodomor was most certainly it.

Maksym Rostotsky, of the Ukraine government's Culture Ministry said, by way of an explanation for the refusal to grant a showing of Romero's comeback hit in the country: "The memory of the Holodomor of 1933 is still fresh in our society. A movie with scenes of people being eaten alive should not be given the go ahead." Given the Ukraine's tumultuous history, Rostotsky may very well have had a highly valid point. As for Romero, twenty years after *Day of the Dead*, not only had he returned in fully fledged force, but his actions and big-screen flesh-eaters were now influencing the decisions of entire nations and governments.

Holy Wars

The Trijicon affair was most certainly not the first in which military commanders have done their utmost to brainwash troops into thinking that the End Times are here when, in reality, the enemy is simply a motley hotchpotch of people that hate us. During the presidency of George W. Bush himself, and when the battle for Iraq's oil was in full swing and the weapons of mass destruction could not be found anywhere, the president received his military intelligence briefings in a very strange fashion: they

Religious Europeans were convinced to go on the Crusades to save the Holy Land because they were made to believe, in part, that the wars were a sign of the coming End Times.

were contained in folders that were emblazoned with words from the books of *Psalms* and *Ephesians* and the epistles of Peter. As just one example of quite literally hundreds, a Pentagon briefing document of April 2003 was prefaced with the following: "Behold, the eye of the Lord is on those who fear Him.... To deliver their soul from death."

This did not go down at all well with the Reverend Barry W. Lynn, who was the Executive Director of Americans United for Separation of Church and State. He noted that U.S. military personnel were not "Christian crusaders," adding that "they ought not be depicted as such. Depicting the Iraq conflict as some sort of holy war is completely outrageous."

The BBC soon got caught up in the debate, too. They revealed that, also during the Iraq war, one Lieutenant General William Boykin chose to deliver speeches at various U.S. churches, in which he emphasized an End Times connection to the wars on Saddam Hussein and Osama Bin Laden. President Bush's buddies were more than happy: Boykin soon found himself elevated in rank, if not quite yet to a realm of heavenly proportions. The BBC noted of all this: "U.S. Defense Secretary Donald Rumsfeld has declined to criticize a senior army officer who told audiences the war on terror is a battle with Satan."

The aforementioned Michael Weinstein, of the MRFF, commented: "There's an eschatology obsessed version of Christianity ... that is trying to make American foreign policy conterminous with their biblical worldview."

Persistent digging by MMRF members turned up the astonishing fact that, in 2007, Operation Stand Up, a definitively evangelical body was on the verge of sending to U.S. troops stationed in Iraq so-called "freedom packages." No-one had a problem with the welcome footwear and tasty treats that the packages contained. More than a few, however, had a *big* problem with the fact that each soldier was due to receive a copy of *Left Behind: Eternal Forces*, a definitively "end of the world"-type video game. It was only when word got out to the media that the Pentagon backed away from endorsing the packages of the apocalypse. Rumors that troops in Afghanistan receive similar packages containing copies of the Armageddon-driven games *Call of Duty: World at War—Zombies* and *Zombie Gunship* cannot be confirmed at this time.

Hoodoo

*See also: **Drug Dealers and Voodoo, Vodun: Mambo and Houngan, Voodoo, Voodoo and the CIA***

As noted by the staff of Haunted America Tours (http://hauntedamericatours .com), Hoodoo refers to African traditional folk magic. This rich magical tradition was, for thousands of years, indigenous to ancient African botanical, magical religious practices, and folk cultures. Mainly enslaved West Africans brought Hoodoo to the Americas.

Hoodoo is a noun and is derived from the Ewe word hudu which still exists today. African-American vernacular often uses Hoodoo to describe a magic spell or potion, the practitioner (Hoodoo doctor, Hoodoo man or Hoodoo woman) who conjures the spell, or as an adjective or verb, depending upon the context in which it is used.

The word can be dated to as early as 1891. Some prefer the term Hoodooism, but this has mostly fallen out of use. Some New Age non-Diaspora practitioners who have taken up Hoodoo as a hobby, employ such synonyms as conjuration, conjure, Witchcraft, or rootwork. The latter demonstrates the importance of various roots in the making of charms and casting spells.

It is important to note that in traditional African religious culture, the concept of spells is not used. Here again, this Afro-botanical practice has been heavily used by the New Age, and Wiccan communities who have little understanding of Hoodoos spiritual significance as it is traditionally used in Africa.

An amulet characteristic of Hoodoo is the mojo bag, mojo hand, conjure bag, trick bag, or tobya small sack filled with herbs, roots, coins, sometimes a lodestone, and various other objects of magical power.

Horror Express

A 1972 movie that starred horror favorites Christopher Lee and Peter Cushing, as well as Telly Savalas of *Kojak* fame, *Horror Express* is a decidedly unusual production. What starts out as a regular movie of the monster kind quickly mutates into a story involving mysterious deaths; the preserved body of an ancient, Bigfoot-like humanoid; a disembodied alien; and, finally, zombies. Handled properly, a movie featuring such a wide and varied body of themes might work. Unfortunately, *Horror Express* is not quite the creature-feature it could have been. That's not to say it's awful. But it's certainly not great either. Rather, it languishes in some middle realm of a less than satisfying kind.

The film is set just a few years after the turn of the twentieth century when one Professor Alexander Saxton—portrayed by Christopher Lee—is bound for England

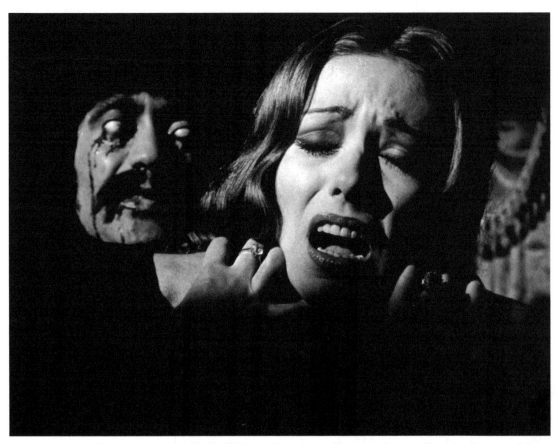

A zombie attacks his victim in the 1972 flick *Horror Express,* a rather mixed-up mish-mosh of monster/alien/zombie genres.

after completing an archaeological expedition on the Russia-China border. In a previously unexplored cave, Saxton and his team stumble on the well-preserved (in fact, the *very* well preserved) remains of an ancient, human-like creature that resembles a cross between a Neanderthal man and a Bigfoot. Or, perhaps, the "missing link" might be more appropriate terminology to use.

Excited by the nature of the groundbreaking find, Saxton wastes no time in securing the utterly frozen monster and loading it aboard a train—the Trans-Siberian Express, which travels from Moscow to Vladivostok. Unfortunately, for those aboard the train, the monster doesn't remain dormant for long. In quick fashion, the beast escapes from the confines of its crate, and the train is hit by a series of mysterious murders. All of the victims display the very same characteristics: their eyes are rendered totally white and their eye-sockets are soaked in blood. A member of the Church traveling on the train—named Father Pujardov, but clearly modeled on the famous Russian "mad monk" Rasputin—asserts that there is downright evil aboard. He is not wrong.

As the hours tick by, the body-count increases. Incredibly, although it soon becomes clear that the ape-man is the culprit; after it is killed, the grisly deaths bafflingly continue. Saxton and Peter Cushing's character—Dr. Wells—come to a startling conclusion. The Yeti-like animal was not the actual cause of the killings. Rather, the real killer is a disembodied, spirit-based, extraterrestrial creature that has the ability to jump from host to host. And, with the ancient ape now dead, the race is on to find in whose body the alien is now hiding.

That's when a platoon of the military becomes involved: led by Savalas' crazed Captain Kazan, they board the Express and prove to be just about as deadly as the body-jumping extraterrestrial. The creature's ethereal form first secretly takes over Father Pujardov and, after he is shot and killed, enslaves the mind of a police officer, one Inspector Mirov.

At this point, an all-out gunfight begins as Kazan and his Cossacks do their very best to wipe out the alien once and for all. Unfortunately, the exact opposite happens. The creature, which is easily able to outwit the troops, slaughters them, as well as even more passengers. The monster from the stars then unleashes its most deadly weapon of all upon Wells, Saxton, and the dwindling number of survivors: it resurrects the recently dead and turns them into mind-controlled killer corpses that stagger—Romero-style—around the darkened corridors of the huge train, exterminating anyone and everyone that gets in their way.

The far from friendly E.T. is finally defeated when Wells, Saxton, and those few still left alive, make their way to the furthest carriage of the train and unhook it. A nearby station is alerted to what is afoot and quickly alters the points on the track, which diverts the speeding train onto a disused piece of line that sends the train—and the alien—over a cliff, resulting in an explosive, pummeling finale. Adios alien, and adios zombies. *Horror Express* is worth a watch, but it's no *Night of the Living Dead*. In fact, with so many threads and themes running through the story, it's difficult to say *what* it is.

The House of Seven Corpses

The early to mid 1970s spawned a number of well remembered and much revered horror movies of both the cinematic and television-based kind. They included *Gargoyles*, *The Night Stalker*, *Race with the Devil* and *Don't be Afraid of the Dark* (which was remade in 2010, with Katie Holmes and Guy Pearce taking the leading roles). From the same era, but far cheesier in nature, were the werewolf-driven *Moon of the Wolf* (that starred David Janssen of *The Fugitive*, and who really should have known better than to have gotten involved) and *The Boy Who Cried Werewolf*, both of which are most definitely best left forgotten. Inhabiting a realm somewhere between revered and downright embarrassing (but certainly much closer to the latter) is *The House of Seven Corpses*—a little known, and largely forgotten, movie that revolves around zombie mayhem and the raising of the dead.

The House of Seven Corpses starred John Ireland (who, interestingly, took the lead in a 1961 episode of NBC's *Thriller* series titled "Papa Benjamin," which was based around Voodoo curses), Faith Domergue (of such 1950s-era productions as *It Came From Beneath the Sea* and *This Island Earth*), and long-time horror movie star John Carradine, who appeared in a number of undead-based films, including the 1940's-era *Revenge of the Zombies* and *Voodoo Man*.

The plotline of *The House of Seven Corpses* is actually quite a good one: filmed in Salt Lake City, Utah, it tells the story of a film director (Ireland) who decides to make a horror movie in a creepy old house that was the site of no less than seven grisly murders. Looking to keep his story as authentic and gripping as possible, Ireland's character—Eric Hartman—directs his cast to read from the pages of an old book that contains certain rituals designed to raise the dead, and which played significant roles in the all too real deaths of earlier years.

Unbeknownst to the crew and actors, the very act of reading the old rites out loud succeeds in bringing the dead to life—or, rather, it brings one dead soul to life that claws his way out of the grounds of an old cemetery and attacks and slaughters the cast, bit by bit. We are talking about shades of *Night of the Living Dead* kind, at least in terms of the cemetery-based shots. Presumably, the clearly limited budget explains why we are treated to just one zombie, rather than to a veritable horde of the nightmarish things.

Ireland, in somewhat noticeably hammy fashion, tries to remain serious in his role, as do the rest of the cast. But, in the end, it matters very little. That not-insignificant lack of money, cheap special effects and bad make-up, and a few stars who really should have taken up careers outside of the world of entertainment, collectively make *House of the Seven Corpses* pretty much forgettable to all but the most obsessive of all zombie fans.

I Am Legend

The only version of Richard Matheson's 1954 novel that kept its original title, *I Am Legend*, hit cinemas all across the planet in 2007. With Will Smith taking on the role of the main character, Robert Neville, it's a film that disappointed as many as it pleased. The film is refreshing in the sense that Hollywood chose not to present Neville as some gung-ho, guns-blazing type of character befitting the likes of the *Die Hard* and *Terminator* franchises. Rather, he is, as one might expect after the apocalypse hits, psychologically damaged and vulnerable in the extreme.

Three years after tragedy strikes, Neville is mentally disintegrating due to being, it seems, the only person left alive in New York City; maybe even in the United States or on the entire planet. He grieves constantly over the death of his wife and daughter. His only friend is Sam, the family dog, and he spends his time talking to mannequins in deserted, downtown stores, while his mind constantly flashes back to the events that led to worldwide disaster.

But that's not all: as a former U.S. Army Lieutenant Colonel, and an expert in the field of exotic viruses, Neville tries to hang on to his sanity long enough to find a cure for the disease that has wiped out billions. As far as Neville can determine, the world's population is now down to less than 600 million, and nearly all of those that survived the plague have been transformed into hideous abominations.

It all began with a search for a cancer cure that involved genetically altering the measles virus. What should have been a cause for planetary celebration turned out to be nothing less than worldwide disaster and death, and the rise of what are called the Darkseekers. They are far less like the vampire-style hordes in Richard Matheson's

Will Smith starred in 2007's *I Am Legend,* the latest adaptation of the Richard Matheson novel that followed the movies *The Last Man on Earth* and *Omega Man.*

novel, and much more akin to the fast-running terrors of *28 Days Later* and the 2004 remake of *Dawn of the Dead.* They only surface at night—hence their name—roaming the ruined and desolate city of New York in search of the last, unfortunate humans on whom they can feed.

As *I Am Legend* progresses, we see Neville throwing himself into his work, which involves capturing an infected woman on who he tests his latest serum in a makeshift laboratory. She is, we learn, the partner of the leader of the local Darkseeker group. They, in turn, set a trap for Neville, which results in Sam getting attacked and bitten by a vicious pack of infected dogs. In a particularly emotional scene, Neville is forced to kill Sam when she begins to mutate into something rivaling the deadly Hound of the Baskervilles itself.

Now utterly alone, Neville descends into an even deeper state of depression. That is until, and to his amazement, he learns that he is not alone after all. While under attack from a pack of Darkseekers, Neville is rescued by a woman named Anna who, with a boy called Ethan, has made her way to New York City from Maryland. Both are free of infection. Anna tells Neville that a colony of survivors is living in Vermont, a statement upon which he pours complete and utter scorn.

The movie culminates with the Darkseekers attacking Neville's heavily protected home, as they seek to rescue the infected woman that is the subject of Neville's experiments. As Neville, Anna, and Ethan race to the safety of the lab, Neville is astonished to see that the woman on who he tested his latest serum is starting to revert to her original, human state. Neville immediately realizes the incredible enormity of the situation unfolding before him: he has found the cure that can bring the human race back from the brink of extinction. Suddenly, the Darkseekers break into the lab and charge headlong towards the terrified trio. Fortunately, they are protected by a thick, glass partition, through which Neville tries in vain to reason with the savage leader of the group.

Realizing that his words are not understood in the slightest, and that the Darkseekers are incapable of comprehending any form of rhyme or reason, Neville gives Anna a test-tube filled with the blood of the woman who is now well on the way to being cured. Neville ushers Anna and Ethan into a coal-chute, slams the door behind them, and kills the Darkseekers, and himself, with a powerful grenade. *I Am Legend* ends with Anna and Ethan finally reaching Vermont, where there really is a colony of uninfected survivors. With the precious cargo of blood in hand, the future looks bright for the human race. Neville becomes, as a result, a legend, albeit a dead one.

While the movie was a massive hit—it has, so far, reaped in almost $600 million—the special-effects left much to be desired. In *28 Days Later*, *The Walking Dead*, and *Dawn of the Dead*, the infected look so impressive because they are portrayed by real people who are skillfully made to appear terrifying via grisly make-up and prosthetics. The Darkseekers of *I Am Legend*, however, are almost exclusively the results of CGI: computer-generated imagery. Unfortunately, it's more than clear to the viewer that they are CGI. It is this factor that, in many respects, lets the film down. The sudden jumps, back and forth, from real actors to CGI-created monsters make for disjointed viewing, and reminds us constantly that we're just watching a movie. With that said, however, it's fair to add that *I Am Legend* is not a bad production. But it could have been better, as could have been the infected.

I Am Scrooge

Written very much in the style and format of Seth Grahame-Smith's *Pride and Prejudice and Zombies*, Adam Roberts' *I Am Scrooge: A Zombie Story for Christmas* is a novel that gives Charles Dickens' classic story, *A Christmas Carol*, a large dose of the apocalypse and plenty of flesh-eating Victorians. It sounds like it wouldn't work, but it actually does—albeit in a very odd and alternative way. Although precisely what Dickens himself might have thought about Robert's unique approach to the story of Ebenezer Scrooge, Tiny Tim, and the ghosts of Christmas past, present, and future, is quite another matter.

It is important to note that Robert's book is not to be taken seriously. This is not Max Brooks' *World War Z* or David Wellington's *Monster Island*. No: this is comedy, satire, and easy and breezy reading. And while not endlessly, hysterically funny, it is still an entertaining and amusing read throughout.

In *I Am Scrooge*, the city of London, England is under siege by endless numbers of hungry monsters. Scrooge, meanwhile, is practically encased in his fortified abode, carefully and greedily counting out his cash and ensuring that the army of the dead never succeeds in darkening his door. As the story progresses, we learn how and why the zombie apocalypse came to be, and how Victorian England is now a shell of its former-self. But, it doesn't necessarily have to be that way. Thanks to that famous trio of specters, none other than Scrooge himself has the ability to change the past to ensure a safe and nightmare-free present and future. But will he? That is the big question. It's a question that has major implications for the Cratchit family—and particularly so for the painfully sick Tiny Tim

Doubtless, there are those who will say—as they most certainly did with regard to *Pride and Prejudice and Zombies*—that *I Am Scrooge* is nothing more than a blatant and distorted rip-off of *A Christmas Carol* and not much else. While such comments might seem logical and justified to those that have not read Robert's book, it should be noted that *I Am Scrooge* makes enough significant changes to Dicken's novella to make it very much a new piece of work—even if it is unashamedly inspired by the 1843 classic.

It's not necessary to read *A Christmas Carol* before devouring *I Am Scrooge*, but doing so is an interesting exercise in seeing how one book can act as the inspiration for another, as well as understanding the concept of what makes a piece of work original, "inspired" by someone else's writings, or somewhere hazily in between both.

Iceland's Resident Man-Eaters

Iceland is an island nation which is situated between the North Atlantic and the Arctic Oceans. As well as being home to around 320,000 Icelandics, the island is also the residency of nothing less than people-eating trolls. And, make no mistake, for the good folk of Iceland such creatures are not just the stuff of legend: they are all too real and deadly. So the old folklore tells it, the trolls can be found in certain, specific locales: forests, caverns, and mountains being their preferred places to hang out. And, if you value your life you should keep well away from them.

Mentioning trolls to most people will likely conjure up imagery of large and lumbering beasts with violent tendencies and profoundly ugly appearances. So much for the legend; the truth, however, is very different. Iceland's trolls are far more human-

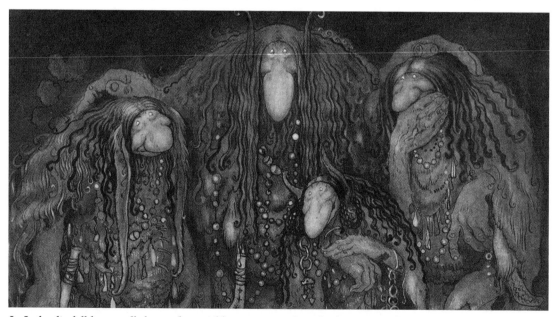

In Icelandic folklore, trolls have a human-like appearance but also have a taste for human flesh (illustration from the 1915 tale *The Boy and the Trolls, or The Adventure* by Walter Stenström.)

like in appearance. It was this aspect of the troll that, centuries ago, allowed it to worm its way into old, Icelandic villages and towns without too much trouble at all, and without being noticed for what it really was. Depending on the circumstances, male trolls would very often abduct human women—either to make them their wife or to eat them for supper. Sometimes it was both. And it was much the same for female trolls: many of them favored human males over those of their own kind for husbands. An abducted human male was in just as much danger as a woman, however, since the female trolls also displayed a diabolical fondness for cooked, human flesh.

Trolls are not the only devourers of humans that lurk in the wilder parts of Iceland, however. There are also the Yule Lads. They are, for all intents and purposes, the Icelandic equivalent of Santa Claus. But, their demeanor is nothing like that of the fat, jolly man dressed in red and white. Thirteen in total, they are the offspring of a hideous, Icelandic she-beast named Gryla, who sports a pair of devilish cloven-hooves, a multitude of tails, and a third eye. Gryla and her offspring, the Yule Lads, are connoisseurs of the flesh and bones of children, which are cooked casserole-style.

If the young kids of Iceland misbehave on Christmas Eve, they are sternly warned by their parents that unless they calm down and wait patiently for their presents, Gryla and the Yule Lads will pay them a visit and eagerly devour them after boiling them alive in a huge cooking pot. Hardly surprising, the warning almost always works!

Immortality

As far as the zombies of cinema and television are concerned, for the most part they are killed off pretty quickly by the living. But, in theory, if left to its own devices and a sufficient amount of food in the form of people, the average zombie can keep on going and going—maybe even forever. In short, a zombified state offers us potential immortality. The major downside is that to achieve everlasting life, one has to give up one's humanity and become a raging monster instead. Then again, maybe there is another alternative, one which still promises a near-endless life, but in a fashion that doesn't involve eating your friends and family. It's here that we have to turn our attentions towards what is known as White Powder Gold.

To fully understand and appreciate the true nature of White Powder Gold, we have to take a trip into the distant past and to the Middle East, one where the power of alchemy—the ability to transform non-precious metals into *very* precious metals, including gold—reigned. While there is a great deal of debate regarding the true nature of White Powder Gold, many students of the mystery suggest it is a by-product of the alchemical process, one which results in the production of a powdery substance that can safely be ingested.

For the ancients, very likely, the powder was "Manna from Heaven" or the "Bread of Presence" as described in the *Egyptian Book of the Dead*. Ingesting White Powder Gold may very well have slowed the aging process to a massive degree, repaired and restored cells, skin, and bone to youthful states, and ensured that old age was a thing of the past. And, let's face it, millennia-old accounts of famous characters that live for centuries abound: Noah lived for 950 years, while Methuselah racked up 969. Everlasting life without having to become a zombie: not a bad deal. The only downside is uncovering the secrets of how to refine White Powder Gold. That may not be quite so easy.

The Incredibly Strange Creatures Who Stopped Living and Became Mixed-Up Zombies

In 1964, Stanley Kubrick's acclaimed movie *Dr. Strangelove* was released across the world to wide acclaim. It tells the darkly comic story of how, in a very short period of time, the Cold War becomes a very hot one, an all-out nuclear war between the Soviet Union and the United States erupts—a war that neither side wins. The only outcome: worldwide extinction of every living creature on the planet. So what does all of this have to do with zombies?

The full title of the movie was *Dr. Strangelove; or, How I Learned to Stop Worrying and Love the Bomb*. Its official release date was January 1964. In production at the time was a zombie-based movie from director and producer Ray Dennis Steckler that surfaced two months later. The title of the movie was *The Incredibly Strange Creatures who Stopped Living and Became Mixed-Up Zombies*. Its working title, however, was one that got Columbia Pictures in a state of fury. It was *The Incredibly Strange Creatures, or Why I Stopped Living and Became a Mixed-Up Zombie*. For Columbia's legal people the similarities in the title were too much and a threat of a lawsuit soon reached Steckler's eyes and ears. He quickly backed down and changed the title.

At the end of the day, however, Columbia Pictures had very little to worry about. First of all, the storylines were totally different: *Dr. Strangelove* was a savage satire on the Cold War mentality of actually believing it was possible to win a nuclear war. *The Incredibly Strange Creatures Who Stopped Living and Became Mixed-Up Zombies* was a chaotic, badly acted, cheaply made (it cost less than $40,000) affair about zombies, strippers, a creepy carnival, and hypnotism. It was hardly, therefore, in competition with *Dr. Strangelove* and came nowhere near matching it in terms of viewing figures. Nevertheless, the news of the-lawsuit-that-never-was ensured that at least some people sat up and took notice of Steckler's cheap yarn.

Today, *The Incredibly Strange Creatures who Stopped Living and Became Mixed-Up Zombies* is lauded by some horror fans in the same way that Ed Wood's movies are: it was so bad it was good. Unfortunately, an unbiased viewing of the movie reveals that, no, it's not so bad that it's good. It's just bad. And whereas *Dr. Strangelove* was all about dropping bombs, *The Incredibly Strange Creatures who Stopped Living and Became Mixed-Up Zombies* merely bombed.

Infection

See also: AIDS, Alien Infection, Alien Virus, Black Death, Creutzfeld-Jacobs Disease

If there is one thing that can be said with any degree of certainty about the fictional zombie virus, it's that it generally takes over its host at an incredibly fast pace. In both *28 Days Later* and *28 Weeks Later*, the "Rage Virus" has control of the victim in a matter of just a couple of seconds. In the movie version of Max Brooks' *World War Z*, it's generally a case of around twelve seconds, but can extend to a few hours. And that's very much the same in *The Walking Dead*: when the character Shane Walsh (played by actor Jon Bernthal) is shot and killed, he turns within mere seconds. When Amy (actress Emma Bell) is fatally bitten during a "Walker" attack, the severe blood loss she experiences kills her very quickly. Her sister, Andrea (Laurie Holden), cradles Amy's body not just for hours, but overnight, before she finally transforms into one of the living dead.

So much for the domain of fantasy, but how quickly do real viruses spread? The good news is, nowhere near as quickly as their on-screen counterparts. Without a doubt, the closest real world equivalent of the zombie virus is the rabies virus, since it is most usually spread via a bite, and by the transmission of the virus in the saliva of the infected. The symptoms of rabies, to a degree at least, are somewhat zombie-like: violent and agitated behavior, delirium, and a significant change in character, to the point where the infected often has to be isolated and restrained. But, even the rabies virus fails to act in the near-instantaneous fashion that the zombie virus so often does.

The first symptoms of rabies are flu-like in nature, but—in stark contrast to the average zombie virus—they do not manifest until, at a minimum, fourteen days after infection, and even as long as three months. There is a zombie parallel, however: when the physical and psychological symptoms set in and become apparent, there is very little chance at all of the victims surviving. As the Centers for Disease Control (CDC) starkly notes: "To date less than ten documented cases of human survival from clinical rabies have been reported."

Then there is the matter of one of the most feared viruses of all: Ebola, or, to give it its correct title, Ebola Hemorrhagic Fever (EHF). Ebola—first identified in 1976, in the Democratic Republic of

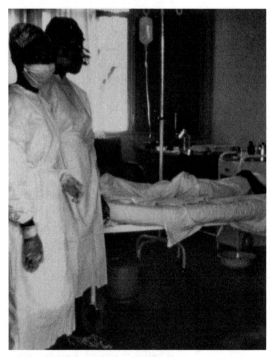

Medical staff watch over an Ebola virus victim in Zaire. The horrifying virus can cause uncontrollable bleeding and death.

the Congo, Africa—is particularly terrifying since, as the CDC admits: "Because the natural reservoir of the virus is unknown, the manner in which the virus first appears in a human at the start of an outbreak has not been determined."

It is hypothesized, however, that when an outbreak does start, patient-zero has likely been infected by an animal, usually via a bite. As for how EHF spreads after the initial infection, it is generally by exposure to blood, bodily fluids, or secretions of the person affected. Since one of the side effects of EHF is severe diarrhea, inadequate protection while cleaning the patient has led to infection of the care giver on a significant number of occasions. For all of EHF's ability to infect its victim, it's most certainly not a fast-acting virus at all. Its incubation period is anywhere from forty-eight hours to three weeks.

Bird Flu—officially termed Avian Flu—is another cause for alarm in many people. Avian influenza primarily affects birds, hence its name, and can jump from species to species. The virus is spread by exposure to infected saliva and feces. In birds, it's an infection that typically kills within two days and with a nearly one hundred percent success rate. Current figures from the World Health Organization show that from 2003 to 2013, there have been 633 confirmed cases of infection by the A(H5N1) virus, of which 377 were fatal. Two to eight days is the general time it takes for the symptoms to appear in people. Presently, the longest confirmed period is seventeen days.

What all of this tells us is that in the real world, viruses do not act in the way that they do in movies, television shows, novels, and comic books—ever. Even in the event that a real-life zombie outbreak of *The Walking Dead* proportions really *does* occur, it is highly unlikely that anyone who is infected will suddenly reanimate and savagely attack the living in mere seconds, or even in minutes or hours. This gives us a significant advantage when it comes to combating a potential apocalypse: the infected can easily be placed into isolation as soon as they are bitten, without fear of them immediately changing into marauding cannibals. Or, so we can hope.

In the Flesh

In March 2013, Britain's BBC broadcast a three-part television series that placed an ingenious and refreshing twist on the whole zombie apocalypse craze. Its title was *In the Flesh*. Most zombie-themed movies and TV shows focus on the terrifying *rise* of the dead and the subsequent apocalypse that rapidly follows. The writer of *In the Flesh*, Dominic Mitchell, however, chose to do something very different with his project. The series is set specifically *after* the outbreak has occurred, and at a time when it has been successfully contained. The dead have been rounded-up and placed in secure facilities, and normality is finally returning to the U.K. where the show is set. Not only that: as we learn from the opening scenes, the British government has found an antidote for the zombie virus. By receiving daily injections of the serum, the dead begin to steadily revert back to human form.

There is a problem, however: even though their original, human personalities resurface, the dead remain exactly what they are: dead. They don't look healthy at all;

their skin is pale and their eyes are a milky color, giving them a decidedly emotionless, anemic, and eerily unsettling appearance. They can no longer eat or drink as we do— ever again. In other words, aside from having their minds restored to their original states, they are, for all intents and purposes, still zombies. The government, however, embarks upon an ambitious plan to try and reintroduce the dead into British society in what is hoped will be an acceptable fashion.

Since millions of people all across the U.K. have graphic and horrific memories of the zombie outbreak, there is a deep fear and distrust of the dead, who are now referred to by the populace as "Rotters." That fear is amplified by the fact that unless the dead keep having their daily shots, they start to return to their murderous, zombie states. So, to try and nullify the concerns and anxieties that the public is clearly exhibiting, the government comes up with a plan. It provides all of those suffering from what the bureaucratic world terms as "Partially Deceased Syndrome" with regular supplies of blue, green, or brown contact-lenses and face make-up to allow them to appear more human and healthy. If they look human, they will be treated like humans, right? In theory: yes. In practice: it's not quite so easy.

In the Flesh chiefly focuses on one undead soul, Kieren Walker, and his relationship with his family, as well as with the people in his home village of Roarton. Displaying high degrees of what might be termed "zombie-phobia," many of the locals want teenage Kieren gone. Some of them want him gone for good, as in a bullet to the head gone. It is on this matter of prejudice, a lack of understanding of what the dead really are, and a fear of the unknown, that *In the Flesh* really scores. Prior to the apocalypse, Kieren was living a secretly gay life. Thus, the prejudice shown towards him by the people of Roarton is, in many respects, an allegory to homophobia.

In the Flesh is far less a zombie story, but one that is much more about the viciousness of human nature, the mob mentality, and how rumors and fear-mongering take hold and often end in deep tragedy. It is the humans of *In the Flesh* that are the violent ones, looking to pierce the brains of all the so-called partially deceased and to end their strange, but now non-threatening, existences. The people have become the monsters. The reintegrated dead just want to be left alone, to cope with their "lives" as well as they can under the fraught circumstances. Seldom has zombie lore been turned completely on its head in such a successful and thought-provoking fashion.

The Invaders

On January 10, 1967, the first episode of a new sci-fi-themed TV series created by Larry Cohen was aired on ABC. Its title was *The Invaders*. Cohen is noted for his writing skills on the likes of such hit shows as *The Fugitive* and *Columbo*. He also directed the notorious and legendary 1974 movie, *It's Alive*, and wrote the hit 2003 film starring Colin Farrell, *Phone Booth*.

The Invaders told the conspiracy-filled and -fueled story of a man named David Vincent, who learns, to his horror and consternation, that hostile extraterrestrials from a dying, faraway planet have secretly come to the Earth and have infiltrated the human race. Advanced alien technology has allowed the relatively small spearhead-style force to appear just like us, aside from a slight, telltale difference in their little fingers and distinctly emotionless appearances on their faces. Vincent, portrayed by actor Roy Thinnes, is pretty much a lone soul, doing all that he can to try and warn the world of the perils it faces from the growing alien menace now amongst us.

Coming across very much like a combination of *The Fugitive* and *Invasion of the Body Snatchers,* and clearly acting as a big-time inspiration for the minds and writers behind *The X-Files* of more than a quarter of a century later, *The Invaders* was an intelligently produced and thought-provoking show that, sadly, only lasted for two seasons, and collectively comprised of forty-three episodes. Nevertheless, even today, nearly fifty years after *The Invaders* ended, the show continues to have a large, cult-like following all around the world, and particularly so in France, where both Roy Thinnes (who had a guest role in *The X-Files*), and his on-screen alter-ego of David Vincent are revered. And there is something else, too.

When *The Invaders* was at its height of popularity, and to help keep the publicity wheels turning at full force, a number of spin-off paperback and hardback novels were published. One of them was definitively zombie-themed. Also demonstrating how *The Invaders* was a clear setter of trends, the title of the novel would most certainly be right at home in today's world in which the zombie rules supreme. The book's name: *Army of the Undead.*

In the story, the zombies are not virally mutated monsters, but humans who are enslaved, mind-controlled and now answerable only to their deadly, alien masters. The author, Rafe Bernard, does a fine job of portraying the zombies in a classically menacing style, as the following extract from *Army of the Undead* acutely demonstrates: "The zombie that had been Danny Hicks thrust Vincent into the small hidden room. Vincent felt a sick horror at the realization that he was helpless in the hands of this creature—once a man, now an automaton doing the bidding of the Invaders."

David Vincent finally manages to save the day, thwarts the latest dastardly attempts of the aliens to gain a greater foothold on our world, and destroys the zombies—one and all—in the process. In view of the above, if a real world, undead-driven Armageddon really does one day unfold, then perhaps we should not look to secret military experiments, or classified biological research programs, for the answers as to how to combat and stop the disaster. Perhaps we should be looking to the distant, twinkling stars right above us.

Isle of the Dead

Imagine a movie, the key ingredients of which revolve around the outbreak of a deadly plague, an island under quarantine, a cast of characters that—one by one—fall victim to the relentless pandemic, and a presumed victim of the plague who returns to life and attacks and kills the living. It sounds like the perfect scenario for a twenty-first century zombie movie. It is not, however. Rather, in abbreviated form, this is the story-line of a 1945 production called *Isle of the Dead*. It is a movie that starred horror movie legend Boris Karloff, who just happened to play—on no less than three occasions—the world's most famous stitched-together zombie of all time: Frankenstein's monster.

The story itself is set in 1912, at the height of as the First Balkan War. It was a deadly confrontation between what was termed the Balkan League (comprised of Bulgaria, Greece, Serbia, and Montenegro) and the Ottoman—or Turkish—Empire. As a small island off the coast of Greece becomes enveloped by a deadly and mysterious plague, the residents and troops are placed under careful quarantine, as part of a concerted effort to prevent the virus from reaching the mainland.

Karloff, as General Nikolas Pherides, is the man chiefly responsible for enforcing the quarantine, something which does not go down well at all with the terrified island folk, all of who are—not surprisingly—wondering who will next fall victim to the lethal outbreak. In no time at all, it becomes very apparent who will be next: pretty much everyone. Amid the concerns about the nature of the hundred percent fatal pathogen, rumors begin circulating that the viral outbreak has less to do with a nor-

An island off the coast of Greece is threatened by a mysterious plague in *Isle of the Dead*. But it is not a disease that is killing people, but rather a vampire-zombie monster called the vorvolaka.

mal disease and far more to do with the actions of an undead, blood-drinking, and flesh-eating monster that preys on the living.

It is a creature that has the ability to infect the living and transform them into horrendous monsters of vampire-meets-zombie proportions. Its name: the vorvolaka. The outbreak, one Madame Kyra suggests, is God's punishment against those on the island that harbored a vorvolaka prior to the eruption of the plague. While some of the survivors—including General Pherides—openly scoff at such an idea, others are not quite as sure it's all nonsense. The possibility that Madame Kyra is correct becomes acutely apparent when one of the characters, Mrs. Mary St. Aubyn, seemingly dies from the effects of the lethal virus and is entombed, but then breaks out and proceeds to violently slaughter the living, including General Pherides, who she fatally stabs.

The audience, however, finally realizes that Mrs. Aubyn was actually free of infection. At the time of her assumed death, she was suffering from catalepsy—a condition that provokes rigidity in the human body and a dramatic decrease in both heart-rate and breathing. But, having finally recovered and broken out of her tomb in a deranged state, Mrs. St. Aubyn is perceived by some as a vorvolaka.

Ironically, one of those is General Pherides, who, with his dying breath, finally becomes a believer in the existence of the monster and maintains that his killer was indeed a crazed vorvolaka. In the end, the viewer is left to make up his or her own mind: God's wrath? Paranormal punishment thanks to a zombie-like monster? Or death by a fast-acting, lethal virus of wholly down-to-earth proportions and, in terms of Mrs. St. Aubyn, a case of catastrophic misdiagnosis?

I Walked with a Zombie

I Walked with a Zombie was made and released by RKO Radio Pictures in 1943. Co-written by Curt Siodmak (the brains behind Universal's 1941 film *The Wolf Man*), and directed by Jacques Tourneur (who also directed the acclaimed 1942 production *Cat People* and the 1957 movie *Night of the Demon*), it's a story driven not by graphic horror, but by a haunting sense of deep menace. The complete lack of on-screen savagery is due to the era in which the movie surfaced. Worldwide apocalypses, strange viruses, monstrous cannibals, and the collapse of civilization were not even specks on the landscape when it came to 1940s-era zombie lore—both on-screen and off it. *I Walked with a Zombie* is very much in the tradition of old-school zombies. That means most of the movie focuses upon such matters as Voodoo rites, Caribbean folklore, curses, and mind-controlled—and mind-altered—characters.

I Walked with a Zombie tells the story of a Canadian nurse named Betsy Connell (played by actress Frances Dee) who travels to a Caribbean island—ostensibly, she is told, to look after one Jessica Holland, the wife of Paul Holland, who makes his living from owning a large sugarcane plantation. It very quickly becomes apparent to Betsy that all is not well with Jessica. In fact, things are far from well with her. Jessica's mind

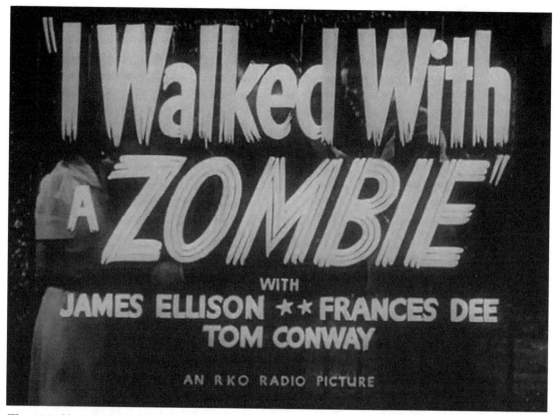

The 1943 film *I Walked with a Zombie* avoids the gore one sees in modern zombie flicks in favor of creating an atmosphere of menace and themes about mind control and Voodoo.

has completely collapsed, she is barely self-aware, and she roams around the creepy old house that she and Paul call home in a zombified stupor. All attempts to cure Jessica of her strange condition—supposedly caused by a tropical fever—have ended in miserable failure.

Betsy—finding herself getting far closer to Paul than might be wise—does her utmost to find a cure for Jessica, including exploring the dark world of Voodoo for the answers. It's at this point in *I Walked with a Zombie* that we are treated to one of the most atmospheric parts of the story: a night-time trek through the windswept sugar-cane plantation to an isolated spot where nothing less than a full-blown ritual of the Voodoo variety is afoot. Ominous drums beat rhythmically, eerie chanting fills the air, and an atmosphere of fear becomes all-dominating. When one of the villagers—a devotee of the disturbing practice—sees Jessica and notes her strange behavior, he pierces her arm with a blade that fails to cause Jessica to bleed. Rumors and fears quickly circulate that she is nothing less than a zombie.

As the controversy surrounding Jessica's strange state of mind and body continues to grow, one of the characters—Paul's mother, Mrs. Rand—admits that she placed a Voodoo curse upon Jessica. The reason was to prevent Jessica from running away with Paul's half-brother, Wesley, who is in love with her. Rather than helping to resolve matters, Mrs. Rand's revelation only serves to deepen the suspicions concerning the true nature of Jessica's condition. Wesley, still deeply in love with Jessica, does his utmost to help her. It's all to no avail; however, the pair is as doomed as were Shakespeare's Romeo and Juliet.

Unable to bear seeing his beloved in such a state—whether a true zombie or simply the victim of a mysterious fever—Wesley fatally stabs Jessica and carries her body into the ocean. The following morning their bodies are found washed up near the shoreline. Was Jessica truly a zombie? Or was she merely the tragic victim of a mystifying fever and superstition that spiralled out of control? The answers are left enigmatically unanswered in a movie that is skillfully unsettling and filled with chills.

Jesus Christ

See also: Lazarus

It is highly ironic that most people consider the zombie to simply be a creature of mythology, folklore, horror-movies, and not much else. Why is it so ironic? Very simple: millions believe in the life, teachings, and actions of the most famous zombie of them all: Jesus Christ. He did, after all—so we are told—rise up from the dead. And rising from the dead transforms a person into one of the *undead*, something which even goes for J.C. too. But, before getting to the matter of Jesus' resurrection, it is essential to have an understanding of the events that led up to it.

Contrary to accepted belief, nowhere in the pages of the Holy Bible does it say that Jesus was crucified on the date that has become known as Good Friday. Even the year is disputed by scholars. All that can be said with a degree of certainty is that the crucifixion took place on a Friday near the Jewish festival known famously as Passover. As for the year, Bible experts suggest anywhere from 30 to 36 C.E. Pontius Pilate—the fifth Prefect of Judea—ensured Christ was put to death by crucifixion. Having been taken into custody in Gethsemane, which is located at the base of Jerusalem's Mount of Olives, Jesus was tried and convicted. It was at Golgotha, a hill outside the city walls of Jerusalem that Jesus was crucified. For hours, he suffered on the cross, finally expiring at around 3:00 P.M.

After Jesus' death was confirmed, his body was removed from the cross by Joseph of Arimathea. There is significant debate regarding where, exactly, the body of Christ was entombed. Of one thing, however, students of the Holy Bible are sure: regardless of the location, Jesus most assuredly *was* entombed. But he didn't stay there for long. On what has become known as Easter Sunday, and three days after his death, Jesus reanimated.

Very interestingly, we are told that after his return from death, Jesus did not appear as he did in life. Mary Magdalene, the apostle Thomas, and Luke the Evangelist all had one thing in common: when Jesus rose from the dead, none of them could recognize him. That is a situation we find in zombie lore all across the world, whether in folklore, mythology, or on-screen entertainment. There are noticeable differences between the appearance of the living and the dead. There may, for example, be a change in skin color. The face of the zombie can appear blank and expressionless. And there is something else too: after his reanimation, Jesus ate. And he ate enthusiastically, too. Doesn't that sound like typical zombie activity?

Jesus Christ did not return from the grave as a maniacal monster, intent on devouring the living. But, it's admittedly very hard to deny the parallels that exist between his death and the subsequent reanimation and the resurrection of the marauding nightmares of the likes of George A. Romero.

Jones, Ava Kay

Voodoo and Yoruba Priestess Ava Kay Jones was an attorney by trade before she chose the path of her true spiritual calling. One of only twenty practicing Voodoo Mambos in the United States, Ava Kay Jones has enthralled locals and visitors alike with her dynamic presentation of authentic Voodoo rituals as practiced in the days of Marie Laveau. Priestess Ava is also the founder and featured performer of the Voodoo Macumba Dance Ensemble, a performance group of drummers, dancers, fire-eaters, and sword and snake dancers. Priestess Ava and Voodoo Macumba have performed in movies, at festivals, and, most notably, in the Superdome, conducting blessing ceremonies for the New Orleans Saints.

Jones, who was raised Catholic, says she is still very much a Christian. She was ordained as a Voodoo priestess in Haiti in 1985, and as a Yoruba priestess in 1989. She is frequently interviewed on the subject of Voodoo, which she says is misunderstood due to inaccurate portrayals, fear, and prejudice. She says she is committed to educating the public about the faith she has so deeply embraced.

The official Ava Kay Jones website can be found at http://yorubapriestess.tripod .com/.

Kikiyaon

Within the ancient folklore and mythology of the people of the Gambia, West Africa, there exist stories of a terrifying creature known as the Kikiyaon. It may justifiably be said that the beast was an African equivalent of other such legendary, monstrous entities of times long gone, such as gargoyles and harpies, in the sense that the Kikiyaon was a humanoid-style beast with the ability to soar the skies. Typically reaching a height of around five feet, and sporting large and leathery wings, glowing red eyes, sharp teeth, and claws instead of toes, the Kikiyaon was a fearsome monstrosity, one best avoided at all costs. It was also an animal that, when one looks at the tales of its actions and exploits carefully and retrospectively, was distinctly zombie-like in terms of its lethal, predatory activities. And, just perhaps, it still is. That's right: the Kikiyaon may have had its origins centuries ago, but reports of the beast still surface from time to time today.

As for those zombie parallels, first, there is the very name of the beast. Kikiyaon translates into English as "soul eater" or "soul cannibal." The title is indeed a most apt one. Kikiyaon is not a literal stealer of souls as such. Rather, it is perceived by Gambian tribes as a creature that can permanently render a person into a soulless state. And how, exactly, does it do that? By quietly and stealthily invading people's bedrooms in the dead of night and, while they sleep, delivering a soft bite to the skin. In practically no time at all, the infected person begins to exhibit the emotion-free, blank-faced characteristics that are most often associated with the zombie of Voodoo and Haitian lore.

The zombie associations don't end there, however. Anyone who sees, or receives a bite from a Kikiyaon, doesn't just become soulless: they also become sick; in fact, they become *very* sick, to the point where they finally die. The reason: when a Kikiyaon bites its victim, it also infects them with a deadly disease, not unlike the zombie virus, it might be said. And, mirroring the likes of the rampaging infected in *28 Days Later* and *28 Weeks Later*, the Kikiyaon is noted for its incredible speed when running across the Gambian plains. Then there is the matter of the odor of the creature, which is described as like rotting flesh, which just happens to be the typical stench of the average zombie. Collectively, these particular characteristics most definitely suggest the Kikiyaon is, at the very least, zombie-like. However, not everyone agrees.

Bernard Heuvelmans, a noted cryptozoologist—one who pursued unknown animals, such as Bigfoot, the Loch Ness Monster, and the Abominable Snowman—suggested that the stories of the Kikiyaon may have been borne out of sightings of a giant, unclassified species of African bird or bat; one which, over time, tribal folklore and legend mutated into an undead monster.

On the other hand, perhaps the old legends of the Gambia were not legends, after all. Just maybe, the stories passed down from generation to generation by the tribal people of the area were a hundred percent accurate. If that is the case, then if one day, a zombie-driven Armageddon really does begin, its point of origin may not be in a top secret, military-controlled bio-weapons lab, but deep in the heart of picturesque West Africa.

King Arthur

There are very few people who have not at least heard of the magical and adventure-filled tales of Britain's famous King Arthur, and his legendary band of knights of the equally legendary round table. The reality of the situation, however, is that very little can be said about this man of great renown and his exploits with any firm degree of certainty. The primary reason being that folklore and mythology combined have become as much a part of the story as have the snippets of facts presently available to us.

The general consensus on the part of scholars and historians is that there really was a King Arthur. He is said to have ruled over certain portions of the wild Welsh countryside at some point in the sixth century, and at a time when the British Isles were under grave peril from invading Saxon hordes that originated in northern Germany. Problematic, however, is the fact that over the centuries Arthur has been elevated from being merely a minor, regional king to an all-powerful ruler of near-supernatural status—in part due to his associations with the famous and mysterious wizard of yore, Merlin, who was allegedly the somewhat sinister offspring of a mortal woman and an unholy demon.

There are tales of the ancient king being immortal; of one of the most famous of all knights, Sir Lancelot taking part in a quest to find the Holy Grail; and of a magical, enchanted land known as Avalon, where Arthur's famous sword—the all powerful Excalibur—was said to have been fashioned, and which was reputedly so bright and gleaming that it had the ability to blind Arthur's foes.

Of the many intriguing legends that surround just about everything of an Arthurian nature, one tells of how the king and his faithful warriors have lain dormant for centuries, deep within the dirt of labyrinthine caves and tunnels below the green fields of England. At an undisclosed time in the future, however, Arthur and his mighty knights will rise up from their graves, zombie-style, to defend the British Isles from attack—whether by hostile nations or by supernatural entities.

One candidate for this legendary resting place is the very appropriately named Arthur's Cave, which is located just north of the town of Monmouth, Wales, the origins of which date back to the tenth century. While no evidence has been found—so far, at least—that the king and his renowned men are buried far below the surface of the cave, it is intriguing to note that the cave contains a number of darkened offshoots, including a twenty-five-foot-diameter room—which, centuries ago, could easily have accommodated that famous round table and a band of knights and their king.

If such a thing ever does occur, it will undoubtedly be a memorable and chilling sight to see the reanimated King Arthur, and his equally reanimated, armored knights of old, doing battle with those forces of evil bent on bringing Britain to its knees. Not only that, it will serve to demonstrate that zombies are not always the bad guys they are almost exclusively painted to be.

King of the Zombies and *Revenge of the Zombies*

King of the Zombies (a 1941 production) and *Revenge of the Zombies* (made two years later) are very much equal parts of the same phenomenon, since the latter was the direct sequel to the former. As one can likely deduce from their age, both movies are driven by matters of a Voodoo nature, Caribbean settings, and creepy old mansions, rather than by modern day issues of the apocalyptic and viral kind. Neither production was likely to win an award for best movie of the year (although *King of the Zombies* did get an Academy Award nomination for best music), but they make for enjoyable viewing, if nostalgia and the past are your things. But, there is something about these particular productions that stands out big time.

The year in which *King* was released, 1941, is intriguing. Only seven months after the movie surfaced, the terrible attack by Japanese forces on Pearl Harbor occurred. Why is the date so interesting? Very simple: there are repeated—and hardly veiled—allusions throughout the film that the villain of the piece, the one man responsible for the zombie outbreak, Dr. Miklos Sangre, is a dastardly Nazi, up to no good at all. In that sense, whether intended or not, *King of the Zombies*, in a curious way, got audiences thinking as much about the threats posed by Hitler's

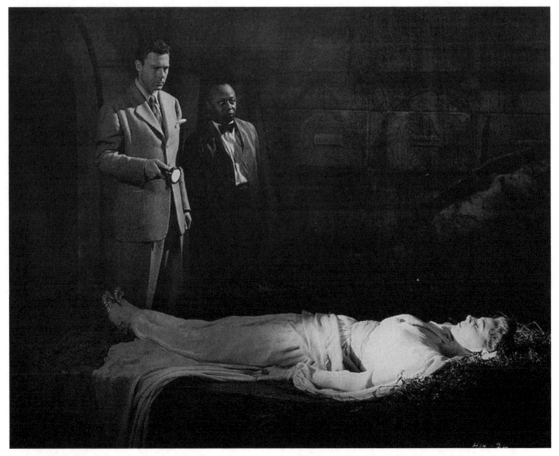

Actors Dick Purcell and Mantan Moreland discover a dead Patricia Stacey in the 1941 zombie flick *King of the Zombies*.

hordes as those posed by Miklos' mind-controlled minions, even though America was not yet at war.

Revenge of the Zombies takes the Nazi connection even further—which is hardly surprising, since by 1943, when the movie was made, the United States and Adolf Hiltler's Germany were bitter foes. In the sequel to *King of the Zombies* the arch-bad guy is Dr. Max Heinrich von Altermann, played by noted horror legend, John Carradine. The evil doctor is doing his utmost to create nothing less than a literal army of zombies for Hitler and his cronies–an army that will be almost invincible on the battlefield. The film, then, is just as much a piece of psychological warfare as was its predecessor, *King of the Zombies*.

Yes, both productions can certainly be watched solely from the perspective of them being entertaining pieces of zombie-based hokum. On the other hand, and specifically at the height of World War II, both *King of the Zombies* and *Revenge of the Zombies* served another, much welcome and even needed purpose: they consciously and/or subconsciously instilled in the mind of the average American the idea that the Nazis were abhorrent, evil, and steeped in matters of a truly dark and disturbing nature—which they really were.

Kuru

Carleton Gajdusek was a virologist who, in 1957, travelled to Papua New Guinea to investigate a mysterious and terrible condition that affected the tribal Fore people of the country. To the Fore, it was known as Kuru, which translates into English as "shiver." As will soon become apparent, the name is a most apt one. The Fore followed a particularly controversial path when it came to the ways by which they honored their dead: they cooked them. They then ate their flesh and brains, not at all unlike the average zombie. Or, it's more correct to say that the women and children ate the brains and flesh, while the men of the tribe, who lived separately, did not. Interestingly, it was chiefly the women and children who became victims of the strange condition. Whereas eating brains feeds and fuels the undead, for the Fore such actions resulted in a far less positive outcome: the development of Kuru.

As Gajdusek began to dig deep into the mystery, he came to note the profound similarities between Kuru and Scrapie, a condition that essentially destroys the brains of sheep. To his horror, Gajdusek concluded—correctly, as history has shown—that the cannibalistic actions of the Kuru had led to the emergence of a human equivalent: a condition that fell under the official title of TSE, or Transmissible Spongiform Encephalopathies. This is the class into which both "Mad Cow Disease" and its human equivalent, variant Creutzfeldt-Jakob disease (vCJD), fall.

The outcome of numerous generations of Fore regularly devouring the brains of the dead proved to be devastating: instead of walking in normal fashion, they shuffled and staggered, rather like a big-screen zombie. Violent mood swings were par for the course. Speech became slurred to the point of being almost animalistic in nature and sound. Uncontrollable shaking and twitching was commonplace—which is what specifically led to the term Kuru, or "shiver" being applied. And, finally, death followed, usually anywhere from six months to a year after infection.

Since the condition was a wholly incurable one, there was only one way to try and save the Fore from extinction, which was to persuade them to stop eating the brains of the recently deceased. Rather wisely, when confronted with the stark facts, the Fore did cease the practice of devouring the brains of their loved ones—and pretty much immediately. Unfortunately, given the long incubation period that often accompanies Kuru, many of the Fore, who believed they had been given a second chance in the 1960s, became victims in the 1970s and 1980s, when the long-dormant, cruel condition finally took its unrelenting hold. A word of careful advice: unless you are one of the reanimated, do not eat a human brain. Doing so will only come back to bite you, so to speak.

LaLaurie, Madame Delphine

Local Voodoosants often tell of how Dr. John really trusted no one living but Madame Delphine LaLaurie, the godmother and wet nurse to the infamous Devil Baby of New Orleans.

Madame LaLaurie was thought to have claimed many lives, and, with her diabolical physician husband, tortured dozens of helpless slaves and others in her attic on Governor Nichols Street and Royal Street in New Orleans.

Recent new discoveries are starting to surface that these poor, gruesome-looking individuals, that many witnesses saw with organs outside of their bodies, were actually zombies that Madame LaLaurie had hidden away so her husband could experiment on them, according to Lisa Lee Harp Waugh. As far-fetched as it sounds, it might just be the truth.

On April 10, 1834, the New Orleans fire department, responding to a call that a fire had broken out at the LaLaurie Mansion, discovered a boarded door on the third floor. Forcing the door open to be certain no smoldering fire lurked behind it, the firemen were horrified to find a number of slaves in the room. Some were dead, but some were restrained on operating room tables, their bodies hideously and cruelly cut open. Firemen were shocked as they found human body parts and organs scattered about the room. In a cage they found a slave whose bones had been broken and reset to make her look like a human crab. Other slaves had been the victims of sex change operations. Some had their faces slashed and distorted so that they were transformed into hideous monsters.

While the firemen were dealing with their terrible discovery, Mary Ellen Pleasant is said to have been seen leaving the house, carrying some charred papers bound tightly with the skin of a cotton mouth snake. Mama Sallie of Compton, California, a present-day member of Mary Ellen Pleasants secret society, claims that all Mary Ellen left them regarding zombification is one document that contains three spells that would turn a living man into a zombie on the spot. According to zombie lore, the most famous blackroot magic hex and spell book of Dr. John's zombification techniques is said to have been walled up in a secret place by Mama Mary Ellen.

One sheet is all that Mama Mary left us, Mama Sallie said. If more spells existed and they were in her possession, then they are hidden fast away.

The dark book of powerful Voodoo secrets, *The Pleasant Book of Dark Deeds*, is said to be kept under lock and key in a secret vault in Marin County, California. The book is reported to contain spells handed down from generations past, and some on zombification are said to be found therein, including the personal account of how Mary Ellen Pleasant made an army of zombies to help build a city.

In 2007, actor Nicolas Cage bought the legendary LaLaurie Mansion for $3.5 million. Cage was well aware that the LaLaurie Mansion had long been known as the most haunted house in New Orleans—some say, the United States.

Cage sold the house in 2008, admitting that he had never slept there. At any given moment, he said, he was aware of six ghosts in the mansion. He and his family had dinner in the mansion on occasion, but he allowed no one to sleep there. He had respect for the spirits, and he said that he had turned down half-a-dozen requests from parapsychologists to come to the house to research the ghostly inhabitants.

Lancellotti, Joseph

About 2:00 P.M. on April 4, 2009, Joseph Lancellotti, sixty-seven, of Metairie, Louisiana, was gardening at his home, enjoying the serenity of the day. Suddenly, he saw a man approaching, shouting angrily. Lancellotti couldn't understand a word the man was saying to him, and he was completely unprepared for the blow that the stranger landed on his head as soon as he was within striking distance.

Lancellotti attempted to defend himself with a rake, but as the two men wrestled with the rake between them, the stranger bit Lancellotti on his forearm, ripping away a large chunk of flesh. Then, to Lancellotti's horror, his attacker chewed the piece of his forearm and swallowed it. Completely stunned by the attack, Lancellotti fell to the ground, his assailant on top of him. As Lancellotti struggled to escape the man's savage clutches, the stranger began to choke him.

Lancellotti's neighbor, Chantal Lorio, director of the Wound Center at East Jefferson General Hospital, came out to investigate what was happening on Lancellotti's front yard. At first, she thought Joseph was having a heart attack and a passerby had come to his aid. Then she saw the pool of blood and the blood issuing from Lancellotti's forearm. Lorio grabbed her medicine bag and ran out to begin dressing Lancellotti's arm. She told the stranger to step back, but he wouldn't release his grip on her neighbor's shirt.

When he caught his breath, Lancellotti told Lorio that the man had bitten his arm, chewed his flesh, and swallowed it as they struggled. The bite mark measured almost 3 by 1.5 inches and was about a quarter of an inch deep. The stranger finally released his hold on Lancellotti's shirt and calmly walked away to an empty lot where a police car was parked. He was still standing there when the deputies returned to their car and took him into custody.

The man who experienced the bizarre Wendigo-type seizure was later identified as Mario Vargas, forty-eight, of New Orleans. Although officials refused to release any details, it was learned that just forty-five minutes before he attacked Joseph Lancellotti, Vargas had been treated for a finger injury at East Jefferson General Hospital. Vargas was booked for second-degree battery, but Mrs. Bonnie Lancellotti wondered if the hospital staff had not noticed anything peculiar when they treated him. She ventured her opinion that a person who goes around eating the skin of people cannot be in complete control of their senses.

Land of the Dead

When George A. Romero's *Land of the Dead* was released in June 2005, it provoked a great deal of anticipation in those domains where the zombie faithful meet and mingle. After all, while this was Romero's fourth foray into zombie world, it was actually his first movie on the subject of the undead since way back in 1985—the year in which *Day of the Dead* appeared. After a full twenty years down the line, could Romero still cut it? Most of his fans wondered and worried to equal degrees, but, after seeing the movie, they considered that the answer was an overwhelming yes: Romero *could* still cut it.

Land ... was much different than *Night ...* , *Dawn ...* , and *Day ...* . However, in the sense that this was the very first time that Romero was working with a big—as in a significantly big—budget. Distributed by Universal Studios, the funding of *Land of the Dead* provided Romero with no less than $15 million with which to go to work. To the delight of everyone involved, the movie went on to make three times that amount at cinemas across the world. Not only was the budget very welcome, the cast was not the usual conveyer-belt-style body of relative unknowns. Starring roles were given to legendary actor Dennis Hopper and to Simon Baker (the latter of the CBS TV series, *The Mentalist*). Even Simon Pegg—Shaun in *Shaun of the Dead*—put in a brief and almost unrecognizable appearance, unsurprisingly as a zombie.

Romero, to the delight of his most loyal fans, did not decide to fill *Land of the Dead* with the super-fast zombies of *28 Days Later*, or its sequel, *28 Weeks Later*, and of the remake of *Dawn of the Dead*, that practically became par for the course in the 2000s.

Land of the Dead (2005) marked George Romero's welcome return to zombie flicks after a twenty-year hiatus.

For Romero, it was very much a case of: if it ain't broken, then let's not even bother trying to fix it. Romero's dead were as slow and as shambling as they always have been.

As for the script, several years after a devastating zombie virus has reduced the human race to utter ruins, the survivors are split into two camps: the rich and the poor, or the haves and the have-nots. In the movie, this new world is played out in the city of Pittsburgh, Pennsylvania, where the wealthy want to cling on to their power and their resources, the poor feel they should have their slice, and the zombies—not being overly discerning—want a slice of everyone, as in literally. Gore, blood, cannibal-like activity, and end of the world-type activity abounded. In other words, Romero was back. And he was back big time.

The Last Man on Earth

The very first movie adaptation of Richard Matheson's 1954 novel *I Am Legend*, *The Last Man on Earth*, was made in 1964, under the careful directorship of Sidney Salkow (who later worked on the 1960s television show, *The Addams Family*) and Ubaldo Ragona. Veteran horror movie star, Vincent Price, took on the role of the sole survivor, Robert Neville, renamed for the movie as Dr. Robert Morgan. Although it is set in Los Angeles, *The Last Man on Earth* was actually filmed in Rome, Italy. In many respects, the movie is faithful to Matheson's original tale, even though Matheson himself was somewhat disappointed by the finished production. Nevertheless, its visual imagery and bleak storyline had an undeniable influence of major proportions on those that immersed themselves in the world of the on-screen zombie, including none other than George A. Romero himself.

By his own admission, Romero "ripped off" Matheson's story while working on what became the 1968 classic, *Night of the Living Dead*. Watching *The Last Man on Earth*, one cannot fail to recognize certain imagery and ideas that, years and decades later, were borrowed from the movie and became staple, iconic ingredients of entire swathes of zombie-themed movies and television shows. Shots of deserted city streets abound. Everywhere is chillingly silent. Something—something terrible—has happened to civilization. A world that was once vibrant and filled with life is now no more.

Night of the Living Dead has become famous for its hair-raising scenes of slow-moving zombies descending upon the isolated farmhouse in which our heroes are hiding out. They relentlessly try to break in, forcing those inside to board-up the windows and create makeshift barricades. It's all very

1964's *The Last Man on Earth* starred horror movie master Vincent Price in the first adaptation of the Richard Matheson novel *I Am Legend*.

impressive and visually striking. It is, however, somewhat eclipsed and shot down by the fact that Ragona and Salkow's production showed *exactly* this four years earlier. Like it or not, *The Last Man on Earth* was the one that thrust open the doors to new imagery, ideas, and paradigms. Romero's zombies merely shuffled through those same doors in Johnny-come-lately style.

The movie kicks off by introducing us to Dr. Morgan, who is played in Vincent Price's typically hammy, over the top, style. Nevertheless, Price does a good job of showing how Morgan's fate as the last man—or, as the last *real* man—on Earth has affected him to a devastating degree. He talks constantly to himself, his life has become little more than an existence, and every waking moment is a dicey battle for survival. That battle is against a horde of creatures that combine the worst parts, or perhaps the *best* parts, of zombies and vampires. Fully aware that Morgan is acutely different from them, and therefore a threat, the undead make their shambling ways to his home every night. They have only one thing on their monstrous minds: Morgan's death. Morgan, not wanting to fall victim to the inhuman things, spends his nights killing the monsters and his days burning their bodies.

The movie then jumps back in time three years. We now learn what it was that led to the catastrophe that has overrun the entire planet: a plague that began in Europe and which, after catastrophically becoming airborne, spread across the surface of the Earth in no time at all. But, this isn't just a plague that kills people. It brings them back, too, in the forms of fiendish, unholy nightmares. It's here that we're introduced to two other aspects of zombie lore that often appear in later movies: (a) attempts by the authorities to hide the truth; and (b) the military trying to control the situation.

When the plague begins, rumors quickly circulate about the dead coming back to life. Dr. Morgan dismisses the controversial stories as nothing but wild and unsubstantiated rumor, as do government agencies. Morgan's wife isn't quite so sure, however, and wonders why the bodies of the newly dead are being quickly burned instead of being given proper, decent burials. Morgan still can't accept such an astounding possibility that the dead aren't quite so dead, after all. That is, until his wife and daughter both fall victim to the outbreak, and he finally sees evidence of the dead roaming the streets of Los Angeles and troops engaged in mass burnings of bodies. The recently deceased really do walk. And Morgan, seemingly immune to the plague, realizes that the old world he once knew so well is forever gone.

As *The Last Man on Earth* progresses, Morgan—to his astonishment—stumbles upon a woman who appears just like him, immune to the effects of the deadly plague. Morgan soon realizes, however, that the woman, named Ruth, is not immune at all. Rather, she has managed to retain her humanity by regularly injecting herself with a serum that keeps the infection at bay. And she is not alone: there are many more like her, all of who have banded together. Unfortunately, unless the infected survivors receive regular shots, the plague takes its icy hold of them again. They quickly die and soon rise up as the unhinged undead.

While the fact that there is a potential antidote is, for Morgan, a very good thing, there is bad news, too. Although nowhere near as affected as those monsters that walk the streets by night, this second group of people—who are no longer fully human—*also* see Morgan as a threat. In the closing scenes of the movie, Morgan is mortally wounded by members of Ruth's people. The world's last man is soon to be no more. In his place are two new types of man: one dead but still walking, and the other a freakish, serum-reliant shell of what it once was. There is no room for Morgan in either society. As he dies, so does the last remnant of what was the true human race.

Laveau, Marie

Perhaps no one single person is more associated with the legends and folklore of zombies and Voodoo than Marie Laveau.

Each year, the reportedly haunted wishing tomb of Voodoo Queen Marie Laveau is visited by thousands of people from around the world. Located in St. Louis Cemetery Number 1 in New Orleans, the tomb is a place where people can photograph ghosts. Others hear messages from beyond the grave on their tape recorders as they attempt to pick up some EVPs (Electronic Voice Phenomena). Almost daily, someone conducts a Voodoo-Hoodoo ritual in Mama Marie's honor. Not too many tourists stay too long after dark, however, for the cemetery has a reputation of being haunted. And, then, of course, there is the restless spirit of Marie herself, who may manifest at any time, seeking someone to zombify.

Mama Sanite DeDe was, in her time, the most powerful of all the Voodoo Queens. As a young woman from Santo Domingo, she bought her secret hexes and Hoodoo-Voodoo to New Orleans. She often would hold rituals in her brick-lined courtyard on Dumaine and Chartres Streets, just walking distance from the St. Louis Cathedral.

Marie Laveau succeeded Sanite DeDe as the Voodoo Queen (High Priestess) of New Orleans sometime around 1830. No one in the hierarchy of Voodoo Priests and priestesses disputed Marie's rise to that prestigious position, for it was widely known that she was gifted with remarkable powers of sorcery.

Marie was a Creole freewoman and a hairdresser by profession. Her prestige among the white establishment was assured when the son of a wealthy New Orleans merchant was arrested for a crime of which he was innocent, although there was much false evidence against him. His father appealed to the Voodoo high priestess to put a spell on the judge to cause him to find the young man not guilty.

Marie took three Guinea peppers and placed them in her mouth before she went to the cathedral to pray. Although she was the recognized Voodoo Priestess of New Orleans, she did not find her beliefs incompatible with Catholicism and Christian charity, and she attended Mass daily. On that particular day, she knelt at the altar for several hours, praying for the young man to be found innocent.

Then, later, by a ruse, she managed to enter the courtroom and place the peppers under the judge's seat. The judge found the prisoner not guilty, and Marie Laveau was handsomely rewarded by the wealthy merchant.

Marie Laveau was the reigning Voodoo priestess of the nineteenth century. New Orleans Voodoo as a social phenomenon came into its heyday during the early 1800s. The population of the city doubled in the 1830s, and, by 1840, New Orleans had become the wealthiest and third most populous city in the nation. The Union captured New Orleans early in the American Civil War, an action which spared the city the destruction suffered by many other cities of the American South.

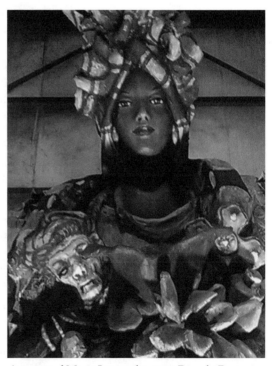

A statue of Marie Laveau by artist Ricardo Pustanio.

As a principal port, New Orleans had a leading role in the slave trade. At the same time, the city had the most prosperous community of free persons of color in the South. The touch of Voodoo-Hoodoo got a firm grasp on the city. Voodooists such as Sainte DeDe, Dr. John, and Marie Laveau prospered.

New Orleans developed its distinctive variety of Voodoo, due in part to syncretism with Roman Catholic beliefs, the fame of High Priestess Marie Laveau, and New Orleans' distinctly Caribbean cultural influences. Under Mama Marie's guidance, Voodoo thrived as a business, served as a form of political influence, provided a source of spectacle and entertainment, and was a means of altruism.

Marie greatly popularized Voodoo by revising some of the rituals until they became her unique mixture of West Indian and African tribal religions and Roman Catholicism. She was certain to invite politicians and police officials to the public ceremonies that she conducted on the banks of Bayou St. John on the night of June 23, St. John's Eve. On other occasions, she would hold Voodoo rituals on the shore of Lake Pontchartrain and at her cottage, Maison Blanche.

Hundreds of the best families in New Orleans would be present at these public celebrations of Voodoo, hoping to get a glimpse of Marie Laveau herself dancing with her large snake, Zombi, draped over her shoulders. For the white onlookers, the music and the dance provided exciting entertainment. For Marie Laveau's fellow worshippers, the rites were spiritual celebrations, and even Zombi was an agent of great Voodoo powers, a physical embodiment of Damballah Wedo.

On other occasions, in private places, the High Priestess celebrated the authentic rites of Voodoo for her devoted congregation, far from the critical eyes of the white establishment and clergy.

Madame Delphine LaLaurie and her third husband, Leonard LaLaurie, took up residence in the mansion at 1140 Royal Street sometime in the 1830s. The pair immediately became the darlings of the New Orleans social scene, which at that time was experiencing the birth of ragtime, the slave dances, the Voodoo rituals of Congo Square, the reign of the great Marie Laveau, and the advent of the bittersweet Creole Balls. Madame LaLaurie hosted fantastic events in her beautiful home that were talked about months afterward. She was described as sweet and endearing in her ways, and her husband was nothing if not highly respected within the community.

At the same time, it is said that Madame's friendship with the infamous Voodoo Queen, Marie Laveau, began to grow. Laveau lived not far from LaLaurie's Royal Street home, and the two women became acquainted when Laveau occasionally did Madame's hair. Under Laveau's tutelage, Madame LaLaurie began to act upon her latent interest in the occult, learning the secrets of Voodoo and Witchcraft at the hands of the mistress of the craft.

Madame LaLaurie and her husband had horrid ways that extended far beyond Voodoo. They began to practice hideous experiments on slaves in a secret room in their attic. Unfortunate black men and women were placed on an operating table where their vital organs were removed while they were still living or their faces were turned into grotesque masks by Dr. LaLaurie's savage scalpel.

Many locals say this is when Madame LaLaurie became the wet nurse or the nanny to the infamous Devil Baby of Bourbon Street.

It is said Madame LaLaurie fled with the cursed creature after it had killed many people and took refuge at the pilot house located on the shores of Bayou St. John. Some say she left the Devil Baby there, and that later she boarded a merchant schooner and escaped to France.

According to one version of the Devil Baby legend, Marie Laveau strangled the horned and murderous demon after it began biting her and her children.

Voodoo lore says that zombie children taken straight from the womb never age as mere mortals do. They may take over thirty years to grow into what appears to be a beautiful girl or a handsome boy in their teens. Many Voodoo cultists insist that Marie Laveau never grew old because she was of zombie birth. The great High Priest, Dr. John himself had performed her zombification on the day that she was born in September 1801.

Although Baron Samedi, the powerful loa of the dead, spends most of his time in the invisible realm of Voodoo spirits, he is notorious for his outrageous behavior, swearing continuously and making filthy jokes to the other loa and Voodooists. He is married to another powerful spirit known as Maman Brigitte, but he often chases after mortal women. It would surprise no one to learn that the Baron soon developed an unbearable desire for Marie Laveau.

In exchange for the hope of one brief romantic liaison, Baron Samedi is said to have revealed the secret of "The Zombie Trance" to Marie Laveau and her followers in a late night necromantic ritual in the 1840s. With this power, Mama Marie was able to instantly zombify anyone of her choosing.

For many years, legend had it that Marie Laveau had discovered the secrets of immortality and that she lived to be nearly 200 years old. Some speak in hushed whispers that she is still alive, conducting Voodoo rituals in the secret shadows of New Orleans.

Such a legend quite likely began when Marie cleverly passed the position of High Priestess to her daughter, who greatly resembled her, at a strategic time when she herself had just begun to age. Marie retired from public appearances to continue conducting the intricate network of spies and informants she had built up, while her daughter, Marie II, assumed the public persona of Marie Laveau, Voodoo Queen of New Orleans. Because she now appeared ageless and could sometimes be seen in more than one place at a time, her power and mystery grew ever stronger among her Voodoo worshippers and the elite white community, as well. As far as it can be determined, Marie Laveau I died in New Orleans on June 15, 1881.

Or maybe not.

It is said that Marie Laveau I is the only person who is able to cross over, back and forth, between the two worlds because she was such a powerful Voodoo Queen. But she is only allowed to be in our world on five or six days of the year. Those days are Christmas Day, New Year's Day, Fat Tuesday, Carnival, or New Orleans Mardi Gras day, All Saints Day, or All Souls Day, St. John's Eve, and her birthday, September 10.

Lazarus

See also: Jesus Christ

In the pages of the New Testament, the most famous person to reanimate after death is, of course, Jesus Christ. He is not the only one, however. There is yet another biblical character that succeeded in living twice: Lazarus, whose story is told in chapter 11 of the Gospel of John. Little is known about the other man who beat the reaper, except that he was a resident of Bethany—today the Palestinian city of al-Eizariya—and had two sisters, Martha and Mary, both of whom had become friends with, and followers of, Jesus, as had Lazarus himself.

When Lazarus became seriously ill—with what, exactly, the Bible does not make clear—Martha and Mary anxiously sent word to Jesus, begging for any help that he

Lazarus' tomb, shown here in a 1913 photograph, is located in the West Bank town of al-Eizariya, where it is a popular pilgrimage site for the faithful.

could provide to their ailing brother. Although Jesus answered the call, it was not until four days after the message reached him that Jesus finally arrived in Bethany. Unfortunately, death had taken Lazarus with great speed. As a result: Lazarus was already dead and laid to rest in a tomb by the time Jesus got there.

"Lord, if you had been here my brother would not have died," cried Martha. Jesus, however, assured her: "Your brother will rise again." Martha interpreted this to mean a reference to the final resurrection of the dead, as prophesized in the holy book. Martha was wrong: Jesus was talking about something very different entirely. Jesus then uttered the following words: "I am the resurrection and the life. He who believes in me will live, even though he dies; and whoever lives and believes in me will never die."

An excited Martha ran to Mary and told her the news. Martha, however, perhaps pondering on the matter to a greater degree when she had the chance to calm down, soon went from being excited to being filled with fear. Reality hit home: her brother was dead. With that in mind, what would happen when Lazarus reanimated? Would he be as he was in life, or would he come back as a zombie-like monstrosity? As a result of her concern at the possible outcome, Martha raced to Lazarus' tomb, which she stood in front of, doing her utmost to prevent it from being opened.

According to what we are told in Chapter 11 of the Gospel of John, Martha had no need to worry. The huge stone that stood in front of Lazarus' tomb—which was in the side of a mountain—was wheeled away. Jesus said a prayer, and before anyone had the chance to say "He has returned!" Lazarus was back on the scene, healthy, vibrant and breathing, just as if nothing had happened.

It's entirely possible, however, that Jesus' actions in reanimating the corpse of Lazarus led to his downfall and crucifixion very soon after. Hardly surprising, it didn't take long at all before word of Jesus' actions got back to certain powerful figures in Jerusalem that wanted to see the son of God gone—as in permanently. The word spread even further when, less than a week before he was crucified, Jesus returned to Bethany and dined with Mary, Martha, and Lazarus. Since there is no word in the Gospel of John that Lazarus dined on human flesh, it seems safe to say his zombification did not extend to becoming a zombie of Romero-style proportions.

For Jesus' foes, there was a big problem: the alleged act of resurrecting Lazarus ensured that more and more people gravitated toward Jesus and his teachings. There was only one answer to the problem: Jesus had to go. And he did, at Calvary, a hill near Jerusalem, where he was crucified. Like Lazarus, however, Jesus failed to stay dead and also came back from the other side, as the Bible famously describes.

Of course, belief in the story is dependent on interpreting the return of Lazarus in literal terms. Christians would argue we *should* take the story literally. On the other hand, perhaps Lazarus was not actually dead when he was placed into his tomb. After all, there are a number of medical conditions that can significantly reduce heart rate, blood pressure, and respiration. Perhaps what was perceived as death actually wasn't. We should not forget, too, that when Lazarus returned after four days of death, he appeared as he did in life. There was no decomposition, as there certainly should have been. Dead, undead, or not quite so expired after all, we'll never really know. For those who follow Christian beliefs, however, only one thing is certain: Lazarus died and returned from the grave as God's zombie.

Lederberg, Joshua

One of the most learned souls that recognized the potential threat posed to the entire human race by lethal viruses of exotic origins was Joshua Lederberg, who was born in New Jersey in 1925, and who obtained his B.A. with honors in zoology at Columbia University. In 1947, Lederberg was appointed to the position of assistant professor of Genetics at the University of Wisconsin, and here he was promoted to associate professor in 1950, and subsequently to full professor in 1954. Stanford University Medical School entrusted to him the organization of its Department of Genetics and appointed him professor and executive head in 1959. Lederberg's lifelong research, for which he received the Nobel Prize in 1958 at the age of thirty-three, was in genetic structure and function in micro-organisms, and he was actively involved in artificial intelligence research, in computer science, and in NASA's experimental programs seeking life on Mars. Lederberg died in 2008 at the age of eighty-two. In 2012, and in Lederberg's honor, a crater was named after him on the planet Mars.

This 1958 photo shows Joshua Lederberg working in his University of Wisconsin laboratory. Lederberg studied the potential for risks to humanity from extraterrestrial viruses.

An eight-page paper written by Lederberg, for *Science*, on August 12, 1960, and titled "Exobiology: Approaches to Life beyond the Earth", focused in part on the potential outcome of a virus from another planet reaching the Earth and provoking a phenomenally rapid worldwide disaster. This, of course, is a scenario that has been used to very good effect in more than a few zombie-oriented novels and movies.

"The most dramatic hazard," said Lederberg, "would be the introduction of a new disease, imperiling human health. What we know of the biology of infection makes this an extremely unlikely possibility. However, a converse argument can also be made, that we have evolved our specific defenses against terrestrial bacteria and that we might be less capable of coping with organisms that lack the proteins and carbohydrates by which they could be recognized as foreign. At present the prospects for treating a returning vehicle to neutralize any possible hazard are at best marginal by comparison with the immensity of the risk."

By the mid-1960s, Lederberg was writing a regular column for *The Washington Post* newspaper. Several of those columns are of both note and relevance to the issues presented within the pages of this book. On September 24, 1966, Lederberg wrote a feature for the newspaper titled "A Treaty on

Germ Warfare" that dealt with his constant worries about biological warfare and its potential for catastrophic misuse.

In part, Lederberg said: "The United States has vehemently denied the military use of any biological weapons or any lethal chemical weapons. However, research on these weapons has continued through and from World War II. The Army has a well-known research facility at Fort Detrick, Maryland, and a testing station at Dugway, Utah. The large scale deployment of infectious agents is a potential threat against the whole species: mutant forms of viruses could well develop that would spread over the earth's population for a new Black Death.... The future of the species is very much bound up with the control of these weapons...."

If, one day, the dead are knocking down our doors, smashing our windows, and feeding on just about anyone and everyone they can get their icy hands on, will Lederberg's words come back to haunt us? They just might do exactly that and much more, too.

Lifeforce

A 1985 movie, *Lifeforce,* was directed by horror legend, Tobe Hooper—who also directed the groundbreaking 1974 movie *The Texas Chainsaw Massacre* and the acclaimed 1979 mini-series version of Stephen King's novel *Salem's Lot.* That the movie featured many well-known actors, including Patrick Stewart (who, in 1987, took on the role of Captain Jean-Luc Picard in *Star Trek: The Next Generation*) should have made *Lifeforce* a big hit. Unfortunately, it was not. Cinema-based earnings didn't even reach half of the $25 million budget that had been allocated for the production of the movie. That said, for zombie fanatics *Lifeforce*—based on Colin Wilson's novel *The Space Vampires*—should not be missed.

The movie begins in outer space, in 1986, the year that Halley's Comet made its most recent appearance. A team of astronauts embark on a mission in a NASA space shuttle called the *Churchill* (named after British Prime Minister Sir Winston Churchill), to rendezvous with the gigantic comet. On doing so, the crew is shocked to find that deep within Halley's Comet there is a huge spacecraft of alien origin. Not only that, the ship is filled with numerous, dead, winged monsters, and three very human-looking beings: two men and one woman.

Unbeknownst to the astronauts, the three entities are not, as is first suspected, fellow *Homo sapiens* who have been abducted by the gargoyle-like creatures. They are one and the same. In other words, the aliens have the ability to morph into human form and back again. It isn't long before all three are secretly brought to London, England, for study at the fictional European Space Research Center. And, despite being heavily guarded by British Army personnel, that's when the trouble begins.

Clearly not dead, the trio of non-humans appears to be in a state of deep, suspended animation. Until, that is, they wake up. The woman, using what might be termed a form of extraterrestrial hypnotism, entrances one of the troops and—utterly

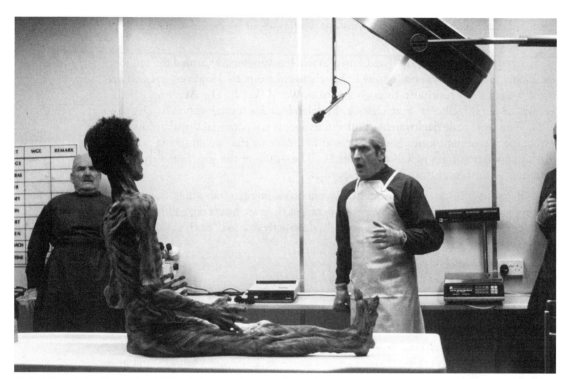

In *Lifeforce* it is aliens who deliberately spread a zombifying disease on Earth, but unlike zombies, the infected drain the life force out of people.

naked—moves towards one man, seemingly to kiss him on the lips. This is no normal kiss, however. As the alien female embraces the soldier, she drains his body of its vital energy—the life force, in other words, of the movie's title. His body falls to the ground, as a withered, shrunken husk, and the alien escapes from the facility. A couple of hours later, a shocking development occurs.

While the military team overseeing the project—and acting to keep everything under wraps and away from the public and the media—tries to figure out what is afoot, word comes in that the body of a woman has been found in nearby woods. She, too, is as withered as an old, leathery Egyptian mummy. When her body is brought to the space center for study, it reanimates—as does the body of the dead soldier. They, too, are now crazed undead entities needing to feed on vital life energy. A doctor is then violently attacked and bitten. He also dies and returns as a savage monster. And with the morphed alien on the loose, it's not long before London is engulfed in an epidemic, one in which the living first become the dead, but who then mutate into something far worse.

In a neat twist, the team comes to believe that these energy-sucking aliens—and the people they infect—are responsible for our centuries-old legends and folklore of bloodsucking vampires. But, in reality, it's energy, and not blood, that the reanimated so badly need. And they don't dress like cloaked Count Draculas, either. One hundred percent zombie-like in appearance, the ragged dead rise up in violent style, rampaging around the streets of London in huge throngs, attacking the living, sucking them dry, and ensuring their victims soon become marauding killers, just like them. The fate of the entire human race is now precariously hanging in the balance.

It's accurate and fair to say that *Lifeforce* is an unusual and highly alternative production that blends together three distinct genres that are generally kept poles apart from each other: zombies, vampires, and science fiction. Notably, however, all three are successfully fused into what is an entertaining—but unfortunately, much underappreciated—storyline.

Live and Let Die

When we think of the world's most famous fictional spy, James Bond, 007, we usually think of martinis (shaken and not stirred, of course), hot girls running around in skimpy bikinis, dastardly super-villains, secret underground bases, and a high degree of adventure and intrigue. We don't usually, however, associate the man with a license to kill with the world of Voodoo and zombies. But, that is exactly what we got in 1973, when *Live and Let Die* (starring, for the first time, Roger Moore, as Bond) was released.

The plotline of *Live and Let Die* revolves around Bond's attempts to get to the bottom of three interconnected murders. The victims are all employees of MI6—the British equivalent of the United States' CIA. And they all have one thing in common: they were engaged in the secret investigation of a certain Dr. Kananga, who rules—in iron-fist style—over San Monique, an island in the Caribbean.

When Bond is ordered to solve the mystery, he finds himself in a world dominated by Kananga's ruthless plans to take over, and control, the world's supply of heroin. Bond also finds himself up to his neck in matters of a Voodoo-based nature. To keep the superstitious locals away from the ever-growing poppy fields that Kananga is cultivating—and distributing under the brilliant disguise of his alter-ego, Mr. Big—he exploits the local fear of Voodoo, curses, and the revived dead.

It all works very well for Kananga until Bond saves the day—but not before almost becoming dinner for more than a few hungry alligators, and racing around the swamps of Louisiana in a speedboat, pursued by Kananga's men and a local sheriff, J. W. Pepper, memorably and amusingly played by Clifton James. Certainly, the most mysterious and sinister character, however, is that of Baron Samedi, a Voodoo-practicing witch doctor who has an uncanny ability to beat the Grim Reaper, time and again.

Neither poisonous snakes nor bullets appear to have a lasting effect on Samedi, who—as one of Kananga's goons—is arguably the star of the show. He pops up throughout the movie in chillingly disturbing fashion and even gets the last hoorah. As the final credits role, we see Samedi—once again, having beaten death or risen from it—sitting on the front of a speeding train, laughing in the same deep and disturbing fashion he does throughout the movie. Bond may have been the hero, but Samedi provided all the zombie-like horror.

Liver-eating Johnson

John Garrison had flaming red hair and beard, stood over six feet tall, and weighed a solid 240 pounds. Born near Little York, New Jersey, around 1824, Garrison joined the Union Army. After he struck an officer, he deserted, changed his name to John Johnson, and decided that he was better suited to life as a mountain man out in the West where there was little or no law officers to interfere with a man's life.

In 1847, Johnson married Swan, a girl from the Flathead tribe, and took her with him to his cabin on the Little Snake River in northwestern Colorado. After making certain that Swan was comfortable and had plenty of food and firewood, Johnson left for his winter trapping grounds with his .30 caliber Hawken rifle, his tomahawk, knife, and backpack. He was unaware that Swan was pregnant with his child.

When he returned as soon as the spring thaws permitted, he was horrified to see vultures circling over his cabin. Inside he found the bones of Swan scattered by birds and animals. Beside her lay the skull of an unborn baby. The markings on a feather lying among the skeletal remains told him that the murderers had been members of the Crow tribe. At that same moment of recognition and rage, Johnson vowed a vendetta to the death, a personal feud that, according to the legends of the mountains, would take the lives of 300 Crow braves.

Whenever he triumphed over a Crow warrior, Johnson would slash open the fallen brave's chest with his knife, rip out the warm liver from within, and eat it raw. Thus the mountain man earned the sobriquet of Liver-eating Johnson.

The rugged lad from New Jersey had peeled away centuries of civilization and allowed the unbridled lycanthrope within his psyche to assume control. Such savagery inspired great terror among the Crow tribe, for it seemed as though they were dealing with a wild beast, something much more terrible than a mere man.

Once, it is said, Johnson was captured by a group of Blackfeet who saw a chance to sell him to the Crow and receive a rich reward. Bound with leather thongs and placed under guard in a teepee, Johnson managed to gnaw through the straps, disarm one of his captors and amputate one of his legs. Fleeing into the deep snows and freezing cold of winter, it required superhuman strength and endurance to survive. But he had food in the form of the Blackfoot brave's leg to sustain him until he reached the cabin of a fellow trapper.

During all the years of Johnson's one-man war against the Crow, they never once managed to catch him unaware. Johnson finally made peace with the Crow, and in 1864, he joined the Union Army and served in Company H, Second Colorado Cavalry. During the 1880s, he was appointed deputy sheriff in Coulson, Montana. He built a home outside of Red Lodge, Montana, and lived to a ripe old age, passing away in a Los Angeles veterans' hospital in 1899.

In 1972, Robert Redford starred as Johnson in *Jeremiah Johnson*, a beautifully filmed tribute to the mountain man. While the plot of the movie was built on the feud between Johnson and the Crow, the motion picture chose not to portray the liver-eating part of his revenge, perhaps deciding that a lot of shooting and tomahawk chopping was blood enough.

Some historians theorize that Johnson only cut out the livers of his victims and pretended to eat them to increase the horror that would spread among the Crow that a madman was stalking them. Others suggest that he may have done it once or twice early on in his revenge killings. To eat the liver of a victim is a symbolic act of revenge and an ancient act of assuming the strength and prowess of one's victims.

And then there are those students of the Old West who maintain that Liver-eating Johnson cannibalized every one of his victims to avenge the murder of his wife and unborn child.

London Underground

As mentioned in a previous entry in this book, for years, rumors have circulated that deep below the city of London, England, lurk savage cannibals—dubbed the "London Subterreanans"—that feast upon unwary passengers on the London Underground rail system. Demonstrating just how far back those rumors go is a story that has its origins in the 1920s. One particular station on the London Underground that is no longer in use is British Museum Station. It was shut down in 1933.

More than a decade before British Museum Station was no more, however, strange tales were told of an unsettling character seen hiding in the shadows of the old tracks. He was described as covered in grime and dirt, and dressed in nothing but a tattered piece of cloth. He was also said to be a man that violently slaughtered anyone that dared to cross his path. The rumor mill suggested he didn't just kill people: he ate them, too. A tattered man-eater: was a zombie staggering around, and feasting within, London's underworld?

Rather oddly, tales soon took shape that the man was an Egyptian—whether a ghostly, ancient one whose remains were held at the British Museum or a psychologically disturbed immigrant who had then recently reached British shores. Such was the interest and concern the story provoked that the local press offered a sizeable number of English pounds to anyone prepared to sleep on the platform-floor of the station overnight. It was all to no avail: the deep fear of the ragged character ensured that no-one was prepared to take the chance of getting murdered—or maybe even eaten—by the mysterious man. Sightings continued through to the late 1920s, although the dirt-encrusted man was never apprehended and identified. For all intents and purposes, he vanished.

In 1935, however, the controversy was reignited. It was in that year that a movie titled *Alias Bulldog Drummond* was released. It starred Jack Hulbert and Fay Wray—the latter of *King Kong* fame. Much of the movie is focused on—and was actually filmed in—the London Underground. Clearly, the screenwriters knew their local folklore, since they incorporated into their story the legend of the ragged Egyptian, as well as tales of hidden tunnels deep below London.

The London premiere of *Alias Bulldog Drummond* was eclipsed, however, by something very weird: on that very night, a pair of young girls vanished into oblivion from a station just one stop down from the old, disued British Museum station. It was not a stunt pulled by the production company (Gaumont International) and, despite the best efforts of the police to wrap things up, the pair was never seen again. Or, maybe *parts* of them were. Whispers abounded that the partly eaten remains of the girls were found somewhere in the deserted British Museum station. Notably, the police did not outright dismiss the story, but suggested the remains were those of an old hobo that had passed away and been gnawed on by rats! Perhaps this was exactly what happened. On the other hand, maybe it was all a carefully executed cover story to hide something worse: savage, cannibalistic humans were wildly on the loose below London and the authorities were unable to do anything about it.

The story is still remembered to this very day. *Tunnel Vision* is a novel penned by author Keith Lowe in 2001. The chief character, Andy, tells his fiancée, Rachel that: "If you listen carefully when you're standing at the platform at Holborn, sometimes—just sometimes—you can hear the wailing of Egyptian voices floating down the tunnel towards you."

Maybe the "London Subterraneans" are not yet done with us and we still provide them with the nourishment they need—although most assuredly not willingly!

Lovecraft, H. P.

There can be no doubt whatsoever that, more than seventy years after his untimely 1937 death from the effects of intestinal cancer, H. P. Lovecraft remains one of the key, integral figures of twentieth century horror-fiction. Ironically, in his short lifetime (he was dead at just forty-six) Lovecraft saw very little evidence that his collective body of work would, one day, generate a fan-base of worldwide, stratospheric proportions. But, that is exactly what has since happened.

With his dark, disturbing, and fantastic tales of ancient cities, magical lands, alien entities of a terrible nature, monstrous beasts such as the now-famous Cthulhu, cavernous realms in which lurked unnamable monstrosities, and much more of a nightmarish nature, Lovecraft developed a loyal but limited audience, thanks to the likes of *Weird Tales* magazine that gave him an outlet for his stories.

Perhaps weirdly appropriate, Lovecraft was himself as strange and controversial as his literary output. His relationships with the opposite sex were practically non-existent, aside from a short, ill-fated marriage that collapsed, in part, due to Lovecraft's refusal to get out of the house and find a real job that actually paid decent money. He was nearly repulsed by the idea of sex and pretty much shunned it. He exhibited bizarre phobias, including fears of both the sea and seafood. He was afflicted with facial twitches and grimaces that made his appearance downright unsettling. And he was an undeniable racist who looked down on Jews, blacks, Asians, and pretty much everyone who wasn't white. Defenders of Lovecraft's stance have suggested that such racism—in early twentieth century America—was hardly rare. But the fact that Lovecraft was hardly alone in his views on what he perceived to be inferior people cannot in any way make his stance even remotely defendable.

While much of Lovecraft's writing revolved around such near-memes as ancient and terrible secrets, arcane knowledge, hidden histories, and foul creatures that lurked by night, he also had a fascination with the issue of reanimating the dead. One might even call him an early literary version of George A. Romero.

One of Lovecraft's most acclaimed series of stories on the matter of reviving the recently deceased is his *Herbert West—Reanimator*, the writing for which began in 1921 and which was published one year later. It very closely parallels today's

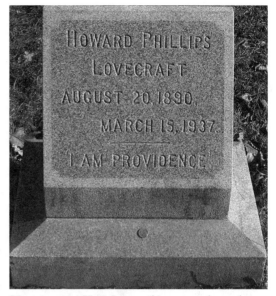

Horror writer H. P. Lovecraft's grave is located at the Swan Point Cemetery in Providence, Rhode Island. Among his many macabre stories are tales of reanimating the dead.

world of the zombie, in the sense that the dead return as crazed killers. The insane and homicidal states of the dead are not, however, due to their exposure to a terrible virus, but to something even more terrible: namely, the afterlife, which is depicted as a domain so awful that the human mind descends into a state of complete and utter madness when fully exposed to it.

Both *The Case of Charles Dexter Ward* and *The Mound* follow similar paths and display undeniable similarities to accepted zombie lore. Interestingly, in the latter, the dead are reanimated and controlled by an alien race that uses them as a slave-species—which is not at all unlike the Haitian accounts of zombified humans exploited as slaves.

Would H. P. Lovecraft have nodded, in approving style, at the likes of *The Walking Dead* and *Night of the Living Dead*? One can never be sure, but it's fair to say that he probably would not have *disapproved*.

MacArthur Causeway Face-eating Zombie

In May 2012, a shocking event occurred in Florida that led far more than a few conspiracy theorists to strongly suspect that the U.S. government had secretly tested a modified virus—possibly one mutated from the rabies virus—designed to mimic the rabid, cannibalistic actions of the army of the undead. If you think that sounds absolutely crazy, well, you just might be wrong.

It was just after midday on May 26 when Rudy Eugene, a thirty-one-year-old man, drove onto Miami's MacArthur Causeway. As Eugene approached the East End of the bridge, his car broke down. His only option was to walk back the way he came, on foot, to seek help. Since the bridge was no less than three miles in length, it was a walk destined to take him a couple of hours. At around 2:00 P.M., and as Eugene reached a ramp that led onto the causeway, he did something very strange, unpredictable, and downright nightmarish.

As footage taken by security cameras on the bridge clearly showed, Eugene's attention was drawn to a homeless man—later identified as one Edward Poppo—who was sprawled out on the ground, below the ramp. Eugene inexplicably, and suddenly, undressed himself, and proceeded down the ramp, towards Poppo. He wasn't about to give the man a few dollars for food, however. In fact, the exact opposite occurred: Poppo became food for Eugene, who, quite out of the blue, violently lunged at Poppo and quickly tore out the eyes of the poor man. Eugene then took hold of Poppo's throat, throttling him until he passed out. Worse was to come; in fact, *far* worse was to come.

Now unconscious, Poppo was completely at the mercy of crazed Eugene, who proceeded to systematically eat Poppo's face, from chin to hairline, no less. Flesh was savagely ripped from both muscle and bone and eagerly devoured. Poppo's nose was bitten clean off. Even one of his eyeballs was chewed and swallowed by Eugene. A horrified police officer, who was quickly on the scene, ordered Eugene to stop. He did not. What Eugene *did* do in response, was to slowly turn and look at the officer and utter nothing less than a low, guttural growl, before returning to continue devouring poor Poppo. The officer had no choice but to bring Eugene down. No luck with that: Eugene continued on, regardless, with his merciless digestion of his victim. In fact, it took an astonishing *five rounds* to finally bring Eugene's carnage to a bloody and decisive end.

Was Eugene possibly under the influence of a mind-altering drug at the time of his maniacal attack? Certainly not according to the autopsy, which only showed a presence of marijuana in his system, and which is hardly known for turning people into crazed cannibals, although it does provoke a craving for potato chips and a comfy couch. And although the media theorized that Eugene was, perhaps, high on "bath salts" at the time—slang term for psychoactive chemicals called cathinones—no evidence of such was ever found in Eugene's body.

Conspiracy theorists quickly jumped on the story and suggested that Eugene had been randomly, and unluckily, selected by a secret government body or military agency. The purpose: to clandestinely expose him to a classified, weaponized virus, one specifically designed to instill rage and cannibalistic tendencies in the targeted individual. Was Eugene hit by a fast-acting pathogen, possibly delivered in airborne form, as he walked across the MacArthur Causeway? We may never know the truth. With Eugene dead, and with no explanation for his sudden homicidal tendencies, the case continues to languish in a realm filled with far more questions than answers. The rise of the zombies just might not be so far away, after all. And, just maybe, it will all begin on the MacArthur Causeway.

Macumba

The Macumba religion (also known as Spiritism, Candomble, and Umbanda) is practiced by a large number of Brazilians who cherish the age-old relationship between a shaman and his or her people. In its outward appearances and in some of its practices, Macumba resembles Voodoo. Trance states among the practitioners are encouraged by dancing and drumming, and the evening ceremony is climaxed with an animal sacrifice.

Macumba was born in the 1550s when the West African tribal priests who sought to serve their people with their old religion were forced to give token obeisance to an array of Christian saints and the god of their masters. As in the cases of Santeria, Voodoo, and other adaptations of original religious expression, the native priests soon realized how complementary the two faiths could be. The African god, Exu, became St. Anthony; Iemanja became Our Lady of the Glory; Oba became St. Joan of Arc; Oxala became Jesus Christ; Oxum became Our Lady of the Conception; and so on. The Africans summoned the Orishas with the sound of their drums and the rhythm of their dancing. In that regard, the West Africans were more fortunate than those slaves in the States, whose masters forbade them to keep their drums.

During this same period, Roman Catholic missionaries were attempting to convince the aboriginal tribes in Brazil to forsake their old religion and embrace Christianity. In many instances, Macumba provided the same kind of bridge between faiths for the native people as it had for the Africans imported to the country by the slave trade. While they gave lip service to the religious practices of the Europeans, they found that they also could worship their nature spirits and totems in the guise of paying homage to the Christian saints.

The ancient role of the shaman remains central to Macumba. The priest enters into a trancelike state and talks to the spirits in order to gain advice or aid for the supplicant. Before anyone can participate in a Macumba ceremony, he or she must undergo an initiation. The aspirants themselves must enter a trance during the dancing and the drumming and allow a god to possess them. As in Haitian and New Orleans Vodou and Santeria, once the dancer has been taken by the spirit, he or she often dances to a state of exhaustion.

A cross fashioned in the Macumba tradition stands in a cemetery in Brazil.

Once the possession has taken place, the shaman must determine which gods are in which initiate so the correct rituals may be performed. The process is empowered by the sacrifice of an animal, whose blood is then smeared over the initiates by the shaman. Once the initiates have been blooded, they take an oath of loyalty to the cult. Later, when the trance state and the possessing god has left them, the initiates, now members of the Macumba cult, usually have no memory of the ritual proceedings.

From the melding of the two religious faiths and the Africans' passion for drumming and dancing, the samba, the rhythm of the saints, was created. The samba became a popular dance, and even today is recognized in Brazil as a symbol of national identity. The dance, synonymous to many as a symbol of Brazil and Carnival, has also become widely accepted throughout the world. One of the samba's derivations is the Bossa Nova.

Mad Cow Disease

See also: Cattle Mutilations, Creutzfeld-Jacobs Disease, Foot-and-Mouth Disease

In 1986, the first signs of a terrifying new disease began to surface in the heart of the British countryside. It was a disease that specifically targeted cattle and made them behave in distinctly zombie-like ways, before finally killing the animals in a deeply distressing fashion. Its official name is bovine spongiform encephalopathy. Unofficially, but far more infamously, it is known as Mad Cow Disease. BSE is caused by a prion—a protein-based agent that attacks and affects the normal function of cells. Worse still, just like the fictional zombie virus of so many movies, prion-inducing BSE is utterly unstoppable and incurable.

By 1987, the British government recognized that did not just have a problem on its hands, but a *major* problem, too. And, it can reasonably be argued, another zombie-based parallel surfaced when the answers as to how and why BSE surfaced and spread chaos and fear across the land became gruesomely clear. In the same way that, in typically fictional format, infected people feed upon the uninfected survivors of the zombie apocalypse, very much the same can be said about the origins of BSE: it was caused by cows being made to eat other cows.

To the complete horror and consternation of the British public—who had previously, and blissfully, been kept completely in the dark—it was revealed by the government that, for years, the discarded remains of millions of cattle that had been put to death in British slaughterhouses had been ground to a pulp and used to create cattle-feed. In stark terms, the UK's cattle herd had been turned into full-fledged cannibals. It was *Soylent Green* for cows. And that is when the problems started.

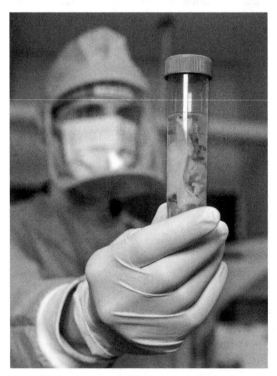

A medical researcher holds up sample brain tissue from a cow infected with mad cow disease.

It quickly became very easy to spot a zombified cow: they shuffled rather than walked; their personalities began to change; they exhibited behavior that varied from confusion to outright rage; and they quickly became unmanageable under normal circumstances. As the crisis grew, and as an even more terrifying development surfaced—namely, that the infection had jumped to the human population, in the form of what is termed variant Creutzfeldt-Jacob disease, or vCJD—the utterly panicked British government took the only option it felt was available.

With close to an estimated 200,000 cattle infected, officialdom decided to play things safe by systematically wiping out no less than 4.4 million cows, all across the entire nation. While such actions were seen as horrific in some quarters, they were also perceived as necessary to ensure that chaos and death did not spread even further—and maybe even overseas, too. For some, however, it was all much too late. Although the cannibalizing process was brought to a halt by the government in 1989, to date, more than 160 British people have died from vCJD. On top of that, the significant increase in Alzheimer's disease in the United Kingdom in recent years has given rise to the disturbing theory that many of those diagnosed with Alzheimer's are, in reality, suffering from a far more mutated form of vCJD.

As all of the above shows graphically, when creatures feed upon their own kind, it's not long at all before apocalyptic scenarios, public panic, strange viruses, and millions of dead (albeit in the form of cows rather than people) become a grim, frightening reality.

Majestic 12

In George Romero's 1968 classic movie, *Night of the Living Dead*, contamination from a NASA spacecraft, returning to Earth after completing its mission of the outer space kind, sparks off the beginning of the end of civilization. Is it truly feasible that something viral, something deadly, and—even worse—something airborne, could come to the Earth from the mysterious realms of outer space and unleash a worldwide plague upon the Human Race?

One person who thinks the answer to that controversial question could very well be "Yes!" is Dr. Robert M. Wood, who received a B.S. in Aeronautical Engineering from the University of Colorado in 1949 and a Ph.D. in physics from Cornell in 1953. Wood worked for General Electric Aeronautics and Ordnance, served in the U.S. Army at the Aberdeen Proving Ground for two years, and then completed forty-three years with Douglas Aircraft and its successors, before retiring in the 1990s.

Dr. Wood, whose work took him into realms where matters of a top secret nature and those having a bearing on national security were commonplace, is someone whose work has a major bearing upon a great deal that is relative to zombie lore. After his retirement, Wood began to more deeply pursue one of his particular, and alternative, passions: the UFO phenomenon. In 1996, Wood received, from a UFO researcher named Timothy Cooper, a number of documents that Wood believes were leaked to Cooper by an Edward Snowden-style whistleblower in government. In part, the documents told a shocking story that was focused on the issue of an outbreak of an alien virus on planet Earth. The leaked papers referred to a highly classified group buried incredibly deep within the U.S. government called Majestic 12, whose job it was to secretly study—and hide from the public and the media alike—the disturbing truths about UFOs.

One of the documents provided to Timothy Cooper by his shadowy, insider-informants, and which ultimately reached Dr. Wood, was titled the *MAJESTIC TWELVE PROJECT: 1ˢᵗ Annual Report*. It told a shocking and controversial story of what supposedly happened when U.S. military personnel and scientists examined the wrecked remains of a crashed alien spacecraft, and its dead crew of alien entities, which were found deep in the deserts of New Mexico in the summer of 1947.

According to the unknown author of the *1ˢᵗ Annual Report*: "BW [Author's note: Biological warfare] programs in U.S. and U.K. are in field test stages. Discovery

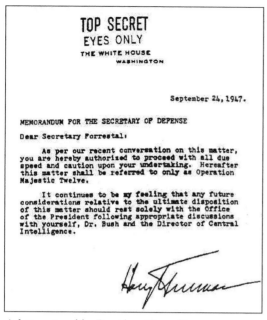

TOP SECRET
EYES ONLY
THE WHITE HOUSE
WASHINGTON

September 24, 1947.

MEMORANDUM FOR THE SECRETARY OF DEFENSE

Dear Secretary Forrestal:

As per our recent conversation on this matter, you are hereby authorized to proceed with all due speed and caution upon your undertaking. Hereafter this matter shall be referred to only as Operation Majestic Twelve.

It continues to be my feeling that any future considerations relative to the ultimate disposition of this matter should rest solely with the Office of the President following appropriate discussions with yourself, Dr. Bush and the Director of Central Intelligence.

Harry Truman

A letter signed by President Harry Truman authorizing Majestic 12.

of new virus and bacteria agents so lethal, that serums derived by genetic research, can launch medical science into unheard of fields of biology. The samples extracted from bodies found in New Mexico, have yielded new strains of a retrovirus not totally understood, but, give promise of the ultimate BW weapon. The danger lies in the spread of air-borne and bloodborne outbreaks of diseases in large populations, with no medical cures available."

The document continues: "The Panel was concerned over the contamination of several SED personnel upon coming in contact with debris near the power plant. One technician was overcome and collapsed when he attempted the removal of a body. Another medical technician went into a coma four hours after placing a body in a rubber body bag. All four were rushed to Los Alamos for observation. All four later died of seizures and profuse bleeding. All four were wearing protective suits when they came into contact with body fluids from the occupants."

Further disturbing data is elaborated upon: "Autopsies on the four dead SED technicians are not conclusive. It is believed that the four may have suffered from some form of toxin or a highly contagious disease. Tissue samples are currently being kept at Fort Detrick, MD."

And most disturbing of all: "In the opinion of the senior AEC medical officer, current medical equipment and supplies are wholly inadequate in dealing with a large scale outbreak of the alien virus."

It must be said that within the field of UFO research, there is great debate regarding the matter of whether the papers acquired by Dr. Bob Wood are the real thing or an audacious hoax. We should, perhaps, *hope* they are the latter, and *pray* they are not the former.

Mambo Sallie Ann Glassman

Counted as one of the twenty most active Voodoo practitioners in the United States, Priestess Mambo Sallie Ann Glassman, a woman of Jewish-Ukrainian heritage, is known for promoting positive thoughts through her Voodoo faith. She is also a historian on Voodoo tradition and its roots in Haitian Vodun.

Mambo Sallie, who was well-versed in the teachings of the Kabala and ritual magic, began studying New Orleans Vodou in 1975. In her New Orleans Voodoo Tarot/Book and Card Set, she writes that she discovered a vibrant, beautiful, and ecstatic religion that was free from dogma, guilt, or coercion.

Mambo Sallie has been practicing Voodoo in New Orleans since 1977. In 1995, she travelled to Haiti and underwent the week-long couche initiation rites. She returned to New Orleans ordained as Ounsi, Kanzo, and Mambo Asogwea High Priestess of Voodoo.

Mambo Sallie is the founder of La Source Ancienne and the Island of Salvation Botanica, a resource for Voodoo religious supplies and a showcase for her Voodoo-inspired art.

You can find her website, Island of Salvation Botanica, at http://www.feyvodou .com/.

Manitou Grand Cavern Mummy

Throughout the United States the mummified remains of men and women from a lost and unknown culture have been found. Some of these mysterious mummies are over seven feet tall and are estimated to be many thousands of years old.

And then there are those accounts of somewhat off-kilter doctors and scientists who have devised their own experiments in embalming and mummification.

Somewhere, right now, at a small country fair, a barker is chanting his old come-on and gullible small town folks are plunking down their hard-earned dollars to take a look at The Marvelous Petrified Indian of Manitou Caverns.

The mummified remains they are viewing may be petrified, if you're willing to stretch a point a little, but by no stretch of the imagination is the shriveled package of skin and bones the remains of a Native American tribal member.

The Petrified Indian is Tom O'Neel, a rugged young Irish railroad worker who met an untimely death in a barroom brawl more than one hundred years ago . His corpse then became the victim of a bizarre experiment in frontier embalming and a pawn in a hoax that has carried his homeless remains across America ever since. A dime store wig gave Tom the needed long tribal warrior hair and an old tomahawk still rests in his mummified hands, but Tom O'Neel is no more Native American than General Custer.

The curious saga of Tom O'Neel began when his life ended during a wild shootout between railroad construction-workers who poured into the suddenly booming town of Colorado City to lay track for the Colorado Midland Railroad in 1885.

The town coroner who pronounced Tom O'Neel dead was an amazing pioneer physician by the name of Dr. Isaac A. Davis, who had some theories about embalming and the preservation of bodies that had brought him a good deal of scientific note in medical circles of the day.

When attempts to locate relatives of the young railroad worker proved futile, Davis decided to use the body for some of his advanced embalming techniques and removed the corpse to a small stone shed in the city cemetery where he had housed chemicals and other instruments used for the normal preparation of the dead.

Dr. Davis believed that soaking a body in certain chemicals he had concocted, then drying the corpse in the mountain sunlight, could produce a cured body that would defy decay, much as the methods employed by Egyptian priests had preserved the remains of the ancient pharaohs.

For more than two years, the frontier scientist alternately soaked and baked poor Tom O'Neel and injected chemical compounds into his lifeless veins.

Soon, the body began to take on the dark brown, leathery appearance of old cowhide, and the once brawny figure of Tom O'Neel shrank to a withered sack of skin and bones that weighed no more than sixty pounds.

It isn't quite certain what ultimate use Dr. Davis hoped to make of what he learned by experimenting on the remains of the young construction man, but death came to claim the doctor himself, and relatives hastened to be rid of the macabre mummy.

The family made a mistake, however, in selecting two local ne'er-do-wells to take the mummy to the cemetery for a decent burial. Quickly assessing the money-making potential represented by the mummy, the pair found themselves a black wig, some old Indian buckskins, several strands of beads, and managed to dress O'Neel's shrunken body. They found an old tomahawk to shove into the jar, and they headed off into the sunset to make their fortune as traveling showmen by exhibiting the remains of the marvelous petrified Indian.

The project almost went awry at once when the two took some of the early proceeds of their ill-gotten gains and got roaring drunk, leaving Tom lying about in a Wyoming railroad depot unclaimed for several days.

When suspicious railroad officials opened the casket-like packing crate and discovered the mummy, sheriff's officers clapped the two budding showmen in irons for grave robbery. Wires sent back to Colorado, however, turned up no incidents of grave robbing and the officials in Wyoming were happy to be rid of the grisly remains. No charges were filed.

The close brush with the law proved enough to discourage Tom's owners, however, and when an opportunity to sell the new circus attraction arose, the two partners leaped at it. Tom O'Neel began a new travelling career, this time with a tent show that also featured a two-headed calf and a five-footed goat.

There is no record of how many times the sun-dried remains of Tom O'Neel changed hands in the years that followed, but old newspapers of the era containing advertisements of the Wondrous Petrified Indian of Manitou Cavern are a witness to the long journey across the country in which Tom suffered the continuing indignity of exhibition at countless country crossroads.

One story has it that an old resident of Colorado City, back east for a visit, encountered the show with which Tom was then travelling and attempted to buy the corpse and provide it with a proper burial. The compassionate man was turned down by the low-budget Barnum in charge, who claimed he was making a fortune with the petrified Indian.

Just where poor Tom O'Neel is right now isn't known, but chances are the long-dead Irish workman is still being displayed and represented as a relic from the mysterious path. His spirit must surely be horribly restless, and his Irish temper at full boil. We can only pity those sideshow tent gawkers if anyone accidentally breaks the jar and frees the Manitou Grand Canyon Mummy.

Man-Monkey

On the chilly night of January 21, 1879, a man was walking home, with his horse and cart in tow, along the tree-shrouded lanes that to this day still link the hamlet of Woodcote in Shropshire to the tiny locale of Ranton, Staffordshire, England. All was normal until around 10:00 P.M., when barely a mile from Woodseaves and while crossing over Bridge 39 on the Shropshire Union Canal, the man's life was plunged into chaos and terror.

Out of the darkened woods there suddenly emerged a frightening beast: it was large, black-haired, monkey-like in appearance, and sported a pair of bright, self-illuminated eyes that glowed eerily and hypnotically. The rampaging monster suddenly jumped atop the cart, then, incredibly, leapt onto the back of the terrified horse, which took off in a frenzied gallop, with the cart careening wildly behind. The man, to his credit, gave chase, and finally caught up with the horse, cart, and beast. On doing so, he proceeded to hit with his whip what was surely the closest thing the British Isles have ever seen to Bigfoot.

Incredibly, the man later reported that on each and every occasion he tried to strike the beast, the whip simply passed through its body—as if the hairy thing was nothing less than a terrible specter of the night. A moment or so later, and without warning, the creature leapt to the ground and bounded away into the safety of the dark woods that loomed on all sides. The shocking event was over as quickly as it had begun.

When word of the story reached the local police, one of the constables remarked to the local media that additional sightings of the creature had been made at the bridge, and that the monstrous matters began after a local man was found drowned in the waters of the canal. What was left unsaid at the time by the authorities, however, was the fact that while the man may very well have drowned, when the police hauled his body out of the water, huge chunks of flesh were missing from the torso, legs, arms, and face.

It may, of course, all have been the work of a large fish—such as a pike, a particularly violent and large fish that can be found all across the U.K.—but, nevertheless, when the full story finally got out amongst the villagers of Woodseaves, the theories for the man's death became far darker. In the late-1800s, and in those parts of England where old traditions and folklore still held firm sway, it was widely believed that executed murderers could return to our world in the form of monstrous animals, not unlike the Man-Monkey itself. Many of these same beast-men of the resurrected kind reportedly fed, cannibal-style, on those that were unfortunate enough to cross their paths. Perhaps one of these very same executed killers returned as the Man-Monkey and made a home for itself in the woods that surround Bridge 39.

Today, the old bridge and canal continue to stand, and sightings of the Man-Monkey still occasionally surface, as it prowls around its old hunting grounds, striking terror into the hearts and minds of those that encounter it. Fortunately, the 1879 case aside, there appears not to have been any more zombie-style feasting on the local populace—that is, unless, and as was certainly the case in 1879, the local police are playing their cards very close to their chests.

Mannequins

In *I am Legend*, the character of Robert Neville (portrayed in the movie adaptations of Richard Matheson's 1954 novel first by Vincent Price, then by Charlton Heston, and most recently by Will Smith) spirals into states of deep depression and psychological illness as a result of a years-long, complete lack of human company. Neville finds a way to overcome this situation of utter loneliness—to a degree, at least, and albeit in strange fashion—by holding conversations with shop-window dummies. For the mentally damaged Neville, his behavior is not unusual in the slightest. And how might any of us cope when faced with spending our days exterminating the risen dead and with not a single living soul to talk to? Perhaps, craving human contact, we too, would resort to doing exactly the same as Neville. It's interesting to note that shop-window dummies turn up in another series of stories that display distinct zombie-based overtones.

Dr. Who is a highly successful BBC television show that first aired in the United Kingdom back in November 1963. And it's still going strong to this very day. Amongst the most memorable and chilling of all the doctor's many alien and diabolical foes are the Daleks, the Cybermen, the Ice Warriors, and the Sea Devils. Then there are the Autons. They first made their appearance in 1970, in the series *Spearhead from Space*, at which time the late John Pertwee portrayed the time-travelling doctor. In the story, the Earth comes under attack from what is termed the Nestene Consciousness—a form of alien life that lacks any physical substance. And the very fact that the Nestene Consciousness is essentially ethereal in nature means it requires a vessel that can be relied on to wipe out the human race. So, it creates what become known as the Autons.

Although the Nestene Consciousness is, essentially, non-physical, it possesses the ability to manipulate plastic. As a result, and all across the United Kingdom, the alien intelligence embeds its homicidal, killer instincts into nothing less than plastic, shop-window dummies. It is a chilling sight indeed to see hordes of the Nestene-controlled, emotionless dummies breaking out of stores and roaming the streets of the U.K.—in distinctly zombie-like fashion—slaughtering anyone and everyone they encounter. Although *Spearhead from Space* is a sci-fi-driven drama, the graphic imagery that leaps out of the television screen practically screams "zombie apocalypse!"

Such was, and still is, the public's love for the Autons, just like the undead, they proved to be pretty much impossible to put down completely. They returned in the 1971 series, *Terror of the Autons*, in the 2005 story *Rose* and in 2010's *The Pandorica Opens*. One suspects that it won't be very long at all before those blank-faced dummies will, yet again, take to the streets, slaughter the public, and do battle with the world's most famous time-traveler, Dr. Who.

Matheson, Richard

Make mention of the name Richard Matheson to most people and you may be on the receiving end of a blank stare and a mere "huh?" Arguably, however, without the fine writing skills of Matheson, zombie culture would not be what it is today. A skilled and atmospheric author who died in June 2013, Matheson wrote regularly for the classic 1959–1964 television series, *The Twilight Zone*. Not only that, he was the brains behind one of the show's most loved and well remembered episodes: "Nightmare at 20,000 Feet," starring William Shatner, better known to all of us, of course, as *Star Trek's* Captain Kirk. Shatner's character, Bob Wilson, has a fear of flying that reaches stratospheric levels when a monstrous beast puts in an appearance—on the wing of the very plane in which Wilson is flying.

Before *The Twilight Zone*, however, there was a certain novel that Matheson penned in 1954. Its title was *I Am Legend*. If it sounds familiar, that's because Matheson's book, in 2007, was made into a blockbuster movie of the very same name that starred Will Smith. It was not the first cinematic version of Matheson's acclaimed story, however. Both *The Last Man on Earth*, which was filmed in 1964, and that featured Vincent Price in the lead role, and *The Omega Man*, of 1971—with Charlton Heston playing the main character—were based on *I Am Legend*.

In Matheson's story, the world has been devastated by human beings transformed into rabid, blood-devouring creatures of a definitively vampire-like nature. Not only do they crave human blood, but they cannot tolerate daylight, and can be killed by the traditional means of exposing them to garlic and thrusting wooden stakes into their hearts. Rather than being steeped in bloodsucking-themed

The late author Richard Matheson (shown here in 2008) penned the story *I Am Legend* that was adapted into the films *The Last Man on Earth* and *Omega Man,* as well as the Will Smith movie that used his original title.

folklore and myth, however, *I Am Legend*, presents the vampire outbreak as having been caused by a mysterious bacteria. It infects the living, takes their lives, and then causes them to soon walk the Earth again. The "*I*" of the book's title is Robert Neville, apparently the only uninfected person left on the whole planet.

Neville does his very best to try and defeat the inhuman hordes that have laid waste to his home city of Los Angeles, but, ultimately, it's all to no avail. Neville eventually realizes that not only is his quest to try and find a cure for the outbreak completely useless, but the worldwide transformation of the human race into something monstrous and terrifying has led to the creation of a brand new society. It is a society in which he, the last real man on Earth, has no place or role. Neville is now the outsider; for the vampire hordes it is he who is the strange and alien one, not them. Faced with such a stark and irreversible reality and a future in which he is now utterly redundant, Neville opts to end his life.

Although Richard Matheson's *I Am Legend* is steeped in matters of a vampire nature, it succeeded in bringing to the fore certain key issues that later found their ways firmly into the heart of zombie lore and entertainment. Namely, the outbreak of a seemingly incurable virus that mutates people into killing machines, the rapid spread of infection, a fruitless search for a cure for the disease, and the collapse of civilization. The writings of Richard Matheson left a significant mark on a young George Romero. Remarking on his first steps to bring *Night of the Living Dead* to life, Romero freely admits: "I had written a short story, which I basically had ripped off from a Richard Matheson novel called *I Am Legend*."

Without doubt, one only has to take a glance at Matheson's writing style to see how, and why, Romero was so profoundly influenced by it. Consider the following words, which are extracted from *I Am Legend*: "He jerked open the door and shot the first one in the face. The man went spinning back off the porch and two women came at him in muddy, torn dresses.... He kept firing the pistols until they were both empty. Then he stood on the porch clubbing them with insane blows, losing his mind almost completely when the same ones he'd shot came rushing at him again...."

Richard Matheson, a legend indeed.

Maya Prediction

If there is one thing that can be said with certainty about society today, it's that far more than a few people are absolutely sure we are living in the so-called End Times. There's barely a zombie movie or a television show on the undead that doesn't have the apocalypse at its heart. There is, however, a major problem when it comes to the controversial matter of the End Times. When we go looking for information on the end of the world, we quickly learn that predictions have been made for absolute centuries that the end of days is near. And it's here that we come to something that should help us all to breathe easier on the matter of the supposedly looming Armageddon: it never, ever comes. The predictions always collapse upon themselves.

You would think, by now, that we would have learned to be highly suspect of such predictions. Millions, however, have short memories and still faithfully believe the end is near, despite evidence to the contrary. Most recently, and ridiculously, this situation came to the fore in December 2012, when—all across the planet—countless people came to believe that the world was due to implode—or possibly explode. It was all the fault of the Mayans, and their beliefs that on December 21, civilization was going to come to a crushing and crashing end. It did not.

Probably the sanest commentator on the whole Mayan controversy is Marie Jones, the author of the book *2013: The End of Days or a New Beginning?* She retains a healthy but balanced skepticism and a welcome sense of humor on the entire matter of how and why we, as a species, are obsessed by world-ending scenarios. Leaving us in no doubt at all as to where she stands on the controversy, Jones begins: "So much of what the public reads about the 2012 enigma is just plain bunk, pure crap. It's either perpetuated for purposes of monetary gain, religious fear, or plain ignorance. But crap nonetheless. And, when it spreads, it can be very frustrating for anyone who has bothered to examine the facts and look for the truth."

She continues: "The Maya were amazingly ahead of their time when it came to observing nature and being able to identify cosmological and astronomical events based upon those observations. But, keep in mind, these are also people who painted each other blue and sacrificed each other to the gods. They had their limits."

With her feet firmly on the ground, Jones adds: "The end of the world predictions we all know and love come not from the scientific acumen of the Maya, but from their mythology, much of which was bastardized when they were conquered by the Spanish. Conquering nations has a tendency to rewrite the myths and original stories of the nations they conquer, as a way to snuff out beliefs that may be pagan or go against those of the conquerors."

Bastardized maybe, but for many, the 2012 phenomenon was still downright petrifying. There was, for example, a whole sub-culture within the 2012 research arena that believed December 21 would mark the terrifying return of Nibiru—or *Planet X*, as it has become infamously and ominously known in those circles where the conspiracy-minded hang out and share their tales of the unlikely kind.

Planet X is a world alleged to be a part of our own solar-system, but whose orbit around the Sun is so massive that only once in an extraordinarily long period of time does it ever come into view. Some said that it was going to do exactly that in December 2012. And guess what: its orbit was going to bring it so close to the Earth that planet-wide disaster would be all but inevitable.

More unfortunate for us, there was to be no last-minute salvation of the type that saw Bruce

Some experts on interpreting the Mayan calendar noticed that its cycle ended on December 21, 2012, and alarmists thought that this meant the Mayans were predicting the end of the world.

Willis saving the world in the 1998 production of *Armageddon*, while *Aerosmith* provided background, musical accompaniment. But some still saw hope on the horizon: If *Planet* X existed, and it was due to provoke worldwide disaster on December 21, 2012, then it should have been viewable via telescope long before. But, here's the thing: it wasn't. And it never has been, before or since.

There is something else too: the Nibiru concept was not on a single person's radar until 1995. That was when a woman named Nancy Lieder, who said she was in contact with extraterrestrials from a faraway world in the Zeta Reticuli system, announced that Nibiru was on its way. And, all thanks to the powerful, magnet-like gravity of Nibiru, our world was about to be turned upside down—and maybe even in *literal* fashion. The doomsayers soon got in a flurry of angst and excitement when Lieder said the end would be upon us in 2003. Well, correct me if I'm wrong (which I'm most definitely not), but didn't we all survive 2003 in just fine and dandy fashion? Yes, we did, which is why we were then told that the first date was incorrect and it was actually going to be December 2012. Ah. That we then proceeded to survive 2012 unscathed, too, is a very good pointer that the Nibiru story is complete and utter garbage.

Most people might simply roll their eyes at such a sorry state of affairs, but, as Marie Jones notes, there is a very serious and sad side to all of this. There are far more than a few fear-filled individuals out there whose lives have been absolutely blighted by what some have said about the ever-elusive *Planet* X and the apocalypse that keeps failing to put in its appearance.

Jones relates one particularly disturbing story: "About a year after my book *2013* came out, I began getting emails from people asking what they should do to prepare for the end. Some of them were heartbreaking, like one from a single mom in the South who had heard me on the radio and thought I would best steer her in the right direction, and wondered if she should sell her home and end her and her children's lives.

"I emailed back immediately to talk her off the ledge, giving her the facts and encouraging her to stay away from media and YouTube sensationalism. We exchanged emails for a few days and she was so relieved to see that what she feared was based upon false interpretation; mainly western apocalyptic tradition piled on the original Mayan mythology."

Well, in a world filled to near-bursting point with fictional zombies, lethal viruses, tsunamis, earthquakes, terrorist-attacks, seemingly never-ending Middle Eastern conflicts, avian-flu, catastrophic oil-leaks, drastic changes in weather, and melting ice-caps, is it actually any wonder that many people, such as the poor soul Marie Jones referred to above, really *do* see the final days as being definitively in the cards before this year is out? And, let's face it, the world of on-screen entertainment has had a big influence on the minds of the populace, too.

AMC's *The Walking Dead* and high-profile movies like *Contagion*; *Children of Men*; *28 Days Later*; *I am Legend*; *Knowing*; *Dawn of the Dead*; and, of course, *2012*, starring John Cusack, are great fun to watch, but they have all given end of the world-type scenarios massive shots of publicity, and mountains of depressing food for thought, over the course of the last decade. And, in the process, those same big-budget productions have also helped further nurture disaster-driven belief systems that the end might be right around the corner, as so many were keen to tell us as December 21, 2012 approached.

And let's face it: "Nothing is going to happen" fails to strike much of a chord with the movers and shakers in Hollywood. It's certainly not what book publishers want to hear either. On the other hand, "worldwide catastrophe is only months away" *does* strike a chord—a very big one too—and gets people into their local cinema, logging onto Amazon, or scanning the shelves of their local Barnes & Noble store.

Marie Jones has a few thoughts of her own on this very issue of apocalyptic entertainment: "The obsession we have with the end, I believe, is partially a subconscious attempt to come to grips vicariously, via movies, books, TV shows, and even prophecies of others, with the fear of non-existence. We all feel that fear. We share it as humans.

"One way to be able to handle our fears, without letting them destroy us, is to embrace them at arm's length or in a way that is safe. I think this same vicarious fear embracing is also responsible for the wave of zombie films that are so popular now, and has always been behind the allure of horror and some sci-fi movies. If we can watch others being killed, tortured, abducted, and eaten by zombies, it serves as an outlet for our own overwhelming fears of it happening to us, even though we consciously know it never would."

Upping the ante even further, she states: "I also believe this collective death wish has some arrogance and narcissism behind it. Those most convinced of their religious beliefs, that include apocalyptic scenarios, use the end of the world as a weapon to wield over those they deem as sinners, or wrong, and, of course, they themselves will be raptured and saved and are the chosen ones who will not die.

"This," Jones believes, "is the ultimate human arrogance, to believe that others deserve punishment for certain behaviors deemed sinful, as if we are able to be the final judge and jury on all of humanity. The funny thing is that these fundamentalists forget that their own Bible states that God is the final judge, not man. So won't they, then, also burn for judging others? Go figure."

And remember this: not a single prophecy in the history of the planet has ever been proven conclusively to have been all true. Not a single, solitary one. It was proclaimed by Nostradamus, the legendary French seer of the 1500s, that 1999 would mark the year in which a "great King of Terror will come from the sky." Sorry Nostradamus, but it didn't happen. Then there were those swirling and dire predictions that suggested when the twentieth century ended and a new one dawned, the dating format on computers that ran everything from cash-machines to our TV channels, and from the world's electrical grid to the nation's nuclear arsenal, would collapse and civilization would descend into anarchy overnight. Yet again, it didn't happen; none of it. As the song says, don't worry, be happy.

How, you might very reasonably ask, could the Maya have gotten so many folks totally convinced that they would not live to see December 22, 2012? To answer that question, we have to take a look at the concept behind the Mayan Long Count Calendar, as it is known. Despite what the gloomy and the end-loving crowd proclaimed, the Maya never predicted that the world was going to come to an irreversible halt on December 21, 2012. Not even once.

What the Maya actually said was that human civilization is defined by various cycles. Our cycle, so the Maya believed, is the fourth. And when was it to end? No prizes for guessing that it was December 21, 2012. But did the end of a cycle mean the end of the world and the extinction of all life on the planet? Well, yes, apparently for many, it *did* mean that. If, however, people had only taken the time to check out the facts, instead of having gotten their information from that bastion of truth and reliability known as the Internet, things might have been very different.

The reality is that no one really knew what the Maya meant by the end of a cycle—it was all very much down to personal opinion and interpretation. Most, however, chose to interpret things in just about the worst way possible. This tells us far less about what was going through the minds of the Maya way back when, and far more about the gloomy, apocalypse-obsessed mindset of people today. The whole 2012 fiasco was not the fault of the Maya. The problem lay with those twenty-first century souls for whom every day is filled with negativity, gullibility, or a high degree of both.

Megiddo

See also: Apocalypse, Armageddon, End Times, Norwegian Armageddon

For decades, tourists from all over the world have visited Tel Megiddo in great numbers, attracted by the site's apocalyptic mystique and the old battlegrounds' significance as the place where the fate of ancient empires was decided with the might of sword and spear. The Israel National Parks Authority works in close coordination with the Megiddo Expedition and the Ename Center for Public Archaeology of Belgium in offering visitors a dramatic perspective of the history of Armageddon.

As the millennium approached in the last months of 1999, Israeli police were presented with an unusual and potentially deadly problem that could affect the entire world. Fundamentalist Christians began to arrive in large numbers so they could be in Jerusalem when Armageddon occurred. These extremist Christians had equated the advent of the new millennium with the end of the world and the return of Jesus, and they wanted to be in the Valley of Megiddo to fight on the side of the angels against demonic hordes when the last great battle between good and evil took place. When it became apparent that some of the more fanatical millennialists were prepared to precipitate a conflict, and initiate Armageddon if the Lord should tarry, Israeli police had no choice other than to escort a number of these Christian warriors to the airport and demand that they leave Israel.

Revelation 16:16 declares Armageddon, the mound of Megiddo, as the battlefield where blasphemers, unclean spirits, and devils join forces for the final great battle of the ages between their evil hordes and the faithful angelic army of Christ. The inspiration for such a choice of battlegrounds was quite likely an obvious one for John the Revelator, for it has been said that more blood has been shed around the hill of Megiddo than any other single spot on Earth.

Located ten miles southwest of Nazareth at the entrance of a pass across the Carmel mountain range, it stands on the main highway between Asia and Africa and in a key position between the Euphrates and Nile Rivers, thus providing a traditional meeting place of armies from the East and from the West. For thousands of years, the Valley of Mageddon, now known as the Jezreel Valley, had been the site where great battles had been waged and the fate of empires decided. Thothmes III, whose military strategies made Egypt a world empire, proclaimed the taking of Megiddo to be worth the conquering of a thousand cities. During World War I in 1918, the British General Edmund Allenby broke the power of the Turkish army at Megiddo.

Most scholars agree that the word Armageddon is a Greek corruption of the Hebrew Har-Megiddo, the mound of Megiddo, but they debate exactly when the designation of Armageddon was first used. The city of Megiddo was abandoned sometime during the Persian period (539–332 B.C.E.), and the small villages established to the south were known by other names. It could well have been that John the Revelator, writing in the Jewish apocalyptic tradition of a final conflict between the forces of light and darkness, was well aware of the bloody tradition of the Hill of Megiddo and was inspired by the ruins of the city on its edge.

This model of Megiddo is located at the Tel Megiddo Museum in Israel. According to the Book of Revelation, this ancient site will be the focal point of Armageddon.

By the Middle Ages, theologians began to employ Armageddon as a spiritual concept without any conscious association with the Valley of Megiddo. Armageddon simply stood for the promised time when the returning Christ and his legions of angels would gather to defeat the assembled armies of darkness.

In the fourteenth century, the Jewish geographer Estori Ha-Farchi suggested that the roadside village of Lejjun might be the location of the biblical Megiddo. Ha-Farchi pointed out that Lejjun was the Arabic form of Legio, the old Roman name for the place. In the early nineteenth century, American biblical scholar Edwin Robinson travelled to the area of Palestine that was held at that time by the Ottoman Empire and he became convinced that Ha-Farchi was correct in his designation of the site as the biblical Megiddo. Later, explorers and archaeologists determined that the ruins of the ancient city lay about a mile north of Lejjun at what had been renamed by the Ottoman government as the mound of Tell el-Mutasellim, the hill of the governor.

Men in Black

Within the controversial field of UFO research there are very few things more menacing than the sinister *Men in Black* (MIB). In the highly successful trilogy of *Men in Black* movies, starring Will Smith and Tommy Lee Jones, the dark-suited ones are portrayed as the secret agents of an equally secret government agency that is doing all that it possibly can to keep the lid solidly on the alien presence on Earth. The Men in Black were not created by, or for, Hollywood, however.

The *Men in Black* movies were based upon a comic book series of the same name, which, in turn, was based upon genuine encounters with these macabre characters dating back to the latter part of the 1940s. The real Men in Black are very different than their movie counterparts, however. They are far less like government agents, and far more like definitive zombies—both in their appearance and their actions. The image that Smith and Jones portray on-screen is just about as far as you can get from the much darker reality of the situation.

Despite what many might think or assume, the real MIB do not force their way into the homes of witnesses to UFO activity. Most witnesses to the MIB note a very curious fact: when the Men in Black make their calls on those who have seen UFOs—calls that usually occur late at night, and long after the sun has set—they loudly knock on the door and, when the door is duly opened by the owner, who usually reacts with a heady mixture of fear and astonishment, they patiently wait to be invited in. Very few people need to be told that this action of not entering a person's home until specifically invited uneasily parallels the lore surrounding yet another undead monster that feeds upon the living: the grotesque, bloodsucking vampire.

Then there is the matter of the attire of the MIB. They wear the typical black suits and fedora-style hats that were chiefly in vogue in the 1940s and 1950s. But it's their physical appearance that matters. They seldom exceed five-feet, five-inches in height, they are very often thin to the point of near-emaciation, and their skin is described as being not just white, but milk-white and very sickly. As for those suits, they're not the cool, chic, expensive types worn by the likes of agents J and K in the films. Rather, they are crumpled and creased and give off a distinct odor very often described as musty and dirt-like—which strongly suggests in the minds of many witnesses and flying saucer enthusiasts that the MIB have been underground for a significant period of time, possibly even in nothing less than a grave.

Interestingly, the late John Keel—the author of the acclaimed book, *The Mothman Prophecies*—called this particular breed of MIB "the cadavers." He carefully noted their distinct, dead-like appearance, their total lack of human emotion, and the fact that many who encountered the Men in Black reported how they seemed to be feeding upon them. Not literally, in the sense of violently devouring them like a movie zombie would, but feeding psychically on their bodily energy, leaving them feeling weak, nauseated, and not unlike a diabetic in crashing mode. Are hostile space zombies in our very midst and living on our life-forces? Don't bet against it, and particularly so if, late one night, you hear a loud, slow and deliberate knocking on your door.

Timothy Green Beckley is someone who has deeply studied the many and varied complexities of the UFO phenomenon for decades. And that includes the mystery of the Men in Black. Beckley believes that the MIB may actually be normal, everyday people who have been placed under a form of mind-control, very much akin to the kind of zombification prevalent in Haitian lore.

Beckley reveals the details of one such example of many from his files: "There was one case where I might have been threatened by a Man in Black. There was a publication I wrote for in the 1970s called *Official UFO*. They published their address in the magazine, so they did get a few crank visitors to the offices. One of these was a gentleman who claimed he was being stalked by the Men in Black."

In time, Beckley met the man, and in the late 1970s and early 1980s, became the unwelcome recipient of a series of very threatening calls from this particular individual. Beckley decided to call the police, and the man was soon traced: it transpired he was a homeless person staying in Grand Central Station. Beckley adds that the man "must have called fifty times and left crazy, threatening messages that would go on and on. I spoke with his parents—who were in Florida—and they said that although he wasn't always like this, something came over him now and again."

Beckley suggests that: "With cases like this guy where something came over him, and with the MIB, it's like a possession, where a paranormal force takes possession of the person and they then *become* the Man in Black, doing what the force wants them to do, but without their knowledge. Afterwards, they might not even remember any of it. These people are living on the fringe of society; they are very simple-minded people who can very easily be controlled and influenced. Someone, say, who might be living in some rundown apartment, is taken over in a kind of trance, and then they become one of the Men in Black. They threaten someone, and then they go back to their normal life after the possession ends, and they don't remember it. But while they are under the control of whatever is doing this—aliens, maybe—they're not quite right. And like a zombie is the best way I can describe it."

Beckley's description is a highly apt one: George A. Romero's cannibalistic zombies in *Night of the Living Dead*—and, indeed in *all* of Romero's subsequent movies in the still-on-going *Dead* series—are utterly driven by two issues: the desire for self-preservation, and an unrelenting need to feed. The MIB are equally and similarly driven; however, their whole goal is to instill fear, rather than feed upon flesh and bone. But, just like the reanimated dead of the big-screen, the Men in Black, too, appear to lack anything more than a basic awareness of why, precisely, they are carrying out the actions they dutifully and never-endingly perform.

Microbiologists' Mystery Deaths

If there is one group of people who might be able to save us from the ravaging effects of a zombie outbreak, it's microbiologists. Their field of research is viruses and bacteria. When the dead rise from the grave or the ground, we will be reliant upon this unique and select body of people to see us through just about the hardest times possible. But, what if there are powerful figures out there that want a real zombie apocalypse to occur, possibly to combat the ever-increasing problems of a rapidly growing population? Having all those microbiologists around, who might very well be able to prevent the outbreak or quash it, would be a big and troublesome problem. It might be a problem that could be solved by killing off the microbiologists in advance of the planned apocalypse. Guess what? That is exactly what is happening.

In 1960, the human population was around three billion. In the 1990s it was in excess of five billion. Today, there are more than seven billion people on the planet. The United Nations estimates that by 2150 the figure may even be as high as *twenty-four billion*. With so many people needing food, water, and shelter, can the Earth offer what is required in terms of resources? The answer could very well be "no, not at all." This possibility has given rise to the idea that plans are secretly afoot to lower the world's population to a far more manageable figure of two or three billion. How to best achieve that without ravaging and irradiating the landscape with nuclear weapons? Well, maybe via having human turn upon human, in the form of the dead upon the living.

But, the chances are we'll all be okay, and particularly so with all those expert microbiologists to help us, right? Nope. In the last decade and a half, numerous people in the field of microbiology have died under very questionable circumstances, something that has given rise to the theory that all of the deaths are the work of government assassins. If someone is about to unleash a real zombie plague on us, now would be the ideal time to take out of circulation all those who might be able to stop that same plague from taking an unrelenting hold on the human race.

Many of those same microbiologists had ties to installations and secret facilities that we have come to know very well in the pages of this book, including the Dugway Proving Ground, Utah; Fort Detrick, Maryland; and the U.K.'s Porton Down. The long list of deaths includes: Dr. Benito Que, an expert in infectious diseases who was murdered on November 12, 2001; Dr. Vladimir Pasechnik, a Russian microbiologist who died under suspicious circumstances less than two weeks later; Harvard biologist Dr. Don C. Wiley, who allegedly killed himself on November 24; another Russian microbiologist, Alexi Brushlinski, who died on January 28, 2002, after being attacked on a Moscow, Russia street; and Dr. David Kelly, a British biological weapons expert who supposedly took his own life in England in July 2003—a suicide that many in the U.K.'s mainstream media had grave doubts about. And that is just the tip of the iceberg.

Today, the figure is in the dozens, demonstrating that microbiology is a hazardous career—not just because of the fact that it requires studying deadly viruses on a daily basis, but also because there are people with dark agendas that want the world's microbiologists gone, as in permanently. And might that be to ensure when the zombies walk there is no one left to come up with a chemical cocktail to counter them? That such a scenario just might be true is both sobering and worrying.

Millan, Mary

Mary Millan, known as Bloody Mary, was born on the bayou and was reared in the Crescent City. Mary, who has earned the title the Poet Priestess of the Spirit of New Orleans, inherited a rich tradition of spirit contact, clairvoyance, and healing.

A recipient of spirit visitation since she was a child, Mary learned to channel these spiritual powers into her work in Vodoun and Magick. Bloody Mary is devoted to educating the cautious public about the teachings of Vodoun and the unique gumbo that comprises the city of New Orleans.

Her official site is http://www.bloodymarystours.com/.

Mind Control

As we have seen, particularly in relation to the research of Wade Davis, and his book *The Serpent and the Rainbow*, sometimes a person can *appear* to be a zombie, when, in reality, they are actually under the influence of powerful, mind-altering drugs and neurotoxins. Davis' work focused to a significant degree on Haitian-based usage of such substances to provoke zombie-like states. Those who practiced Voodoo rituals and instilled zombie-style behavior in their victims were not alone, however. In the 1950s, none other than the CIA secretly delved into very similar territory—and in highly controversial fashion, too.

After its creation in 1947, the CIA established a number of highly classified programs designed to try and control and manipulate the human mind. The most notorious of all the many operations was known as Project MKUltra. Control of the psyche

The Serpent and the Rainbow **author Wade Davis.**

was achieved via chemical cocktails, psychedelics, and subliminal programming. The purpose of the project was to create armies of individuals who would be utterly under the control of their CIA masters, who would lack any and all self-will, and who, as a result of their programming, would follow just about every order under the sun, no matter how dicey or deadly they might turn out to be. They would, for all intents and purposes, be old-school zombies. To understand the sheer extent to which the CIA not only sought to harness the mind, but actually succeeded in doing so beyond its wildest dreams, we have to go back to 1953. On April 13 of that year, MKUltra was officially, albeit very secretly, approved by the CIA. Its goals were, to say the absolute very least, grim in the extreme.

They included creating "substances which will promote illogical thinking and impulsiveness;" "materials and physical methods which will produce amnesia for events preceding and during their use;" "physical methods of producing shock and confusion over extended periods of time and capable of surreptitious use;" "substances which produce physical disablement;" "a knockout pill which can surreptitiously be administered in drinks, food, cigarettes, as an aerosol, etc., which will be safe to use, provide a maximum of amnesia, and be suitable for use by agent types on an ad hoc basis;" and "a material which can be surreptitiously administered by the above routes and which in very small amounts will make it impossible for a man to perform any physical activity whatsoever."

Moreover, the development of substances that could induce large scale amnesia, altered thinking, and changes in bodily movements and physical abilities, collectively create in the mind's eye imagery that harks back to the days of the enslaved zombies of the Haitian variety. The CIA's zombies, however, were to be used for something more than Voodoo-based practices. For the Agency, one of the main goals of MKUltra was to have an army of mind-controlled 007's; secret agents who would be programmed to assassinate just about anyone the CIA wanted gone, and who, after they had performed their murderous assignments, would have no recollection of their actions. And even if, by chance, they did remember, they would be at a loss to explain why they seemingly, illogically, and out of the blue, went on sudden and violent killing sprees.

In light of the above, it's not at all surprising that many conspiracy theorists suspect that certain infamous assassins—including Lee Harvey Oswald, Sirhan Sirhan, and Mark David Chapman—may have been hypnotized and chemically controlled to target famous figures, such as President John F. Kennedy, his brother, Robert, and former Beatle, John Lennon. This trio of Oswald, Sirhan, and Chapman may not have been the lone gunmen that many assume them to have been. They may have been something entirely different: definitive CIA zombies.

The Monkey's Paw

A deeply atmospheric, and undeniably fear-filled tale, *The Monkey's Paw* was penned in 1902 by author William Wymark Jacobs. It tells the tragic saga of the White family. They are friends with one Sergeant-Major Morris of the British Army, who, while visiting them, reveals the strange story of the withered and shriveled monkey's paw that he has acquired. Possessed of, or cursed by, Voodoo-style magic, the old paw has the power to grant three wishes. Morris guards against anyone using the old paw, however, as doing so only provokes tragedy—and very often death. Unwisely, and unknown to Morris, Mr. White retrieves the paw after Morris throws it into a blazing fireplace. That's when dire trouble begins.

The Whites are in need of a considerable sum of money to pay for their house— money they do not have. Mr. White takes hold of the paw and asks that it help him out of his woeful financial situation. The power of the paw does exactly that, but most assuredly not in the fashion that Mr. White was expecting or hoping for. In the wake of White's unwise pact of the paranormal kind, his son, Geoffrey, is killed in horrific fashion while at work—his body is violently disfigured after he falls into machinery. As a result, the White family receives financial compensation from their son's employer, eerily in the very sum needed to pay off the house mortgage.

Mrs. White, utterly distraught and deranged at the death of her son, very unwisely asks her husband to make use of the monkey's paw once again—namely to bring their son back to life. Seeing how devastated his wife is, Mr. White grudgingly agrees to have the deadly paw grant him a second wish. It works all too well. There is a loud banging on the front door of their home. Mrs. White rushes to the door, overjoyed that her son has returned. Her husband, however—knowing that Geoffrey has been rotting in the ground for eight days, and was hideously mutilated at the time of his death—realizes he should never have asked for his son to return and wishes him to be back in his grave. Sure enough, the pounding on the door ceases and Geoffrey is gone. The three wishes have resulted in nothing but death and disaster. *The Monkey's Paw* is a decidedly cautionary tale, one that reminds us to be very careful about what we yearn for. We may get it, but not in the way we expect it or want it.

Monster Island, Monster Nation, **and** *Monster Planet*

Even the most cursory search of a good, online bookseller will demonstrate that zombie-themed novels are just about as widespread as the dead are twenty-four hours after the apocalypse has kicked in. Certainly, there are literally dozens upon dozens of such titles. Many of them, however, are hastily, and very badly written, and are usually only available in e-format. In other words, respectable publishers won't touch them with the proverbial pole. That's not to say there aren't a few exceptions to the majority: there certainly are. Take, for example, David Wellington's trilogy of the flesh-munching variety: *Monster Island*, *Monster Nation*, and *Monster Planet*. If you want a lesson in how to write a good, entertaining zombie novel, check out Wellington's books.

The first book in the three-part series quickly plunges us deep into the heart of the reanimated action, as the world steadily collapses and the dead savagely turn upon the living—or, far more correctly, upon the ragged remnants of all that is left of the living. In *Monster Island*, we are introduced to a trio of memorable characters: Dekalb, who was a weapons-inspector for the United Nations before things went straight to hell; a teenage Somali girl named Ayaan, who is an expert when it comes to using a gun; and one Gary Fleck, a zombie whose mind is certainly focused on devouring the living, but who, incredibly and near-uniquely, still possesses his pre-zombie faculties. That's right: Fleck's mindless zombie is not quite so mindless, after all. As for the action, it's chiefly focused on Ayaan and Dekalb's sterling attempts to reach the heart of ravaged New York City and find vital meds that will hopefully help stave off the escalating cataclysm. Things don't quite go to plan, however, which means—for the reader—a great deal of entertaining mayhem, carnage, and death in what is now a city of the dead.

Although *Monster Nation* is the second book in the series, the story it tells is a prequel to *Monster Island*. In this book, Wellington takes us right back to the very start of the zombie outbreak. Panic and fear are erupting all across the United States, as reports surface of violent, murderous attacks on the living by people that are now something far more, or something far less, than their fellow Americans. Military personnel valiantly struggle, but ultimately fail, to control the growing disaster, Los Angeles is about to fall victim to the flesh-eaters, and there are—maybe—just a few, key characters left that stand a chance of saving the day. Or do they? Well, given that a third title follows, it's fair and accurate to say that *Monster Nation* hardly has what could be termed the most pleasant of all endings possible. But, come on, who wants "pleasant" when you're reading a zombie novel?

There is a nice twist to the final installment in Wellington's trilogy. Rather than following directly on from the events chronicled in *Monster Island*, the third and concluding chapter is set more than a decade down the line. This is, without a doubt, Wellington's most alternative, and outrageously entertaining, of all three books in the series, as it takes accepted zombie lore and firmly turns it on its head. Ayaan is still very much with us, having managed to survive twelve years of continuous zombie mayhem, as are not just the brainless dead, but the highly intelligent and evil dead, too. Add to that a wizard from Wales and you have a mind-warping tale that takes the reader to a final confrontation and a final countdown. Zombies vs. humans: the last battle is on.

Monster of Glamis

Situated just west of Forfar, Scotland, Glamis Castle is referred to by Shakespeare in *Macbeth*; Macbeth of its title having killed King Duncan there in 1040. And it is also at the castle where assassins murdered King Malcolm II in 1034. In addition, Glamis Castle was the childhood home of both Queen Elizabeth II and the Queen Mother, and the birthplace of Princess Margaret. And then there is the castle's very own monster.

Jon Downes, the director of the British-based Center for Fortean Zoology—one of the few full-time groups dedicated to the search for unknown creatures, such as Bigfoot, the Loch Ness Monster, and the Abominable Snowman—notes that "the castle is the site of a well known and semi-legendary beast known as the Monster of Glamis. It's said that the creature was supposed to have been the hideously deformed heir to the Bowes-Lyon family and who was, according to popular rumor, born in about 1800, and died as recently as 1921."

Jon digs further into the puzzle: "Legend has it that the monster was supposed to look like an enormous flabby egg, having no neck and only minute arms and legs but possessed incredible strength and had an air of evil about it. Certainly, there is a family secret concerning the monster, which is only told to the male heir of the Bowes-Lyon family when they attain majority."

He continues: "But according to the author Peter Underwood, who has looked into this case, the present Lord Strathmore knows nothing about the monster, presumably because the creature has long been dead, but he always felt that there was a corpse or coffin bricked up behind the walls."

So says local folklore and oral tradition, the existence of the terrifying creature was allegedly known to only four men at any given time, namely the Earl of Strathmore, his direct heir, the family's lawyer, and the broker of the estate. At the age of

Glamis Castle in Scotland has long been the home of royalty, and it is also the home of the Monster of Glamis, who was supposedly the malformed member of the wealthy Bowes-Lyon family who lived during the nineteenth century.

twenty-one each succeeding heir was told the truth of the terrible secret and shown the rightful—and horrendously deformed—Earl, and succeeding family lawyers and brokers were also informed of the family's shocking secret.

As no Countess of Strathmore was ever told the story, however, one Lady Strathmore, having indirectly heard of such tales, quietly approached the then broker, a certain Mr. Ralston, who flatly refused to reveal the secret and who would only say by way of a reply, "It is fortunate that you do not know the truth for if you did you would never be happy."

So, was the strange creature of the castle a terribly deformed soul with some bizarre genetic affliction or something else? While the jury, inevitably, remains steadfastly out, it's an intriguing fact that in 1912, in his book, *Scottish Ghost Stories*, Elliott O'Donnell published the contents of a letter that he had received from a Mrs. Bond who had spent time at Glamis Castle and who underwent an undeniably weird encounter while staying there.

In her letter to O'Donnell, rather notably, Mrs. Bond described a somewhat supernatural encounter with a beast that was possessed of nothing less than distinct ape-like qualities, rather than specifically human attributes. Might it be the case, then, that the beast of Glamis was not simply a man with appalling genetic abnormalities, but some terrifying ape-like beast—a definitive wild-man or ape-man, perhaps?

That the man-beast lived for more than 120 years, and was deemed to be so violent that it had to be kept imprisoned for all of its life has led to the development of an even more controversial theory: that the Monster of Glamis was a zombie, one kept alive by its family, who could not bear to see its life ended, even if it was no longer truly human. Here we see something very much akin to the scenario in AMC's *The Walking Dead* television series, in which the character known as the Governor (played by actor David Morrissey) keeps his zombified daughter locked in a small room, chiefly because he simply cannot face killing her—even though she is one of the definitive undead.

The truth—whatever it may one day prove to be—remains hidden behind closed doors. Just like the creature, or zombie, itself.

Morley, Anthony

In April 2008, Anthony Morley, thirty-six, a handsome chef from Leeds who had won the Mr. Gay UK title in 1993, killed Damian Oldfield, thirty-three, a former lover, then carved flesh from his body and made a meal of it. Morley, it could be argued, was sexually confused, for at the time that he won the Mr. Gay UK title he also had a steady girlfriend. There seems to be nothing at all to indicate why he suddenly became a murderer and a cannibal.

On the day of the murder, Morley and Oldfield went to the chef's apartment where they had sex, then cuddled in bed to watch the film *Brokeback Mountain*, a 2005 film about two men who find they are attracted to each other.

Suddenly, it seemed, without any provocation, Morley slashed Oldfield's throat and stabbed him several times. When his sometime lover was dead, Morley sliced sections of his thigh and chest and set about making a meal of the cuts. Police, investigating a complaint from neighboring apartments, found six pieces of human flesh on a chopping board, cooked so they were raw in the middle and browned on the edges. Some olive oil and seeds were found on the kitchen's work surface and a frying pan was waiting on the stove. Morley was chewing a piece of flesh when the police apprehended him.

Morley told the Leeds Crown Court in October 2008 that he had no memory of killing Damian Oldfield. His barrister argued that Morley was not guilty on the grounds of diminished capacity. It took the jury two hours and twenty minutes to find Anthony Morley guilty of murder.

Such cannibals as Anthony Morley, who was found guilty of a solitary slaying, are hardly worthy of mention when compared to Fritz Haarman (1879–1925). The famous Hanover Vampire bit and slashed his victims to death, then ate their flesh. What he didn't eat himself, Haarman sold as fresh meat in his butcher shop.

Jeffrey Dahmer (1960–1994) killed, dismembered, butchered, and ate portions of at least 18 of his human victims. When police entered his apartment, they discovered nine severed heads, seven in various stages of being boiled, four male torsos stuffed into a barrel, and several assorted sections of male genitalia stored in a pot. At his trial, Dahmer described how he cooked the biceps of one of his victims and seasoned it with salt and pepper and steak sauce.

Mouths

If there is one part of the anatomy of a zombie that should be avoided at all cost, it is, without any shadow of doubt, the mouth. When the savage jaws of the undead clamp down on the living, it is pretty much the end of the line for the victim. In no time at all—and as a result of the virus of the dead now coursing and swirling through their bloodstream—they, too, will very soon join the rank ranks of the revived monsters. But it's not just the people of today that recognize it is far from wise to get close to, and kissy with, a zombie. The people of ancient Ireland were deeply aware of those very same hazards, and centuries ago, too.

In 2005, a series of excavations undertaken by archaeologists began in County Roscommon, Ireland. The ambitious program was part of a survey of medieval churches throughout the area. During the course of the excavations, an old graveyard was uncovered, something which led to a startling and sinister discovery. Some of the bodies contained in the graveyard—which were estimated to have been laid to rest between the seventh and fourteenth centuries—had been buried in a very unusual fashion.

The team-leader, Chris Read, of the Sligo, Ireland-based Institute of Technology, noted that, of the bodies in question: "One of them was lying with his body straight up. A large black stone had been deliberately thrust into his mouth. The other had his head turned to the side and had an even larger stone wedged quite violently into his mouth so that his jaws were almost dislocated."

Read added, rather notably, that: "The stones in the mouth might have acted as a barrier to stop revenants from coming back from their graves," as the mouth was perceived in earlier times as being "the main portal for the soul to leave the body upon death." There was a longstanding belief, Read expanded, that an evil spirit could enter the body of the dead, via the mouth, and then do nothing less than revive it.

One might also be inclined to suggest that the stones were firmly inserted into the mouths of the newly deceased for a very different reason: to prevent them from fatally attacking and biting the living after reanimation set in.

Mummies

See also: Burial Traditions, Cemeteries and Tombs, Funerals

Perhaps of all the classic monsters that have terrified theater audiences and groups gathered around campfires, the two most likely to be confused with one another are the mummy and the zombie. One thinks of curses and spells associated with both of these beings. Of course, the principal difference is that the mummies pronounce curses upon those who disturb their elegant tombs, while zombies lie for a time in crude graves because a curse has been placed upon them.

When Boris Karloff emerged as Im-ho-Tep in *The Mummy* (1932), his 3,700-year-old reanimated body set out to punish those who had disturbed his tomb, as well as to reclaim his reincarnated lover. In *The Mummy's Hand* (1940), Universal Studios initiated the first of a series of films featuring the mummified High Priest Kharis, who is revived by a mixture of tana leaves. Kharis, first played by Tom Tyler, slowly shuffles toward his victims, but always manages to catch them, even though he is dragging one leg, and one arm remains bound to his mummy wrappings.

In each of the four entries in the Kharis series, the lovely actresses who played his reincarnated lover from ancient Egypt were never able to escape his clutches, despite their appearing sound of body enough to easily outrun the shambling mummy. In 1942, Lon Chaney, Jr. took over the role of Kharis in *The Mummy's Tomb*. Chaney wrapped himself in gauze again in *The Mummy's Ghost* (1944) and *The Mummy's Curse* (1945), always assuming the same shuffling gait that actors impersonating the undead have used in nearly every mummy and zombie movie made until quite recently. In *28 Days Later*, (2002) the zombies definitely run as they chase the survivors of a plague that has afflicted London.

As early religions began to teach that there was a spirit within each person who died that might someday wish to return to its earthly abode, it became increasingly important that efforts be made to preserve the body. Burial ceremonies, which had at first been intended solely as a means of disposing of the dead, came to be a method of preserving the physical body as a home for the spirit when it returned for a time of rebirth or judgment.

The ancient Egyptians as a culture were preoccupied with the specter of death. There was never an ancient people who insisted upon believing that death was not the final act of a human being, that it is not death to die, with more emphasis than the Egyptians.

Today, in many countries such as the United States, Canada, Great Britain, and the European nations, bodies are embalmed and every effort is made to preserve the body as long as possible. Coffins are sold to the bereaved families as dependable containers that will be able to preserve and protect the body of their beloved for centuries. The wealthier bereaved can afford crypts and vaults that are placed above ground and constructed of concrete or granite to contain family coffins.

Famous actor Boris Karloff is at his creepy best in 1932's *The Mummy* in which he portrays a 3,700-year-old Egyptian brought back to life.

Embalming the body of the deceased was practiced in ancient Egypt where the warm, dry climate assured its success. The Egyptians anointed, embalmed, and buried their dead, and made mummies of the men and women of power, rank, and importance.

To mummify, the Egyptians extracted the brain and the intestines, cleaned out the body through an incision in the side, and filled the body cavities with spices. The body was then sewn up and set aside to lie in salt for a period of seventy days. Then it was placed in gummed mummy cloth and fastened into its ornamental case. The poorer classes were not mummified but merely salted.

If the body of a vengeful mummy moves bereft of brain and other vital parts, there has to be a powerful spirit residing in or near the deceased that drives it. That spirit is known as the Ka. In the cosmology of the early Egyptians, humans were considered the children of the gods, which meant that they had inherited many other elements from their divine progenitors than physical bodies. The ba or soul was portrayed on the walls of tombs as a human-headed bird leaving the body at death. During a person's lifetime, the ba was an intangible essence, associated with the breath. In addition to the ba, each person possessed a ka, a kind of ghostly double that was given to each individual at the moment of birth. When the person died, the ka began a separate existence, still resembling the body that it formerly occupied, and still requiring food for sustenance. Each person also had a ren or name, which could acquire a separate existence and was the underlying substance of all ones integral aspects.

In addition to the facets listed above, there was the khu or intelligence, the ab or will, the sakkem or life force, the khaybet or shadow, the ikh or glorified spirit, and the sahu or mummy. But the most important of all these was the ka, which became the center of the cult of the dead. It was to the ka that all offerings of food and material possessions were made.

When death came to the Egyptians, the physical body did not decay, for the greatest care was taken to preserve the body as a center of individual spirit manifestation. The body was carefully embalmed and mummified and placed in a coffin, on its side, as if it were only asleep. In the tomb with the mummy were brought all the utensils that a living person might need on a long journey, together with toilet articles, vessels for water and food, weapons and hunting equipment to protect against robbers, and to provide food once the initial supply was depleted.

About 1580 B.C.E., the Pyramid Texts, the oldest extant funerary literature in the world, dating back to as early as the Fourth millennium B.C.E., and certain revised editions of those texts called the Coffin Texts, were brought together, re-edited, added to, and painted on sarcophagi, and written on papyrus. This massive literary effort, the work of many authors and compilers, is known to us as the Book of the Dead, but to its creators as The Chapters of Coming Forth by Day. Although there are many known copies of this ancient work, no one copy contains all the chapters, which are thought to number around 200.

By the time the text of the Book of the Dead was being copied on rolls of papyrus and placed in the tombs of the dead, a great social and religious revolution had taken place. Whereas the Pyramid Texts were meant only to be inscribed on the sarcophagi of the royals, it was now decreed that any one commoner or noble-born who could afford the rituals would be entitled to follow the god Osiris into the afterlife.

The most important ceremony associated with the preparation of the dead was the opening of the eyes, mouth, ears, and nose of the deceased. This rite guaranteed life to the body and made it possible for the ba to re-enter its former dwelling.

The Book of the Dead also contained certain holy incantations that were designed to free the ka from the tomb and allow it to be incarnated again. The spirit might experience an existence as a hawk, a heron, or even a plant form, such as a lotus or a lily, moving along through various expressions of the life force until, after about 3,000 years, it could once again achieve rebirth as a human.

When an ancient Egyptian died, he or she expected to appear before Osiris, who would be waiting to pass judgment on him or her. The deceased would be led in by the jackal-headed god Anubis, followed by the goddess Isis, the divine enchantress, representing life, and the goddess of the underworld Nephthys, representing death. There were forty-two divine judges to assess the life of the one who stood before them, and the deceased would be allowed to deny forty-two misdeeds. Once the deceased had presented his or her case, Osiris indicated a large pair of balances before them with the

This Egyptian mummy can be seen at the Philadelphia Academy of Natural Sciences. The process of mummifcation mastered by these ancient people successfully preserved bodies for centuries.

heart of the deceased and the feather of truth, one in each of the pans. The god Thoth read and recorded the decision. Standing in the shadows was a monstrous creature prepared to devour the deceased should the feather of truth outweigh his or her heart. In those instances when the heart outweighed the feather and few devout Egyptians could really believe that their beloved Osiris would condemn them, the deceased was permitted to proceed to the Fields of Aalu, the real world, where the gods lived. Because humans were the offspring of the gods, the ancient Egyptians had no doubt about their immortality.

Mutants

A zombie-based love story that actually works very well is hardly the easiest of things to achieve, and particularly so for discerning cinema audiences with plenty of movies of the undead to choose from. But, writers Louis-Paul Desanges and David Morlet did exactly that, and much more too, with their film *Mutants*. A French production made in 2009, *Mutants* tells the tumultuous tale of Sonia, who is an ER doctor, and Marco, her boyfriend, portrayed by actors Helene de Fougerolles and Francis Renaud.

Made very much in the mayhem-filled mode of the 2004 version of *Dawn of the Dead*, *Mutants* is stuffed to the brim with fast-running zombies and lots of gore and blood. It could be said that *Mutants* is, perhaps, one of the most violently graphic of all films dealing with the hordes of the undead. Added to the fact that the pace of the film is easily as manic as the infected themselves, and you have on your plate a production well worth watching, if you can stomach it, that is.

Whereas in many zombie productions the cast are simply there to provide welcome food for the zombies and high entertainment for the viewers, Sonia and Marco are very much fleshed out for the audience. In short, we quickly begin to care for them and about them. When a planet-wide outbreak of a deadly virus erupts—one that, as if you hadn't already guessed, transforms people into violent, murderous maniacs— Sonia and Marco do all they can to beat the odds. Sadly, those odds are inevitably stacked against them and it's not long at all before Marco quickly becomes infected. In an unforeseen twist, however, Marco swallows tainted blood, rather than succumbing to a savage bite, which has the effect of lessening the speed at which the infection spreads throughout his body.

Sonia, seemingly immune to the disease, tries her very best to save her beloved Marco and keep their love intact. Sonia's very best isn't anywhere near good enough, however. It never is in these situations. It is as matters deteriorate for Marco that we see why, exactly, the movie is called *Mutants*. Not unlike Jeff Goldblum's equally ill-fated character, Seth Brundle, in the 1986 remake of *The Fly*, the infected of *Mutants* go through a terrible, physical transformation: Marco's teeth, for example, fall out; his hair drops out in clumps, and he pees large amounts of blood. A change in life isn't necessarily always a good thing.

Matters become even more downright nightmarish for Sonia when, thanks to the unstoppable march of the infection coursing through his veins, Marco finally becomes her deadly enemy. The virus has now taken its horrific, unrelenting hold upon him. A fight to the death is firmly on the cards in a movie that makes one thing very clear: not even the power of love itself can overcome the zombie virus. *Romeo and Juliet* for the zombie era? No, *Mutants* is not. But it *is* just about the closest thing to it that you will find.

Naegleria fowleri

When it comes to the subject of the eating of brains—and specifically *human* brains—the zombie has a fierce and deadly competitor. Its name is *Naegleria fowleri*. Unlike the average member of the undead club—which is easy to spot, but far less easy to escape—*Naegleria fowleri* is, for all intents and purposes, invisible. There's a very good reason for that: it's an incredibly minute, single-celled amoeba. Nevertheless, it arguably wreaks more havoc upon the human brain than any zombie ever could.

Although it is extremely rare for someone to have a close encounter of the very worst kind with *Naegleria fowleri*, it is a bleak reality that the vast majority of people who fall victim to this tiny, lethal organism do not recover: death comes swiftly. And not surprisingly, since this deadly amoeba has but one goal in mind: to utterly destroy brain-tissue, bit by bit, and step by step.

Since *Naegleria fowleri* is primarily located in freshwater locations, such as rivers and lakes, it is typically swimmers that find themselves bitten by the beastly bug, so to speak. Typically, *Naegleria fowleri* enters the body via the nose, and from there it immediately makes its unstoppable way to the brain. At that point, death is already, albeit unknowingly, nearly inevitable. Rather ironically, the initial symptoms—that typically begin to manifest barely a day or so after infection—are not unlike those portrayed in zombie-themed movies and television shows when infection first occurs. They include: a raging fever, a pounding headache, constant nausea, and—as *Naegleria fowleri* begins its zombie-like devouring of the brain—violent seizures and hallucinations that can result in rage and fear. Within five days, or thereabouts, it's all over. Entire portions of brain tissue are gone. The victim is dead and the brain-eater is fully sated—just like its undead counterpart is after a typical attack on the living.

Fortunately, there is one very big difference between the brain-eaters of horror-based entertainment and *Naegleria fowleri*: infection does not spread beyond the initial host. Not even saliva can transmit the deadly amoeba from person to person. That is certainly not to say, however, that its potential seriousness should be ignored. Currently, the average survival rate for people who are diagnosed with *Naegleria fowleri* is less than one percent. Of the nearly 130 U.S. citizens who have died after becoming infected since 1962, only one has survived to make a full recovery. With statistics like that, you would very likely have a better chance of fighting off a brain-eating zombie than you would a brain-eating amoeba.

NASA and Super Plagues

In *Night of the Living Dead*, George A. Romero used—to excellent effect, it must be said—the scenario of a contaminated U.S. space vehicle returning to Earth and, as a result, unleashing something highly infectious and undeniably deadly on the world's population. As a result, in a shockingly short space of time the world is plunged into unending chaos. Those who think that such a thing could never happen might want to think twice about that, particularly in light of certain statements that were made by NASA—the National Aeronautics Space Administration—in September 2012.

Imagine the scene: it's just a few decades from now and NASA launches a manned-mission to our nearest, neighboring planet, Mars. While on the red planet, the crew is unknowingly infected with a deadly pathogen of extraterrestrial origin. When the mission is over, and as they prepare to begin their journey back to Earth, the effects of the alien virus begin to take hold. It soon becomes apparent that the astronauts are infected. The big question, however, is: infected with what? And this begs an even bigger question: if there was a fear that the astronauts were infectious, and that the possibility was discussed that no cure might be found for the alien plague, would the crew even be allowed to return to Earth? Or, would the perhaps half a dozen brave explorers be sacrificed to prevent potentially billions of people dying as a result of an alien outbreak?

Here we come to the work of Catharine "Cassie" Conley, who is NASA's Planetary Protection Officer. As well as ensuring that any planets that NASA may visit in the future remain free of contamination by human pathogens, it is part of Conley's work to ensure that the opposite does not occur: the outbreak of an alien super-plague on our home-world. So far, thankfully, there appears to be a lack of any hard evidence suggesting that a strange and unearthly virus of outer space proportions has ever affected the human race. The fact that NASA has staff engaged in "planetary protection" research to prevent the unthinkable from happening, however—and to take steps to ensure that all possible scenarios are considered— suggests that we might be wise to keep a careful eye on the heavens above.

If, one day, we find ourselves plunged into an apocalyptic world where the dead roam and rule, it may not be the result of reckless dabbling by the scientific and medical communities. Death and reanimation may actually result from nothing less than a Martian invasion. This invasion, however, may not occur via the use of fantastic spaceships and mind-boggling, advanced weaponry of the alien variety. Instead, the zombie hordes may rise up as a result of an invisible-to-the-eye Martian virus.

Native American Cannibals

Although the Aztecs were well-known for their ritual cannibalism, only the Karankawa tribe of southeast Texas was accused of practicing cannibalism on their defeated enemies. None of the other 1,200 Native American tribes engaged in the eating of human flesh ritual or otherwise. Of course, as happens on occasion in contemporary times, there may have been times when groups of individuals were stranded in snow storms or other situations of enforced isolation when cannibalism was prompted by necessity. Other than such extraordinary situations, cannibalism was not a culturally approved practice by any tribe and those who were caught in such a perversity were put to death. The Mohawk tribe was called the man-eaters, but contemporary tribal leaders insist that was due to their ferocity as warriors, not their dietary preference.

Nazis

See also: Adolf Hitler, World War II

Experiments in reviving the dead through the use of electrical stimulation were not lost upon Nazi scientists. We do know that the doctors in the various concentration camps were under orders from the Fuhrer to conduct experiments on reviving the dead and to learn anything about the human body that could aid the German people in becoming superior examples of the species.

In Auschwitz experiments were conducted on prisoners to see how long it would take to lower the body temperature until death came. Next, several methods were employed to see if it were possible to bring the victims back to life. Such tests were deemed important because of the German troops suffering the terrible cold of the Eastern front in the invasion of Russia.

Other prisoners, selected largely from groups of Jews or Gypsies, were submerged in water and timed to determine how long a person could survive under such conditions. This was deemed an important experiment that could aid Nazi aviators shot down over oceans, rivers, and lakes and keep them alive after ditching. Experienced aviators were becoming scarce as the war progressed, and every effort had to be made to keep them afloat and alive in the water.

Nazis SS officer Dr. Josef Mengele used imprisoned Jews, gypsies, and other minorities to perform sadistic and bizarre medical experiments.

Dr. Josef Mengele, the infamous Angel of Death, conducted his horrible experiments primarily to learn if the Master Race could be improved genetically. For example, blue eye color was preferred, so he sought a means of altering eye color by injecting various dyes. Unfortunately, such procedures resulted only in painful infections and blindness in his test subjects.

Mengele also infected healthy individuals with numerous viruses to see how long they might live untreated. Cruelly, he removed prisoners' limbs without anesthesia to see how long they would survive unattended.

Mengele often selected his victims by deciding that they possessed satanic bloodlines. Many hapless individuals for his experiments were selected because they came from orphanages, foster care homes, or incestuous families, and were pronounced as expendable, meaning, if any of them should die during the experiments, they would not likely be missed. They were fulfilling their destiny as the chosen ones, those who had been selected to give their lives so the Third Reich could achieve perfection. This cold-hearted dismissal of accidents which resulted from the consequences of harsh experiments is said to have been coined by Mengele at Auschwitz.

All of these cruel and sadistic experiments were conducted in order to help keep the Nazi soldier healthy and strong. Hitler and his inner circle did not want to lose any more fine examples of the Master Race than necessary. Early on in their master plan for world dominance, the hierarchy of the Third Reich had decided that it would be far less risky to find some means of enslaving the minds of those opposed to their politics and their treacherous invasions rather than having to endanger members of the stalwart German youth by fighting bloody wars.

Near Death Experience

In March 1968, a man named Paul Garratt was involved in a near-deadly car crash while driving to work in Santa Cruz, California. Thankfully, an ambulance was on the scene very quickly—which was incredibly good news for Garratt, as at one point his heart stopped beating. Fortunately, and thanks to the work of the hospital staff, he was brought back from the edge unscathed. Actually, it's more correct to say he was brought back *physically* unscathed. Mentally and psychologically, Garratt was traumatized in the extreme.

Most people will be aware of the concept of so-called Near Death Experiences, or NDEs. Typically, people report that at the moment of death, and before resuscitation occurs, they find themselves moving towards a bright white light. It is an experience that is often accompanied by sightings of dead relatives, friends, and even deities of varying religions. Skeptics argue that this is all due to the complex nature of the human brain and a dwindling lack of oxygen as death approaches. Try, however, telling that to those that have experienced NDEs. The experience is generally an uplifting, life-changing, and transformative one that has a profound, positive effect on the person. But not always: take the case of Paul Garratt, whose experience was memorably horrific in nature.

According to Garratt, while his NDE began with an encounter with the typical bright white light that so many other people have reported, he suddenly found himself plunged into a dark realm of terrible and nightmarish proportions. It was, he said, as if he was lifted, without warning, high into the air by an invisible force, and then unceremoniously dropped a great distance. There was nothing positive about the place in which Garratt suddenly found himself. It would be very apt to say it was downright hellish, since that's exactly where Garratt quickly came to believe he had been dispatched: hell. This was not, however, the traditional and fairy-tale-like hell of fire, brimstone, and a fork-tailed devil that so many envisage it to be.

Still able to recall the events years later, Garratt described a world in which the never-ending sand-like landscape was of a light-blue color, while the sky was of a deep purple hue. And, also unlike the typical imagery of hell, this place was not just cold but absolutely frozen. But, worst of all, was the sight of what Garratt estimated were hundreds of thousands of naked people, all lying flat on the ground, but screaming in a mixture of pain and terror. Above them were huge numbers of saucer-shaped objects of a light brown color—around the size of an average car—that looked like machines. Garratt, however, for reasons he could not explain, believed the machines were living creatures, about to perform some awful task. He was right on target. And just how awful quickly became apparent.

Only a few minutes after Garratt was thrust into this obscene dimension, the earsplitting screams of the multitude stopped—as in instantly—and their writhing bodies lay still. At that point, the strange, living machines descended to heights of around fifty or sixty feet above and changed in color from brown to green. The craft then began to shimmer, giving them an almost transparent appearance. This was followed by something that terrified Garratt to his core: the objects, perhaps seventy or more of them, bathed the entire throng of people in a pale, green light. As each person—man, woman, or

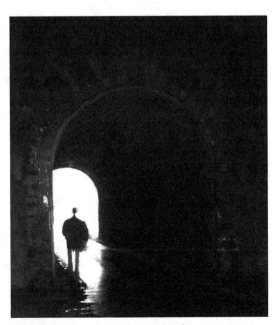

In near-death experiences people often report seeing a tunnel, light, and initially shadowy figures who reveal themselves to be departed loved ones.

child alike—was hit by the green light, a small brightly colored ball of silvery light exited through their heads, and was sucked into tentacle-like suckers that hung below the bizarre machines.

Then something even more terrifying occurred: in utter silence, the mass of people rose to their feet in decidedly staggering fashion. One and all, in unison, began walking across the unearthly landscape in the direction of a large, gaping hole that seemed to open out of nowhere. The only way Garratt could describe it was as a dense, vertical shadow with no originating source. In a fashion that, with hindsight and years later, reminded Garratt of something straight out of a zombie movie, the thousands of dead marched, in a weird, almost drunken, fashion towards their final destination: hell, which existed on the other side of the shadowy portal.

Suddenly, the experience was over and Garratt found himself lying in a hospital bed. The medical team had prevented Garratt from breathing his last. After a lengthy period of rehabilitation, he finally recovered. The memories of that fear-filled experience never left him, however. Not surprisingly, Garratt pondered deeply on the experience. If it was not some form of strange nightmare borne out of his own subconscious, Garratt could only come to one scary conclusion: hell was not the place that traditional teachings maintained it to be. Instead, it was another dimension, one that co-existed with ours, and in which sentient machines harvested the souls of the human dead as a form of energy to feed their mechanical lives.

It must be said that Garratt's story is very similar to the scenario that plays out in the 1999 movie, *The Matrix*, in which the human race of the late twentieth century unknowingly exists in a dream world, an incredibly sophisticated hologram created by machines that feed on the electrical energy that the human body creates. But, whereas in Garratt's story, the harvesting of soul-energy takes place at the gateway to hell, in *The Matrix* the reaping occurs in huge factories, where billions of people lie in dormant states, in pods, acting as fuel for the machines. It's important to note, however, that despite the similarities between the plotline of *The Matrix* and Garratt's memories, Garratt first related his experiences to family and friends days after his traumatic encounter with hell's zombies.

Paul Garratt died in 1986. One earnestly hopes that the reality of life after death is not that which Garratt was briefly exposed to back in 1968.

Night of the Living Dead

There can be absolutely no doubt that when it comes to zombies of the movie genre, matters are firmly split into two camps. There are the mind-controlled zombies brought to life via Voodoo (such as those that appeared in *White Zombie* and *I Walked with a Zombie*), and there are the crazed and cannibalistic undead, whose actions result from exposure to mysterious viruses. And, there is a specific timeframe in which the Caribbean zombie gave way to the viral zombie: 1968. That was the year in which George A. Romero's acclaimed movie, *Night of the Living Dead*, was released.

Although there were, admittedly, a couple of pre-1968 movies that, at least, gave a nod to the viral angle of the zombie (such as 1945's *Isle of the Dead* and *The Plague of the Zombies*, of 1966) it was Romero's ground-breaking production that changed pretty much everyone's perceptions about zombies. Such was the powerful imagery of the infected as presented in *Night of the Living Dead* it's unlikely that the old-school zombie of Voodoo and Haitian settings will ever reclaim its long-lost crown.

For a movie that was made on a budget of less than $120,000, *Night of the Living Dead* has surpassed all expectations, having now grossed close to $300 million. It was directed by Romero, who took much of his inspiration from Richard Matheson's 1954 novel, *I Am Legend*. It should be noted, however, that the story was not Romero's alone. Rather, it was the combined work of Romero and a screenwriter by the name of John Russo. At the time, along with actor/producer Russell Streiner, Russo, and Romero headed a movie-production company: The Latent Image.

With financial help from local investors—and with friends and acquaintances taking on the roles of the hordes of the risen corpses—*Night of the Living Dead* soon came to fruition. It also received widespread acclaim, thanks to the cast of relative

George A. Romero's 1968 movie *Night of the Living Dead* is widely considered to be *the* classic zombie film.

unknowns that proved to be far more than capable actors, including Judith O'Dea (Barbra), Duane Jones (Ben), and Karl Hardman (Harry Cooper). As for the filming, it occurred in the nineteenth century-era Evans City, Butler County, Pennsylvania.

As well as effectively changing the way in which zombies were perceived— namely not as Voodoo-controlled slaves but as infected killers—*Night of the Living Dead* achieved something else, too: its bleak and graphic imagery forever associated zombies with the collapse of civilization and the end of the world as we know it. Certainly, take a look at the post-1968 cinematic zombie and you will see that Voodoo-themed productions are noticeably and starkly absent. Thanks to *Night of the Living Dead*, bites, infection, death, reanimation, and a planet-wide Armageddon were quickly—and collectively—the order of the day. And they still are.

Nearly half a century after it was made, George A. Romero's *Night of the Living Dead* retains its chilling air of menace and terror, as well as its apocalyptic theme that so many other movies have tried to emulate—some more successfully than others

Night of the Living Dead Cast

There's no doubt that George Romero's *Night of the Living Dead* of 1968, absolutely defined—and continues to define—the celluloid image of the zombie, as it is generally perceived today. The movie would not have been what it was, however, without its cast. Given the tight budget that Romero was working with, there was no chance of securing big-name stars, for what ultimately turned out to be a production of legendary proportions. *Night of the Living Dead*, however, propelled the main cast of chiefly unknown actors to absolute stardom—at least, within the domain of zombie fandom. Leading the pack is without doubt Judith Odea, who played Barbra.

In her early twenties when she got the part of Barbra, Odea was not prepared for, and did not anticipate, the way in which she would forever be associated with Romero's first, and without doubt best, foray into the dark world of the undead. Ironically, she had a deep fear of horror movies, which may explain why her screams and terrified appearance throughout the movie came across as so lifelike. Odea continued to make movies in the aftermath of her experience on *Night of the Living Dead*. She had roles in a number of additional horror-themed productions, including a 2003, serial-killer-themed film, *Claustrophobia*, and 2005's *October Moon*. Today, she runs Odea Communications; it's a company which helps clients to "fine tune their oral presentation skills." And some of those clients are prestigious, indeed, including the Hughes Aircraft Company and the Raytheon Company.

Russell Streiner, who played Barbra's ill-fated brother, Johnny, in *Night of the Living Dead*, has had a varied career, both as an actor and as a producer. He appeared in a 1986 serial-killer-type movie titled *The Majorettes*—a reference to the majorettes of a high-school that fall victim to the deranged psychopath. Streiner also had a role in the 1990 remake of *Night of the Living Dead*. Not—as you might imagine—as Johnny returned from the grave, however, but as Sheriff McClelland, played in the original version by George Kosana.

Duane Jones, Ben in Romero's film, died in 1988, at the tragically young age of fifty-one. Nevertheless, he will not be forgotten. Aside from the fact that he was an integral part of *Night of the Living Dead*, Jones achieved a true first in the field of cinematic horror: never before had an African American taken on a lead role in an American horror movie. Jones was also a prime mover in the world of New York-based theaters in the 1970s, serving as director of the Black Theater Alliance and as a teacher at the American Academy of Dramatic Arts.

Karl Hardman had a lead role in *Night of the Living Dead*, as unlikeable Harry Cooper, who was just about as much a danger to the cast as were the zombies. Hardman performed another, vitally important role, too: he also produced the movie. He died in 2007 at the age of eighty. Hardman's daughter, Kyra Schon—who played Harry Cooper's daughter, Karen, in the movie—said that her father was "nothing like old Harry in real life, thank God, yet he agreed that the cellar was the safest place."

The Night Stalker

In January 1972, the American Broadcasting Company (better known as ABC) aired a new "made for television" movie entitled *The Night Stalker*. It starred Darren McGavin in the lead role of newspaper reporter Carl Kolchak, who investigates a spate of bloody killings in Sin City itself, Las Vegas. It turns out that the culprit is nothing less than a real-life vampire. Such was the success of the movie—at the time, it was the highest rating made for a TV movie ever broadcasted on American television—that it spawned a sequel: *The Night Strangler*, which aired one year later, in January 1973.

Enthused by the response of the viewers to both productions, ABC quickly decided to commission a full series. And thus was born: *Kolchak: The Night Stalker*, a show that first aired in September 1974. During the course of the series, McGavin's character investigated everything from swamp monsters to Jack the Ripper, hostile aliens to a murderous werewolf, and witchcraft to mummies. Kolchak also found himself taking on a deadly zombie, one that almost cost him his life.

Although the episode in question—somewhat unimaginatively titled *The Zombie*—post-dated George A. Romero's *Night of the Living Dead* and *The Crazies*, the writers and producers of the show chose to stick to traditional zombie lore. That's to say, the episode revolved firmly around Voodoo, graveyards, sacrificial rites, and the raising—and controlling—of the dead. When the zombie of the title embarks upon its violent killing spree, Kolchak is there to capture the facts, and the photos, thank to his ever-present, pocket-sized camera. As was nearly always the case with *Kolchak: The Night Stalker*, however, much of the story was prevented from reaching the public. The reason: a police clampdown to prevent panic and attendant embarrassment resulting from officialdom's mishandling of the strange case.

With a cameo spot from Antonio Fargas—who, in the following year, took on the role of Huggy Bear in *Starsky and Hutch*—*The Zombie* is an atmospheric, memorable, and nostalgia-driven production that pays homage to the likes of old-school movies of the undead, such as *I Walked with a Zombie* and *King of the Zombies*. Despite the fact that *Kolchak: The Night Stalker* was a well-produced show, and had an engaging cast of regulars, it was not destined to last. In March 1975, after twenty episodes were aired, the show was cancelled. Nevertheless, its fan-base has not diminished and, today, it remains a cult-classic amongst devotees of on-screen horror. In 2005, ABC resurrected the show, with Stuart Townsend taking on the role of Kolchak. It was not a hit with the viewers and lasted just six weeks, despite the fact that ten episodes had been filmed. Unlike its much-loved original, the twenty-first century Kolchak is not missed.

Noriega, Manuel

Shortly after Panamanian dictator Manuel Noriega's fall from power in 1989, U.S. intelligence sources revealed that the real ruler of Panama had been a Voodoo practitioner named Maria daSilva Oliveira, a sixty-year-old priestess from Brazil who practiced Candomble and Palo Mayombe.

U.S. Drug Enforcement agents escort the captured General Manuel Noriega aboard a Navy plane in this 1990 photo.

Witnesses stated that Noriega relied blindly on his Voodoo necklace, a pouch of herbs, and a spell written on a piece of paper to protect him. Journalist John South, writing from Panama City, Panama, said that those close to the dictator were aware that he did not make a single move without first consulting Maria.

When U.S. soldiers searched the house that Noriega had provided for his Voodoo priestess, they found evidence of spells attempted on former Presidents Ronald Reagan and George H.W. Bush. Maria had written out special ritual chants for Noriega to repeat over photographs of his enemies as he burned Voodoo candles and magic powders.

According to U.S. intelligence, Noriega's own spy network had informed him that U.S. forces would invade Panama on December 20, 1989. The dictator ordered Maria to conduct an immediate sacrifice to determine the validity of such intelligence reports.

During a ritual ceremony, Maria sliced open the bellies of frogs in order to study their entrails. Her interpretation of the entrails caused her to predict a U.S. invasion on December 21.

Placing more confidence in his Voodoo Priestess than in his intelligence network, Noriega believed Maria. Consequently, he had not yet moved his troops into position when the U.S. military forces attacked on December 20, a day earlier than Maria's sacrifice had prophesied. Even worse, from the dictator's perspective, he also missed the opportunity to escape in advance of the invading army.

Norwegian Armageddon

See also: Apocalypse, Armageddon, End Times, Megiddo

In 2010, a very strange letter was splashed across the Internet. It read as follows:

"I am a Norwegian politician. I would like to say that difficult things will happen from the year 2008 till the year 2012. The Norwegian government is building more and more underground bases and bunkers. When asked, they simply say that it is for the protection of the people of Norway. When I enquire when they are due to be finished, they reply before 2011. Israel is also doing the same and many other countries too. My proof that what I am saying is true is in the photographs I have sent of myself and all the Prime Ministers and ministers I tend to meet and am acquainted with. They know all of this, but they don't want to alarm the people or create mass panic. Planet X is coming, and Norway has begun with storage of food and seeds in the Svalbard area and in the arctic north with the help of the U.S. and EU [European Union] and all around in Norway. They will only save those that are in the elite of power and those that can build up again: doctors, scientists, and so on. As for me, I already know that I am going to leave before 2012 to go to the area of Mosj en where we have a deep underground military facility. There we are divided into sectors: red, blue, and green. The signs of the Norwegian military are already given to them and the camps were already built a long time ago. The people that are going to be left on the surface and die along with the others will get no help whatsoever. The plan is that 2,000,000 Norwegians are going to be safe, and the rest will die."

Was all of the above someone's idea of a bad joke? Clearly it was, since no such disaster ever occurred and we are now talking about the matter, and discussing it, years after the end was supposed to arrive. At the time the document surfaced, however, it provoked major anxiety in paranoia-filled circles, and led more than a few to worry about what was on the horizon. It turned out that *nothing* was on the horizon.

O–P

The Omega Man

The Omega Man was the second cinematic version of Richard Matheson's 1954 novel, *I Am Legend*. With Charlton Heston taking the lead-role, it was released in 1971. Interestingly, it was one of no less than three apocalypse-themed movies that Heston starred in between 1968 and 1973; the other two being *Planet of the Apes* and *Soylent Green*. *The Omega Man* broadly sticks to the plot of Matheson's acclaimed tale, although there are more than a few significant changes.

In Matheson's story, the world is turned upside down by a mystifying disease that rapidly mutates people into savage monsters. In *The Omega Man*, however, the cause of the deadly outbreak is a war, in 1975, between the former Soviet Union and China. Weapons of a biological-warfare nature are used on a massive scale during the conflict, something which results in the emergence and spread of an unstoppable plague that quickly kills most of the Earth's human population. Notably, the decision to bring biological-warfare into the equation was that of Joyce Corrington, the screenwriter of *The Omega Man*, and who has a doctorate in chemistry.

Almost all of those that survive the effects of the plague in *The Omega Man* are transformed into cold-hearted creatures. They are utterly crazed albinos, filled with hatred of not just the human race, but of the old world and of our now-redundant technology, too. Worse, they are bent on the destruction of the small, isolated pockets that still remain human. One of the latter is Charlton Heston's character, Robert Neville, who, unlike in Matheson's book, is a colonel and a doctor with the U.S. military. Hiding out in a ruined Los Angeles, Neville watches, anxiously and fearfully, the rise of the plague-infected survivors—or "The Family," as they become known. Two years pass, and the immune Neville is still doing his very best to steer clear of the mutants who, as a result of being unable to tolerate sunlight, only surface when darkness descends on the dead city. By this time, Neville, saved from a terrible fate by a vaccine created just before civilization collapsed, believes he is the very last man standing. To his amazement, he soon learns that he is not.

Neville comes across a straggling band of people—led by a man named Dutch—who are infected, but who have not yet physically or psychologically mutated. Neville has an idea to create a serum from his blood that, at the very least, will hopefully keep infection at a minimum and allow the survivors to retain their humanity. When one of the group's members, a young man named Richie, begins to slowly transform, Neville realizes there is no alternative and no time to waste: he injects Richie with the antidote, hoping and praying it will reverse the symptoms. It does exactly that. Tragedy soon follows, however. Richie visits the Family and pleads with them to make peace with Neville; he implores them to take the serum that will return them to human form. Outraged by the very idea, they kill Richie. His sister, Lisa, then begins to turn and quickly allies herself with the Family, which ultimately leads to Neville's downfall and death.

In his final moments, after being speared in the torso by one of the Family, Neville gives Dutch the precious serum. As Neville breathes his last, Dutch grabs Lisa and, with the rest of the group, they leave the city, and the Family, far behind. The

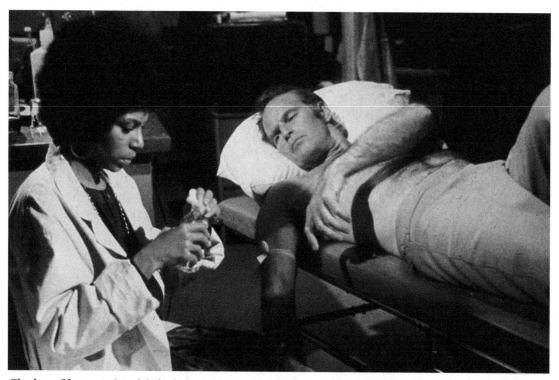

Charleton Heston is (nearly) the last man on Earth, until he is helped by Rosalind Cash, in 1975's *The Omega Man*. In this version, much of humanity is wiped out by a biological war between Russia and China.

implication is that thanks to Neville's actions and the creation of an antidote, humanity will be restored and the terrible physical and psychological effects of infection will be reversed. In Matheson's novel, Neville, weak and psychologically pummeled, opts to commit suicide after bleakly accepting that nothing can be done to change the new order. In *The Omega Man*, however, Neville is the savior of the future. We hope.

Operation Resurrection

In this secret project, implemented from 1965 to 1966, the CIA replicated the isolation chamber that had been constructed earlier by Dr. Donald Ewen Cameron, the brain butcher, at the Allen Memorial Institute in Montreal and rebuilt it at the National Institutes of Health. In Operation Resurrection, the experiments would not be with humans, but with apes.

The apes were first lobotomized, then placed in total isolation. After a time, the experimenters, adapting the radio telemetry techniques developed by Leonard Rubenstein, directed radio frequency into the brains of the apes. Those apes that appeared to receive the frequencies were decapitated and their heads transplanted to another ape's body to see if the radio frequency energy could bring them back to life and thus the name Operation Resurrection. The apes that were not selected for possible resurrection from the dead were bombarded with radio waves until they collapsed and became unconscious. Autopsies yielded the information that the apes' brain tissue appeared to have been literally fried.

It is difficult to see how Operation Resurrection could possibly have produced information of any value to any study of behavior control, behavior modification, or mind control. Researchers will probably never know the rationale behind the belief that dead apes could be resurrected if you switched heads and bodies, though the experiment seems another step toward the creation of human zombies.

Orford Zombie

Was a savage zombie on the loose on the east coast of England more than eight hundred years ago? Incredibly, it just might have been. The facts of the strange affair were chronicled in the year 1200, in the pages of a mighty tome titled *Chronicon Anglicanum*. The author was a monk and an abbot at Coggeshall, Essex, England, known only as Ralph, who penned the following words on the mysterious affair, which occurred at the ancient Suffolk town of Orford:

> In the time of King Henry II, when Bartholomew de Glanville was in charge of the castle at Orford, it happened that some fishermen fishing in

the sea there caught in their nets a Wildman. He was naked and was like a man in all his members, covered with hair and with a long shaggy beard. He eagerly ate whatever was brought to him, but if it was raw he pressed it between his hands until all the juice was expelled. He would not talk, even when tortured and hung up by his feet. Brought into church, he showed no sign of reverence or belief. He sought his bed at sunset and always remained there until sunrise. He was allowed to go into the sea, strongly guarded with three lines of nets, but he dived under the nets and came up again and again. Eventually he came back of his own free will. But later on he escaped and was never seen again.

Or, maybe it—or, far more likely, given the large passage of time, one of its off-spring—*was* seen again, albeit hundreds of years later. At some point during the summer of 1968, one Morris Allen was walking along the coast near, of all places, the town of Orford when, in the distance, he saw someone squatting on the sand and leaning over something. As he got closer, Allen said, he could see that the man was dressed in what looked like an animal skin and was tearing into the flesh of a dead rabbit. The man was dirt-encrusted, with long, tangled hair and had wild, staring eyes. Morris could only watch with a mixture of fascination and horror.

Suddenly the man held his head aloft and quickly looked in Morris' direction, as if he had picked up his scent. The wild man quickly scooped up the rabbit, bounded off into the grass and was lost from sight.

Some might say that the creature seen all those centuries ago was simply the unfortunate victim of a medical condition that made him appear, and act, as something definitively wild and monstrous. On the other hand, just like a zombie of the cinematic variety, the wild man of Orford was far from averse to a tasty bit of raw meat, never spoke, and could seemingly spend extensive time underwater—which is precisely what the undead of such movies as *Land of the Dead*, *Zombie Honeymoon*, and *Zombie Lake* were able to do—and with overwhelming ease, too. On top of that, Morris Allen's experience at Orford in 1968 provokes an interesting scenario: given that, in theory, the average zombie can go on "living" forever, providing it has sufficient food supplies; perhaps Allen's zombie and the creature whose actions were recorded back in 1200 by Ralph of Coggeshall were one and the same. Take great care if you ever decide to visit Orford.

Outer Space

See also: Alien Infection, Alien Virus, Extraterrestrials

On March 5, 2006, it was reported in the world's media that, five years previously—on July 25, 2001, to be exact—a strange form of "rain" fell from the skies over India, specifically in the state of Kerala situated in the western part of the country. What made this particular rain so strange and terrifying to the people that called Kerala their home was its color: that of human blood. For more than eight weeks, the red deluge continued, in near-endless fashion. Clothes were stained, trees were burned, and water was contaminated by the bizarre liquid. Godfrey Louis, a physicist at Mahatma Gandhi University in Kottayam, commented on the strange state of affairs: "If you look at these particles under a microscope, you can see they are not dust, they have a clear biological appearance." Indeed, Louis concluded that the rain was made up of bacteria-like material that had been swept to Earth from a passing comet.

A study of the red rain was undertaken by one Milton Wainwright, a microbiologist at Sheffield, England, who said: "It is too early to say what's in the phial. But it is certainly not dust. Nor is there any DNA there, but then alien bacteria would not necessarily contain DNA."

Godfrey Louis added: "If anybody hears a theory like this, that it is from a comet, they dismiss it as an unbelievable kind of conclusion. Unless people understand our arguments—people will just rule it out as an impossible thing, that extraterrestrial biology is responsible for this red rain."

In George A. Romero's 1968 movie, *Night of the Living Dead*, the zombie apocalypse was believed to have been caused by alien contamination. Maybe fact and fiction are closer together than many assume—or hope and pray.

Panteón de Belén

Situated in the pleasant confines of Guadalajara, Mexico, Panteón de Belén is a large cemetery constructed in the 1840s. Like a lot of cemeteries all across the world, this one has more than a few stories of the undead attached to it. And, although many of the tales concerning Panteón de Belén revolve around spirits and specters, one such story is focused far more upon matters of a zombie nature. It was in the latter part of the 1800s when Panteón de Belén was hit by a wave of bloody mayhem. While visiting the cemetery, grieving relatives of the dead reported finding the blood-drained corpses of numerous animals, primarily dogs and cats, all around the graves.

In addition, there were reports of a savage looking man roaming the grounds, dressed in rags and acting in violent fashion. Late one night, three weeks or so after the wave of attacks on the animals began, a shocking discovery was made in the cemetery: whatever, or whoever, had targeted the animals had suddenly decided to start feasting on people. That much was very clear from the two torn-apart male bodies that lay outside of one particular crypt.

In both attacks, it seemed that the killer was intent on securing huge amounts of blood from its victims. This was very much in evidence when the pale corpses of the dead were carefully examined. But there was something else too: whereas the average vampire is generally content to drain its victim of blood and leave it at that, such was most definitely not the case with the deadly predator of Panteón de Belén. Organs and

Mexico's Panteón de Belén cemetery is associated with a number of zombie stories.

even bones had been savagely torn from the bodies of the two murdered men, giving every indication that the attacker was cannibalistic—and voraciously so, too.

Quite understandably, the locals became filled with fear and were determined to quash the outbreak of flesh-eating that was afoot in their very midst. On several occasions, the mysterious figure was seen prowling around the cemetery, always after the witching-hour had struck and presumably while the terrible thing was on the hunt for human meat. Finally, however, the townsfolk caught up with the carnivorous killer and, as several men pinned it to the ground, another thrust a wooden stake into its heart. The snarling, snapping fiend of the night did not go quietly or quickly, however. Only decapitation finally ended its reign of terror.

There's no doubt at all that this case is ripe with vampire lore, but, we are still left with that one important question: how often does a vampire dine on the flesh, bones and internal organs of its victim? The answer is very seldom, if, in fact, ever. If a true zombie, then the actions of the beast give whole new meaning to the famous Mexican festival of the Day of the Dead.

Papa Jaxmano

The following is according to Lisa Lee Waugh, a well-known necromancer:

Voodoo-Hoodoo Sin Eaters seem to be the outcast of the group of religious practitioners, making up five percent of the more devout individuals in the United States. Their sin-eating ritual differs in many ways from those of the nineteenth century. It has been related to me over the years that Marie Laveau was visited by a Sin Eater several years before she died and she was one of the few individuals who had their sins eaten while still alive. This is why many say she turned pious and renounced Voodoo.

Displaced by hurricanes Katrina and Ike, several of these individuals who eat their meals off of the bodies of the dead now live throughout Texas. As a result many have been noticeably in the spotlight in recent months. I happened to meet the King of all the Voodoo-Hoodoo Sin Eaters just recently.

A Sin Eater known as Papa Jaxmano, a former New Orleans resident, is revered by many as the lord of all Hoodoo-Voodoo Sin Eaters. This man has been eating sins since the age of seven when he had to eat the sins of his father after his untimely death. Now sixty-eight years of age, Papa Jaxmano lives in Dallas, Texas, where he applies the ancient art for individuals of all races, faiths, and social strata. He does charge a fee for his services, but the price depends on the amount of sins carried by the individual who has passed on.

At one time Papa Jaxmano was a close friend of the Voodoo King Chickenman, and he is said to have eaten the sins of the Witch Queen of New Orleans Mary Oneida Toups.

Papa Jaxmano also tells of eating sins publicly and privately for many well-known celebrities and politicians around the world.

Public ceremonies, he relates, often consist of laying cakes or candies in the coffin with the deceased prior to the viewing of the corpse. They are then removed and given out, or placed in a bowl at the door of the funeral home or the coffee room.

Relatives and friends are then told to take a candy and eat it before the corpse is buried. This custom is still widely practiced today. Many use donuts and even packets of sugar instead of candy. Many of the funeral goers are not aware that they are eating the sins of the deceased, and Papa Jaxmano says this is more of a sin than one might imagine. In Texas, cupcakes, brownies, pastries, tacos, burritos, and even store-bought canned goods are placed alongside the body inside the coffin during the wake or funeral and later taken home and offered guests.

"I charge no fee for what I do for the poor," says Papa Jaxmano. "I do it because I do it. Others charge a fee all the time. If someone is poor, I might just ask for a ride or a friendly handshake."

Then he added with an expression of distaste, "Still, there are others that you could not pay me to eat their sins."

Papa Jaxmano next stated an important afterthought: "If you are the one who contacts a Sin Eater to eat someone's sins, then you need your sins ate too, or you is going to hell also!"

In the past week, I have watched Papa Jax, as I call him, eat the sins of over forty dead individuals. He often brings food home with him to offer to others.

In his brand of Voodoo-Hoodoo, there is a group of individuals who gather each week to eat the sins of others. Papa Jax's group has over fifty members who assemble in a Dallas suburb to eat the food and sins of the dead. These Sin Banquets are very trendy and only rarely are individuals like myself invited.

In doing research, I discovered that such Sin Eating parties go back to the late 1700s in New Orleans. A Voodoo congregation would gather each Saturday night and eat the sins of others, then go to Mass first thing Sunday morning and go to Confession. Thus their savory sins were forgiven.

Parsons, Jack

Jack Parsons was one of the most revered characters in the early years of the U.S. military's research in the field of rocketry. Parsons made such a name for himself that, in the mid 1940s, he was given a top secret clearance with the Army, Air Force, and Navy. Without Parsons' work, NASA's Jet Propulsion Laboratory at Pasadena, California would not exist. Parsons even has a crater named after him on the surface of the Moon. And on top of that, he was a noted occultist and a devoted follower of the "Great Beast," Aleister Crowley.

In the mid-1940s, Parsons became friends (albeit for a short while) with one of the most controversial figures of the twentieth century: L. Ron Hubbard, the brains behind the Church of Scientology. Parsons told Crowley: "I deduced that [Hubbard] is in direct touch with some higher intelligence. He is the most Thelemic person I have ever met and is in complete accord with our own principles."

Such was the admiration that Parsons had for Hubbard, the man behind Scientology moved in with his new friend. There was, however, a hidden reason for this: Hubbard had more than a passing interest in Parsons' girlfriend, the teenaged Sara Northrup. It was while Parsons and Hubbard were living together that the pair engaged in a complex ritual termed the Babalon Working. The goal was a grand one: nothing less than to create life in the form of an elemental entity. And it may very well have worked. Just a couple of weeks later, a striking and mysteriously alluring woman appeared in Parsons' life: Marjorie Elizabeth Cameron. An occultist, she would become Parsons' wife. "I have my elemental!" Parsons advised Crowley. This was not the only occasion upon which Parsons tried to create life via magical means.

Noted rocket scientist Jack Parsons was also an occultist who tried to create a life form of an elemental entity.

On the day of his death—which occurred on June 17, 1952, when he accidentally blew himself up in his Pasadena lab—Parsons tried to create yet another form of life.

Moviemaker Renate Druks, who was a friend to Marjorie Elizabeth Cameron, made the following, intriguing statement: "I have every reason to believe that Jack Parsons was working on some very strange experiments, trying to create what the old alchemists call a homunculus, a tiny artificial man with magic powers. I think that's what he was working on when the accident happened."

In times now long gone, those that practiced the ancient art of alchemy had a particularly curious way of bringing life to the things that should not be, such as the homunculus. It all revolved around nothing less than the mandrake plant. According to centuries-old lore, the mandrake plant had the magical ability to bring life to inanimate materials. The process, however, was a highly complex one. It was widely accepted centuries ago that mandrakes only grew on areas of ground where the semen of recently hung criminals was deposited. The key to creating life lay in the root of the plant, which had to be pulled out of the ground by nothing less than a black dog, and only early on a Friday morning. It then had to be nourished via a curious combination of blood, honey, and milk. Then, over time, the root would take on human form, develop into a diminutive humanoid entity, and faithfully act as a guardian to its creator.

A second way to give life to the homunculus was described—back in the 1700s—by Dr. David Christianus of the German University of Giessen. An egg, one specifically laid by a black-colored hen, was the key to life. The egg required piercing, just enough to make a tiny hole. Then, a small amount of egg white had to be removed and replaced with semen, after which the hole had to be closed, and the egg buried in the ground on the very first day of the March lunar cycle. Exactly one month later, the tiny homunculus would break out of the egg, force its way through the dirt, and make its way to the surface. It would remain a devoted protector of its initiator, providing it was given a regular supply of worms and seeds to fuel its strange, paranormal form.

Pet Cemetery Zombie

See also: **Pet Sematary**

In 1983, horror-maestro Stephen King penned a novel titled *Pet Sematary*. Made into a movie in 1989, it told of distinctly dark goings-on—including the rise of the dead in homicidal, crazed, zombie form. Rather chillingly, there is a real-life story that parallels King's tale.

It is a little known fact—to outsiders, at least—that hidden deep within the sprawling and heavily wooded Haldon Hills that overlook the English city of Exeter, there exists what might accurately be termed an unofficial pet cemetery. A distinctly tranquil and gentle locale, it has for years acted as the final resting place for many a deceased and much loved pet—whether dog, cat, rabbit, canary, hamster, guinea-pig, or something far more exotic.

In reality, such pet cemeteries are utterly illegal in Britain: the passing of the Environmental Protection Act of 1990 made it a serious crime to bury animal corpses on Forestry Commission land. Up until the early part of 2001, however, at which point rural England was utterly ravaged by a devastating outbreak of Foot-and-Mouth Disease that decimated the nation's cattle-herd, the authorities were content to turn somewhat of a blind eye to what went on in the old pet cemetery. But it is two events that occurred five years earlier that we must now turn our attention.

In 1996, the cemetery was suddenly transformed from a place of tranquility to one of outright terror. A number of stories surfaced of a pale faced, raggedly dressed man prowling in and around the pet cemetery late at night. On one occasion, he was actually seen digging in manic and frantic style into the soil of the burial grounds. And worse was to come. Pet graves were found disturbed, as if a wild, carnivorous animal had been trying to dig up the rotting corpses that were buried deep below the surface.

Until 2005, Jon Downes, the director of the British-based Center for Fortean Zoology—one of the world's few full-time groups dedicated to the study and investigation of unknown animals, such as Bigfoot, the Loch Ness Monster, and the Chupacabras—lived very close to the old cemetery and, as a result, collected many stories pertaining to this unholy, zombie-like humanoid and his predilection for digging up the dead and—wild rumor had it—devouring their corpses.

Fortunately, the incidents did not last. The last known sighting of this demented thing occurred on a summer morning in 2004, when a young woman, named Janice Parker, was visiting the cemetery. She was there to take photographs of a small gravestone that her grandmother had created, decades earlier as a child, for her beloved pet spaniel dog, Sally. As Parker entered the cemetery, the man, dressed as always in torn and tattered clothes, charged out of the surrounding trees, came to a sudden halt about twenty feet in front of her, and stared malevolently in her direction. Janice did not hang around to see what might happen next. She quickly raced down the hillside, never, ever to return.

As for what happened to the zombie of the Haldon Hills' pet cemetery, we may never know. Maybe he moved on, perhaps to feast on the dead of yet another cemetery, one that—just like the old pet cemetery itself—offered him cover, camouflage, and a plentiful supply of meat.

Pet Sematary

See also: Pet Cemetery Zombie

It's accurate to say that, in most zombie-themed movies, the cast of characters want the dead to stay dead. When the worst scenario occurs, however, and the deceased prefer not to stay quite so deceased after all, swift and violent action is taken to put them down. But not always: sometimes, there is a deep desire on the part of the stars to bring back those that really should be left underground. Such actions, however, rarely end in anything but overwhelming disaster. A perfect example is *Pet Sematary*.

Based upon Stephen King's 1983 novel of the very same title, the movie, a Paramount Pictures production, was released in 1989. It starred Dale Midkiff, Denise Crosby, and Fred Gwynne, the latter better known to fans of comedy-horror as bumbling Herman in *The Munsters*. Midkiff and Crosby's characters, thirty-something Louis and Rachel Creed, elect to move—with their young children, Ellie and Gage—from hectic Chicago to a sleepy little town in Maine called Ludlow. They really should have stayed where they were. Shortly after the Creed family arrives in town, their neighbor, Jud Crandall (played by Gwynne) takes them to an enchanting, but eerie, place hidden in the nearby woods. It is nothing less than a pet cemetery, containing the buried remains of the beloved, furry, hairy, and feathered friends of decades' worth of Ludlow locals.

As Louis settles into his new job at the University of Maine, violent tragedy unfolds before his very eyes. One of the students at the university, Victor Pascow, is fatally injured as a result of a traffic accident. As Pascow's rapidly life ebbs away, he whispers to Louis to keep away from the cemetery. Later that night, Louis has a nightmarish dream in which Pascow takes him to the cemetery and again warns him that the place is steeped in evil and negativity. Or is it a dream? Perhaps not: Louis wakes the next morning with his feet utterly caked in dirt.

Further tragedy strikes the Creeds when Ellie's cat, Church, is hit and killed by a speeding trucker. Jud takes Louis back to the pet cemetery, along with the body of Church. Jud then quietly reveals something more: behind the cemetery is another burial ground, one that was built centuries earlier by First Nation Micmacs. The pair duly buries Church on the Micmac's sacred land. Louis wonders out loud if anyone had ever buried a human at this very site. Jud is both appalled and scared witless at the very thought of such a thing.

Death continues to dominate the Creed family in just about the worst way possible: Gage—Louis and Rachel's beloved little son—is also hit and killed by a speeding truck. The family quickly descends into a state of mental collapse. Louis, becoming more and more deranged by the death of Gage, decides to dig up his corpse from the graveyard in which it is buried and re-bury it in the Micmac's ground. Jud pleads with him to reconsider and explains why: whatever is buried in the Micmac burial ground does not stay dead. That includes Church, who returns from the grave as a violent, aggressive, zombie-cat. Jud also explains how, decades earlier, a local man, Bill Bateman, buried his son, Timmy, in the Micmac's sacred land, after the latter was killed

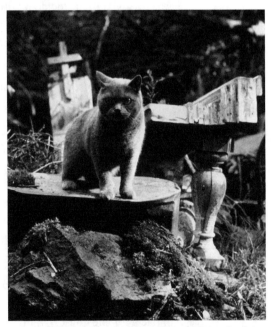

It sounded like a good idea, at first, to bring back beloved pets from the dead by burying them in a special cemetery, but the idea backfires horribly in the 1989 adaptation of the Stephen King novel *Pet Sematary*.

during World War II. Timmy, like Church, was not long for the ground. He returned to town, a zombie-like shell of his former self, crazed and psychotic.

Louis fails to heed the warning and places Gage's remains into the ground. Sure enough, he rises up. Gage is not the Gage that he once was, however. Rather, he is an abomination. He slaughters both his own mother and Jud, something which forces Louis to take the reanimated life of his own child. Now plunged even deeper into madness, Louis buries Rachel at the unholy site, hoping that she will return as she was. She does not. Rachel, now a fully paid-up member of the walking dead, makes her way back to the family home where, in the final moments of the movie, she plunges a knife into the back of completely deranged Louis. As the credits roll, the Ramones' *Pet Sematary*—which was written specifically for the movie—kicks in and Joey Ramone sings: "I don't wanna be buried in a pet cemetery; I don't want to live my life again." They were, and still are, wise and cautionary words, indeed.

Photographing a Zombie

Back in the 1960s, paranormal investigator and author Timothy Green Beckley was involved in an incident with nothing less than a Man in Black of a definitively zombie-style nature. Beckley recalls the strange, now long gone, events, which are still very much in his mind: "I had my own experience with a Man in Black, when me and Jim Moseley [Author's note: A long-time UFO researcher who died in 2012] photographed a strange individual one day back in 1968. There was a fellow by the name of John J. Robinson—Jack Robinson to his friends—who was the secretary for the National UFO Conference, the organization that Jim had started. Jack lived over in Jersey City. He was known as the point man as far as UFOs went on the other side of the Hudson, and had a *massive* UFO library. Jack was married to Mary. She was the psychic in the family, whereas Jack was more of a nuts-and-bolts UFO guy."

For several days, Mary had seen an ominous-looking character lurking in the shadows of a building directly opposite the one in which she and Jack lived. All in black, with a pair of black sunglasses, a fedora-style hat, and pale skin, the man made for a distinctly strange sight. That was in itself more than a bit unsettling. That the strange character did nothing beyond stand there, utterly rigid, staring at the windows of the Robinson's apartment for hours on end, was downright sinister. So, Mary took a bit of decisive action: she called Beckley and Moseley to check out the man and try and figure out what he was up to.

Beckley recalls: "Mary told me and Jim he seemed to be oddly dressed, and kind of like a zombie—just standing there, very rigid. She had never engaged him in dialog but he seemed to be surveying those going in and out of the building."

The very next morning, Beckley and Moseley were on the scene and, sure enough, there was the staring zombie. The intrepid duo managed to snap a quick photo of the man, who seemingly vanished into nothingness as the two tried to find a place to park their car. What happened to the man, and who or what he was, remains a mystery to this very day. Of course, there was one big difference between the zombies of the big screen and that which hung out by Jack and Mary Robinson's home: it was a well-dressed zombie, but a zombie all the same! And, of course, we should note of the year: 1968, the very year in which George Romero's *Night of the Living Dead* took the world of the zombie to previously unheard of levels.

The Plague of the Zombies

From the latter part of the 1950s to the early years of the 1970s, the U.K.'s Hammer Film Productions absolutely dominated the world of cinematic horror. The somewhat tame, black and white movies of the 1930s and 1940s were by now long gone. Hammer was all about entertaining its audiences with full color, over the top gore, and glamorous, buxom babes. Let's not forget bright red blood, and lots of it, too. *Dracula*, *The Curse of Frankenstein*, and *The Mummy*—all starring Hammer regulars Peter Cushing and Christopher Lee—were major hits with the general public. It is truly ironic, then, that one of Hammer's most memorable and fear-filled productions lacked both of its major, much loved stars. It was *The Plague of the Zombies*, made and unleashed in 1966. Predating George A. Romero's apocalyptic masterpiece *Night of the Living Dead* by two years, *The Plague of the Zombies* lacked any kind of end of the world-style storyline. Rather, Voodoo was the dominant theme of the movie.

The Plague of the Zombies starred Andre Morrell, who had previously played Dr. Watson opposite Peter Cushing's Sherlock Holmes in Hammer's 1959 version of *The Hound of the Baskervilles*. In a small, old village in the wilds of Cornwall, England, people are reportedly dropping from a mysterious disease like flies. They aren't staying dead, however. Rather, they are returning in zombie form and doing what zombies have always done best: namely, attacking and killing the living. It is all the fault of the evil and deadly Squire Clive Hamilton, portrayed in fine and menacing fashion by John Carson. A devotee of Voodoo, the sinister squire spent a number of years living in Haiti, where he learned the terrible secrets of how to both raise and command the dead.

The film contains a particularly memorable, and very creepy, scene in which one of the chief characters—Dr. Peter Thompson, brought to life by actor Brook Williams—has a nightmarish experience in the village's cemetery. As a typical English fog rolls in and engulfs the area, the dead start to slowly claw their way out of the old, grimy graves. As they make their staggering way towards a frozen-with-fear Dr. Thompson, eerie, hypnotic music adds to the bone-chilling atmosphere. Fortunately for the doctor, a nightmare is all it was. But not for significant portions of the rest of the cast: *The Plague of the Zombies* culminates in a battle for life and death in a series of tunnels in an old tin mine deep below the Cornish countryside.

With a black-arts-based theme at its heart, *The Plague of the Zombies* definitively tipped its hat in the direction of the likes of Jacques Tourneur's 1943, masterful pro-

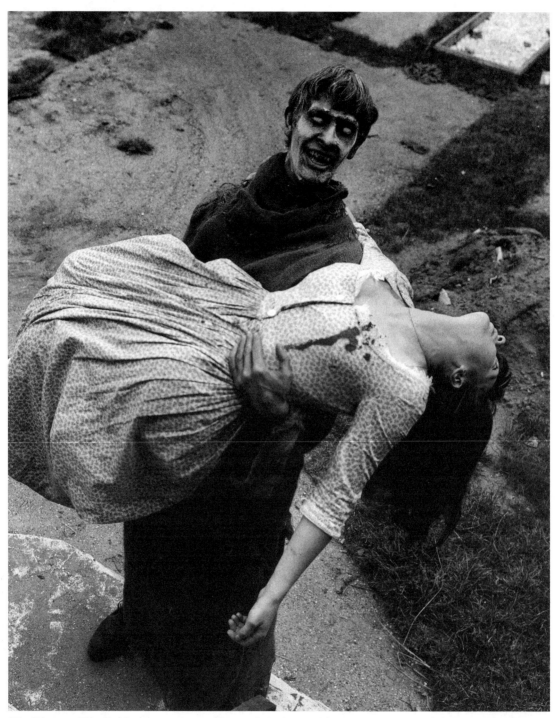

The Hammer Film Productions company *Plague of Zombies* involves a scourge of zombies in a village near Cornwall, England, that is caused by Voodoo.

duction, *I Walked with a Zombie*. The reference to the zombie outbreak having been caused by a mysterious disease—albeit one provoked by Haitian rituals—ensured that Hammer's zombie-themed classic significantly helped pave the way for future productions in which matters of a viral, rather than of a Voodoo, nature were all-dominating.

Planet Terror

When you combine the directing skills of Robert Rodriguez (*Machete* and *Sin City*, to name but two) with the production talents of Quentin Tarantino (*Pulp Fiction* and *Reservoir Dogs*) it's more than safe to assume that the end result is going to be a great one. And it certainly was, when the two paired-up to make 2007's *Planet Terror*. Instead of simply jumping on the zombie bandwagon that had been raging ahead in full-force in the wake of both *28 Days Later* and the remake of *Dawn of the Dead*, the duo chose to do something very different with their blood-filled, splatter-fest.

Planet Terror is nothing less than a full-on, zombie-dominated homage to the infamous "exploitation" movies of the 1970s, most often shown in so-called "grind-house" theaters and cinemas. The film is not, however, an exercise in nostalgia, or one that wallows firmly in the past. No: it very much uses the movies of decades long gone as springboards to the present, and in a very skillful fashion, too. Moreover, *Planet Terror* was Rodriguez's and Tarantino's way of demonstrating that, with cheap and mediocre zombie flicks surfacing just about everywhere, it was still possible to be 100 percent original and make something fresh and inspiring.

So, in true grindhouse-feel, we have a movie that is filled with women wearing very little, women behind prison bars, women in shiny black boots and miniskirts, and women who like women. In a nice touch, Rodriguez and Tarantino insert deliberate, on-screen scratches, flashes, and flickering reels to the film, which gives the impression that it is playing at a seedy, dive-style cinema with less than reliable projection equipment. Add to that a one-legged stripper (whose replacement limb is nothing less than a fully functioning machine-gun), cool motorbikes, violent shoot-outs, huge amounts of blood pumping out of the bodies of both the living and the dead, and a couple of maniacal baby sitters, and you have all the perfect ingredients for a wild ride into the land of the dead.

A zombie-themed movie, even one of a grindhouse nature, still requires certain tried and tested archetypes, of course. There is a deadly gas that turns people into insane, violent monsters, there is a military contingent struggling to keep things under control, and there is a band of survivors attempting to survive the Armageddon-style situation that is wreaking unrelenting havoc all around them.

With fine and witty performances from the likes of Rose McGowan (playing sassy, one-legged stripper Cherry), Freddy Rodriguez as Rose's beloved, Bruce Willis as the lunatic Lieutenant Muldoon, Josh Brolin as the deeply creepy Dr. Block, and Marley Shelton as Block's suffering wife, Dakota, *Planet Terror* is a carnage-saturated journey into a world where the guys and girls are all bad-ass, the zombies are just bad, and the soldiers are even worse. We even get to see zombie legend Tom Savini and the Black-Eyed Peas' Fergie—the latter looking suitably hot, of course, for such a movie— chomped on in bloody fashion. And, after all that is said and done, you really can't go wrong with a movie that tells you, in relation to Cherry's deadly leg: "Humanity's last hope rests on a high power machine gun!"

Pleasant, Mary Ellen

Mary Ellen Pleasant (who died on January 4, 1904) was a nineteenth-century female entrepreneur of partial African descent who used her fortune to further the cause of abolition. She worked on the Underground Railroad helping slaves to escape across many states and eventually helped expand the escape route to California during the Gold Rush era. She was a friend and financial supporter of John Brown, the fierce anti-slavery crusader who attacked the Federal Arsenal at Harpers Ferry, West Virginia (then Virginia), on October 16, 1859, and she became well known in abolitionist circles.

After the Civil War, Mary Ellen took her battles to the courts and won several civil rights victories, one of which was cited and upheld in the 1980s and resulted in her being called The Mother of Human Rights in California.

But only a few know the great dark secrets she kept and that she was one of Dr. John's greatest pupils. According to researchers at Haunted America Tours (http://hauntedamericatours.com), Mary Ellen Pleasant pried more secrets from him than any of her contemporaries. The old stories handed down often claim that she was Dr. John's favorite lover, but in spite of their physical passion and admiration for one another, it is supposed that during their affair, his zombification book was hidden in the LaLaurie Mansion.

Mary Ellen Pleasant, who was known as the Mother of Human Rights in California, kept secret the fact that she was a pupil of Voodoo practitioner Dr. John.

Poland Zombies

In July 2013, a shocking and controversial discovery was made in Gliwice, Poland. Workmen, then engaged in the building of a new road in the area, stumbled upon a large number of human remains. There was actually nothing too unusual about that, as skeletons have periodically been found buried in and around the wilds of Gliwice for years. The area was one of widespread confrontation and carnage between Nazi and Allied troops during World War II. And, due to the chaos and severity of the war, many of those who lost their lives in battle were hastily buried right where they fell. But, there was something very different about the corpses that were uncovered in 2013.

Before burial, each and every one of the bodies had had their heads removed and carefully balanced upon their legs. Dr. Jacek Pierzak, who personally oversaw the excavation of the beheaded bodies, noted that there were no identifying remains that could help to accurately date when, exactly, the burials occurred. The bodies did, however, show clear indications of wear and tear, suggesting strongly that they had been in the ground for a long time. Moreover, that none of the bodies displayed any evidence of bullet wounds was a clear indication that whenever the deaths occurred, they probably significantly predated World War II of 1939 to 1945.

In centuries long gone, all across Europe there were widespread beliefs that decapitating a corpse would prevent it from rising from the grave in the form of a monstrous, homicidal ghoul. Many of those same beliefs initially grew out of fears relative to vampirism and blood-sucking monsters. Removing the head of a vampire, it was widely accepted, would ensure that its nightly ritual of feeding on the blood of the living would come to an irreversible end. But was it really vampires that so terrified the people of Gliwice? Might their fear actually have been of zombies, not of blood-drinking creatures of the type befitting the likes of *True Blood*? Was there an undead outbreak in the area, centuries ago? If so, did that same outbreak cause terrified townsfolk to secretly take matters into their own hands and prevent a localized eruption from turning into something on a larger, possibly even worldwide, scale?

As any and all fans and devotees of zombie lore know all too well, the most vulnerable part of a walking corpse is its head. Pumping bullets into the body of a zombie will simply not work, aside from slowing it down for a few seconds. The creature will pretty much keep on marching regardless, driven solely by a never ending need to feed, no matter how many shots might slam into its torso, arms or legs. A bullet to the head, however, will bring a zombie down in an instant. And it will not get back up, either. Decapitating a zombie will prevent it from attacking anyone else, too, since the head will effectively be rendered immobile. That is not to say that a decapitated zombie is totally harmless, however. In fact, exactly the opposite is the case. Unless or until the brain of a zombie is penetrated, the severed head remains alive, still wildly snapping its jaws and snarling at anyone that dares to get close to it. That is, until it finally expires from starvation, due to no longer having a connecting stomach in which it can digest human meat.

Perhaps, in light of all the above, we might want to consider an astounding possibility: namely, that the walking dead of Gliwice were not infected with a vampire virus, but were, themselves, the victims of zombie attacks. And, once infected and duly transformed, they too quickly turned upon the living. Removing the head of the zombies of Gliwice would certainly have incapacitated them, providing the still-animate heads were handled very carefully after their removal and before the heads were placed on the legs. Just maybe, one day, we will learn to our amazement that the people of Gliwice successfully nipped in the bud the first wave of what threatened to turn into a full-scale zombie apocalypse of *Dawn of the Dead* proportions.

Porton Down

In more than a few zombie movies and television shows, before the bloody apocalypse becomes overwhelming, the military does its utmost to wipe out the undead. Very often, however, doing one's utmost is simply not good enough and the soldiers, too, become members of the zombie club. But what about real life zombie troops: do they actually exist? Well, yes, incredibly, in a strange way they do. For the proof, we have to turn our attentions to a highly classified installation, one whose path we have already crossed Porton Down, Wiltshire, England.

While the origins of Porton Down date back to World War I, when the British military was working on programs to combat German "mustard gas" attacks, it wasn't until the 1940s—when Nazi Germany and Japan began developing nation-threatening biological warfare programs—that Porton Down really left its mark. That was when scientists at the base began to dig ever deeper to find ways of combating both biological- and chemical-based weapons of the Axis powers. Following the defeat of Adolf Hitler, Porton Down's staff turned their attentions to the growing menace of the Soviet Union. As the Cold War developed, so did the installation and its work. In

At the classified installation at Porton Down, England (shown here circa 1917), research was conducted to combat mustard gas and, later, biological weapons the Nazis were developing.

1957, it became officially known as the Microbiological Research Establishment. Today, its title is the Defense Science and Technology Laboratory Porton Down.

While the staff at Porton Down has done its utmost to present the work of the base in a wholly positive light, there is a side to the research that is downright disturbing. In the early 1950s, Porton Down scientists began clandestinely experimenting with LSD, to determine how it might be used as a weapon against enemy personnel. And how did Porton Down's people determine the drug's ability to affect the enemy? By secretly testing it on unknowing and unsuspecting members of the British Army, that's how.

Of particular relevance to this matter—and also to tales of zombified military personnel—is a now-declassified piece of Top Secret, decades-old black and white film-footage showing British Army troops surreptitiously hit with a wealth of mind-bending drugs, and all in connection to this highly controversial experimentation. The film graphically shows numerous stoned soldiers jerkily roaming around the woods of southern England in confused states as they try—but spectacularly fail—to retain control of their normal faculties. To say their shambling, staggering movements parallel those of cinematic reanimated soldiers would be an understatement. There has, perhaps, never been anything closer to a real-world zombie army.

Potion to Make Zombies

Warning: Do not try this. It will not work unless you know the actual chants, prayers, and invocations to the Great Baron Samedi.

- One Human Skull
- Assorted Bones from a Water Rat
- A Pure White Cat
- An Iguana Tail
- The Teeth of a Man nineteen years dead
- A good dose of pure Vegetable Oil
- A dash or two of Datura
- Two Blue Agama Lizards of the male sex
- One Big Toad called Crapaud Bonga (Bufo Marinus) that must weigh one pound
- One Sea Snake's brain and sex organ
- Several Pods of Itching Pea, Pois Gratter
- Two (Preferably Female) Puffer Fish
- Add Tarantulas, Millipedes, and White Tree Frogs to taste

The potion should be prepared in June, when the female Puffer Fish contains its greatest quantities of Tetrodotoxin. Be careful not to touch the mixture at any time as it can act through skin.

Tie the snake to the toad's leg. Put them in a jar and bury it.

This is so that the toad dies of rage, which increases the concentration of its poison. Place its skull in a fire with Thunderstone and some blessed oil and burn till black.

Roast the animal ingredients and grind with the uncooked plants in a pestle and mortar. Add unheated shaving of the bones.

A few sacred spells (Juju), now grind your mixture to fine powder, place in a jar and bury in the coffin with the rest of your source skeleton, if possible, for three days.

You now have coup poudre or zombie potion. It is traditionally sprinkled in a cross on the threshold of the target. It can only be introduced by touching the skin. If taken internally, death will be final.

Upon the zombies awakening from the grips of death, one must bite the tip of the tongue as some Voodoo-Hoodoo practitioners prefer the entire tongue. The tongue should be kept always in the company of the person who owns the zombie, because the zombie will obey only the person who has it.

If the tongue is swallowed, the zombie is bound only to the boukur (bokar), or Voodoosant who created it. The zombie will obey someone else's commands if their master tells them to do so.

Pride and Prejudice and Zombies

Jane Austen's 1813 novel, *Pride and Prejudice*, is considered to be one of the finest literary titles of all time. It tells the story of the lives, loves, and very often turbulent times of five young sisters, the Bennets (with the bulk of the novel focused on the life and adventures of just one of the sisters, Elizabeth), who live in the town of Meryton, Hertfordshire, England. It is also a novel that has crossed over into the world of Hollywood on more than a few occasions, with the most well known and regarded examples being a 1940 movie with Sir Laurence Olivier and Greer Garson, and a 2005 film starring Keira Knightley as the lead character, Elizabeth Bennet. The BBC made their own versions of Austen's books, too: the first in 1980 and the second in 1995. But, the weirdest—yet, undeniably, the most entertaining—take on *Pride and Prejudice* came in 2009, with the release of a very strange and highly engaging novel titled *Pride and Prejudice and Zombies*.

Whether or not the novel would have had a rage-filled Jane Austen turning in her grave—or, perhaps, more appropriately, rising from its dirt-filled depths—we will never know. But readers loved Seth Grahame-Smith's take on the two-hundred-year-old saga, to the point where it became a *New York Times* bestseller. The author took an ingenious approach to his book: first of all, Grahame-Smith actually credited Jane Austen as the co-author! Not because she reanimated and assisted in the writing, but because *Pride and Prejudice and Zombies* was, to a very significant degree, still Austen's original work—at least, in terms of the characters, settings, and plot development. And also in terms of the words, too: Grahame-Smith didn't rewrite the book, but instead inserted his own text into the pages of Austen's original. Grahame-Smith did something else, too: he turned the original tale right on its head. In the reinvented story, nineteenth century England is a land awash with nothing less than deadly zombies.

There is a very good reason why the dead walk in this particular version of Jane Austen's saga: the England of *Pride and Prejudice and Zombies* is not the England of our world. Instead, it is an England of a very different dimension to the one that we inhabit. So, we see a lot of hysterically funny situations in which the dead intrude upon, and upset, the plans of the Bennet girls to come to grips with their emotions, their development as ladies of the landed-gentry kind, and their loves and lovers. Amusingly referred to by the Regency-period Brits as "the unmentionables," the dead are just about everywhere, even to the extent that London has been transformed into a fortified city, one surrounded by huge walls to keep the cannibalistic dead at bay. Much hilarity ensues as the Bennet girls deal with the issue of trying to remain demure and ladylike, but at the same time learning to prepare for action when the unmentionables appear on the scene, baying for flesh and blood at every opportunity. Although *Pride and Prejudice and Zombies* is filled with laughs, it is also packed with violent and bloody confrontations with the reanimated monsters, something which makes Seth Grahame-Smith's book a notably dark and humorous one.

Not only did *Pride and Prejudice and Zombies* become a big hit with readers, but it got Hollywood interested in turning it into a movie. At the time of this writing, plans are still very much in the discussion and planning stage, even though the rights have been purchased by an unnamed movie company. Lily Collins, the daughter of singer Phil Collins, is tipped to take the lead role as Elizabeth Bennet. Until the movie rolls around, however, fans can indulge in a graphic-novel and a video game, both based on *Pride and Prejudice and Zombies*. There is also a prequel to Seth Grahame-Smith's novel available. Written by Steve Hockensmith, and with the title of *Pride and Prejudice and Zombies: Dawn of the Dreadfuls*, it takes us back to the time when Elizabeth Bennet was a young girl, still—of course—,doing her best to remain as a demure zombie-killer.

Prison Cannibals

Up until the end of season four of *The Walking Dead*, we were familiar with seeing our straggling bunch of heroes hunkered down in a fortified Georgia prison, doing battle with both the dead and their arch-villain, the Governor. But the resurrected dead, people feeding on people, and prisons also have a place in the real world. In the latter part of the sixteenth century, London's Newgate Jail was the site of a horrific series of deaths that would have made the average zombie proud in the extreme—if such creatures possess significant amounts of brains to be proud.

Due to a pronounced lack of regular food, on more than a few occasions the prisoners targeted the weakest members of the pack and turned *them* into food. It was very much a case of eat the living to avoid becoming one of the dead. We are, then, talking about cannibals in the cell block. One of those savagely killed and partially eaten by the prisoners was an unnamed man, but one that—according to an 1812 document titled *The Discovery of a London Monster, called the black dog of Newgate*—was apparently something of a scholar.

With his body mutilated and semi-devoured, the man did exactly what the bitten and the equally semi-devoured of the prison of *The Walking Dead* did on so many occasions: he rose again. Not, however, as a voracious devotee of raw, human flesh, but as a ghastly and ghostly black dog with a pair of blazing red eyes. The actions of this zombie hound were not at all unlike those of its television-based equivalents. The creature violently slaughtered those that had taken its human life by savagely biting down on their necks with its immense and powerful jaws. Death swiftly followed for the guilty. Reanimation, however, did not. When the deed was done, the man—in spectral dog form—vanished, never to be seen again.

Then there is the very similar, and very weird, tale of William and David Sutor. The dark saga all began late one night in December 1728, when William, a Scottish farmer, was hard at work in his fields and heard an unearthly shriek that was accompanied by a brief glimpse of a large, dark-colored dog, far bigger than any normal hound, and one possessed of a pair of the ubiquitous, glowing red eyes. On several more occasions in both 1729 and 1730, the dog returned, always seemingly intent on plaguing the Sutor family. It was, however, in late November of 1730, that the affair ultimately reached its paranormal pinnacle.

Once again the mysterious dog manifested before the farmer, but this time, incredibly, it was supposedly heard to speak, in rumbling tones, and directed William to make his way to a specific, nearby piece of ground within thirty minutes William did as he was told, and there waiting for him was the spectral hound of hell. A terrified William pleaded to know what was going on. The hideous hound answered that he was none other than David Sutor—William's brother—and that he had killed a man at that very spot some thirty-five years earlier.

As David had directed his own savage dog to kill the man, David had himself—as punishment—been returned to our plane of existence in the form of a gigantic hound. The dogman instructed William to seek out the buried bones of the murder victim, and then place them within consecrated ground, which William duly did, in the confines of the old Blair Churchyard. The ghostly black dog—the spirit of David Sutor in animalistic form—vanished. Like the beast of Newgate Jail, when its work was done, it never made a re-appearance.

Psychomania

It is without a doubt one of the oddest movies of the undead ever made. Its name is *Psychomania*. Filmed in the United Kingdom in 1972, and released the following year, *Psychomania* is a British production starring Nicky Henson and directed by Don Sharp, who was responsible for such horror outings as *Kiss of the Vampire* and *The Curse of the Fly*. The plotline revolves around the actions of a biker gang that, very appropriately, call themselves "The Living Dead," and that have the name emblazoned prominently on the back of their black leather jackets.

Henson's character—Tom Latham—is an unlikable, spoiled, early twenty-something brat, one whose main form of entertainment is inflicting both emotional and physical pain on others. The Living Dead regularly take to the roads, creating havoc and mayhem for other drivers. But that's nowhere near enough for Latham. He has something else on his mind: death and resurrection. Latham's mother, played by English actress Beryl Reid, is an expert in the world of the occult, and as a result, Latham himself comes to know a great deal about the dark realm of the supernatural. Not only that, Latham enjoys hanging out with his biker buddies at the Seven Witches, which is a small, Stonehenge-like circle of ancient standing stones that are featured heavily in the movie.

Biker gangs like this one often embrace a tough-guy culture embracing death; such is also the case in the 1972 British film *Psychomania.*

Using the directions of an ancient supernatural ritual, Latham purposely kills himself by driving his motorcycle off a highway bridge and into the waters below. He is killed instantly. He does not, however, stay that way. The leader of the Living Dead becomes, quite literally, one of the *real* living dead. After being buried within the grounds of the Seven Witches (and atop his motorcycle, no less!), Latham soon returns from the grave and his violent actions quickly become murderous as he goes on a homicidal killing spree. It isn't long at all before the rest of the gang follow suit and take their own lives, before returning from the grave as equally crazed killers. The only one who is not enthused by the infernal situation is Latham's girlfriend, Abby, who finally confides in the police what is going on. At first the police view the whole thing with a high degree of skepticism and doubt—until it's all very much too late and the investigating officers also end up dead.

That's right: not even the powerful world of law enforcement is a match for matters of an occult nature, and the lethal living dead continue to provoke death and mayhem. Latham's murderous spree takes on even greater proportions when, right in the heart of the Seven Witches, he tells Abby that she will either have to pledge herself to the gang, take her own life and return as one of the undead, or the bikers will kill her—as in permanently and with no chance of reanimation. Unknown to Latham, however, his mother—by now completely appalled at his actions—enlists the help of her butler, Shadwell (played by actor George Sanders, who committed suicide shortly after the filming of the movie was completed), to perform a complex rite that will bring the terrible activities of Latham and his gang to a sudden and irreversible halt. As Abby looks on with fear, thinking that there will be no way out for her, the living dead are, one by one, turned to stone. Finally, they are indistinguishable from the original "seven witches" of their favorite hang-out. The reign of terror is finally over. With its almost dream-like qualities that border upon the psychedelic, and its focus on old stone circles and ancient rituals, *Psychomania* has attained cult-like status amongst horror and undead aficionados.

Public Health Services

Such was the concern shown by the possibility of the United States' cattle-herd becoming infected by deadly viruses in the post-World War II era, even the FBI got in on the act. A confidential memorandum to FBI Director J. Edgar Hoover on May 9, 1950, from Raymond P. Whearty, the Chairman of the Interdepartmental Committee on Internal Security, and titled *Alerting of Public Health Agencies re Biological Warfare*, states:

> The Public Health Services has a long-established relationship (direct or through regional offices) with official State—and through them to local—health agencies. Accordingly, the Public Health Service should be the chief agency on which NSRB [The National Security Resources Board] will rely as a source of advice to these agencies on biological warfare [BW] matters in so far as they are a part of civil defense of people. NSRB will rely on the Bureau of Animal Industry in the same manner for defense of animals against BW. The National Security Resources Board has kept the Public Health Service fully informed as to biological warfare plans.

> In developing these plans the NSRB created an Interdepartmental Committee on Defense Against Biological Warfare. The Public Health Service and BAI [Bureau of Animal Industry] are, of course, represented on this committee. Definite plans are being made in this field, as shown by the two attached "Restricted" documents. The Public Health Services and Bureau of Animal Industry are planning the training course for civil defense against biological warfare and will conduct such courses if and when appropriations are available. Approximately fifty Public Health Service top administrative officers recently spent one week at Camp Detrick for orientation in BW as part of the training, for Public Health Service officers in this particular field.

Quarantine Station

Viruses, widespread panic, death on a large scale, the deceased returned from the grave, disease, and the isolation of the infected: they are all the key ingredients of any good, self-respecting zombie saga. They are also the key ingredients of an old facility in Sydney, Australia called Quarantine Station. Back in the 1830s, much of Australia was ravaged by the effects of widespread infection which was provoked by a multitude of deadly conditions, including cholera, plague, and smallpox. As the situation grew worse, hundreds of the infected were rounded up and transferred to the most appropriately named Quarantine Station, where they were forced to remain, like it or like it not. This was not done to try and save the infected, however. Rather, it was seen as a last resort-style attempt to prevent the rest of the population from also falling sick. Those bitten by the bug were destined for nothing less than death in the isolated rooms of Quarantine Station.

In an attempt to try and relegate the horrors of Quarantine Station to the world of the past, the old facility has been given a significant overhaul. It is now nothing less than a first-class hotel and restaurant. But, just like the dead of zombie lore rise from the grave, so the victims of Quarantine Station do exactly likewise. Whereas the infected zombie returns in literal, physical form, however, the deceased diseased of Quarantine Station do so in ghostly form. Indeed, ghostly phenomena, poltergeist activity, and the manifestation of those who succumbed to lethal viruses all those years ago still dominate the old facility.

It's all very good news for the hotel, however, the staff of which embrace its dark history as much as they do the resident, spectral dead. Nighttime tours of the most haunted parts of Quarantine Station are incredibly popular. And, ghost-hunting groups have a collective field day trying to find specters of the infected type. While the controversial deaths of hundreds of people at Quarantine Station are admittedly disturbing, one has to look at things from the other perspective too: had the infected not been contained and isolated from the rest of the population, it's not at all impossible that Australia would have seen its population decimated by near-unstoppable disease.

Queen Bianca

Queen Bianca has been the reigning Voodoo Queen of New Orleans since 1983, when she received the title from Liga Foley, her aunt by marriage who claimed to be a granddaughter of Marie Laveau.

Queen Bianca has presided over the secret Sosyete (society) that the Laveaus originally founded, carrying on the legacy of true New Orleans Voodoo. Bianca has said that the Grande Sosyete did not die with Marie Laveau I or Marie II, it just went underground; therefore, only the inner circle of followers and devotees know of its secrets, rites, and ritual locations.

Queen Bianca has been the reigning Voodoo Queen of New Orleans since 1983. (**Art by Ricardo Pustanio**).

Each year, sometimes twice a year, Queen Bianca will host a ritual in which the Monkey and Cock Statues created in honor of Marie Laveau are blessed and charged. In this ritual, which always takes place outdoors in a highly secret location, Queen Bianca will invoke the spirit of Marie Laveau, becoming possessed by the powerful Voodoo Queen. Through Bianca, her modern day counterpart, Marie Laveau is able to be present with her devotees and personally blesses the Monkey and Cock Statues, which protect the followers from evil and any curses directed against them during the course of a year.

The highly secret vodusi of Queen Bianca's Sosyete present the living, channeled Marie Laveau the first Monkey and Cock Statue of each year as an offering. This ritual is said to take place once each year, usually around April 30 or May 1. Other offerings preferred by Marie Laveau are also presented and accepted by her spirit through the powerful Queen Bianca.

The first Monkey and Cock Statue remains with the powerful Mambo throughout the year until the time of the next ritual when it is ceremoniously broken in favor of another. Often, however, Queen Bianca and her vodusi will repeat the ritual in the fall of the year, coinciding with harvest festivals and

Samhain rituals. The location for each ritual is a closely guarded secret, shared only with members of the Sosyete at the very last minute when they are summoned to assemble. This is one of the most powerful examples of continuing devotion to the great Marie Laveau surviving in New Orleans today.

Bianca began learning the ways of New Orleans Voodoo and Santeria at a very young age. Because she devoutly studied numerous ancient paths and traditions, she quickly became very well known as one who specialized in rare New Orleans original Voodoo occult items and personally made magical fetishes, small Voodoo statues, and good luck charms.

Go to the official Bianca the Voodoo Queen of New Orleans Website at http://www.thehouseofVoodoo.com/.

Rabbits of the Dead

Soviet and Czechoslovakian Parapsychological Research is a lengthy U.S. Defense Intelligence Agency (DIA) document that was written in September 1975, and which is now in the public domain, thanks to the provisions of the Freedom of Information Act. Intriguingly, but also disturbingly, the document reveals evidence of a deep fascination for the domain of the dead on the part of the DIA. Much of that fascination was for the work of a Russian scientist, one Pavel Naumov, whose fringe research suggested that physical death for animals was not actually the end, after all.

The *Soviet and Czechoslovakian Parapsychological Research* document states in part: "Dr. Naumov conducted studies between a submerged Soviet Navy submarine and a shore research station: these tests involved a mother rabbit and her newborn litter and occurred around 1956. According to Naumov, Soviet scientists placed the baby rabbits aboard the submarine. They kept the mother rabbit in a laboratory on shore where they implanted electrodes in her brain."

The writer of the DIA report continued: "When the submarine was submerged, assistants killed the rabbits one by one. At each precise moment of death, the mother rabbit's brain produced detectable and recordable reactions."

Of equal—and perhaps even more—interest, Defense Intelligence Agency staff recorded that: "As late as 1970 the precise protocol and results of this test described by Naumov were believed to be classified." Precisely why the government of the Soviet Union chose to hide its findings on the matter of an afterlife in animals remains unknown. Let us all hope, however, that it wasn't because they intended bringing them back from the other side. Anyone who has ever watched a zombie movie will know that when the dead return they are far from what they were in their original lives. Perhaps someone needs to tell the Russians before we see hordes of flesh-eating zombified animals roaming the planet.

Rabies

In the 1997 movie *Conspiracy Theory*, Mel Gibson's character—a paranoid cab-driver named Jerry Fletcher, who has been the subject of CIA-sponsored mind-control experiments—states that a good conspiracy theory is one that can never be proved. Perhaps the very same thing can be said about one of the most controversial of all the zombie-based conspiracies currently in circulation. It suggests that, right now, deep in the heart of Fort Detrick, Maryland—home to a dizzying amount of secret research into biological warfare and exotic viruses, and the American equivalent of the U.K.'s Porton Down—a terrible cocktail is being secretly concocted. It is one based around a mutated version of the rabies virus, one that will, in the near future, be unleashed upon enemy forces and cause them to attack each other in violent, homicidal fashion. They won't be literally dead, but trying to tell the difference between the real-life infected and those of television and cinema will be no easy task in the slightest.

Could it actually be true? Are dark forces really at work, trying to create a virus that will mimic—as closely as is conceivably possible—the effects of a real zombie apocalypse? Certainly, rabies radically transforms the character and actions of an infected individual. Its name is highly apt, too: it is a Latin term meaning nothing less than "madness." Rabies spreads from animal to animal, via bites, and provokes inflammation in the brain, as Ozzy Osbourne almost learned to his cost when he very unwisely bit the head off a bat at a Des Moines, Iowa gig in 1982. Left untreated, disturbing characteristics develop anywhere from weeks to months after infection, including violent outbursts, manic behavior, aggression, and a fear of water. Death usually occurs within 48-hours to two weeks after the first symptoms surface.

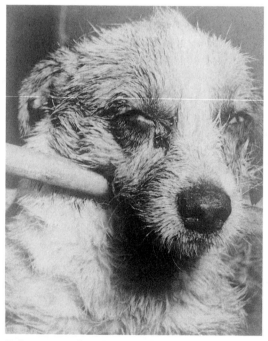

Rabies is usually a death sentence for an unfortunate animal like this dog. Some say the CIA is working on a mutated form of rabies to be used as a weapon.

Rumors among conspiracy theorists suggest that a rage-instilling, highly infectious, airborne version of rabies is, right now, being secretly developed. It will not quickly kill the infected individuals, however. Instead, their lives will be prolonged, albeit in violent, murderous, rage-filled states. That might seem like an ideal weapon to release on enemy troops, and then sit back and watch as they tear each other to pieces. But what happens when the wind blows hard and weaponized, airborne rabies—mutated into something even more nightmarish—begins to spread far and wide, and outside of the confines of the battlefield? Our cities will be faced with a veritable army of rabid, infected killers, indiscriminately murdering and infecting everyone that has the distinct misfortune to cross their paths. As Mel Gibson's Jerry Fletcher pointed out, however, a good conspiracy theory such as this one can never be proved. Or, maybe more correctly, *not yet it can't*.

Rammbock

Rammbock: Berlin Undead—a 2010 movie, and one that was clearly inspired by the brains behind *28 Days Later* and *28 Weeks Later*—is a German production that is well worth watching, but unfortunately very much under-appreciated. It is certainly not the greatest zombie movie out there, but it is one that is most definitely highly recommended.

In *Rammbock* the rapidly growing bands of infected are not the recently deceased risen from the grave. Actually, they are the exact opposite: they are still alive, but grossly infected with the German equivalent of the "Rage Virus" that made the maniacal killers of the *28 ...* movies so terrifying, and even plausible and believable. And just like those same infected that overran the United Kingdom in both *Days* and *Weeks*, so the rabid, deranged hordes of *Rammbock* charge around in maniacal fashion, as they seek out the uninfected.

For the most part, the entire movie is set within the confines of a large apartment complex—and its attendant courtyard—in the heart of the city of Berlin, Germany's capital city. That the movie does not—geographically speaking, at least—take us far and wide, ensures that a deep sense of claustrophobia and isolation quickly develops, as those who are still human do their very best to barricade themselves in their homes, while the far-more-than-angry mob tries to force its way in. Unfortunately, the latter usually succeeds.

The chief characters are Michael and Harper. Michael has traveled to Berlin to visit his girlfriend, Gabi, while Harper—a plumber by trade—is working at Gabi's apartment. Both men—middle-aged Michael and teenaged Harper—have chosen just about the worst time possible to make their appearances. And when the infected attack, they quickly band together to try and find a way out of the growing disaster in their very midst.

The movie works extremely well, and for several reasons: the frantic pace rarely lets up, the infected look suitably menacing, and there is far more than a bit of character development. This is not, then, a cheap piece of zombie tat in which the characters are only there to entertain the audiences by getting bitten, eaten or torn apart. A high degree of thought clearly went into the storyline, and, for that reason alone, *Rammbock* scores majorly.

As is so very often the case in zombie movies, the finale is distinctly bittersweet, where survival and infection become inextricably intertwined and one of our heroes unfortunately fails to retain his humanity. *Rammbock* has an ending that is handled very well and in a welcome, low-key fashion, to the credit of the writing/production team. Rather than going out in a guns-blazing, zombies-charging fashion, the movie ends on a theme that is not seen too often in zombie productions: love. A copy of the movie would not be out of place at all on the Blue-Ray or DVD shelves of any discerning zombie fan. To be sure, *Rammbock* is infectious.

Reanimation Experiments

Experiments in the Revival of Organisms is the title of a highly controversial film that dates from 1940. The very title alone suggests strong zombie-like overtones. Such an analogy is not altogether wrong. An approximately twenty minute long production, it chronicles the work of a Dr. Sergei Brukhonenko, who was an expert in the field of open-heart surgery in the Soviet Union. Such was Brukhonenko's success that he was awarded the prestigious Lenin Prize, which acknowledges major achievements in a wide body of disciplines, including science and medicine. But, it is the aforementioned *Experiments in the Revival of Organisms* for which Brukhonenko has become not so much famous, but downright notorious.

The film is, to say the very least, graphic. Imagery of both a canine lung and heart existing outside of the confines of the body—and kept alive via a variety of medical techniques—are just the start. The *piece de resistance*, however, far surpasses such already unsettling footage. It also involves a dog, one that dies a particularly horrific death. As the film makes very clear, the dog is deliberately and decisively drained of all its blood. After death has been fully confirmed, the corpse of the dog is left to rest in peace, so to speak. About ten minutes later, however, the body of the dog is attached to a machine that is designed to kick-start both the heart and the lungs, and to ensure the flow of new blood into the body of the dead dog. Remarkably, the dog reanimates, all thanks to an injection of that very same new blood. Its heartbeat starts somewhat erratically, but in no time at all, the lucky hound is enjoying its brand new lease on life.

While the dog is not, of course, a literally zombified dog, the fact is that in the film it is indeed confirmed as being deceased, and it does return from that usually terminal condition. And although the dog does not display the savage behaviour of a typical zombie, let's not forget that it was blood—something which zombies have a particular penchant for—which brought the dead dog back from the point of (almost) no return.

Redneck Zombies

Sometimes, a movie is deemed to be so bad and inept that it ultimately takes on definitive cult status. And, as a direct result, it becomes a skewed, but much lauded, masterpiece. Writer and director Ed Wood, as a perfect example, became an undeniable legend, all from putting out overwhelming tripe like *Night of the Ghouls*, *Orgy of the Dead*, and *Necromania*. Other times, however, a movie is just plain bad—period. For fans of the undead, the walking dead, and the racing around like crazy dead, 1987's *Redneck Zombies* is a film that well and truly divides its audience into one of the two above-camps.

If you are inclined to take your zombies very seriously, then this is probably not the movie for you. On the other hand, if you are looking for a break from heart-thumping, adrenalin-pumping mayhem, something that lacks the intensity of *The Walking Dead*, and something that, instead, will give you a chuckle or several, chiefly as a result of its engagingly amateurish nature, *Redneck Zombies* just might appeal. In fact, it probably will appeal.

For a comedy-based production, the plot is actually not a bad one at all: a bunch of good ol', genial, moonshine-swigging boys and gals—the Clemson family—are given a discarded barrel that had been used to store something that is all but guaranteed to provoke a devastating zombie outbreak: toxic waste of just about the very worst kind there is. Being the definitive redneck buffoons that they are, the family decides to brew their potent, favorite drink in that very same barrel; as we all would, of course.

Then something terrible, but hardly surprising, happens to that merry band of Elly May, Jethro, Ma, Pa, and Junior. After knocking back the grog, the rednecks quickly become the dead necks. Worse still, the Clemson clan has shared its drink of the undead with just about everybody around town. Before you can play even a single, solitary note on a banjo in the woods, blood-filled anarchy has broken out. That's when the other members of the cast—a bunch of campers consisting of Bob, Andy, Theresa, Wilbur, and Sally—are forced to fight for their very lives.

The film does, admittedly, have its amusing moments, and there are a couple of good, gory and (literally) eye-popping shots that will keep most zombie aficionados more than happy for a while. But, it's very much a case of far too little, and far too late. Or is it? If you're looking for a well-acted, very funny, and skillfully made comedy about the crazed, the cannibalistic, and the infected, then it's probably wise to stick to the likes of *Shaun of the Dead* or *Zombieland*. If, however, you want to hang out on a Friday night with your buds, knock back more than a few potent brews, and watch a zombie movie that has a great sense of fun to it, which doesn't take itself seriously in the slightest, and that will certainly never win any Oscars, then *Redneck Zombies* is ideal viewing. And it will also teach you a valuable lesson: never, ever drink anything brewed in a container marked "Hazardous Waste."

Religious Sacrifice

Blood sacrifice, whether of humans or animals, is the oldest and most universal propitiatory act of the pious seeking favor from a benevolent or a wrathful god. An ancient Hittite cylinder seal from the second millennium B.C.E. depicts a human sacrifice in intricate detail.

The Abrahamic God strictly prohibited his followers from imitating their neighbors in the offering of human sacrifices (Lev. 20:25; Deut. 18:10). The one God placed a high value on human life and forbade this practice (Lev. 20:25; Jer. 32:35).

The Old Testament book of Leviticus acknowledges (17:14) that blood is the life of all flesh, the blood of it is the life thereof, but the children of Israel are instructed that they shall not eat of the blood of no manner of flesh; for the life of all flesh is the blood thereof: whosoever eateth it shall be cut off.

Again, in Deuteronomy (12:20–24), the Lord warns thou mayest eat flesh, whatsoever thy soul lusteth after. Only be sure that thou eat not the blood: for the blood is the life; and thou mayest not eat the life with the flesh.

While the Hebrew God on the one hand repeatedly emphasized that He, as Spirit, did not need or require food and that the true gift that He required was that of man's love, commitment, and service, the Laws of Moses did require the blood of animals and the sacrifice of grain to God. These sacrifices were conducted for three basic reasons: Consecration, to dedicate oneself; Expiation, to cover one's sin or guilt; Propitiation, to satisfy Divine anger.

Consecration sacrifices were vegetable or grain offerings, but they could not be brought to God unless they had been preceded by an expiatory offering of a blood sacrifice. There was no consecration or commitment to God apart from expiation. According to the law, man could not approach God and be right with Him without the shedding of blood that of a bull, a lamb, an ox, and so forth. The sacrifice itself could only be carried out by a High Priest under the strictest obedience to the law. The High Priest himself had to be consecrated before entering the innermost part of the temple or Holy of Holies where the sacrifice was offered to God.

Resident Evil

Make mention of *Resident Evil* and it will inevitably, and correctly, provoke imagery of the on-going series of phenomenally successful movies starring Milla Jovovich. So far, there have been no less than five films in the series. From 2002 to 2012, they are: *Resident Evil, Resident Evil: Apocalypse, Resident Evil: Extinction, Resident Evil: Afterlife*, and *Resident Evil: Retribution*. Collectively, the movies tell the on-going story of Alice, Jovovich's character, who is a former employee of a sinister organization called the Umbrella Corporation. In a post-apocalypse world, a deadly pathogen—known as the T-Virus—has escaped from the confines of the Umbrella Corporation's labs, devastated the entire planet, and led to the terrifying, worldwide rise of the dead. Alice and her varied bands of comrades are forced to do battle with violent, marauding zombies, while at the same time trying their very best to stay just as far away as possible from the surviving remnants of the Umbrella Corporation.

The *Resident Evil* movies have proved to be massive hits with zombie fans: so far they have earned close to an incredible $1 billion worldwide. *Resident Evil: Retribution*, alone, raked in an excess of $200 million. There is, however, far more to *Resident Evil* than just a highly successful film series. It is fair and accurate to say that *Resident Evil* is a veritable phenomenon. Its origins date back to 1996, when Capcom released, in Japan, a video game called *Biohazard*. It proved to be a huge hit, and an English version quickly followed in its apocalyptic wake. It was, of course, titled *Resident Evil*. Right now, there are more than twenty video games in the series, with overall sales having surpassed fifty million. Ironically, Alice—a huge hit with the fans of the movies—is absent from the games. In other words, while the films and the video games are very much part and parcel of each other, the plots and the characters differ to highly significant degrees.

Just like the zombies of *Resident Evil*, the franchise is just about near-unstoppable too. More than a dozen novels, based either on the games or the movies, have been released. Marvel Comics and WildStorm Productions have published *Resident Evil* comic books. There are even *Resident Evil* action figures available. And, on top of that, two CGI-based movies—*Resident Evil: Degeneration* and *Resident Evil: Damnation*—have been released, much to the delight of hardcore fans.

In a unique twist, it is an evil corporation, and not Voodoo or a natural or space plague, that sets off a zombie and monster apocalypse in 2002's *Resident Evil*, the first movie in a multi-film franchise.

It appears that the future of the *Resident Evil* enterprise is safe and secure: A sixth installment in the movie series is slated for release in 2015. And there's even talk of a seventh production. Further video games are planned by Capcom. On top of that, Samuel Hadida, the producer and brains behind the movie spin-offs of the video games has said that after the seventh movie, he is "sure" the series will be "rebooted." As he notes: "*Spiderman* did. Why not *Resident Evil*?" Why not, indeed? Whether in game format, novels, or big-bucks movies, the marauding dead of *Resident Evil* are clearly here to stay.

Romero, George A.

If there is one person who is, and forever will be, inextricably linked to the domain of the zombie, it is George A. Romero. The brains behind *Night of the Living*

George Romero in 2009.

Dead, The Crazies, Dawn of the Dead, Day of the Dead, Land of the Dead, Diary of the Dead, and *Survival of the Dead,* Romero is, for all intents and purposes, solely responsible for the fascination for zombies that began in the late 1960s and that, today, has reached stratospheric proportions. There is, however, far more to Romero than those slow-walking monsters of the big screen.

Born in 1940, in New York City, Romero studied at, and graduated from, Pittsburgh's Carnegie-Mellon University. In the 1960s, Romero and several friends and colleagues established Image Ten Productions, which went on to make the 1968 zombie classic, *Night of the Living Dead.* Three years later, Romero's *There's Always Vanilla* surfaced. Unlike most of Romero's output, this one is based around two topics generally absent from his other productions: comedy and romance. It bombed. One year later, Romero returned to safe ground: horror. *Season of the Witch* (sometimes billed as *Hungry Wives*) was, as the title suggests, a movie filled with covens, spells, and satanic suburbia.

The Crazies of 1973, while not strictly a zombie movie per se, most assuredly pleased fans of the undead with its plotline of a town of people turned into marauding, deranged killers after being exposed to a lethal biological agent.

In between 1978's *Dawn of the Dead* and 1985's *Day of the Dead,* there was a very unusual movie from Romero: *Knightriders.* Running at a lengthy two and a quarter hours, the plotline of this 1981 movie revolves around a band of motorcyclists who entertain the crowds at fairs by jousting on their bikes. *Knightriders* is very much a drama, filled with love, death, passion, and an engaging nod towards the folkloric tales of England's legendary King Arthur. It may not be Romero's most famous piece of work, but it is watchable all the same. One year later, Romero directed the movie, *Creepshow,* for which horror maestro Stephen King wrote the screenplay. It was a film packed with famous faces, including Ted Danson, Leslie Nielsen, and Adrienne Barbeau. It made a healthy profit, too: in excess of $21 million.

Between 1984 and 1988, Romero served as executive producer on no fewer than seventy-seven episodes of the popular television series, *Tales from the Darkside.* He was also the executive producer of *Deadtime Stories,* volumes 1 and 2. In 1993, Romero's cinematic version of Stephen King's *The Dark Half* was released, and in 2000, *Bruiser* surfaced, which is an unusual horror story about a man who wakes one morning to find his face is no more. In its place is a mysterious white mask.

Of course, zombie fans were itching for another sequel in the *Dead* series. And Romero did not disappoint: no less than three new movies in the zombie genre—*Land of the Dead*, *Diary of the Dead*, and *Survival of the Dead*—followed in the 2000s. And Romero is still not done with zombies: his voice appears in the 2012 video game *Zombie Squash*. Just like the flesh-eating creatures for which he has become so famously known, Romero is a nearly unstoppable force.

Russian Zombie Pigeons

When we muse upon the notion of zombies, reanimated corpses, and the undead rising from their coffins, most of the time we think, or assume, that it is going to be the *human* dead that come back to plague and terrorize us. But, how about animals: could they, too, return to provoke mayhem and death on a worldwide scale? Zombie lions, zombie gorillas, or zombie wolves would all be formidable, terrifying killers. Without a gun or several to take them down, they would probably be nearly unstoppable, too. Sadly, for those who think that such things might be infinitely cool to see (although not up close and personal, of course!), they don't exist, or at least not yet they don't. But zombie pigeons do, of a sort, anyway.

In the summer of 2013, and almost overnight, something strange and unsettling occurred on the streets of Moscow, Russia. The resident pigeon population began to change in a dramatic and bizarre fashion. The usually cooing and strutting birds started displaying the sorts of behavior far more in line with the collective works of George A. Romero. Konstantin Ranks, a Russian journalist, said of what was going on: "Before death, they start to resemble zombies; they lose their orientation and fly without a sense of direction, then fall, already lacking the strength to get up."

One witness to the actions of what quickly became known as "the pecking dead" came straight to the point and said: "They're just not normal." Too right: as the days and weeks progressed, hundreds of the feathered creatures were seen staggering around Moscow, all in what appeared to be near-drunken style. There was not a single drop of vodka in sight, however. The pigeons would twist and contort their heads and necks in extraordinary style, while exhibiting sudden and violent outbursts of rage and manic behavior. On top of that, they showed no fear of people and stood their ground when approached, rather than hurriedly and panicky flying away. At the height of the mystery, there was even controversial, whispered talk about secret government experiments involving pigeons brought back from the dead. Why, however, Russian scientists might want to secretly reanimate a bunch of pigeons was anyone's guess.

When further rumors spread around Moscow, to the effect that the birds were infected with a secret, mutated version of Newcastle disease, the levels of concern and worry grew ever larger by the day. No wonder, since Newcastle disease is a highly contagious bird-based virus that can spread to humans, causing serious flu-like symptoms if it is left untreated. Concern and worry reached near-panic levels when the government's Federal Veterinary and Phytosanitary Inspection Unit (FVPIU) *officially* suggested that Newcastle disease was the cause of all the feathery fuss.

According to a Russian sanitary official named Gennady Onishchenko, however, everything was down to nothing stranger than an outbreak of salmonella poisoning. Was this a case of damage control, an attempt to try and allay fears that a deliberately altered version of Newcastle disease was on the loose, possibly all across the entirety of Moscow itself? To this day, the Russian government continues to steadfastly play the matter down, stating that although it has no plans to investigate the ongoing pigeon puzzle, it advises people to keep well away from the birds. You know: just in case.

Scotland Baboon Infection

In the hit 2002 movie, *28 Days Later*, the dawning of the infected is caused by a number of well-meaning animal-rights activists that break into a secret lab and release a chimpanzee infected with what is termed the "rage virus." In no time at all, the United Kingdom is overrun by the virus and millions are transformed into zombie-like killers. Three years before *28 Days Later* was released, however, a significant number of sightings were made of a baboon on the loose in Scotland, something that provoked fears that the animal had escaped from a research lab and, just like its fictional near-counterpart, had been used in some kind of bizarre, biological warfare program.

It all began in January 1999, when a Scottish newspaper, the *Ayrshire Post*, published a story of a distinctly eye-catching nature. It read: "A motorist spotted what he believed was a 'Baboon-like creature' on the Shaw Farm Road in Prestwick, not far from the airport. Police rushed to the scene, and as the officers got to within thirty yards of the animal it disappeared into the undergrowth." As it transpired, the sighting had actually occurred almost two weeks before the newspaper reported the facts, and so when the *Ayrshire Post* revealed the details, it prompted other people who had seen the beast to come forward with their own accounts. Clearly something unusual was afoot in bonny Scotland.

Even Strathclyde's police force became embroiled in the saga: "We received a call from a local man who said he'd narrowly avoided hitting a baboon-like creature on Shaw Farm Road, Prestwick. A patrol car was sent out, and after a search of the area, the officers reported seeing an animal of some sort, although they couldn't be sure what it was."

That a number of police officers had even seen the creature raised the credibility of the reports considerably. As a result of the fact that the creature had been seen near Prestwick Airport, very in-depth and careful checks were made to determine if the creature had illegally entered Scotland via an international flight. Not an impossible scenario, but unlikely, to say the least. Notably, checks by the local police revealed, airport staff *did* receive a large cargo of animals, and only just days before the sightings began, but none of them even remotely resembled a baboon. Checks were then made with every single zoo and animal sanctuary in Scotland. No luck there, either.

As press interest increased, the police did their very best to play the matter down and make light of it. The Scottish media was told by one particular senior officer that not only did the mysterious baboon threaten to overtake the Loch Ness Monster in terms of publicity, but that the police officers who had themselves seen the creature were "very careful" in regard to how they reported their encounter. The spokesman added: The officers were cautious about how they phrased the sighting over the radio. "The mickey-taking could have been merciless and they didn't want to make monkeys of themselves." Quite!

While all of this was excellent fodder for the Scottish press, behind the scenes officialdom was very worried about the affair. Thanks to the terms of the British government's Freedom of Information Act, official documents have surfaced showing that numerous checks were quietly made by the police with government-sponsored laboratories where monkeys were routinely used in experimentation. And not just in Scotland: animal-based research facilities all across England were contacted. They all came up blank. Perhaps the most interesting documents relative to this affair, however, are not the ones that *have* surfaced, but the ones that specifically *haven't*.

Amongst those that the police are known to have spoken with on several occasions in relation to the wild baboon sightings were staff at a facility in the English county of Wiltshire: Porton Down, a well-guarded facility from where the British government undertakes all manner of controversial research in the domains of biological warfare, chemical warfare, and lethal viruses. While scant documentation has surfaced showing that more than fifteen calls were made by a senior Scottish police officer to Porton Down, the details of those conversations remain classified—rather tantalizingly.

Was the distinctly out-of-place baboon an animal that had escaped from Porton Down, or, perhaps more likely, released from the base and then secretly driven to Scotland and let loose into the wilds of the countryside? If so, for what kind of experimentation might the baboon have been used? One hopes the animal was not exposed to some form of exotic, fast-acting pathogen of the type that broke out in *28 Days Later*. Since Britain did not plunge into a nightmarish real version of the high-tech horror movie, it seems safe to assume that the animal was either uninfected or, perhaps, died as a result of the cold, harsh Scottish weather. One question still remains, however: why do the details of those conversations between personnel at Porton Down and the Scottish Police Force still remain classified, more than a decade after the first sightings of the baboon? It is a question that no-one is willing to answer.

Seabrook, William

The 1932 movie *White Zombie* was written by Garnett Weston. It was, however, based upon a book penned by a man named William Seabrook. The latter was, to say the very least, quite a character. He was one who travelled the world having all sorts of Indiana Jones-style adventures, and mixing with Voodoo practitioners, witch doctors, head hunters, and occultists. Seabrook was far more, too, however: he was, very briefly, a full-fledged member of the cannibal club. In other words, the man who wrote about Voodoo and the undead succeeded in becoming just about the closest thing one can to the real thing.

Born in Maryland in 1884, and having fought bravely for his country during World War I—and for which he was prestigiously decorated—Seabrook went on to become a noted journalist. It was Seabrook's love of two issues that really defined his life, however: world-travel and new and novel experiences. On one particularly memorable occasion, both of those matters crossed paths in controversial and noteworthy fashion.

With his wartime career behind him, Seabrook chose to head off to the wilds of Africa for a life of adventure. It was while specifically in West Africa, in the early 1920s, however, that Seabrook developed a distinct taste for a certain type of meat that it's most unwise to get acquainted with: human meat. In an effort to try and understand what life was really like in the region, Seabrook spent time with, and gained the confidence and friendship of, a group of people called the Guere, who just happened to be cannibals. Not wishing to offend the Guere, when it came to feasting on the body of a member of the tribe who was newly dead, Seabrook wasted no time in tucking in heartily. Seabrook's own words on the near-unique experience—extracted from his 1931 book, *Jungle Ways*—make for eye-opening, and even amusing, reading:

"It was like good, fully developed veal, not young, but not yet beef. It was very definitely like that, and it was not like any other meat I had ever tasted. It was so nearly like good, fully developed veal that I think no person with a palate of ordinary, normal sensitiveness could distinguish it from veal. It was mild, good meat with no other sharply defined or highly characteristic taste such as for instance, goat, high game, and pork have. The steak was slightly tougher than prime veal, a little stringy, but not too tough or stringy to be agreeably edible. The roast, from which I cut and ate a central slice, was tender, and in color, texture, smell as well as taste, strengthened my certainty that of all the meats we habitually know, veal is the one meat to which this meat is accurately comparable."

Just to confuse matters, however, there is a story that Seabrook only *watched* the Guere devour the body, and that his own experience with cannibalism occurred not in Africa, but in France, several years later. So the story goes, Seabrook succeeded in getting hold of a fresh corpse—all thanks to the help of an intern at the Sorbonne—which Seabrook roasted on a spit and devoured eagerly. We may never really know where, precisely, Seabrook dined on the dead, but by all accounts, his description of the texture and taste of cooked, human meat was right on target.

Seabrook was far from finished with the domain of the dead, however: as well as having become acquainted with arguably the world's most famous occultist, Aleister Crowley, Seabrook took a lengthy trip to the heart of Haiti to investigate Voodoo lore. It was his experiences and research into the realm of the undead, the reanimated, and the hypnotically controlled that led Seabrook to write two books that detailed his experiences and thoughts on the matters of Voodoo, cannibalism, and zombies. They were *The Magic Island* and *Jungle Ways*, the former being the title on which the 1932 movie, *White Zombie*, was specifically based.

Although William Seabrook was a skilled and atmospheric writer, one with a distinct flair for telling a wild story, his life was not destined to be a long one. He was dead at sixty-one, by his own hand no less, and after years spent fighting both mental illness and alcoholism.

Shaun of the Dead

If you are going to try and make a zombie movie that is hysterically funny, then you had better do a very good job of it. *Zombieland* (starring Woody Harrelson and Bill Murray) was a great example of how the dead can be side-splitting, in a good way. *DeadHeads* and *Juan of the Dead* are okay and good for a chuckle or several. But it's *Shaun of the Dead* that remains the definitive, zombie comedy. The 2004 movie tells the story of Shaun and Ed, two friends living in London, England. Shaun (actor and co-writer of the film, Simon Pegg) has a dead-end job and a rocky relationship with his girlfriend, Liz. Ed (Nick Frost) is a slacker whose main activities are hanging out at home during the day, playing video games, and smoking dope. Most nights are spent at the local pub, the Winchester. That is, until the zombie apocalypse has the bad timing to intrude and truly upsets the applecart.

Shaun of the Dead takes more than a few affectionate leads from established zombie lore, and genially and skillfully pokes fun at modern day society in general, too. Before the hordes of zombies hit the streets, we are treated to amusing scenes of morose, bored, and half-asleep people making their weary way to work—the implication being that acting like a zombie does not necessarily require getting bitten by one and transforming. Indeed, when Shaun and Ed spot the first wave of the shambling dead, they assume that they are just a few drunks on their way home from the pub. Unfortunately, they are not.

Pretty much overnight, the streets of London are filled with the dead arisen from the soil. Taking the zombies out of circulation, however, is no easy task for our two heroes. For the most part, guns are outlawed throughout the British Isles. So, delivering a bullet to the brain of a zombie or several becomes more than a bit of a problem. It becomes a very *big* problem. Shaun and Ed are not without a few resources, however. They improvise by hurling—Frisbee-style—old vinyl records at the hungry hordes, or beating them soundly to the ground with cricket-bats. They then set about making sure that Liz and Shaun's mom, Barbara, are okay. As the zombies increase in number, Shaun, Ed, Barbara,

Simon Pegg (far right) stars in the tongue-in-cheek zombie film *Shaun of the Dead*.

Liz, and her roommates, David and Dianne, realize they have to try and make a final stand, Alamo-style, no less. There's only one thing for it: they head to the Winchester and barricade themselves inside. If you are going to fall victim to an army of zombies, then you might as well knock back a few pints of beer before everything goes to hell.

It is in the latter part of *Shaun of the Dead* that the humor becomes decidedly dark and the movie takes on a poignant tone, particularly when Shaun is forced to kill his own mother. She is bitten by one of the undead earlier in the film, but chooses to keep the terrible news from Shaun until she finally begins to turn. When the zombies inevitably break in, the death toll increases even more, with only Shaun and Liz making it out of the Winchester alive. Even Ed becomes a victim of the marauding flesh-eaters. Fortunately, however, we haven't seen the end of him. Months later, and after the British government has at last managed to overcome the near-irreversible apocalypse, we learn that a semi-tamed, and chained, Ed lives blissfully in Shaun and Liz's garden shed, still playing his beloved video games. Sometimes, a zombie movie does have a happy, and a funny, ending, after all.

Shelley, Mary

See also: Andrew Crosse, Frankenstein

She was born Mary Wollstonecraft Godwin on August 30, 1797. She is, however, far better known to horror aficionados as Mary Shelley, who penned what was not just one of the greatest literary classics of all time, but a gothic saga of true zombie-like proportions. It was *Frankenstein*, published in 1818. It is a story that tells of a crazed doctor—named Victor Frankenstein, hence the title—who engages in dark and disturbing experiments. They revolve around creating a hideous man out of various and sundry body parts of the recent dead and departed. That's to say, Frankenstein goes on a body-snatching spree: an arm here, a leg there, a purloined pair of hands, and so on. Then, having stitched together all of the various limbs, he animates and breathes life into his terrible creation via electricity. It all ends horrifically, of course, as the monster—just about as crazed as Frankenstein himself—goes on a murderous rampage. Most people know at least something of the tale of *Frankenstein* (whether via the book or from the countless movie spin-offs that Shelley's novel has provoked), but what of its author?

Mary Shelley's life began in tragedy: a little more than a week after she was born, her mother—Mary Wollstonecraft—died as a result of complications caused by puerperal fever, a bacterial infection that was all too common during pregnancy back in the 1800s. As a result, Mary and her half sister, Fanny Imlay, were raised solely by their father, William Godwin, a noted and respected philosopher. In 1814, things suddenly changed when Mary met the man who was destined to help define her life and career: the acclaimed poet Percy Bysshe Shelley. Immediately captivated by young Mary, Shelley whisked both her, and her stepsister, Claire Clairmont, off to Europe for fun, adventure, and wild times.

While traveling throughout Europe, a dramatic and unforeseen development in the life of then sixteen-year-old Mary occurred: she became pregnant by Shelley. Since Shelley was already married, the pair was soundly ostracized by those around them. The outcome was that the pair soon descended into poverty and debt. The biggest tragedy of all was that their prematurely born daughter died. Soon after, Shelley and Mary married, but that too was an event steeped in death and doom. The only reason the marriage could go ahead was because Shelley's wife, Harriet, took her own life, thus leaving the poet free to wed Mary.

Not surprisingly, feeling a need for new and fresh surroundings, in the summer of 1816, and along with Claire, poet Lord Byron, and John William Polidori (a physician and the author of a proto-tale of blood-sucking monsters, *The Vampyre*), Mary and Shelley traveled to Switzerland and rented a large manor house on Lake Geneva. It was while staying at the spacious home—Villa Diodati—that Mary began to work on her now-famous novel. And there is a very good reason why she did so. Polidori, Shelley, and Mary had one thing in common: a fascination for an eighteenth century poet and physician named Erasmus Darwin, who had supposedly succeeded in reanimating a human corpse. Filled with enthusiasm and ideas, and with Shelley guiding her,

Mary Shelley, author of *Frankenstein*.

Mary plunged herself into the story and created an undeniable masterpiece. In spite of her literary success, however, even more tragedy awaited the now-famous novelist.

Of Mary and Shelley's three children, only one survived to reach adulthood: Percy Florence. And even worse was to come. In 1822, and at the age of just twenty-nine, Shelley himself died. It was during a violent storm, and while sailing to the Italian town of Lerici that Shelley met his end when his ship, the *Don Juan*, sank due to the pummeling might of the pounding waves. Utterly crushed, Mary returned to England and devoted the rest of her life to raising her son and continuing her career as a writer. And tragedy was waiting in the wings for Mary, herself, too: in February 1851, and at the age of only fifty-three, she died from the effects of a brain-tumor. How ironic that Mary Shelley's most famous creation—Dr. Frankenstein's monster—should have been successfully brought to life, when Shelley herself was surrounded by nothing but death.

Sin Eating

Brad Steiger's friend Lisa Lee Harp Waugh, an expert on many aspects of the paranormal, necromancy, and Voodoo, grew up in Marshall, Texas, and went to school with a daughter of a well-known local Sin Eater.

At the ripe old age of fourteen, Lisa Lee said, "I witnessed her father practicing the Sin Eaters' trade on her grandmother before the mortuary hearse came to retrieve her body."

According to Waugh: "The body was laid naked on the kitchen table, and all the food in the house had been prepared and set out alongside and on top of this sixty-nine-year-old woman's nude corpse. It was explained to me that in Texas Voodoo-Hoodoo Sin Eaters had a redemptive role in the religious practices of American civilization. At the end of an individual's life, he was allowed to confess his misdeeds to this Soul Eater, and according to legend, the Soul Eater would cleanse their dirty soul by eating its filth."

Waugh learned that while many believed the old custom to be abandoned, in many parts of Louisiana and southern Texas, it is still a common practice that occurs regularly.

As she grew up, she discovered that Marshall alone was home to many Sin Eaters and that there

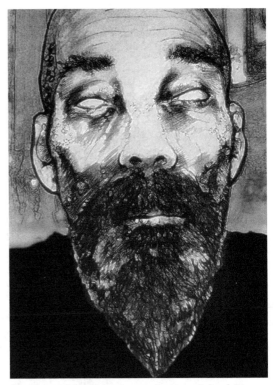

Sin Eaters literally consume the sins of the dying so that they may travel to the afterlife without the burden of a guilty soul.

were no less than twenty-two adept Sin Eaters across the United States who ate the many awful assorted sins of those who could not rightfully go to heaven unless their evil sins were gone.

Waugh has met a wide variety of paranormalists in her life, but she says, "Actual Sin Eaters are very much more interesting than the average ghost enthusiast." And many times during the process of the actual eating of the sins, it is said that the ghost of the deceased is seen and witnessed, moving and crying around the room. "I will tell you that this has been witnessed by many besides myself."

Singh, Rev. Mother Severina Karuna Mayi

Rev. Mother Severina Karuna Mayi Singh practices Vodoun and Yoruba traditions, as well as Sufism and metaphysical practices. She is also the founder of the New Orleans Voodoo Crossroads Dance and Drum Ensemble, a popular troupe performing at festivals, Voodoo weddings, and other events.

Reverend Mother Severina Karuna Mayi Singh is the founder of the New Orleans Voodoo Crossroads Dance and Drum Ensemble. (*Art by Ricardo Pustanio*).

The Voodoo Crossroads was founded in 1991 as a vehicle for the dissemination of true and accurate information about the beliefs and practices of the Voodoo religion in New Orleans. She offers products and services in the tradition of New Orleans Voodoo.

The official site is http://www.neworleansVoodoocrossroads.com.

Snake Zombies

Located on the northern coastline of South America and the Caribbean Sea, Guyana is a captivating and mysterious land that is noted for its dense jungles, huge mountains, deep caves, and varied wildlife. And it doesn't get any more mysterious than the village of Taushida, which has a story attached to it of definitive zombie proportions. The dead of Taushida are not people, however, but huge and marauding snakes. According to local lore, centuries ago, the villagers of Taushida suffered attacks from a local tribe and sorely needed to find a way to combat the escalating problem. Thus it was that they turned to their shaman for the answers. Skilled in understanding and utilizing the powers of the supernatural world, he invoked from some unearthly realm a supernatural snake-god possessed of terrible and awesome powers.

With a series of animal sacrifices duly made to the terrible snake-god, it, in return, revealed an equally terrible secret to the shaman: how to create an army of deadly, unstoppable killers in the form of giant snakes. The process involved catching and killing baby anacondas and then, using a mixture of spells and incantations, having them return from the grave in the form of giant-sized snakes with just one thing on their evil minds: devouring people, as in the enemies of Taushida.

Since only the shaman could command and control the mighty creatures, when opposing forces closed in on Taushida, all aside from the man of magic retreated to a fortified cavern in the hills and patiently waited for the all clear. It was the shaman's job, and his alone, to recite an ancient verse provided to him by the snake-god, one which would cause the slaughtered anacondas to rise from the dirt and the grime. Transformed from their original lengths of a couple of feet into massive beasts of around forty-feet in length, the reanimated snakes obeyed the commands of the shaman to destroy the enemy, which they did in violent fashion.

As Taushida's foes closed in on the village, the snakes—which were hidden in the deep grass surrounding the locale—reared up in their dozens and tore the aggressors to pieces. Never again were the people of Taushida bothered by agressors; or, at least, not by human aggressors.

As is so very often the case when one makes a pact with a deadly supernatural entity—in this case a snake-god—there is a snag. To prevent the zombified snakes from turning their lethal attentions towards the people of Taushida, once a year, and for the next twenty years, the village folk had to sacrifice a new-born baby to the snake-god. It was a most high price to pay for their safety.

It may be said that the story is nothing but a legend, and that certainly could be the case. Very often, however, a legend will develop out of some semblance of reality. And the reality is that on more than a few occasions, giant-sized snakes *have* been spotted roaming in and around the caves and forestland of Taushida, and specifically in an area called Corona Falls.

For example, in 2007, a British adventurer named Richard Freeman traveled to Guyana to investigate such reports and came across numerous sightings of snakes of such a size that they dwarfed the largest snakes ever recorded. Freeman, who gained the trust of the people of the area, learned of sightings of immense snakes, in the order of fifty feet long and with bodies thicker than oil drums. They weren't zombie-snakes, but they were so lethal they just might as well have been. That these huge creatures led to the development, centuries ago, of stories about supernatural zombie-snakes lurking in and around Taushida seems more than likely.

Solomon Island Cannibals

The Solomon Islands, situated east of Papua New Guinea, are captivating and enchanting. And there are far more than a few of them; in fact, in excess of nine hundred. As for a human presence on the islands, it dates back tens of thousands of years. Back then, the people were primitive and savage in the extreme, very often resorting to cannibalism to fuel and feed their bellies. It was not until the 1500s, when Alvaro de Mendana y Neira—a Spanish explorer—became the first European to reach the islands and duly christened them "Islas Salamon," that stability and civilization came to the area and the savage days of the past began to recede. What did not recede, however, were the old beliefs of the islanders.

While, today, more than ninety percent of those that call the Solomon Islands their home are Christians, the traditions of centuries long gone still hold sway for many. Reincarnation was, for many years, a deeply accepted reality by the islanders. For the people of the Solomon Islands, however, there was a belief that the soul was comprised of two parts—only one of which would reincarnate, while the other would be banished to an island filled with savagery or a land of light and enchantment.

The folk of the Solomon Islands believed in something else, too: the presence in the forests of troll-like monsters that displayed a significant number of zombie-like traits. The beasts—which fed voraciously on the human population—were extremely violent and required beheading to bring their attacks to sudden halts. It was important to avoid getting bitten by one of the ogre-style monsters of the Philippines, too, since this would provoke the sudden emergence of a terrible disease that would quickly infect, ravage, and kill their victims. As for how the creatures were able to so successfully attack the islanders, the answer was born out of shape-shifting: they had the ability to transform their bulbous, hideous forms into those of people, thus making it easy for them to move among the unwary and the unsuspecting—before launching a lethal attack.

Clearly, we should not interpret all of this literally. Much of it, no doubt, was born out of myth and folklore. But, the image of crazed beasts, spreading infection and devouring the living, does, admittedly, provoke significant parallels with today's zombie. Were the Solomon Islands, in times long gone, the abode of something not unlike the walking dead? Given that most folklore is born out of at least a bit of truth, perhaps the amazing answer is: Yes.

Somaliland

In early 1999, the Central Intelligence Agency (CIA), followed closely—and with a high degree of concern—a story that came out of Somaliland without any warning. As incredible as it may sound, it was a story that contained far more than a few zombie parallels. Thanks to the provisions of the United States' Freedom of Information Act, a number of documents relevant to the story have now surfaced into the public domain. Certainly, the most significant paper of all is one titled *Somaliland President Egal Speaks on Mysterious Bomb Blast*. The document—which was forwarded to the State Department, Defense Intelligence Agency, and Wright-Patterson Air Force Base, Dayton, Ohio, among other agencies and departments—includes an interview extracted from a *Focus on Africa* radio show that CIA analysts carefully transcribed. That transcript reads as follows:

"There have been reports this week of mysterious explosions in the remote eastern region of the self-declared republic of Somaliland. They apparently occupied in December, but because of the remote nature of the area have been slow coming to light. The blasts have been attributed to various causes from unidentified flying objects, UFOs, to rocket tests. Well, Somaliland Leader, Mohamed Egal, has been looking into the matter. On the line to Hargesa, Timothy Ecott asked him what he thought had been going on.

"Begin recording Egal [sic]: We have these mysterious reports from our nomadic population there, and then, I sent a four-man commission, two doctors, a veteran doctor, and one minister, and they have submitted to us a report, which is very, very alarming. They said that they went there almost a fortnight after this thing had taken place and the found most of the animals in the area are still in a sort of a demented stage. They were not grazing, they were just stampeding all over the place.

"Ecott: You said the animals were demented. What about the people living there?

"Egal: Some of them, who were very close to the area, have got skin rashes, and some of them are almost shredding their outer skin. There are boils all over the place, and some of them are having stomach aches, you know, and very unusual motions—stomach motion—and a lot of symptoms have been reported. We are sending back some doctors to actually evaluate the human damage and the animal damage that has been done.

"Ecott: Did anyone get an eyewitness account of what this explosion might have been caused by?

"Egal: The people who were there, you know, the stories they tell is [sic] that they heard no noise. Apparently whatever exploded was moving at a supersonic speed, because there was no prior noise or anything like that. You know, they just heard a very, very, very loud explosion which has taken place and the light, you know, the light of the explosion in the air. The area is so big that they didn't have the capability or the time to investigate the whole ground and try and pick up any debris that might have fallen. They haven't been able to do that.

"Ecott: Whatever your authority is claiming that this might have been, some of the news agencies are talking about UFOs.

"Egal: No, no, no, no. We are not making any claims of that or any fantastic claims like that, you know. What we think happened is that there must have been a missile fired from somewhere, which has exploded either deliberately over our country or whether it has exploded inadvertently, we can't tell. So, what we are asking now, people like the English, and French, and especially the Americans who monitor the world, they must know what happened, you know. They definitely know what happened. If it was Saddam Hussein who fired the missile, it would have been in the headlines all over the world. But apparently whoever fired the missile is still in the good books of those who know, and they don't want to publicize it. But we want to know what happened to us so that at least we will know how to deal with it.

"Ecott: Is anybody offering you help to investigate and to look after the people you say have been injured?

"Egal: Well, we have sent it ... yes ... to the American Embassy. You know. We have sent it to the British Embassy, we have sent it to the French Embassy, and we have sent to the BBC, and to the Reuters and people like that, you know. Nobody has yet responded, but we have made the appeal and we are still making it."

There ends one of the transcripts that not surprisingly so intrigued the CIA. Rather interestingly, additional papers—ones that were *heavily* censored before their release via the Freedom of Information Act—refer to additional reports of not just animals, but also of people acting in "demented" fashion. And in the same way that the affected animals were said to be "stampeding" around the area, so the deranged people—when infection set in—were said to exhibit what were described as "sudden bursts of speed." What became of the rampaging infected, we do not know. The story died as quickly as it surfaced. Did the U.S. military, alerted by the CIA, secretly and quietly dispatch a Delta Force-type team to extinguish the threat of the infected? We simply don't know. But, if nothing else, this episode does serve to demonstrate one important thing: The fast-running zombie may not just be a creation of novelists and screenwriters after all. It may also be something about which the CIA secretly knows a great deal. Whether the CIA will one day choose to share what it knows with the rest of us, however, is a whole different ball game.

Soul-Stealers

In Tobe Hooper's 1985 movie *Lifeforce* the reanimated dead look like zombies, return just hours after getting attacked and killed, and provoke apocalyptic carnage all across London, England. They are just regular zombies, right? No: wrong. In *Lifeforce* the dead are alien-controlled monsters that do not feed on the flesh of the living but on their souls, which is converted into a form of life-sustaining energy for the malevolent extraterrestrials. It may well be, to the eternal horror of everyone, that such soul-stealing zombies are not just a fantasy.

In the film, Sharon is a secretary employed at the Kennedy Space Center at Merritt Island, Florida, who, for as long as she can remember, has had encounters of the so-called "alien abduction" kind. For the most part, the abductions have followed the standard motif: Sharon finds herself transported onto a UFO where she becomes the subject of distressing medical and genetic experimentation by large-headed, dwarfish creatures with huge black eyes. By the time Sharon reaches her thirties, however, matters changed—but certainly not for the better.

On several occasions, Sharon experiences something even more traumatic than diminutive ETs messing around with her body. She develops an acute fear that the bug-eyed creatures are trying to extract her soul from her body. How, exactly, Sharon knows this she is unable to explain, but it is such an intense feeling that she has no doubts about the overall goal of the abductions: to allow her captors to feed on her, in somewhat of a zombie-like style. Not on her body, bones, or blood, but on her very essence, her life-force, her soul.

A few days after casually mentioning her experiences to several colleagues at the space center, Sharon is approached by a woman who displays NASA credentials, but whom Sharon does not recognize as an employee of the installation. That's because she is not. As Sharon listens intently, and somewhat nervously, the woman tells her that she works for an arm of NASA ("out of Arizona") that covertly monitors the UFO phenomenon, and particularly to accounts of alien abduction.

When the woman asks Sharon to meet and discuss her experiences in-depth, Sharon agrees. Rather oddly, it is an off-the-record meeting in the staff car park. Despite the undeniably cloak-and-dagger atmosphere, Sharon is happy to discuss her experiences, and particularly so with someone seemingly working on a program devoted to the very issue that has so dominated and affected Sharon's life. It's fair to say that what Sharon hears is not what she was expecting. It is her assumption that the woman (dressed all in black, no less—definitive shades of the Men in Black) would reveal all that NASA knows about alien abductions and the apparent genetic and medical aspects of the phenomenon. What Sharon *does* hear is very different— and outright terrifying.

According to the woman, NASA had deduced—although how, exactly, is not made clear—that our supposed extraterrestrials are actually nothing of the sort. Instead, they are inter-dimensional beings, acutely hostile to the human race, and that take far more than a passing interest in the human soul. Having studied "hundreds of reports," Sharon is advised, NASA's ultimate conclusion is that we are all in danger of being "harvested" by poorly understood creatures of some mystifying realm that, for all intents and purposes, are here to "eat us."

In view of all this, maybe the apocalypse will come not via undead monsters that crave our flesh but life-force-stealing nightmares that yearn for our souls.

Soylent Green

Two years after he starred in *The Omega Man*—the 1971 movie adaptation of Richard Matheson's novel, *I Am Legend*—Charlton Heston took on the lead role in another movie of undeniably apocalyptic proportions. Its title was *Soylent Green*. The film is set in 2022, when the Earth is in deep and dire straits. The planet's population has risen to such gigantic levels that its resources can no longer sustain us—or, in fact, sustain *anything*. The decades-long and reckless use of fossil fuels, widespread pollution, dwindling food supplies, and a stifling temperature caused by man-made global-warming, have all ensured that the Earth as we once knew it is no more. Forests, jungles, lakes, rivers, and the rich diversity of animals that once populated the planet are all but gone. Even the world's oceans are rapidly becoming barren and sterile. Pretty much all that is left is the human race. And while its numbers are growing, society is

In a world ravaged by overpopulation and shrinking resources, humanity takes to harvesting human beings for food in the dystopian society portrayed in *Soylent Green.*

collapsing. New York City, where *Soylent Green* is set, is in chaos and resembles nothing less than a Middle Eastern war-zone. People live in cramped and crowded conditions; millions of them are on the streets, begging for food and shelter. Rioting is commonplace and the police resemble the Gestapo.

While a small elite group of people still has access to such luxuries as meat, vegetables, cheese, and the many and varied food items that we take for granted today, the billions upon billions of people that now swarm the Earth derive their entire sustenance from a product called Soylent—named after the powerful and mysterious Soylent Corporation that produces it. Resembling a wheat cracker in appearance, Soylent comes in three colors: red, yellow, and green. It is the latter which is the most popular.

Heston's character, Robert Thorn, is a police officer who, while investigating the killing of one of the directors of the Soylent Corporation—a man named William Simonson—uncovers the terrible truth about Soylent Green. Officially, Soylent Green is made from plankton, taken from the ocean and refined into food. That certainly was the case in earlier years; by 2022, however, the oceans are so polluted that there is almost zero plankton left. This begs an important question: with the plankton gone, and the Earth's resources all but spent, exactly what is Soylent Green now being made from? The answer is as simple as it is terrifying: As Officer Thorn learns to his horror, the bodies of the newly deceased are being secretly transferred to huge processing plants. It is at these plants that the remains of the dead are converted into the world's tastiest food, Soylent Green. The movie ends in memorable fashion, as a shot and seriously injured Thorn cries out to anyone who will listen: "Soylent Green is people!"

Although *Soylent Green* is clearly not a zombie-themed movie, it is a production that has relevance to the undead, albeit in a strange and alternative fashion. In the cinematic world of the zombie, the dead feed voraciously upon the living. In the world of *Soylent Green*, however, the living feed equally voraciously upon the dead, even though, admittedly, the overwhelming majority of the population assumes they are eating modified plankton. In other words, the people of *Soylent Green* are the collective mirror image of the monsters of *Night of the Living Dead*. In a curious way, the human race has become the army of the undead.

Spanish Flu

See also: Black Death, Infection, Creutzfeld-Jacobs Disease

To have an understanding of just how quickly a real zombie apocalypse might take a solid, unrelenting grip on the human race—and ultimately decimate it in the process—it is necessary to take a leap back in time to 1918, when one of the most devastating viral outbreaks of all time occurred. Such is the speed with which the past soon gets forgotten; however, many are completely unaware of the terrible events that saw the rise of a deadly virus and tens of millions dead from infection. It is the fear-filled affair of what has become infamously known as Spanish flu. This was no normal kind of flu virus, however. Rather, it was one that mutated to such an astonishing degree that practically no-one on the planet was immune to, or safe from, its deadly power.

In 1914, World War I began and led to countless deaths all across battle-scarred Europe. The carnage finally came to its end in 1918, when Germany was finally defeated. Since, however, the first wave of infection began in early 1918—when the war was still being fought, and when tens of thousands of troops were dying from the carnage of warfare—its scale, and its attendant implications for the human race, went by largely unnoticed or under-appreciated. That is, until it was all way too late to do much about it.

As is often the case in zombie-themed TV shows and movies of today, the origin and the eruption of the outbreak are matters of deep controversy and mystery. Confusion reigns and wild rumors spread regarding what is afoot. Such was the case with Spanish flu in 1918. Interestingly, and also paralleling established zombie lore, there were suspicions on the part of Allied soldiers that it was all the work of the dastardly Germans. There was an undercurrent of belief that they had created a deadly virus and then, using carefully placed agents all across the planet, had unleashed it to wipe out any and all enemy nations. And there is a third zombie-based angle, too:

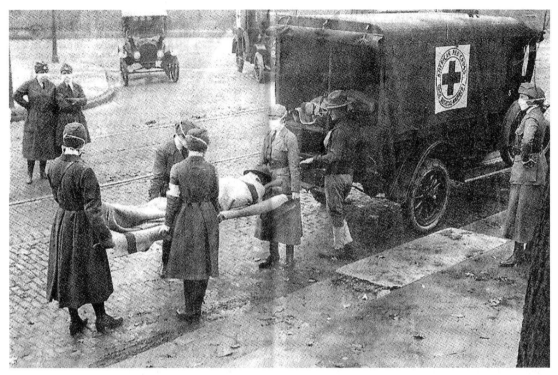

Spanish flu victims are tended to by Red Cross workers in this photo taken in St. Louis, Missouri, in 1918. There are no exact figures, but between thirty and fifty million died of the pandemic worldwide, including about 650,000 in the United States.

when infection from Spanish flu set in, its effects could be seen in mere hours. Profuse bleeding from the mouth and nose was typical. A raging fever and pneumonia-like symptoms soon overwhelmed the infected. Death was not far behind. The only thing missing with Spanish flu was reanimation.

What is known for sure about the outbreak is that military personnel in training camps in Kansas were amongst the very first fatal victims. This has led to a theory that Spanish flu had its origins in the Kansas-based Fort Riley, where chickens and pigs were bred by the military for food. It is suspected that a form of avian flu, present in the chickens, may have "jumped" to the human race, thus resulting in the anarchy and death that very quickly followed. Certainly, it was not long at all before the rest of the world was in the icy grip of the deadly virus: parts of South America, Asia, Europe, the United States, and Africa were soon overwhelmed. One might think that such a powerful, mutated form of the flu virus would chiefly take its toll on the old and the sickly. Not so, actually the opposite: nearly all of the victims were under the age of thirty-five.

Incredibly, at the height of the epidemic, no less than twenty-five percent of the entire U.S. population was infected, as was around eighteen to twenty percent of the rest of the planet. To put that in some form of perspective, we are collectively talking about around 500 million people, worldwide. It's hardly surprising, then, that Spanish flu ultimately took the lives of around *forty million people*. In late 1918, and for reasons that still remain very much unclear to this day, the death toll began to drop at a significant rate and to the point where, by 1919, the epidemic was finally, and thankfully, on its last legs. By the time the outbreak was declared over, Spanish flu had killed more people than had the hostilities during all of World War I.

Stumpp, Peter

Beyond any shadow of doubt at all, one of the most notorious serial-killers of all time was Peter Stumpp. He was a German farmer who became infamously known as the Werewolf of Bedburg. Born in the village of Epprath, Cologne, Stumpp was a wealthy, respected, and influential farmer in the local community. But he was also a man hiding a truly dark and diabolical secret—one that surfaced graphically and sensationally in 1589, when he was brought to trial for the heinous crimes of both murder and cannibalism.

Having been subjected to the extreme torture of the rack, Stumpp confessed to countless horrific acts, including feasting on the flesh of sheep, lambs, and goats, and even that of men, women, and children, too. Stumpp further revealed to the shocked court that he had killed and devoured no less than fourteen children, two pregnant

A woodcut showing the execution of Peter Stumpp in Cologne, Germany, in 1589 using the "breaking wheel" method.

women and their fetuses, and even his own son's brain. Stumpp, however, had an extraordinary excuse to try and explain and account for his vile actions and cannibalistic behavior.

Stumpp maintained that since the age of twelve, he had secretly engaged in black magic, and on one occasion had succeeded in summoning up none other than the devil, who provided him with a "magical belt" that gave him the ability to morph into "the likeness of a greedy, devouring wolf, strong and mighty, with eyes great and large, which in the night sparkled like fire, a mouth great and wide, with most sharp and cruel teeth, a huge body, and mighty paws."

While the devil may have been impressed by Stumpp's explanation, the court most assuredly was not. Stumpp was put to death in brutal fashion: flesh was torn from his body, his arms and legs were broken, and, finally, he was beheaded. The Werewolf of Bedburg was no more. Stumpp was not alone, however, in terms of feasting on the dead while in a homicidal state.

Equally as horrific as the actions of Peter Stumpp were those of an unnamed man who, in the final years of the sixteenth century, became known as the Werewolf of Chalons. A Paris, France-based tailor who killed, dismembered, and ate the flesh of numerous children he lured into his shop, the man was brought to trial for his heinous crimes on December 14, 1598. Notably, during the trial, it was claimed that on occasion the man also roamed nearby woods in the form of a huge, predatory wolf, where he further sought out innocent souls to both slaughter and consume. As was the case with Stumpp, the Werewolf of Chalons was sentenced to death and duly burned at the stake.

Sumanto, the Indonesian Cannibal

When Sumanto, an Indonesian farmer in rural Central Java, was about to be released from prison in July 2009, he promised his neighbors in his home village that he was no longer going to be eating people. His cannibal days were over, he assured them. He was now going to eat only spinach and vitamins. His old neighbors rejected his request to come home. The memories of Sumanto digging up an old lady and eating her were far too fresh in their minds.

In his room at a Muslim mental rehabilitation center, Sumanto said that he loved meat and that the corpse of the elderly woman that he had dug out of her grave was very tasty. Even though eating the deceased made for inexpensive meals, Sumanto argued, he would restrain himself from ever again stealing another body to put into his stew pot.

Neighbors in the village rejected Sumanto's plea for understanding. A woman who had been his next-door neighbor had the unpleasant experience of investigating a terrible smell coming from Sumanto's house. She said that she would never forget the stench of death and the sight of Sumanto eating from a bowl of whitish-yellow human flesh dripping with soy sauce.

Survival of the Dead

It hit cinemas in 2009 and was George A. Romero's sixth production on the matter of those pesky undead. It was *Survival of* (what else?) *the Dead*. Romero's previous titles in the *Dead* series (*Night, Dawn, Day, Land,* and *Diary*) got rave reviews and reaped in respectable profits. *Survival,* however, achieved neither. The lack of success of *Survival of the Dead* was not due to poor marketing, however. It was due to something else: quite simply, the movie is not a very good one.

The storyline is unusual, focusing as it does on a pair of Irish clans who are bitter enemies: the Muldoons and the O'Flynns. The tension between the two grows ever bigger when, with the dead roaming far and wide, the O'Flynns learn that their archfoes are keeping their infected family members alive in the hope that a cure might be found for their cannibalistic conditions. For the O'Flynns there is only one way to deal with the dead: bullets to the brain. Not surprisingly, this antagonizes the hatred between the two families even more, and particularly so as the death count grows and the zombie army increases in number. And that's pretty much the entire plot: families fighting each other when they are not combating the infected.

What makes *Survival of the Dead* particularly odd is that it presents itself as a combination of a zombie movie and a "shoot 'em up"-style western, of the likes of *Gunfight at the O.K. Corral.* Had Romero taken the best parts of *Night of the Living Dead* and blended them with the likes of the Clint Eastwood-starring *A Fistful of Dollars,* he would have been onto a winner. Unfortunately, that was not the case. And the fans knew it all too well: despite a budget of around $4 million, *Survival of the Dead* has yet to bring in even $200,000 in earnings. In the world of the zombie, you can't win them all—and that goes for both on-screen and behind the camera.

Survivors

Survivors was a British television series, made by and aired on the BBC, that ran from 1975 to 1977. It had at its heart two things that are absolutely integral to the domain of the zombie in today's world: a deadly virus and the end of civilization. While the dead themselves remain dead in *Survivors,* the show offers a good indication of how life might really be in the events of a fast-spreading plague that kills nearly all of the human race.

Survivors begins in London, England, at a time when a mysterious illness has begun surfacing amongst the population. At first, and due to the small number of deaths, the British government is able to successfully hide the truth from the public and the media. But matters don't stay like that for long, however. The deadly virus, released in error by a Chinese scientist, soon takes its grip not just on the U.K., but on the entire planet. World authorities do their very best to retain control, but it's all to no avail. In no time at all, the death rate rises from the dozens to the thousands and, ultimately, from the millions to the billions. The human race is all but extinct, aside from the few survivors of the show's title.

It must be said that *Survivors* is a highly watchable and gripping series, primarily because it pulls no punches. The entire tone of the show is bleak, as one might expect it to be in the real world when society and civilization are nothing but a memory. The regular cast—not unlike those of AMC's *The Walking Dead*—constantly find themselves dealing with the devastating effects of the deadly virus and the ragged remnants of society that will do all they can to survive. And doom and gloom dominate the entire storyline, as does violent murder—something which quickly takes hold all across the nation, as people struggle to survive, no matter what the cost in human lives.

Survivors ran for three series and thirty-eight episodes and, typical of its entire theme, ended in a fashion that, while providing some degree of hope for the straggling bands of people across the U.K., also left the door open for further anarchy and descent into savagery. In 2008, *Survivors* was resurrected from the grave. It was not a hit with the viewing public and was cancelled after just twelve episodes, proof that ratings (or, in this case, a lack of them) can be far more powerful than even the deadliest of all viruses.

Taigheirm

Centuries ago, in some of the wilder and darker parts of Scotland, occultists began engaging in a ritual designed to provide them with endless riches, wealth, good health, and power. It was a ritual that became known as the Taigheirm. It stands out in the sense that the process of ensuring good fortune involved the invoking of huge and malevolent, zombie-style cats.

Without a doubt, the most detailed description of this archaic and highly disturbing rite can be found in the pages of J.Y.W. Lloyd's 1881 book, *The History of the Princes, the Lord's Marcher, and the Ancient Nobility of Powys Fadog and the Ancient Lords of Arwystli, Cedewen, and Meirionydd*. Since Lloyd's words are vital to understanding and appreciating the weird story, it's important that they are understood in their entirety:

"Horst, in his *Deuteroscopy*, tells us that the Highlanders of Scotland were in the habit of sacrificing black cats at the incantation ceremony of the Taigheirm, and these were dedicated to the subterranean gods; or, later to the demons of Christianity. The midnight hour, between Friday and Saturday, was the authentic time for these horrible practices and invocations; and the sacrifice was continued four whole days and nights, without the operator taking any nourishment."

In the words of Horst himself: "After the cats were dedicated to all the devils, and put into a magico-sympathetic condition, by the shameful things done to them, and the agony occasioned to them, one of them was at once put alive upon the spit, and amid terrific howlings, roasted before a slow fire. The moment that the howls of one tortured cat ceased in death, another was put upon the spit, for a minute of interval must not take place if they would control hell; and this continued for the four entire days and nights. If the exorcist could hold it out still longer, and even till his physical powers were absolutely exhausted, he must do so.

"After a certain continuance of the sacrifice, infernal spirits appeared in the shape of black cats. There came continually more and more of these cats; and their howlings, mingled with those roasting on the spit, were terrific. Finally, appeared a cat of a monstrous size, with dreadful menaces. When the Taigheirm was complete, the sacrificer [sic] demanded of the spirits the reward of his offering, which consisted of various things; as riches, children, food, and clothing. The gift of second sight, which they had not had before, was, however, the usual recompense; and they retained it to the day of their death."

Let's return to the words of Lloyd: "One of the last Taigheirm, according to Horst, was held in the island of Mull. The inhabitants still show the place where Allan Maclean, at that time the incantor, and sacrificial priest, stood with his assistant, Lachlain Maclean, both men of a determined and unbending character, of a powerful build of body, and both unmarried. We may here mention that the offering of cats is remarkable, for it was also practiced by the ancient Egyptians. Not only in Scotland, but throughout all Europe, cats were sacrificed to the subterranean gods, as a peculiarly effective means of coming into communication with the powers of darkness.

"Allan Maclean continued his sacrifice to the fourth day, when he was exhausted both in body and mind, and sunk in a swoon; but, from this day he received the second-sight to the time of his death, as also did his assistant. In the people, the belief was unshaken, that the second-sight was the natural consequence of celebrating the Taigheirm."

Lloyd once again turned to Horst: "The infernal spirits appeared; some in the early progress of the sacrifices, in the shape of black cats. The first glared at the sacrificers and cried "Lachlain Oer" [Injurer of Cats]. Allan, the chief operator, warned Lachlain, whatever he might see or hear, not to waiver, but to keep the spit incessantly turning. At length, the cat of monstrous size appeared; and, after it had set up a horrible howl, said to Lachlain Oer, that if he did not cease before their largest brother came, he would never see the face of God. Lachlain answered, that he would not cease till he had finished his work, if all the devils in hell came. At the end of the fourth day, there sat on the end of the beam, in the roof of the barn, a black cat with fire-flaming eyes, and there was heard a terrific howl, quite across the straits of Mull, into Morven."

Lloyd then continued: "Allan was wholly exhausted on the fourth day, from the horrible apparitions, and could only utter the word "Prosperity." But Lachlain, though the younger, was stronger of spirit, and perfectly self-possessed. He demanded posterity and wealth, and each of them received that which he has asked for.

"When Allan lay on his death-bed, and his Christian friends pressed round him, and bade him beware of the stratagems of the devil, he replied with great courage, that if Lachlain Oer, who was already dead, and he, had been able a little longer to have carried their weapons, they would have driven Satan himself from his throne, and, at all events, would have caught the best birds in his kingdom.

"When the funeral of Allen reached the churchyard, the persons endowed with second-sight saw at some distance Lachlain Oer, standing fully armed at the head of a host of black cats, and everyone could perceive the smell of brimstone which streamed from those cats. Allan's effigy, in complete armour, is carved on his tomb, and his name is yet linked with the memory of the Taigheirm.

"Shortly before that time also, Cameron of Lochiel performed a Taigheirm, and received from the infernal spirits a small silver shoe, which was to be put on the left foot of each new-born son of his family, and from which he would receive courage and fortitude in the presence of his enemies; a custom which continued till 1746, when his house was consumed by fire. This shoe fitted all the boys of his family but one, who fled before the enemy at Sheriff Muir, he having inherited a larger foot from his mother, who was of another clan. The word Taigheirm means an armoury, as well as the cry of cats, according as it is pronounced."

Another old document, from 1893, adds, rather notably, in relation to the zombie comparisons: "Those who were witness to the black cats of the Taigheirm described a sense of death and a smell of the corpse about them." And maybe they are still with us. Carl Van Vechten was the author of a 1922 book, *The Tiger in the House*, which details how the author had carefully studied the ritual of the Taigheirm and learned from various contacts in Scotland that, at the time he wrote his book, the terrible rite was still practiced. It had not died out in the slightest. Perhaps, then, the zombie-cats of Scotland still roam, even to this very day.

Tay Bridge

According to a Glasgow, Scotland electrician named Danny Thomas, on a particular evening in January 1879, his great-great-grandfather, who apparently suffered from some form of severe mental affliction, committed suicide by hurling himself off Scotland's Tay Bridge, and right into the harsh waters of Dundee's Firth of Tay. In the immediate days that followed the family's tragic loss, ominous reports began to quietly circulate within the close-knit confines of the neighborhood of a shaggy-haired man-beast that was seen roaming the Tay Bridge late at night, and that came to be known locally as the Shuggy—a word which is derived from an old English word, "Scucca," which means "demon." But there were far more ominous things to come—things that some said were directly linked to the presence of that shaggy-haired monster.

Almost two miles in length and carrying a single railtrack, the bridge—which was completed in February 1878, to the plans of Sir Thomas Bouch—was the longest in the world at that time. Proposals for such a bridge dated back to 1854, and its foundation stone was laid with ceremony on July 22, 1871. The first engine duly crossed the bridge on September 22, 1877, and the bridge was officially opened by Queen Vic-

The Tay Bridge in Scotland is where many people reported seeing a demon of some sort appear immediately after a mentally unstable man committed suicide there.

toria on June 1, 1878. Ulysses S. Grant worded it correctly when he commented that it was "a big bridge for a small city." But that situation soon changed—and most definitely not for the better.

It was an appropriately dark and stormy night on December 28, 1879 when, at around 7:15 P.M., and as a veritable storm of truly deluge-style proportions was blowing right down the length of the estuary, the central navigation spans of the Tay Bridge collapsed and plummeted into the Firth of Tay—taking with them a train and six carriages that resulted in no less than seventy-five untimely and tragic deaths. Legend and urban-myth that still circulate in Dundee to this very day hold that—had illness not intervened—none other than Karl Marx himself would have been aboard the doomed train.

A Court of Inquiry set up at the time decided that: "… the fall of the bridge was occasioned by the insufficiency of the cross bracing and its fastenings to sustain the force of the gale." Had the wind-bracing been properly concluded, said the Court, the bridge might very well have withstood the intense battering of the mighty storm. Regardless of the real nature of the tragedy, however, the trail of death was far from over. Plans were duly made for a new bridge to be built—according to the designs of one William Henry Barlow. The first stone was laid on July 6, 1883; and, by the time of its completion, no less than fourteen of the construction workers were dead, all from a variety of accidents.

It must be said that Danny Thomas was most definitely not an adherent of the theory that the Tay Bridge disaster, and all of the attendant deaths, could be attributed to something as down to earth as the stormy and relentless British weather. No: It was his firm belief that the dark and sinister forces of the Shuggy were at work on that most tragic of all nights. Moreover, Danny was of the opinion that the precise cause of the Tay Bridge disaster of December 1879 was his great-great-grandfather; reanimated, after his January 1879 death, to our plane of existence in the spectral form of some vile man-beast that haunted the darkened corners of the bridge—positively oozing negative energy and creating an atmosphere of death, doom, tragedy, and decay as it did so, albeit briefly for a few weeks following the collapse of the once-mighty bridge.

Thames Terror

In September 2001, someone made a ghastly discovery in the River Thames, London, England. Floating in the water was the mutilated torso of a small black boy. His head, arms, and legs had been viciously hacked off.

Investigators of the grisly crime had nothing to work with in their attempt to reveal the young victim's identity. An autopsy yielded little additional information except for an estimate of his age to be between four and seven years.

The detectives were shocked by the crime and maddened that they had no face, fingerprints, or dental records to assist them in their investigation.

Enough of the boy's neck remained to permit a forensic expert to conclude that his throat had been cut and that the body had been deliberately drained of blood.

Scotland Yard called in additional forensic experts from various universities to assist them by using the latest scientific methods to examine the boy's bones, stomach, and intestines for any clues at all.

Ken Pye, a forensic geologist at the University of London, found traces in the victim's bones of strontium, copper, and lead that were two and a half times greater than would be normally expected of a child living in Britain. Pye's meticulous research revealed that the boy had recently arrived from West Africa.

The forensic team, working on the contents of the boy's stomach and intestines, discovered unidentifiable plant material, not at all native to England. In addition, the team attempted to analyze a strange mixture of sand-like material, clay pellets, and flecks of gold. Plant anatomists identified the strange plant material as coming from the calabar bean, a highly toxic vine that could be found in West Africa.

Writer James Owen said that Wade Davis, an anthropologist with the National Geographic Society, immediately noted the use of the calabar bean as a plant that was often used in West Africa to create a variety of poisons, many of which result in total paralysis and a very painful death.

A U.K.-based expert on African religions and Voodoo, Richard Hoskins, commented that the calabar bean, in combination with other ingredients in the boy's stomach and intestines, indicated the West African country of Nigeria. Witch doctors commonly used such potions for black magic.

After an exchange of data, the investigators and the forensic experts agreed that the boy had been smuggled into the country for the sole purpose of serving as a human sacrifice.

While Hoskins said that human sacrifices are not common occurrences in contemporary celebrations of Voodoo or Black Magic rites, they still do take place. Animal and fowl sacrifices are regularly practiced, but the ceremonial sacrificial killing of a human is considered a vital element in the most empowering of magical rituals. Special police teams in Southern Africa have estimated that there may be as many as a hundred human sacrifices a year and the most powerful magic of all is created when a child is placed on the altar.

In many parts of Africa, certain witch doctors practice a traditional form of medicine called muti. The more unscrupulous of these witch doctors use body parts of children to increase their powers.

According to James Owen, Ken Pye and his forensic team were finally able to trace the murdered black boy's bones to locate his birthplace near Benin City in southwestern Nigeria. According to many authorities, vodun began 350 years ago in Benin. In 1996, vodun, or Voodoo, won state recognition. January 10 was inaugurated as National Voodoo Day, and the religion that is practiced by sixty-five percent of the 5.4 million Beninese took its place alongside Christianity and Islam.

Voodoo (vodou, vodoun, vudu, or vudun in Benin, Togo, southeastern Ghana, Burkina Faso, and Senegal; also vodou in Haiti) is a name attributed to a traditionally unwritten West African spiritual system of faith and ritual practices. Like most faith systems, the core functions of Voodoo are to explain the forces of the universe, influence those forces, and modify human behavior. Voodoo's oral tradition of faith stories carries genealogy, history, and fables to succeeding generations. Adherents honor deities and venerate ancient and recent ancestors. This faith system is widespread across groups in West Africa. Diaspora spread Voodoo to North and South America and the Caribbean.

On the inauguration of National Voodoo Day, Sossa Guedehoungue, the eighty-six-year-old High Priest of Voodoo, held an audience at his hometown of Doutou, on the Togo border, and scoffed at those who considered Voodoo dangerous. Sossa made a sweeping gesture with his arm to indicate his twenty-four wives, more than one hundred children, and three hundred grandchildren and declared that if Voodoo were evil, none of them would be there.

Numerous practitioners of Voodoo insist that the practice developed a more sinister side only after the slave trade shipped millions of West Africans to Haiti, Cuba, and the Americas. The Old Gods followed their captive people to help them survive and to cast evil spells upon those who enslaved them. At the same time, the people who were carried far from their home villages cleverly began to use the names of Catholic saints to disguise the ancient ones in their pantheon of gods under the names of those whom their captors deemed holy.

Tulpas

Among the secret lore of the Tibetan adepts is the claim that phantoms or Tulpas may be created by those who have attained high mental and spiritual ability; they are sent to accomplish tasks or missions assigned to them by their creators. Once the adept has endowed the Tulpa with enough vitality to assume the form of an actual physical being, it frees itself from its creator's psychic womb and leaves to complete its assignment.

According to certain Eastern metaphysicians, thoughts, emotions, and mental emanations add to the strength of the Tulpa, enabling it to accumulate power and grow. The Tulpa may manifest apparent solidarity and vigor, and Yogis claim that they may even carry on intelligent conversations with these creatures born of their own minds. The duration of a Tulpa's life and its vitality are in direct proportion to the tension and energy expended in its creation.

Sometimes, however, even the most accomplished of adepts and magicians confess that the phantom, the Tulpa, becomes rebellious and may conduct itself independently of its creator. On occasions, the Tulpa may become something of a zombie-like monster. And in certain instances, the highly developed Tibetan magicians have been forced to admit that they have unconsciously set loose a phantom zombie to wreak havoc on unsuspecting victims.

28 Days Later

In 2002, the world of the cinematic zombie received a major overhaul, one that changed our perceptions of zombies big-time and practically overnight. The slow-moving, shambling flesh-eaters, so famously thrust upon the world by George A. Romero in *Night of the Living Dead*, were suddenly gone. In their place was a new and even deadlier breed of creature: it has become famously known as the fast-running zombie. Director Danny Boyle's movie, *28 Days Later*, has all of the staple ingredients of a definitive zombie fest: the emergence of an unstoppable virus that transforms people into monsters, the rapid collapse of society, and the terrifying rise of the infected. There is just one key ingredient missing in *28 Days Later*: zombies. Although the film—which is set in a devastated and ravaged Britain—has since become a firm part of zombie culture, those with whom the straggling survivors are forced to do battle are not actually the dead risen from the grave at all.

The movie begins with a team of animal-rights activists who attempt to free a group of caged chimpanzees held in a secret research lab in Cambridge, England. Unknown to the team, the chimps have been deliberately infected with a manufactured virus that provokes irreversible, homicidal rage in those that are exposed to it—whether animal or human. When one member of the group is bitten by a savage simian, in seconds she is turned into a marauding killer. The person she attacks rapidly transforms, too. The nightmare has duly begun.

Things then jump forward twenty-eight days—hence the name of the movie—when the "Rage Virus," as it is termed, has escaped from the lab and has laid waste to Britain and its people. To prevent the virus from spreading across the whole planet, the nation is quarantined from the rest of the world. And as this green and pleasant island quickly becomes filled with savagery, the remnants of society are left to their own devices and to do whatever is necessary to survive.

28 Days Later focuses on Jim, Selena, Frank, and his daughter, Hannah: four people who are thrust together under terrifying circumstances. They quickly discover that it's not just the infected they have to worry about. After Frank becomes a victim of the virus and is quickly killed, Selena, Hannah, and Jim are rounded up—in definitive martial law-style—and held in an old country mansion by a band of British Army soldiers. The tumultuous events of the past four weeks, however, have psychologically damaged the troops, to the extent that they are as much a threat to our heroes as are the infected. The soldiers want Selena and Hannah for one thing only: sex. As for Jim, the platoon secretly plots to have him executed. Fortunately, none of this comes to pass.

Jim learns that an infected soldier, Mailer, has been kept alive to try and determine how long those with the virus can survive without nourishment. Late at night, Jim stealthily releases Mailer from his shackles. Mailer then goes on a violent rampage around the mansion, infecting the rest of the troops one by one. Jim and the girls flee the spacious building and head for the safety of the countryside. Unlike many zombie movies, *28 Days Later* offers a positive future: a further twenty-eight days down the line, the infected are finally dying due to the lack of food. The film ends with Jim, Hannah, and Selena on the verge of being rescued by far friendlier military personnel. Rapid-paced, in just about every sense possible, *28 Days Later* firmly set the scene for a plethora of further movies in which fast-running zombies were all-dominating.

28 Weeks Later

Such was the phenomenal success of 2002's *28 Days Later* that it spawned an equally apocalyptic sequel, *28 Weeks Later*. It was released in 2007 and, to date, has earned more than $60 million in profits—proof that infection is, well, highly infectious. As the title of the movie suggests, *28 Weeks Later* is set specifically after its predecessor. As we learn in the follow-up production, all of those originally infected with the Rage Virus died from the effects of starvation a month or so after the initial infection began. Weeks later, a U.S. led NATO contingent heads a massive operation which is designed to repopulate the U.K., and return all those British residents who managed to flee the country immediately after the disastrous events started. A full twenty-eight weeks after the initial outbreak occurred, Britain is finally deemed free of infection and the repopulation eventually begins, in the East End of London.

Amongst the returnees are Tammy and Andy, two young children who were vacationing in Spain with their school friends when the virus spectacularly exploded all across the U.K. Their father, Don, managed to escape the apocalypse, unscathed. Their mother, Alice, did not. When the old cottage in which the pair is hiding gets overrun by the raging mob, Don, to his regret, flees for his life, leaving Alice all alone. Incredibly, however, while Alice is shown to have become infected, she does not succumb to the terrifying symptoms. In short, and amazingly, she is completely immune

Actor Robert Carlyle flees a rotting zombie in director Juan Carlos Fresnadillo's *28 Weeks Later,* a sequel to *28 Days Later.*

to the effects of the Rage Virus. When Don and Alice are reunited, Don pleads for-giveness and kisses her on the lips. The exchange of saliva seals Don's fate almost immediately. In seconds, he is a homicidal killer. Don quickly kills Alice and infects more and more of the newly returned Brits, who, in turn, quickly infect others. In mere moments, the Rage Virus, thought by NATO to have been first contained and then completely obliterated, is wildly on the loose again.

A panicked U.S. military quickly orders everyone, whether they seem to be dis-playing symptoms of the Rage Virus or not, to be shot and killed on sight. With the help of military personnel who refuse to go along with the indiscriminate slaughter, however, Tammy and Andy manage to flee the scene. Suspecting that one or both of the children might be immune to the virus, too—which is confirmed when Andy is attacked by Don, but does not fall victim to the effects of his bite—a Major Levy decides that the survival of the children is paramount to finding a cure for the deadly plague. A military helicopter pilot, Flynn, agrees to fly the children out of the U.K., to France, where hopefully a cure can be found—and quickly, too. There is no hope, however, none at all. The final scenes of the movie show the helicopter abandoned somewhere in the French countryside, followed by images of marauding infected charging along a tunnel that opens up in front of Paris' Eiffel Tower. The Rage Virus, previously contained in the U.K.—an island—has now reached mainland Europe.

The ending of *28 Weeks Later* left the door wide open to a further follow-up to the 2002 original. Danny Boyle, the brains behind the *28 …* movies, has confirmed as late as 2013 that while a third production in the series, possibly to be titled *28 Months Later*, is not entirely out of the question, for now, things are in a state of limbo. Just maybe, however, and not unlike the Rage Virus itself, we have yet to see the last of Britain's fast-running infected—and, now, of France's, too.

V–W

Vodun: Mambo and Houngan

See also: Drug Dealers and Voodoo, Hoodoo, Voodoo and the CIA

A male priest of Vodun is called a houngan or hungan; his female counterpart is a mambo. The place where one practices vodun is a series of buildings called a humfort or hounfou. A congregation is called a hunsi or hounsis, and the hungan cures, divines, and cares for them through the good graces of a loa, his guiding spirit.

The worship of the supernatural loa is the central purpose of vodun. They are the old gods of Africa, the local spirits of Haiti, who occupy a position to the fore of God, Christ, the Virgin, and the Saints. From the beginning, the Haitian Voodoo priests adamantly refused to accept the Church's position that the loa are the fallen angels who rebelled against God. The loa perform good works, and guide and protect humankind, the hungans argue. They, like the saints of Roman Catholicism, were once men and women who lived exemplary lives and were given a specific responsibility to carry out to assist human spirituality. Certainly there are those priests, the bokors, who perform acts of evil sorcery, the left-hand path of vodun, but rarely will a hungan resort to such practices.

The loa communicates with its faithful ones by possessing their bodies during a trance or by appearing to them in dreams. The possession usually takes place during ritual dancing in the humfort. Each participant eventually undergoes a personality change and adapts a trait of his or her particular loa. The adherents of Vodun refer to this phenomenon of the invasion of the body by a supernatural agency as that of the loa mounting its horse.

There is a great difference, the hungan maintains, between possession by a loa and possession by an evil spirit. An evil spirit would bring chaos to the dancing and perhaps great harm to the one possessed. The traditional dances of vodun are conducted on a serious plane with rhythm and suppleness but not with the orgiastic sensuality depicted in motion pictures about Voodoo or in the displays performed for the tourist trade.

All vodun ceremonies must be climaxed with a sacrifice to the loa. Chickens are most commonly offered to the loa, although the wealthy may offer a goat or a bull. The possessed usually drinks of the blood that is collected in a vessel, thereby satisfying the hunger of the loa. Other dancers may also partake of the blood, sometimes adding spices to the vital fluid, but most often drinking it straight. After the ceremony, the sacrificed animal is usually cooked and eaten.

The traditional belief structure of the Yoruba envisioned a chief god named Olorun, who remains aloof and unknowable to humankind, but who permitted a lesser deity, Obatala, to create the Earth and all its life forms. There are hundreds of minor spirits whose influence may be invoked by humankind, such as Ayza, the protector; Baron Samedi, guardian of the grave; Dambala, the serpent; Ezli, the female spirit of love; Ogou Balanjo, spirit of healing; and Mawu Lisa, spirit of creation. Each follower of vodun has his or her own met tet, a guardian spirit that corresponds to a Catholic's patron saint.

In Haiti and in New Orleans, Papa Legba is the intermediary between the loa (also referred to as lwa) and humanity. He stands at a spiritual crossroads and gives (or denies) permission to speak with the spirits of Gine; he translates between the human and angelic and all other languages of the spheres.

Papa Legba is also commonly called Eleggua and is depicted as an old man sprinkling water or an old man with a crutch accompanied by dogs. He is also known as Legba or Legba Ati-Bon in other pantheons. In any vodon ceremony, Legba is the first loa invoked, so that he may open the gate for communication between the worlds. The dog is his symbolic animal, moving with him between the worlds and across the waters of the Abyss.

When it comes to the protection of one's domicile, Voodoo practitioners place representations of Papa Legba, similar to those of St. Michael and St. Peter, beside the back and front doors of their homes. Legba will keep evil from entering the home unchecked.

Voodoo

See also: Drug Dealers and Voodoo, Hoodoo, Vodun: Mambo and Houngan, Voodoo and the CIA

According to some of its more passionate adherents, Vodun/Vodoun is not a magical tradition, not an animistic tradition, not a spirit tradition neither, and should it be seen as a pagan religion. The deities of Voodoo are not simply spiritual energies and the path of Voodoo should not be followed for the sake of power over another. Although the Voodoo religion does not demand members proselytize, anyone may join. However, ninety-nine percent of its priesthoods are passed from generation to generation.

The same individuals who esteem their Voodoo religion so highly, insist that it is neither dogmatic nor apocalyptic. Whatever outsiders may make of their faith, the sincere Voodoo follower declares that it has no apocalyptic tradition that prophesizes a doomsday or end-of-the-world scenario.

Although one might suspect that these same true believers are a bit dogmatic when they emphasize that Voodoo was not created as a result of captive West Africans being transported to Roman Catholic countries as slaves, a closer look reveals that Voodoo is not really a blend of African religions and Catholicism, but a clever mask that disguised the ancient deities of the Old Religion.

One point the believers in Voodoo make that cannot be disputed is that the religion did not originate in Haiti. Vodun/Voodoo definitely emerged out of Africa.

Voodoo means spirit in the language of the West African Yoruba, and the religion is an assortment of African beliefs and rites that may go back as many as 6,000 to 10,000 years. Slaves, who were snatched from their homes and families on Africa's

Voodoo drummers in New Orleans demonstrate that Voodoo is still practiced and respected in the Big Easy.

West Coast, brought their gods with them. Plantation owners in Haiti and other West Indian islands purchased the slaves for rigorous labor and had no interest in their religious beliefs if they even had any at all. In the minds of their owners, the African slaves were simple savages from the jungle who probably were not even at the level of a culture in which a kind of worship of God would even be comprehended.

In spite of their indifference to any possible theologies that their slaves might hold, the plantation owners in Haiti were compelled by order of the lieutenant-general to baptize their slaves in the Catholic religion. The slaves were in no position to protest their forced conversion, but by the time the West Africans submitted to mass baptism, the wise priests among them had already discovered simple segues from worshipping the old jungle family of gods and goddesses into bowing and praying to their newly acquired Catholic saints.

As the black population increased and the white demand for slave labor was unceasing, vodun began to take on an anti-white liturgy. Several messiahs emerged among the slaves, who were subsequently put to death by the whites in the big houses. A number of laws began to be passed forbidding any plantation owner to allow night dances among his employees.

In 1791, a slave revolt took place under the leadership of Toussaint L'Ouverture which was to lead to Haiti's independence from France in 1804. Although L'Ouverture died in a Napoleonic prison, his generals had become sufficiently inspired by his example to continue the struggle for freedom until the myth of white supremacy was banished from the island.

After the Concordat of 1860, when relations were reestablished with France, the clergy fulminated against vodun from the pulpits but did not actively campaign against their rival priesthood until 1896, when an impatient monsignor tried, without success, to organize an anti-vodun league. It wasn't until 1940 that the Catholic Church launched a violent campaign of renunciation directed at the adherents of vodun. The priests went about their methodic attack with such zeal that the government was forced to intercede and command them to temper the fires of their campaign.

Today there are over eighty million people who practice vodun worldwide, largely where Haitian emigrants have settled: Benin, Dominican Republic, Ghana, Togo, various cities in the United States (primarily New Orleans), and, of course, Haiti. In South America, there are many religions similar to vodun, such as Umbanda, Quimbanda, or Candombl.

Anthropologist Walter Cannon spent several years collecting examples of Voodoo death, instances in which men and women died as a result of being the recipient of a curse, an alleged supernatural visitation, or the breaking of some tribal or cultural taboo. The question that Cannon sought to answer was: How can an ominous and persistent state of fear end the life of a human?

Fear, one of the most powerful and deep-rooted of the emotions, has its effects mediated through the nervous system and the endocrine apparatus, the sympathetic-adrenal system. Cannon has hypothesized that, if these powerful emotions prevail and the bodily forces are fully mobilized for action, and if this state of extreme perturbation continues for an uncontrolled possession of the organism for a considerable period, dire results may ensue.

Cannon has suggested, then, that Voodoo death may result from a state of shock due to a persistent and continuous outpouring of adrenalin and a depletion of the adrenal corticosteroid hormones. Such a constant agitation caused by an abiding sense of fear could consequently induce a fatal reduction in blood pressure. Cannon assessed Voodoo death as a real phenomenon set in motion by shocking emotional stress to obvious or repressed terror.

Dr. J.C. Barker, in his collection of case histories of individuals who had willed others, or themselves, to death (*Scared to Death*, 1969), saw Voodoo-like death as resulting purely from extreme fear and exhaustion, essentially a psychosomatic phenomenon.

Voodoo and the CIA

See also: *Drug Dealers and Voodoo, Hoodoo, Vodun: Mambo and Houngan, Voodoo*

We have seen how, in the mid 1960s, the CIA was influenced by the imagery of subservient zombies of old-school movies (such as *King of the Zombies*) and, as a result, established *Acoustic Kitty*—an espionage-based program involving the use of mind-controlled cats. Only a couple of years later, the CIA's staff were taking a great deal of notice of yet another aspect of the world of old-school zombies: Voodoo. It was all thanks to one Sydney Gottlieb, Ph.D., a man who made his mark with the CIA in the early 1950s. At the time, he ran the agency's Chemical Division, which was devoted to developing mind-warping cocktails designed to manipulate the human brain and control the psyche.

By the early 1960s, Gottlieb was on a new track: he had developed a fascination for the world of the occult and the paranormal. And, as someone who recognized that psychic phenomena, extra-sensory perception, and black magic, might make excellent tools of espionage. In late 1968, he submitted to the director of the CIA, Richard Helms, a proposal for a project designed to dig deep into the domain of the supernatural. Helms enthusiastically gave it the go-ahead. Within weeks, Operation Often opened its darkest of all dark doors. As unbelievable as it all sounds, in no time at all the staff of Operation Often was mixing with astrologers, clairvoyants, witches, warlocks, mediums, Satanists, and Voodoo practitioners.

To date, very little—beyond the basics—has surfaced from the labyrinthine archives of the CIA on Operation Often and its Voodoo-driven research. But, consider this: a great deal of Gottlieb's work on the program began in 1968—the very year that George Romero's *Night of the Living Dead* was giving cinemagoers chills, thrills, and sleepless nights. One has to wonder if Gottlieb, perhaps deeply inspired by

Romero's work, developed a deranged plan to try and raise the dead for the CIA and unleash an army of unstoppable killers on the former Soviet Union. It might seem outlandish to even suggest such a possibility, but consider this: the release date of *Night of the Living Dead* was October 1, 1968. The proposal for Operation Often was submitted by Gottlieb to Helms on October 16, which was plenty of time for Gottlieb to have watched the movie and mused on its contents and potential implications for future warfare of the flesh-devouring type.

Walking Corpse Syndrome

It will, no doubt, excite and please zombie enthusiasts everywhere to know that there exists a medical condition called Walking Corpse Syndrome. Its official title, however, is Cotard's Syndrome. It's also a condition that is steeped in mystery and intrigue. Very disturbingly, and bafflingly, Cotard's Syndrome causes the victim to believe that he or she is dead, or that their limbs are no longer living or even theirs. The condition takes its name from one Jules Cotard, a French neurologist who died in 1889 from diphtheria, and who spent much of his career studying and cataloging cases of Walking Corpse Syndrome (WCS). Not only do those affected by WCS believe they are dead, they also fall into spirals of psychosis and fail to take care of their personal appearance—which only serves to amplify the zombie/undead parallels even more.

One of the most disturbing accounts of Walking Corpse Syndrome surfaced out of the United Kingdom in May 2013. A man, referred by the medical community only as "Graham," found himself descending into a deeply depressed state, to the point where he ultimately came to believe he was literally a member of the walking dead club. As Graham's condition rapidly worsened, and as he actually spent his days and nights wandering around graveyards, his family was forced to seek medical treatment. For a while, Graham became convinced that his brain was clinically dead—or, at the very least, was "missing" from his skull. Fortunately, treatment finally brought Graham back to the world of the living.

Just recently, new light has been shed on the nature of Cotard's Syndrome as a result of its connection to Zovirax, generally used in the treatment of herpes-based conditions, such as cold-sores. Although Zovirax is known for having an extremely small and insignificant number of side effects, approximately one percent of all patients prescribed the drug develop and suffer from psychiatric conditions, including Cotard's Syndrome. Intriguingly, most of those taking Zovirax and who experienced Walking Corpse Syndrome, were suffering from renal failure at the time. Studies undertaken by Andres Helden, of the Stockholm, Sweden-based Karolinska University Hospital, and Thomas Linden, based at the Sahlgrenska Academy in Gothenburg, Sweden, have uncovered remarkable, albeit unsettling, data on this curious phenomenon.

Their case studies include that of a woman who was prescribed Zovirax after having a bout of shingles. When the drug took hold of the woman, who also happened to have renal failure, she began to act in crazed and concerned fashion, believing—or suspecting—that she was dead. When given emergency dialysis to cope with the effects of kidney failure, her strange beliefs began to fade to the point where she finally came to accept she was not dead, after all. For hours, however, she remained convinced that "my left arm is definitely not mine."

While the Zovirax-Cotard's connection is still not fully understood, administering the drug to those that are susceptible to it in such a strange fashion—and then medically treating those same patients to ensure their firm beliefs that they are dead are removed—may allow for Walking Corpse Syndrome to be turned on and off at will. Might this allow for an unscrupulous mad scientist of Dr. Frankenstein-like proportions to create the closest thing possible to a real legion of the dead? Let us hope not.

The Walking Dead

There can be absolutely no doubt that much of the fascination—and, perhaps, even the obsession—that people have today with all things of a zombie nature stems directly from AMC's hugely successful television show, *The Walking Dead*. But long before the series began there was *The Walking Dead* comic book. It all began back in 2003 when Robert Kirkman and Tony Moore (writer and artist respectively) got together with a brand new concept: a comic book series not focused around the actions of superheroes, but on the world of the zombie. It was a concept that worked extremely well, with Image Comics of Berkeley, California, publishing what is now a much sought after title, and particularly so the early originals. Today, the series is still very much ongoing: well over one hundred issues are now in print, and it shows no sign of stopping any time soon.

As for the television spin-off, AMC secured the small-screen rights in 2009 and wasted no time at all in commissioning a pilot and a first series. It aired—highly appropriately—on the night of Halloween, 2010. It quickly became clear to AMC's staff that they had a big winner on their hands, and a second series was soon commissioned. Precisely like the infected of the show, *The Walking Dead* does not stop: not only have four seasons already been broadcast, a fifth was ordered in October 2013, for broadcast in the following year.

While the comic book and the television show are very much tied to each other in terms of concepts, characters, locations, and storylines, there are significant differences too. The comic book series contains characters that never made it to the show and the show features characters that never appeared in the comic book. Thus, for those that might want to check out the comic books to try and figure out what the show may have in store for them in episodes still to come, it's not quite as easy as it might sound. In fact, due to certain variations in characters and settings, the comic book and the series can be perceived as entirely separate entities.

Much of the public's enthusiasm for AMC's *The Walking Dead*—and particularly so those that may never previously have given the world of the zombie much time

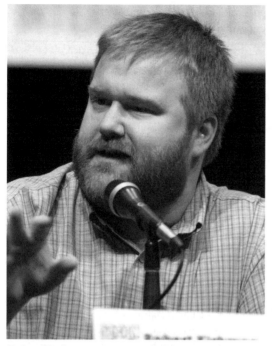

Robert Kirkman, co-creator of the popular television show *The Walking Dead,* is seen here at the 2013 Comic-Con.

or thought—stems from the fact that the show is actually far less about zombies than it is about the plight of the characters that the viewers have come to like, appreciate, and even love. Yes, *The Walking Dead* is full of gruesome gore and knuckle-clenching tension and terror, but it's also very much about people, and about how, in dire circumstances, we band together and help each other—or, in some circumstances, how people coldly turn on one another, doing whatever is necessary to stay alive and one step ahead of the dead.

The Walking Dead also makes the viewer ponder on important questions: how would I react when faced with a real zombie apocalypse? Would I retain my humanity? Would I help my fellow people? Maybe you would take the approach of: "It's every man for himself." And such is the high quality of the acting in the show, there is surely no viewer of the series that, when the on-screen carnage is at its height, has not looked around their living room, wondering if their home is secure and strong enough to withstand a real zombie assault.

The Walking Dead—both television show and comic book—does something else too: it keeps the viewer on his or her toes by killing off leading characters at any given moment. Most television productions that have a high success rate take the cynical approach of "if it's not broken, then don't fix it." So, we see the same old faces season after season and year after year, to the point where, finally, it all becomes very tiresome and predictable, ratings drop, and the show is cancelled instead of going out on a high. *The Walking Dead* is very different in the sense that no main character is safe from the walkers, something which has the fans hoping and praying it won't be their favorite who goes this week.

Such is the success of *The Walking Dead,* the viewer and the reader can now engage in video games, too: *The Walking Dead* and *The Walking Dead: Survival Instinct.* And if you want to curl up with a good book, there are the novels *The Walking Dead: Rise of the Governor* and *The Walking Dead: The Road to Woodbury.* The dead, it seems, are going to keep on walking, and walking, and walking, no matter what.

Long before AMC's phenomenally successful television show, *The Walking Dead* was on anyone's radar, there was … *The Walking Dead.* Moreover, the original was also based around the recently deceased rising from the dead and wiping out the living, albeit in a somewhat distinctly different fashion. *The Walking Dead* in question was a 1936 movie, shot in moody black and white and starring Boris Karloff—most famous for his portrayal of the patchwork living-corpse in Universal Pictures' *Frankenstein* of 1931.

In *The Walking Dead,* Karloff's character is one John Ellman. We are introduced to him just as he has been released from prison, after serving a lengthy sentence for killing a man. Unbeknownst to Ellman, a group of hoods is looking to murder a certain Judge Roger Shaw, who they fear knows a great deal about their criminal activities. But how can they kill the judge and also escape detection? Very easily: they learn that Judge Shaw was the very man that sentenced Ellman to his sentence. So, with Ellman newly released from prison, the gang sets out to frame Ellman, by making it look like he killed Shaw as revenge for his lengthy time spent in jail. The ruse works all too well: one of the gang murders the judge, and Ellman quickly becomes the fall guy and is arrested, tried, and found guilty of the crime. The hoodlums have gotten away scot-free. Or so they assume.

As fate would have it, a young couple, Nancy and Jimmy, witness the murder and come forward when they realize that Ellman is about to be executed for a crime of which he was innocent. Unfortunately, their actions are too late to save Ellman. He is put to death in the electric chair before Nancy and Jimmy can raise the alarm. As luck would have it, however, Nancy and Jimmy work for a Dr. Evan Beaumont, a somewhat eccentric scientist obsessed by death, the afterlife, and the reanimation of human corpses.

When it quickly becomes clear to the authorities that Ellman was innocent of the death of Judge Shaw, Dr. Beaumont is given permission to try and bring Ellman back to life—which he succeeds in doing. Ellman is not the man he once was, however. He has no memory of his life prior to his execution, and he exists in a strange, almost zombi-

The cast of the 2010 season of *The Walking Dead* included (left to right) Emma Bell, Jon Bernthal, Steven Yeun, Chandler Riggs, Sarah Wayne Callies, Andrew Lincoln, Jeffrey DeMunn, and Laurie Holden.

fied, state. For reasons that are never made clear, however, Ellman has an eerie awareness of the gang responsible for his death. By night, he visits them, one by one, and, while staring malevolently in their direction, asks: "Why did you have me killed?"

Soon after the question is posed, the gang members die in grisly accidents—and not unlike the scenarios played out so successfully in the *Final Destination* movies. As Ellman closes in on the final two hoods that were responsible for his death, one of them fatally shoots him in, rather appropriately, the confines of an old, creepy cemetery. They escape from Ellman, but cannot avoid the Grim Reaper. The pair dies in a fiery car accident. Nancy and Jimmy do their best to keep Ellman alive, while Dr. Beaumont pleads with Ellman to tell him what he encountered during his brief time spent in the afterlife. It's to no avail, however. Ellman takes his last breath without revealing the secret of the world beyond this one. The viewer is left with the impression that there are certain things about which we should not know until it's our time, and turn, to find out personally.

Waugh, Lisa Lee Harp

Necromancer and Voodoo reactionary Lisa Lee Harp Waugh. (**Art by Ricardo Pustanio**).

Lisa Lee Harp Waugh, the great American necromancer, reports that on many occasions she has been in the company of Baron Samedi, the infamous master of the dead who escorts souls from the grave to the underworld. She suggests that many people in the paranormal field fear or have not investigated the sacred rites of Voodoo and the many spirit and ghost contacts that occur.

Waugh, a Voodoo reactionary herself, was called upon to help discover if a young Haitian woman in Miami, Florida, was actually possessed. Her case drew a lot of local attention in early 2009. The young woman had been held by the spirit since Halloween 2008. The case has been documented and will be featured in a forthcoming documentary on Voodoo-Hoodoo possession and exorcism.

Welsh Zombies

Oll Lewis is a respected researcher of the world of the paranormal who hails from Wales. He has a zombie-based story with a difference: it suggests real-life equivalents of today's cinematic zombies have been roaming our world for centuries. The story begins in a small Welsh village in Nant Gwynant, which is a truly picturesque valley situated in Snowdonia, Gwynedd, North Wales.

Lewis' research has revealed that long, long ago, villagers and shepherds in the area of Nant Gwynant were plagued by a silent and stealthy thief who broke into their homesteads under the protective covers of shadow and darkness on a disturbingly regular basis. Those same villagers and shepherds would awaken to find that their goats and cows had been inexplicably milked, much-needed food was stolen, and a number of sheep were taken during the night, their bodies savagely devoured, and with nothing but discarded scraps of flesh and bone left strewn across the fields and pastures. The carnage and thievery, says Lewis, went on for some years, and every time anyone laid a trap for the thief it never took the bait and the finger of popular suspicion passed from ne'er-do'-well to ne'er-do'-well, with each suspect's guilt eventually being disproved.

So, what—allegedly, at least—was the true nature of the nightmarish beast said to have roamed the densely treed, ancient valley? According to North Wales-based legend, it was a creature of undeniably primitive proportions and terrifying appearance, one that seemed intent on tormenting the people of the picturesque area whenever, and however, possible, as Lewis notes:

"One day a shepherd was returning from the mountains later than usual and spotted something strange; a huge, burly naked man covered from head to toe in thick red fur was resting on a neighboring hill. The shepherd suspected that this out of place and strangely hirsute giant might be the thief that was plaguing the village, so the shepherd snuck past the man without being detected and ran back to the village as soon as he was out of sight."

The story continued that when the shepherd in question breathlessly reached the heart of Nant Gwynant, he persuaded all of the available men-folk of the village to join him in a quest to, once and for all, rid the area of the creature that had elected to descend upon it and its people. Evidently, and unfortunately, not much thought went into this particular exercise. It basically involved little more than the hysterical posse charging up the green hill, and towards the wild man with crude, homemade weapons in-hand, while simultaneously screaming at him at the top of their lungs. Not surprisingly, alerting the hairy man-thing to their presence was hardly the cleverest of all moves that the group could have made. The mighty beast shot away—on all-fours, interestingly enough—and, as Oll noted, in a fashion that suggested "the skill and precision of a deer." Or, maybe, the speed and agility of the fast-running infected of *28 Days Later*.

A close and careful watch of the hill and its immediate surroundings was made from that day onward, in the event that the man-beast might return to once again wreak diabolical havoc upon Nant Gwynant and its frayed and fried populace. It was, without doubt, a most wise decision. Barely a few days passed before the menacing entity returned, to both feed voraciously and spread fear and chaos across the immediate land.

This time, however, the villagers took a new and novel approach to tackling their quarry. The plan was to let loose a pack of vicious hounds upon the British Bigfoot-type animal, in the hope that the dogs would succeed where the men had over-whelmingly failed. Unfortunately, this action proved utterly fruitless, too. As soon as it caught wind of the scent of the hounds, the hairy thing was gone, once again bound-ing away in almost graceful fashion as it made its successful escape, easily leaving the snarling dogs far, far behind.

Lewis reveals that a distinctly alternative plan of action was then put into place: "One man came up with the idea of consulting a magician. The magician told the vil-lagers to find a red haired greyhound without a single hair of a different color and this would be able to catch the man. After much searching and bartering with local towns and villages the people of Nant Gwynant found a dog that fit the bill and proudly took him home. When the villagers next saw the hairy man they were ready with the red greyhound and it was set loose to catch the hairy man. The hairy man escaped again by leaping down a small cliff."

Were the people of Nant Gwynant cursed to forever have the marauding thing in their very midst? No. If the men, the dogs, and even the supernatural powers of a renowned and mysterious purveyor of ancient magic had failed to put paid to the mon-ster-man and its terrible actions, then, quite clearly, another approach was sorely need-ed. It fell upon one of the women of the village to come up with a plan of attack to rid the area of the terrifying beast. Lewis demonstrates what happened next:

"One woman was so angered by her frequent losses she decided to stay up every night and hide herself in the front room of her farmhouse to wait for when the hairy man decided to pay a visit. Sure enough, after a few weeks, the hairy man paid a visit to the wrong house and the lady was waiting with a hatchet. She remained hidden, until the man had squeezed his bulky frame half way through the window, before she struck the hairy man with her hatchet. The unexpected blow cleaved off the hairy man's hand in one blow and he recoiled back out of the window before the woman could smite him with a further whack. The brave woman dashed out of her door, hatchet in hand ready to finish the man off but by the time she had gotten outside he had fled."

The wretched terror that had descended upon Nant Gwynant had finally reached its end, much to the overwhelming relief of the entire neighborhood, as Oll reveals: "When the village awoke the next day and the men learned what had hap-pened they followed the trail of blood the hairy man had left behind to a cave beneath a local waterfall. As the big hairy man was never seen again it was assumed by the villagers that he had died in the cave, so the cave was named 'the cave of the hairy man.'"

But that was not quite all: old documents show that some of the village folk—and specifically those that had seen the marauding character at close quarters—said that the hairy thing resembled a villager that had died several months before the first outbreak of attacks began. His name was Tom Fowler, a man who was killed in a pub brawl, late one drunken night. Is it possible that Fowler didn't stay dead, but rose from the grave, and went on a violent rampage, slaughtering and devouring animals and having the intriguing ability to outrun just about one and all? The evidence seems to suggest that is precisely what happened. A centuries-old *28 Days Later*-style outbreak in North Wales may sound fantastic, but we might be wise to keep such a possibility under careful consideration.

Wendigo

On the night of July 30, 2008, a twenty-two-year-old Canadian man named Tim McLean was killed and mutilated under truly horrific circumstances while on-board a Greyhound Canada bus as it neared Portage la Prairie, Manitoba. According to the shocked passengers, McLean was sleeping when suddenly, and without any warning whatsoever, the man next to him pulled out a large hunting-knife and began to wildly and viciously stab McLean in the chest and neck—no less than forty times, police were later able to graphically determine.

Needless to say, complete and utter pandemonium broke out on the bus, as people clambered to quickly escape from the lunatic in their midst. But far, far worse was to come. Several of the terrified passengers held the door of the vehicle firmly shut from the outside to prevent the man from leaving the scene of the crime. As they did so, they were shocked to the absolute core to see that he had by now decapitated McLean and was calmly walking towards them down the aisle of the bus, with his victim's head held in his hand no less.

"There was no rage in him. It was just like he was a robot or something," said Garnet Caton, one of the passengers who had the misfortune to be aboard the bus. Royal Canadian Mounted Police quickly arrived on the scene and arrested the killer—who was identified as forty-year-old Vince Weiguang Li. For most people, the incident was seen as just another further example of the overwhelming violence and rage that seems all too prevalent in today's world and society; and, particularly so when police revealed that Li had, apparently, even devoured some of his victim's flesh while on the bus. As the investigation progressed, however, it moved away from being simply an infinitely violent crime, and took on decidedly ominous and almost paranormal overtones.

It transpired that a little more than a week before he killed McLean, Li had been delivering copies of the *Edmonton Sun* newspaper to homes in the area. Interestingly, the very issue in question contained an extensive article written by Andrew Hanon that profiled the work of a historian named Nathan Carlson, and his authoritative research into a monstrous beast known as the Wendigo.

A creature that appears prominently within the mythology of the Algonquin people—the most populated and widespread of all the North American Native groups, with tribes originally numbering in the hundreds—the Wendigo is an evil, cannibalistic and rampaging creature with the ability to possess human souls and minds, forcing them to do their dark bidding. Humans have the ability to transform into a Wendigo, especially if they have engaged in cannibalism. Notably, in centuries past, those who were suspected by the Algonquin of being Wendigos were decapitated after death

The Wendigo is an evil, cannibalistic, and rampaging creature into which humans have the ability to transform.

to prevent them rising from the grave and attacking the living. Shades, of course, of *The Walking Dead*, one might say.

In the wake of the terrible and tragic death of Tim McLean, Nathan Carlson noted that there were a number of similarities between Li's actions and those of the Wendigo, and told the *Edmonton Sun* on August 11, 2008, that: "There are just too many parallels. I can't say there's a definite connection, but there are just too many coincidences. It's beyond eerie."

Eerie is without a doubt the right word for what took place on that fateful evening in July 2008. And while for many people, this particular affair was perceived as being just yet another example of how our society is becoming ever more violent; some were of the opinion that matters extended into far stranger territories. For some, this particularly notorious and savage incident was suggestive of the sensational possibility that Li himself had become a zombie-like Wendigo.

Whatever one's own views on this admittedly curious case, it perhaps serves to demonstrate one thing more than any other: Even in today's fast-paced world, with our technological marvels, and our sprawling concrete cities, when circumstances dictate it, it does not take long at all before our minds swing back to the paranormal-themed fears and superstitions of cultures and eras long gone—including those focused on the dead rising from the grave and eating the living.

In today's world of the zombie, the process of turning man into flesh-eating monster results directly from the effects of a lethal, fast-acting virus. In 1879, a man, whose terrible actions of the cannibalistic kind remains as notorious today as he did more than 130 years ago, claimed that his transformation into a deranged devourer of people was caused by something very different: a Wendigo.

In the early part of 1879, a member of the Native American Cree group, named Swift Runner, made his way to a Catholic Mission in St. Albert, a city situated in Alberta, Canada. He proceeded to tell a controversial and unlikely story to the resident priests. Swift Runner claimed to be the last, surviving, and starving member of his family—which had lived, he said, in a camp in woods northeast of Edmonton. His mother, brother, wife, and no less than six children had all succumbed to the cold and the lack of food.

Fearing that he too would soon meet the Grim Reaper, Swift Runner decided to take on the harsh elements and make his way to St. Albert. There was a big and glaring problem with Swift Runner's story, however, which the priests could not fail to notice when they saw him. The new arrival certainly didn't look as if he was starving to death. In fact, he was decidedly chubby—almost as if he had been dining far more than heartily over the winter months. This, as it transpired, is exactly what had happened.

When the suspicious priests contacted local police, and Swift Runner found himself grilled by the officers, the shocking and awful truth tumbled out in spectacularly horrific style. The Cree admitted that he had devoured each and every one of his family, limb by limb. And, just for good measure, he had even sucked the marrow from their bones. The police wasted no time in racing to the family home, where, sure enough, a scene of utter carnage was found.

Faced with inevitable execution by hanging, Swift Runner had a unique defense for his cannibalistic actions: his mind was possessed by, and in the grip of, a deadly Wendigo. Given that the existence of the Wendigo was something utterly accepted by the people of both the era and the area, many were not inclined to doubt Swift Runner's words. That included the priests to whom he first shared his story. They told the police of how, while at the mission, Swift Runner descended into savage states that bordered upon outright, rage-filled fits.

Swift Runner's line of defense was to no avail, however. He was hung by the neck, in Fort Saskatchewan in December 1879, still insisting to the very last moment that his terrible actions were due to the malicious manipulations of a supernatural Wendigo. It must be stressed that there are a few zombie-like overtones to this bizarre affair. Just like the undead, Swift Runner's mind was taken over—not by a mysterious virus, but by a malicious, paranormal beast. He was driven to devour the living, which is practically all that a zombie ever aspires to do. His rage-filled seizures provoke imagery very much like that of the infected in *28 Days Later*. And, finally there was his name: for today's zombies of the athletic kind, could there be a better description than Swift Runner? No, there could not.

White Zombie

A 1932 movie written by Garnett Weston and starring Bela Lugosi, *White Zombie* was not a particularly good production. While the sets and scenery are actually very well constructed, and have a distinct air of creepiness about them, the cast's noticeably amateurish overacting, of which even Lugosi was guilty, pretty much lets the whole thing down. Nevertheless, *White Zombie* does stand out for one particular reason: in practically all of the zombie-based movies of the 1930s, the creatures themselves are presented as mind-controlled slaves, but ones that are, nevertheless, still alive. In *White Zombie*, however, and practically from the outset, the viewer is led to believe that the zombies are the resurrected dead, ones of a kind typically seen in *Dawn of the Dead* and *The Walking Dead*.

This belief is amplified even further when we get to see the undead up close and personal: gaunt, wide of eye, staggering, and with psychotic—rather than blank—looks on their faces, they slowly roam the landscape in a fashion not unlike the flesh-eaters of *Night of the Living Dead*. But, it's all a brilliant ruse. The dead aren't really as dead as they seem to be, despite what the audience is initially told. In reality, Voodoo is afoot.

White Zombie tells the story of a young couple, Neil and Madeline, who travel to the West Indies, where they are to be married. As a precursor to what is soon to follow, the arrival of the happy couple, late one dark and shadowy night, is marred by menace. As their coachdriver takes them to the Beaumont House—a huge, sprawling old building very befitting the storyline—they cross paths with one "Murder Legendre," played by Lugosi, and who stealthily steals Madeline's scarf. There's no time for Madeline to notice Legendre's sleight of hand, however, as the landscape is quickly filled with zombies, all making their unsteady way towards the carriage and horses. The terrified driver cracks the whip and hits the road. As he does so, we see a large cemetery in the background, emphasizing the idea that the zombies are well and truly dead.

The owner of the house, one Charles Beaumont, takes the kind of liking to Madeline that is far from recommended on the eve of a bride's wedding. Crazed by his love for her, Beaumont enters into a distinctly Faustian pact with Legendre, the man who commands the zombies that work as slaves in his Haitian mill. Legendre provides Beaumont with a potion that, Beaumont believes, will kill Madeline, but then return her to life as a mind-controlled member of the undead club, and as someone who will remain forever faithful and devoted to Beaumont.

WITH THESE ZOMBIE EYES
he rendered her powerless

WHITE ZOMBIE

WITH THIS ZOMBIE GRIP
he made her perform his every desire!

A poster announces the 1932 Bela Lugosi movie *White Zombie*.

Sure enough, Beaumont slips Madeline the lethal cocktail, which, shortly after her marriage to Neil, causes Madeline to collapse and die, right in front of her distraught husband. Or, rather, that is what *appears* to happen. An utterly traumatized Neil is faced with burying his bride on their wedding day, which he does in a creepy crypt on the island. While Neil tries to find some degree of comfort in copious amounts of booze, Legendre and Beaumont are on a mission: they steal Madeline's body from the tomb and reanimate her. But, she comes back as a very different person: completely emotionless, pale, and, for all intents and purposes, undead.

Beaumont, initially the bad guy, has a drastic and sudden change of heart: seeing the terrible effects of reanimation on Madeline, he begs Legendre to restore her to original human form. Legendre refuses and, unknown to Beaumont, even infects him with the paranormal potion. In a short time, Beaumont too begins to feel the strange effects of the drug of the dead. Neil, in his drunken state, makes his way to the vault where Madeline was buried, only to find her gone. A Dr. Bruner tells Neil of Legendre's zombie army that runs his mill and how, in reality, the dead are actually the victims of a potent cocktail that only *mimics* death, a state from which they awake in mind-controlled form.

Matters come to a final confrontation at Legendre's castle, which stands on the edge of a steep set of cliffs that overlook a churning ocean. As Neil seeks to rescue Madeline from the clutches of Legendre, the latter's zombie hordes come staggering onto the screen, ready and eager to kill Neil. Fortunately, it doesn't happen. Beaumont, finally realizing that he is destined to become one of the walking dead, attacks Legendre, and both of them plunge to their deaths in the waters below. With Legendre gone, his psychic control over Madeline and the zombie army is also gone. The undead follow their master over the cliffs—this time *really* dying. As for Neil and Madeline, it's a case of happy ever after.

Wild Man of the Navidad

It was a truly horrific and nightmarish beast that provoked both overwhelming fear and intense alarm within the minds and hearts of the fine folk that lived in the small, and somewhat isolated, Texan town of Sublime throughout the 1830s. It roamed the dense and mysterious thickets and fields of an area whose people became terrified of the unknown entity in their midst. It may have lived on local folk, picking their bones clean, not unlike the average undead. And it rapidly became known to those that were forced to live in its dark shadow by the memorable moniker of the Wild Man of the Navidad.

So the notable legend goes, at the turn of the 1830s, strange and hard-to-identify barefoot tracks of two so-called "wild people" were often found both in and around the varied settlements of Texas' lower Navidad, and specifically in the area of Sublime, which can be found roughly halfway between the cities of San Antonio and Houston. Generally speaking, the tracks were relatively small, and consideration was given to the possibility that there was both a male and a female on the loose. Keen and alert guard dogs on local ranches and properties would on occasion react both violently and furiously when the strange and unidentified visitors were believed to be quietly and carefully prowling throughout the area late after nightfall had enveloped the entire area. And there were even reports of the mysterious pair breaking into people's homes and stealing food.

According to the legends and tales that inevitably surfaced in the wake of the initial wave of mysterious reports and encounters, a human skeleton was later discovered in the area—something that led a number of commentators to conclude that the wild woman's larger, male companion had possibly died. Or, perhaps, that the pair had turned their attentions to eating people, Zombie style. Precisely what happened to the skeleton—if indeed it ever really existed, of course—remains unknown and has unfortunately been lost to the inevitable fog of time. An initial attempt, organized by a group of men in the area, to hunt down the other mystery hominid utterly failed. On the second occasion, however, there was an intriguing development in this early, somewhat zombie-like affair.

As inevitably is the case in camp-fire-style tales such as this one, it was a distinctly dark and stormy night, and a shadowy, monstrous, and mighty form loomed perilously into view. Whatever he, she, or it was, the unidentified visitor was relatively slim and unclothed, but was curiously and notably described as having a body that was covered—head-to-toe—in short brown hair. The brave band of men valiantly tried to seize the beast; however, it skillfully bounded out of the area with what was later described as truly astonishing speed.

The odd event remained utterly unresolved until a group of locals allegedly cornered a runaway male slave in the same area. This latest development in the strange saga seemingly satisfied local newspaper editors, who unanimously concluded that the wild man and woman of the Navidad were actually nothing of the sort at all. In reality, the media asserted, the tales were merely based upon nothing stranger than misidentifications of the aforementioned unfortunate slave—who had presumably escaped from his "masters" and who had been living in the harsh wilds of the Navidad for years.

Taking into careful consideration the fact that certainly not everyone was in agreement with that particularly down-to-earth conclusion, however, yet another valiant attempt was initiated to try and resolve the mystery of the unknown entities and their identities, and this time once and for all. A team of experienced hunters from Sublime decided that a complete check of the nearby thick, atmospheric woods was the only real, viable option left available to them if matters were ever to be firmly laid to rest.

After several fruitless searches, the group truly hit the absolute jackpot when one of them reported seeing what looked to be a wild-looking human racing along an adjacent prairie. Men with lassos urgently pursued their quarry; while others with dogs ensured that there was no chance of it escaping into the heart of the dense woodland. Nevertheless, and initially at least, the hunters were wholly outwitted by the hairy man-thing. It was destined not to remain missing for too long, however.

Under a bright, moonlit sky of a type that would be welcome in any self-respecting horror movie, the heart-thumping excitement of the previous several hours was finally beginning to subside, when the hounds suddenly became agitated and nervous. Not only that: something, or someone, was loudly crashing through the thick bushes—and in the specific direction of the hunters, no less. The creature suddenly appeared again, bounded across the prairie, and raced for the protection and cover of the dense forest. Whatever it was, it was most certainly no normal human being. Indeed, the nearest hunter reported that his horse was so afraid that it refused to go anywhere near the hairy monstrosity.

By this time, the wild thing was coming perilously close to the forest, and the lead hunter realized that it was quite literally a case of now or never. He excitedly spurred his horse on and threw his lasso. Unfortunately, it missed its target; the beast made good its escape, deep into the heart of the darkened forest. Although the attempted capture of the beast of the Navidad had ended in complete failure, one important point should not go without observation or comment.

The hunter in question had an excellent opportunity to note the physical appearance of the creature as both he and it charged wildly across the open prairie. Precisely like others who had come before him, the hunter described the man-thing as being naked, with bright staring eyes and a body covered in short, brown hair. It was also said to be carrying something in its hand. Interestingly, nothing less than a five-foot-long, carefully fashioned wooden club was reportedly later found in the same area where the furious and famous pursuit had taken place. And thus was born the dark and unforgettable legend of the Wild Man of the Navidad.

The Witches

Made by Hammer Film Productions—the company behind numerous classic horror-movies of the 1950s to the 1970s—*The Witches* is a 1966 film that tells of distinctly occult goings-on in the English countryside. It starred the acclaimed actress Joan Fontaine, who, in 1942 won an academy award for best actress for her role in Alfred Hitchcock's 1941 movie, *Suspicion*. As *The Witches* begins, we see Fontaine's character, a schoolteacher named Gwen Mayfield, employed as a missionary in Africa—that is, until the compound at which she works is invaded late one dark and stormy night by a group of nightmarish figures clearly displaying a devotion to the world of Voodoo. Such is the traumatic nature of the violent attack on Mayfield, she suffers a psychological collapse and is forced to return to her native England. When finally recovered, she accepts a position as a schoolteacher in what appears to be just an old, picturesque English village. The truth, however, is far more unsettling. Within the pleasant-looking hamlet of Heddaby, disturbing Voodoo-based activity is secretly being practiced.

All seems normal until Mayfield finds evidence of toy dolls being used in a ritualistic fashion, uncovers evidence of widespread, local beliefs in the world of the occult, and even learns of whispered talk of human sacrifice. On this latter point, as *The Witches* progresses, Mayfield discovers to her horror that a local schoolgirl who has gone missing—Linda Rigg, played by Ingrid Boulting—is about to be sacrificed. Mayfield does her very best to prevent such a thing from taking place. She succeeds, but not before one of the most bizarre scenes to have ever graced a Hammer Films movie occurs.

As the high-priestess of the Voodoo cult—a rich and powerful local named Stephanie Bax—prepares to have young Linda sacrificed to infernal, supernatural entities, the villagers descend into a strange, almost psychedelic, dance that evokes imagery of the famous zombie-themed dancing that is featured in the video for Michael Jackson's hit song of 1983, "Thriller." Fortunately, Mayfield saves the day. Linda is rescued before high-priestess Bax is able to thrust a knife into her chest, and normality is finally returned to Heddaby. Although not strictly a movie of zombie proportions, the eerie, jerky dancing of the cast—as the sacrificial rite comes to a head—coupled with the many and varied references to Voodoo-themed magic, most assuredly makes *The Witches* a movie that fans of the undead will want to check out.

Wolves That Are Immortal

The June 2, 1888, edition of the *Dallas Morning News* told a strange tale with the eye-catching headline of "A Huge Wolf Killed, Big as a Yearling." According to the journalist that wrote the story: "Frank Boshore, a farmer living near the city, killed and brought to town yesterday one of the largest gray wolves that was [sic] ever killed in this country. It was nearly as tall as a yearling calf. These animals have been a great disadvantage to the community, one man saying that he had been damaged at least $1,000 by them on sheep."

While the story, initially at least, suggested that the wolf was simply a distinctly oversized one and nothing stranger, than that Boshore himself believed the creature to have had distinctly supernatural origins. His reasoning was simple yet undeniably bizarre. It was also quite logical: Boshore claimed, incredibly, that he killed the giant wolf no less than *twice*. On the first occasion, he maintained with complete seriousness, the animal was felled by three shots to its body and fell to the ground, utterly dead. It apparently didn't stay that way, however. After he dumped the corpse in an old dried up pond, Boshore was amazed when, two days later, the creature returned to his farm, and killed seven of his sheep. Could it not simply have been a very similar wolf, but one also of extreme size? Not according to Boshore: he said that he could clearly see the bullet wounds on its torso that identified it as the very same animal he had previously shot and killed.

Somewhat amazingly, and undeniably pre-empting the zombie craze by decades, Boshore maintained that the only thing which ended the wolf's reign of terror permanently was a bullet to the head! More amazing is the fact that the story was not over. Twenty years later, something eerily similar occurred in Texas and again caught the attention of the *Dallas Morning News*.

"Hunt for Phantom-Like Animal" was the bold heading that leapt off the front page of the January 29, 1908, issue of the *Dallas Morning News*. The newspaper recorded that an unknown, large creature—that some described as a massive dog and others as a huge wolf—was causing overwhelming carnage across the city of Waco, and had been up to its infernal activities for at least four weeks.

Farm animals were being eaten by the dozen, no one was able to kill the creature, and dark rumors began to surface suggesting that the creature might actually have paranormal origins, rather than ones of a definitively flesh and blood nature—something which famously echoed the concerns of Frank Boshore, two decades previously. A staff-writer for the *Dallas Morning News* recorded that one person whose path had unfortunately crossed with the animal said it seemed to pass "like a phantom, jumping fences from one lot to another, elusive and shadowy, except where the use is made of teeth and claws."

The press additionally stated: "The McLennan County Fox Hunters' Association, with their best hunters, declare that while they have been able to capture big wolves, red and gray foxes, bob cats, and catamounts, they are baffled by this peculiar beast." Despite an intense search, the creature was never caught or firmly identified.

And, soon after, it evidently moved on to new pastures, as the slayings came to an abrupt and mysterious halt.

Were zombie wolves roaming around the Lone Star State more than a century ago? Just maybe, they really were.

Woolpit's Wonders

While it's true to say that just about every single zombie—whether of television, movies, or of Voodoo-based origins—looks menacing, it is perhaps zombified children that look the most disturbing of all. There's something decidedly unsettling about seeing a young child transformed into a homicidal cannibal. George A. Romero's 1968 movie, *Night of the Living Dead,* pretty much gave birth to the concept of the zombie child—in a suitably creepy cellar where nothing but death awaits the living. Then there were the opening scenes of carnage in the 2004 remake of George A. Romero's *Dawn of the Dead,* in which a young, infected girl named Vivian rips open the throat of Luis, a character who dies in seconds and who then returns in seconds, too. And who can forget the gut-wrenching scenes in the very same movie when the star, Anna, played by actress Sarah Polley, is forced to shoot a newborn zombie baby in the head?

But what of zombified children: are there such cases in the real world? Amazingly, the answer is "yes." One case that very possibly falls into this category is that of the "Green Children" of Woolpit, a village in Suffolk, England, situated between the towns of Bury St. Edmunds and Stowmarket. So the story goes, back in the twelfth century, a young girl and boy, of strangely green-hued skin and dressed in rags, staggered into Woolpit one day, claiming to have come from a magical place called St. Martin's Land, which existed in an atmosphere of permanent twilight, and where the people lived underground.

It is not just adults who are affected by the zombie plague but also, very disturbingly, children.

There was something else about the children, however: for some of the villagers the pair provoked an unsettling sense of menace and unease, a feeling that they were not all that they seemed. For some, the girl and boy were corpses returned to life. Certainly, their oddly colored skin, their ragged clothes, and their staggering motions practically bellowed: "Zombie!" Or, it would have done, had the term been coined in the twelfth century. But, is it possible that the undead appearance of the pair may actually have been due to something very different than the zombie virus? Yes, it is.

While the saga—told by Ralph of Coggeshall, an abbot and monk who lived in the 1200s, and the author of a massive tome titled *Chronicon Anglicanum*—has been relegated by many to the realms of both myth and folklore, it may not be just that. It may, actually, be much more. According to the legend, the two children remained in Woolpit and were ultimately baptized by the villagers, who accepted them as their own. And although the boy ultimately grew sickly and eventually died, the girl did not. She thrived and finally lost her green-tinged skin to normal, healthy-looking skin. She also, somewhat in defiance of the disapproving attitudes of certain members of the village, became "rather loose and wanton in her conduct," as it was amusingly termed.

That both children were reportedly green-skinned and lived underground in a mysterious locale, has led many to disregard the tale out of hand as one of fairy-based, mythological proportions and nothing else whatsoever. That, however, may not actually have been the case. The pair may have been suffering from a condition called Hypochromic Anemia, in which the sufferer—as a result of a very poor diet that, in part, affects the color of the red blood-cells—can develop skin of a slight, but noticeable, green shade. In support of this scenario, Hypochromic Anemia was once known as Chlorosis, a word formulated in the early 1600s by a Montpellier professor of medicine named Jean Varandal. And why did Varandal choose such a name? Simple: It came from the Greek word Chloris, meaning "greenish-yellow" or "pale green."

Therefore, we might very well, and quite justifiably, conclude that the strange children of Woolpit were definitively wild in nature. And given their state of poor health, they may certainly have lived sad and strange lives, very possibly deep underground with others of their kind, in and around Suffolk, England, just as they had claimed to the villagers of Woolpit; all the while struggling to survive on the meagre supplies of food available to them.

Sometimes, a zombie child may simply be just a tragic victim of circumstances of a very down to earth kind.

World War II

See also: Adolf Hitler, Nazis

In the early 1930s, certain of Hitler's scientists learned of some experiments with fluoride that had been conducted in England in which infinitesimal doses of fluoride in drinking water would, in time, reduce an individual's power to resist domination. Since the dosages would be small, the victims would unknowingly be slowly poisoned and a certain area of the brain would be narcotized, thereby making the victims submissive to the will of those who wished to govern them. The Nazi masterminds envisioned worldwide domination through mass medication of drinking water supplies.

The first of the Nazis' secret zombie-making potions was demonstrated by mixing fluoride in the drinking water in Nazi prison camps in order to subdue the more unruly inmates into calm submission. Repeated experiments indicated that the addition of fluoride appeared to produce excellent results in calming the most troublesome of the prisoners.

Nazi scientists confidently projected that their early experiments enabled them to predict that entire cities could be made submissive to the Hitler gospel. Rebellious regions could be made passive and be commanded to enter work programs as if they were zombies. And, as a marvelous bonus, entire regiments of soldiers could become a zombie army, never questioning their officers, never resisting any order, never complaining about lack of comfortable living conditions.

Sodium fluoride is a hazardous waste by-product of the manufacturing process of aluminum. The fluoride contamination of the environment comes from the following things: coal combustion, cigarette smoke, pesticides such as cockroach and rat poison, animal feeds, fertilizer, plastics, nonstick cookware,

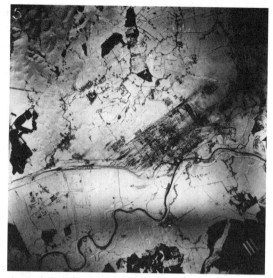

An aerial shot of the I. G. Farben complex at Auschwitz during World War II. The chemical company produced poisons for the Nazi regime.

soft drinks, juices, and other drinks (both canned and bottled), and unfathomably, in an astounding number of pharmaceutical products, including anesthetics, vitamins, antidepressants, hypnotics, psychiatric drugs, and of course, military nerve gas.

A prominent German chemist who worked in the massive I.G. Farben chemical company testified after the war that when the Nazis under Hitler decided to go into Poland, the German General Staff planned to accomplish mass control through the process of water medication.

German scientists boldly declared that any person who drank artificially fluoridated water for a period of one year or more would never again be the same person mentally or physically. Large numbers of German soldiers had fluoride introduced into their daily supply of drinking water. It is quite possible that the slavish devotion that so many Nazi troops had to their Fuhrer was due to the submissiveness induced by fluoride.

After fluoride had been used on the German people for a number of years, researchers, scientists, doctors, neurosurgeons, and other professionals began to notice, during autopsies, a rise in the presence of the chemical within the human brain. Since fluoride was known to have effects on the right temporal lobe, hippocampus, and the pineal gland, some of the professionals began to ask similar questions: Was the fanatical rise in the worship of the Fuhrer due to the fluoride placed in the water? Had a combination of the chemical and the Fuhrer's fiery speeches that emphasized the German people being the true Master Race begun to take great effect on large numbers of the mass public? Had he truly achieved his goal of submissive, compliant, zombies with no true will of their own?

One cannot resist pointing out that in 1945 fluoride was introduced into the public water supply and drinking water of select cities across the United States. Eventually, most cities across North America followed suit, believing it was the healthy thing to do. The wonder-working benefits of fluoride were taught to dentists and dental/hygienists and to children in elementary school health classes. Soon, families across the United States spent extra money and time making dental appointments for their children and themselves, in an effort to have strong, healthy, and hopefully, cavity-free teeth.

As early as 1954, some doctors have suspected and reported fluoride to be harmful. Dr. George L. Waldbott, M.D., observed that his fluoridation patients became forgetful, drowsy, lethargic, and incoherent. Comparable cases of impaired cognition and memory have been reported to the government by many other dental professionals. Government reports themselves indicate similar findings of impaired cognition and memory. Contrary to popular belief, fluoride has never been approved by the FDA for ingestion, only for topical use.

Mixing fluoride with drinking water remains controversial. On December 18, 2009, Graham Demeny, who had served fifteen years at the Glenmore Water Treatment Plant in Rockhampton, Queensland, Australia, resigned his position because he questioned the safety of adding fluoride to the city's water supply. Graham told reporter Allan Reinikkaar that until that time all processes adopted by the city council had made the water clean or safe to consume. Fluoride addition does neither, he said, and questionably compromises the safety aspect.

World War Z

When, in 2007, Brad Pitt's production company, Plan B Entertainment, obtained the rights to Max Brooks' bestselling novel, *World War Z*, there was much debate and anticipation among zombie enthusiasts about how the movie version of the book would be handled. Would it stay completely faithful to Brooks' novel? How would the dead be portrayed? Who would take on the lead role? Well, the answers to those questions and concerns—and many more—finally surfaced on June 2, 2013, when *World War Z* had its premiere in London, England.

One of the things that surprised, and worried, many undead aficionados was the fact that *World War Z* was given a "13" certificate. Taking into consideration the sheer level of blood, gore, and chaos that appear in Brooks' story, did this mean that the on-screen imagery would be less than what could be termed graphic? Well, yes it did. There's absolutely none of the blood and guts of *The Walking Dead* variety in *World War Z*. And there's a very good reason for that—it is primarily the reason why the production was so successful.

In the book, Brooks (who is also the author of *The Zombie Survival Guide: Complete Protection from the Living Dead*) presents the dead in typical zombie fashion: they spend a great deal of time not just infecting the living, but eating them, too. In the Brad Pitt version, however, the dead do not feed on the human race at all. Instead, they are merely, and solely, driven to spread the zombie virus, as far and wide as possible. Thus, while we see a lot of biting and infecting, we don't see the living devoured in horrific fashion—hence the "13" certificate. It's important to note, however, that when we realize that the zombies of *World War Z* are very different to those of most cinematic productions, the lack of graphic, cannibal-style mayhem is not a problem. Nor does it detract from what is a very entertaining and solid story.

There is one more big difference between Max Brooks' book and the movie: in the former, the dead are of the slow-walking and staggering variety. In the movie they are not just fast running, but, at times, they are *beyond* fast. While some devotees of the novel baulked at the idea of mutating Brooks' dead into creatures akin to those of *28 Days Later*, they were wrong. The frantic pace of the zombies ensures one thing that, for the viewer, is a major plus: the movie, too, charges along at a frantic pace.

In keeping with the theme of the book, the story races from place to place: it begins in Philadelphia, jumps to New York, makes its way to South Korea, descends upon the city of Jerusalem, takes the audience to Wales, and finally concludes in Nova Scotia, Canada. If there is one thing that many zombie productions are guilty of, it's not showing the viewer the worldwide scale of the undead pandemic. *World War Z*, however, does *exactly* that. Without a doubt, the scenes in which the zombie hordes overrun Jerusalem, in full-throttle fashion, are among the most memorable and spectacular in the movie.

Brad Pitt stars as the man charged with solving the world-wide zombie crisis in 2013's *World War Z*.

And despite the fact that some commentators had concerns about Brad Pitt taking the lead role as Gerry Lane, an investigator for the United Nations, they shouldn't have. Pitt brings believability to the role, as Lane frantically tries to find a way to combat the virus that threatens to overwhelm the planet. While *World War Z* is obviously based directly upon Brooks' novel, it should be stressed that it's also very much its own unique entity. And that's how it should be watched and interpreted.

Xara

Brad Steiger's friend and colleague Paul Dale Roberts interviewed Julie, who told him that she had encountered a zombie while she was visiting friends in Biloxi, Mississippi in March 2009.

Julie was driving down the road towards her friend's house, when she saw a dark-haired woman in a white flowing gown walking alongside the road. She looked through her rearview mirror and saw that this lady had no pupils and her skin was ash white. Finally the woman faded away into nothingness.

Paul said that the mysterious woman at the side of the road sounded to him to be more like a ghost than a zombie.

Julie agreed, but then proceeded to tell him the story of Xara the Zombris. Yes, she knew there was no such word as zombris, but that's what the locals called the entity.

Julie said that she did her own investigating and started talking to people on the streets about her encounter. Jeff, fifty-two, told her that back in the early 1980s, Xara, who was originally from Nicaragua, was practicing Santeria. The story goes that she traveled to New Orleans to obtain various ointments and potions from a Voodoo priest. The Voodoo priest and Xara became entangled in an affair.

When the Voodoo priest discovered that Xara was cheating on him with his own brother, he poisoned her with toxins from the puffer fish. With various rituals, he was able to turn her into a zombie.

Xara became a zombie prostitute on the streets of New Orleans. Her mind was under the complete control of the Voodoo priest turned pimp. Eventually the Voodoo priest released Xara, and she returned to Biloxi.

Paul Dale Roberts

Xara was never the same again. She always seemed like she was in a daze. The last time anyone saw Xara is when she was picked up by a trucker in a Mack truck. Xara was never seen or heard from again. Many people thought she was killed by a trucker serial killer.

One year later, Xara was seen walking the road side, staring blankly ahead and if anyone watched her long enough, she would dissipate into nothingness.

Xara learned to her everlasting sorrow that it can be extremely detrimental to one's health to anger a Voodoo Priest, perhaps especially in New Orleans, the center of Voodoo practice in the United States.

Zombie Child

Who could guess that the tale of the Zombie Child would be revived in the aftermath of Hurricane Katrina? But that is just what happened.

A couple renovating a cottage in the old Rampart section of New Orleans are said to have been hard at work, scraping years of plaster from the gabled ceiling of what was once the old kitchen when suddenly what appeared to be a small door was revealed.

Assuming it went into the attic, the owners put some elbow grease into the work and by the time they wrapped up that evening, they could both see the outline of a little trap door. It had been painted shut under a heavy plaster coating and had the appearance of having been sealed for generations.

Leaving off their work for the night, the owners cleaned up and enjoyed a well-deserved dinner before relaxing and going to bed. Late in the night, however, they were awakened by what sounded like cats yowling. Thinking that perhaps a stray had wandered in during the day while the doors were wide open, the owners got up and searched but found nothing.

The sounds continued for the next several nights and soon were compounded by small grunts and scratchings. The owners became convinced that they had somehow disturbed a family of rats lurking in the old frame house.

When at last the weekend arrived and the renovating work could be resumed, the owners decided to investigate the little door again, thinking it might hold the secret to some of the unusual night noises. Together they chipped at the paint and plaster holding the trap door in place and finally were able to pry it open. A gust of unwholesome air, full of dust and the passage of years, wafted into their faces;

when the dust cleared the owners took a flashlight in hand.

Peering into the darkness of the attic gable, pushing aside the bones of dead pigeons and rats, sorting through a rusty pile of antique toys, metal plates, and tattered rags, they came upon what appeared at first glance to be an old doll. It was the size of a young child, but it appeared for all intents and purposes to be a doll wrapped in layers of tattered cloth like a mummy. There was even a kind of gauze around the face. What caught their eyes though, even in the dim light of the attic, was the dazzling purple flash of a pair of amethyst earrings, still brilliant and still attached, even after all the intervening years.

Something about the discovery greatly disturbed the homeowners and they debated for days about what to do with their find. Soon, however, a decision was about to be made for them.

As Hurricane Katrina was poised in the Gulf of Mexico to strike New Orleans, massive evacuations were called. So disturbed by their attic find were the young couple that even in the midst of the evacuation mayhem, they took the time to replace and nail shut the trap door to the attic. Their house secured, they joined the mass of humanity fleeing the storm of the century.

When they were finally allowed to return to their home after the storm, they discovered that although the house had not flooded, there was

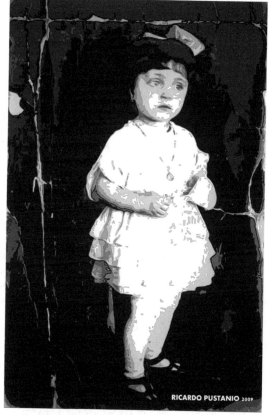

A couple renovating a home in New Orleans stumbled upon what looked like a doll but was, they strongly felt, actually the corpse of a real child. (**Art by Ricardo Pustanio**).

minor damage to one side, where a collapsed Chinaberry tree had pierced the roof. Their hearts fell when they saw this and not just because of the horror of insurance claims and Federal Emergency Management Agency (FEMA) paperwork. It was as if, they said, they knew the broken roof meant trouble.

Reluctantly, they moved aside the branches of the fallen tree and went to the little attic door. With a feeble flashlight they peered inside.

Horror and dismay overcame them when they saw that the mummified doll, which they now fully believed was really the body of a dead child, was nowhere to be found. There was nothing in the attic but the bones, the rusting toys and plates, and swatches of the decaying rags that had once encased the awful little body. It was gone.

I can think of nothing now except the words of Madame Popleuse saying: You can't kill what's already dead!

Where, I wondered, in all of Katrina-ravaged New Orleans, would such a thing go? Where would it hide now that the whole landscape was as surreal as the world it was called back from? I shudder to think, to this day, that somewhere, in the tattered remains of Old New Orleans.

Zombie Dogs of Texas

See also: Black Dogs, Chupacabras, Dog of the Dead

For the last decade or so, reports have surfaced out of the Lone Star State—and particularly so in the vicinity of the rural areas around the cities of San Antonio and Austin—of creatures that have become infamously known as "Texas Chupacabras." They are less well known, bur certainly far more intriguingly known, as "zombie hounds." Looking sickly, skinny, lacking in hair, and reportedly having a taste for blood and raw meat, they have struck fear into the folk of Texas. One of the world's leading researchers of the "dogs of the dead" phenomenon is Ken Gerhard, a San Antonio resident, and the author of a number of acclaimed books, including *Encounters with Flying Humanoids*.

Gerhard notes: "I first learned of the Texas Chupacabras in 2004." Gerhard's source for the story: Jon Downes, the director of the British-based Center for Fortean Zoology, one of the few full-time groups in the world dedicated to the study of unknown animals, such as Bigfoot, the Loch Ness Monster, and the Abominable Snowman.

The story continues: "As we sat and drank cold Shiner Bock beer in the courtyard of San Antonio's haunted Menger Hotel one evening," says Gerhard, "Jon told me about how he had been driven to a town called Elmendorf earlier that day, in order to meet a rancher named Devin McAnally. Apparently, Mr. McAnally had dispatched an inexplicable, bluish-gray animal that had been slaughtering his chickens. After looking at some photos of its strange corpse, Jon had deduced that the creature was obviously some type of canine, but beyond that he was unable to make a definitive identification."

Gerhard expands further: "People often ask me: 'Are the Texas Chupacabras merely mangy coyotes?' I personally feel to simply say 'Yes' is an oversimplification. Examination of their physical remains, and DNA tests and analysis, has confirmed that these animals belong to the genus Canis. It's also true that the closest genetic matches have been with coyotes; though the Elmendorf Beast may have been a hybrid. It seems plausible to theorize that an extreme type of mange is being passed from mothers to their offspring, causing their hairless condition. My associate, naturalist Lee Hales, has pointed out that adaptations happen all the time in nature. And maybe their baldness has even given them an advantage on the hot plains of Texas. Perhaps it is even being written into their genetic code."

But there seems to be far more going on. "As of yet," Gerhard astutely notes, "no one has been able to sufficiently explain their other abnormal characteristics, which have included grossly enlarged fangs and claws, irregular skulls, disproportionate limbs, and unusually long tails. These are all traits that seem inexplicable. These creatures might possess cataracts in their eyes, resulting in poor vision. This would certainly explain why so many of them have been shot so easily, or run over by cars. There is also the issue of their sinister behavior, which seemingly revolves around lapping up the blood of helpless poultry. There could be specific nutrients in blood that these animals crave, due to their affliction."

Despite all the years of study, as Gerhard admits, we are still left with one, overridingly important question that remains tantalizingly unanswered: "Exactly what are these blue, zombie dogs that roam the grasslands of Texas?"

Zombie Honeymoon

Imagine the scene: you have just gotten married, you are sitting on a warm, sandy beach, looking out on an inviting ocean, and you are thinking of all the fun, love, and adventures that lie ahead of you. Then, suddenly, your world crumbles around you, all thanks to the sudden surfacing from the waters of a deadly zombie that quickly seals the fate of your loved one. That's what happens in *Zombie Honeymoon*, a 2004 production of Hooligan Pictures. The terrified onlooker is Denise, played in fine form by Tracey Coogan. Her doomed, new husband is Danny, played by actor Graham Sibley.

Unlike many movies of the undead—in fact, unlike practically *all* movies of the undead—*Zombie Honeymoon* is not filled with hundreds and thousands of rampaging monsters. One is far more than enough to provoke deep tragedy for our newlyweds. As Denise and Danny are hanging out on a stretch of New Jersey beach, a tattered-clothed figure comes striding out of the ocean. A terrified Denise screams as the far from healthy looking man lunges at Danny, who is snoozing under the sun. The zombie holds Danny down and, rather than delivering a deadly bite to the neck or arm, proceeds to vomit up a sickly looking black substance directly into Danny's mouth. Irreversible infection has begun. A crazed race to the nearest hospital follows, but it's no good: the fast-acting virus quickly kills Danny. As a doctor somberly relates the terrible news to Denise, however, Danny returns to life—or, more correctly, to a new life as a zombie.

For Denise, Danny is still Danny, no matter what. Well, for a while he is. Certain, very noticeable, changes quickly occur: Danny, a vegetarian, soon gets a taste for red meat. Heck, let us get right to the point: a taste for *human* meat. Denise,

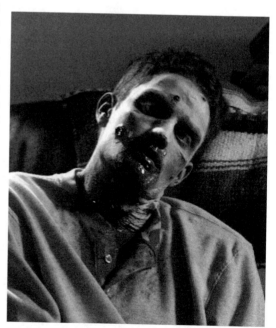

Graham Sibley plays Danny, an ill-fated newlywed who is infected by a zombie and struggles to maintain his humanity and his love for his bride.

appalled by what Danny has become, is in a state of deep conflict. In her heart, she knows that Danny is becoming a monster and that his cannibalistic actions cannot be allowed to continue. But, on the matter of her heart, Denise is still deeply in love with Danny, no matter what he may be rapidly transforming into.

Matters come to a nerve-jangling conclusion when Danny, by the end of the movie, now having lost practically all of his humanity and with his body decomposing at a rapid rate, targets Denise. He throws her to the ground and is just about to spew forth some of the very same black stuff all over Denise that transformed him into a zombie when he suddenly pulls back and turns his head to one side. The small speck of Danny that is still left is mortified and asks Denise for forgiveness. She realizes that Danny is not at fault for the situation in which they have now found themselves and can only watch with devastation as Danny dies for a second time. Denise gives Danny a respectful, loving send-off and returns to that stretch of beach where tragedy occurred, and where she now ponders on the life that might have been, but which now never will be.

For some, the idea of a zombie movie focused solely upon the lives of a pair of new-lyweds might seem bizarre or downright ridiculous. It is, however, to the credit of the cast—and particularly so Coogan, who gives an emotional performance—that a nearly unbelievable storyline becomes all too believable. *Zombie Honeymoon* is a very different love story to *Mutants*; however, it does have something in common with it: even when the world is falling apart, love still survives, even if it doesn't necessarily triumph.

Zombie Lake

While many may find it understandably tasteless, more than a few scriptwriters have weaved their zombie-themed stories around the actions of the Nazis, both during and after World War II. It has to be said, however, that combining Hitler's hordes with the undead is not an automatic guarantee of a huge box-office success. In fact, the exact opposite is the case. Nevertheless, that has not prevented just such an entire sub-genre from "developing," if that's the correct term to use, which it probably is not. Such Nazi-themed productions include *Dead Snow*; *Oasis of the Zombies*; *Outpost*; and *Shockwaves*. And then there is a 1981 French production, *Le Lac Des Morts Vivants*, or in its literal English translation, *Lake of the Dead*. It was, however, titled for English-speaking audiences as *Zombie Lake*.

Without a doubt, *Zombie Lake* is just about one of the worst zombie movies ever made; perhaps even *the* worst. Bad acting, extremely poor special effects, and what appears to be a near-non-existent budget, collectively ensure that *Zombie Lake* should be avoided at all cost. Certainly, it is not even worth watching from the "it's so bad, it's good" perspective. To put it succinctly, the movie is just plain bad. The storyline is not without a few merits, however, and, handled properly, could have been a winner. It ends up, however, very much a loser.

During World War II, a band of German troops is killed by a group of resistance fighters, who dump the bodies of Hitler's goons in the lake of a typically picturesque French village—one which, years later, is used for devilish rites. The result: the lake soon gives up its dead, and the village teems with flesh-devouring monsters, all still adorned in their German uniforms, and all intent on making a feast of the locals. The level of nudity on the part of the female cast-members is taken to such levels of overkill that any sense of eroticism is non-existent. And as for those special effects: well, what could be worse than seeing what is clearly *green paint* rubbing off the faces of the zombies and onto the clothes and skin of their victims? One thing could be worse, and is: watching fake-blood squirt out of less than well hidden plastic tubes that are affixed to the necks of the "actors."

Zombie Lake is utterly gross, but for all the wrong reasons.

Zombieland

Chiefly as a result of the huge success of *Shaun of the Dead*, more than a few comedy-based zombie movies surfaced in its immediate wake, such as *Juan of the Dead*, *Black Sheep*, and *Zombie Strippers*, which, while not laugh out loud hysterical, are at least entertaining and fun to watch. There are, however, far more, so-called zombie comedies that are actually nothing of the sort and which do not deserve, and will not get, a mention here. One movie that *will* get a mention, however, and that is right up there with *Shaun of the Dead* is 2009's *Zombieland*. Whereas the humor in *Shaun* is very much of the slapstick, in your face, variety, in *Zombieland* it's far darker.

In a neat twist, and something that echoes previous entries in this book, the rise of the infected is not caused by alien viruses, Voodoo, or matters of an occult nature. Instead, it's provoked by bovine spongiform encephalopathy (BSE), or, as it is most familiarly known: Mad Cow Disease. In *Zombieland*, when the human equivalent of BSE, variant Creutzfeldt-Jacob disease (vCJD), mutates to a terrifying and catastrophic degree, the Land of the Free becomes the land of the zombies.

As is the case in nearly all post-*Night of the Living Dead* movies on reanimated flesh-eaters and the end of the world, *Zombieland* unites a wide and varied cast of characters, who bond together—or, more correctly, who are *forced* to bond together—if they want to stay alive. In this case, those characters are the Twinkie-obsessed Tallahassee (actor Woody Harrelson), Columbus, a student, (played by Jesse Eisenberg), and savvy teenage sisters, Wichita and Little Rock (actresses Emma Stone and Abigail Breslin).

The movie begins in the gun-toting state of Texas, which is not faring well as the zombie hordes are increasing day by day. When their paths cross, Tallahassee is doing his utmost to make it to Florida, while Columbus wants to get back to his family, in Ohio. That all changes, however, when the pair runs into Wichita and Little Rock and things go from bad to worse. Not only do the girls fool Tallahassee and

Woody Harrelson (with bat) and Jesse Eisenberg (center) fight off zombies after fast food burgers have infected people with a form of mad cow disease in the darkly humorous *Zombieland*.

Columbus into feeling sorry for them—by brilliantly making it look like Little Rock is infected, when she actually isn't—they also steal Tallahassee's vehicle and guns and hit the highway for Los Angeles. Suddenly, Tallahassee's plans to make it to Florida have gone right out of the window. Enraged almost as much as a genuine zombie, he vows to track down the sisters and make them pay for crossing him. Finding a Hummer, he and Columbus head west, in hot pursuit of the conniving teens.

It's not long before paths cross again and, despite being in a state of almost *28 Days Later*-style anger proportions, Tallahassee realizes that there is safety in numbers, and, as a result, and somewhat reluctantly, the four agree to tough it out as one, unified, fighting force. And they're soon bound for Hollywood. It's when they arrive that we are treated to one of the funniest sections of the movie: they make their way to the huge home of actor Bill Murray, playing none other than himself. Murray has found an ingenious way to outwit the dead when he needs to leave the house: he acts just like them, moaning and growling and staggering around in unsteady fashion. Unfortunately for Murray, he does such an excellent job of it all that Columbus, assuming Murray to be infected and deadly, turns a gun on him. A word of warning for all budding stars of Hollywood: method-acting can, it seems, be fatal.

Zombieland comes to a nail-biting conclusion, but one filled with humorous asides too, in a Los Angeles amusement park, where our four heroes are forced to fight off a near-army of vCJD-infected monsters. They finally do so and realize that they do pretty good together as a team and hit the road to start a new life, far away from the deadly dead. Will we see how Tallahassee, Columbus, Little Rock, and Wichita fare in the future? Well, maybe or, perhaps, maybe not: rumors abound of *Zombieland 2*, although, right now, nothing is cast in stone.

Zombie Preparation

It might sound like just about the wildest science-fiction story of all, but it most assuredly is not. It is actually nothing less than astounding reality. On Halloween 2012, at Mission Bay, San Diego, elements of the U.S. Marines, along with an elite unit of U.S. Navy personnel, took part in a training operation that revolved around a tumultuous, but fictionalized, zombie onslaught. And it was all taken very seriously, too, as is evidenced by the words of one Brad Barker. The president of the Halo Corporation—which is a security-based organization that was formed in 2006 and that is made up of personnel with backgrounds in special operations, intelligence, and national security—Barker told the media that: "This is a very real exercise. This is not some type of big costume party."

Echoing the deadly seriousness of the exercise, none other than a retired U.S. Air Force four-star general, former CIA director, and former National Security Agency director named Michael Hayden was in attendance. On top of that, more than a thousand military personnel, dozens of police officers, and a sizeable number of government officials all took part in the event, which occurred on more than forty-acres of land that was specifically transformed into, among other things, an Iraq-style town.

Barker added, admittedly rather intriguingly: "No doubt when a zombie apocalypse occurs, it's going to be a federal incident, so we're making it happen." He also noted that, from his personal perspective at least, there was one major downside to the publicity that had been given to the exercise of the undead: "Every whack job in the world" had been emailing and phoning, demanding to know what, exactly, was afoot and why.

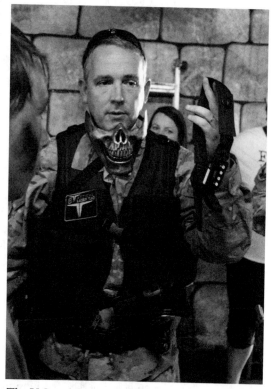

The U.S. military, as well as the CIA, have taken part in exercises to prepare for a possible zombie apocalypse.

Officially, the scenario of a zombie outbreak, that the military had to quash at all costs, was utilized as a result of the enormous popularity in which the risen dead are presently bathing and basking. Adding the flesh-eating abominations to the mix, in the collective mind of the Halo Corporation anyway, was a sure way of alerting people's attention to the importance of being prepared for a *real* disaster, such as one caused by war, by terrorists, or by the harshness of Mother Nature, herself.

Not surprisingly, however, the conspiracy-minded were of a very different opinion. When the story surfaced, they voiced their deep suspicions that the government would soon be releasing a nightmarish, airborne virus all across the nation—and maybe across the world. It was to be a virus that would turn the populace into zombie-style, psychotic killers, and which would require the military to be fully prepared, and trained, to wipe out tens upon tens of millions of crazed infected. The reason behind all of the mayhem: to massively lower population levels and permit the government to place the now far more manageable, and much smaller, population under a never-ending state of grim, *1984*-style, martial law.

Given that Michael Hayden is a former director of the NSA, and that in September 2013, it was revealed in the media that the Big Brother-style NSA secretly refers to the millions of Americans who own smart-phones as "zombies," perhaps there really *was* more to this exercise than meets the eye. If the NSA's headquarters in Maryland suddenly goes into lockdown mode in the near future, it may not be because of the fall-out from the Edward Snowden affair. It could be due to something far, far worse: the real undead.

Zombie Stay-Away Powder

When vampires are reported prowling the darkened midnight streets, one can attempt to ward them of by wearing a crucifix or by sleeping in front of a large mirror to terrify the bloodsucker by forcing it to glimpse its own ghastly image. When werewolves howl at the full moon to demand it light the creature's way to a victim, the pursued human prey can wear a garland of wolfbane or carry a pistol loaded with silver bullets. But is there anything that will banish a member of the living dead?

Yes, there are many ingredients in Zombie-Stay-Away Powder that Voodoo priests and priestess recommend to keep the moldering creatures at bay.

Ichintal (chayote root) is used in making Zombie-Stay-Away Powder. The zombies are said to freeze in their tracks and cannot cross over a buried chayote root.

Although most people are familiar only with the fruit itself, the root, stem, seeds, and leaves are all edible. If you feed any part of a chayote (merliton) to a zombie, the spell will be broken for nine days. The person will then resume a normal life, but at the end of nine days it will return to being a zombie or die.

The act of feeding a chayote to a zombie to break the spell will only work once every seven years.

The chayote (Sechium edule), also known as sayote, tayota, choko, chocho, chow-chow, christophene, merliton, and vegetable pear, is an edible plant that belongs to the gourd family Cucurbitaceae, along with melons, cucumbers, and squash. The plant has large leaves that form a canopy over the fruit. The vine is grown on the ground, or more commonly, on trellises.

Costa Rica is a major exporter of chayotes worldwide. Costa Rican chayotes can be purchased in the European Union, the United States and other places in the world. Chayote is a very important ingredient in the Central American diet.

Zombie Strippers

Ah, yes: if you are aiming for a hit movie, then what could be better than combining zombies with hot, gyrating strippers? Probably *nothing* could be better—providing, of course, that the end result actually works well. Sadly, *Zombie Strippers*, Jay Lee's 2008 production, falls short in many respects. It must be said that the premise, at least, is a very good one, and particularly so in the sense that the story relies to a great extent on satire and laughs. But, the satire doesn't work so well and the laughs are seldom of the laugh-out-loud kind.

Zombie Strippers portrays a world that has, basically, gone to hell. In a situation that many might view as even more horrific than an undead apocalypse, President George W. Bush is serving his *fourth* term in office, and American society has been reduced to the worst combination of George Orwell's *1984* and Aldous Huxley's *Brave New World*. On top of that, the U.S. war-machine is wildly out of control, engaging in battle with anyone who dares to question its foreign policy, which includes France, no less.

As the need for more and more troops increases, a project is initiated to try and find a way to return to life the many American soldiers who are being killed on the equally many battlefields. That way, in theory, the U.S. military will never run short of personnel. That's great—or, it is until the virus that has been created to give some degree of life back to the army of the dead escapes from its confines. It's then time to bring in the backup: an elite team of military personnel whose job it is to wipe out the zombies and contain the outbreak. It would probably have all worked very well, had one of the

Zombie Strippers makes an attempt at black humor with a combination of zombies and, well, strippers, but doesn't make the grade.

men, Birdflough, not got bitten. Unfortunately, he *does* get bitten. And, just like any other regular zombie, in his undead state he decides to pay a visit to a strip club, *Rhino*, which is managed by Robert "Freddy Krueger" Englund.

Legendary porn star, Jenna Jameson, becomes a victim of Birdflough's deadly bite, but that doesn't prevent her character, Kat, a stripper at the club, from giving an erotic dance or several. In fact, the audience, much preferring her dead to alive, practically eats her up—if you will pardon the pun. When it becomes clear that being a zombie stripper is far more profitable, money-wise, than just being a regular human stripper, the other pole-dancing babes follow suit. Of course, overwhelming carnage, and the devouring of the living, quickly erupts when the girls trade in their dollars for fresh meat.

In essence, that is the theme and story of *Zombie Strippers*. It could have been a great grindhouse-style satire, combining the best bits of the 2006 movie *Idiocracy*, and Robert Rodriguez's zombie-dominated *Planet Terror*, of 2007. *Zombie Strippers*, unfortunately, has all the ingredients, but none of the substance. The girls, however, look great, even when they're dead. And, admittedly, the blurb for the movie is worth its weight in gold: "They'll dance for a fee, but devour you for free."

Zombie Walks

Civilization is over and the hungry dead have taken control of the world's cities. Zombies are rampaging their way through the streets. Like a tidal wave, they overwhelm just about everyone and everything in their monstrous path. And there is no stopping them. But, we're not talking about cinematic zombies. In fact, the exact opposite: real-world zombies, of a kind, anyway. Not content with simply watching the deeds of the dead on television or at movie theaters, whole swathes of the population have developed deep desires to *become* zombies—albeit temporarily. Welcome to the escalating phenomenon of Zombie Walks.

The premise behind Zombie Walks is very simple yet great fun: throngs of zombie fans get together, at a specific time, and at a particular location, and roam around town dressed as the undead. And they take the whole thing very seriously. Torn and ragged clothes, coupled with plentiful amount of fake blood and white face-paint, make for a seriously horrific combination. And for anyone who has ever seen a Zombie Walk—and particularly one where the numbers of the "dead" are in the thousands—it's quite a sight to experience just about the closest thing possible to a real zombie epidemic exploding all around you.

Zombie Walks date back to August 2001, when the first such event was organized in Sacramento, California. Since then, and just like their fictional counterparts, the pretend dead of the real world have grown at alarming rates and their rotting tentacles are spreading all across the planet. In 2005, and in the wake of the success of the 2004 remake of *Dawn of the Dead*, more than 400 people took part in a Zombie Walk in Vancouver, Canada. Double that amount transformed themselves into hun-

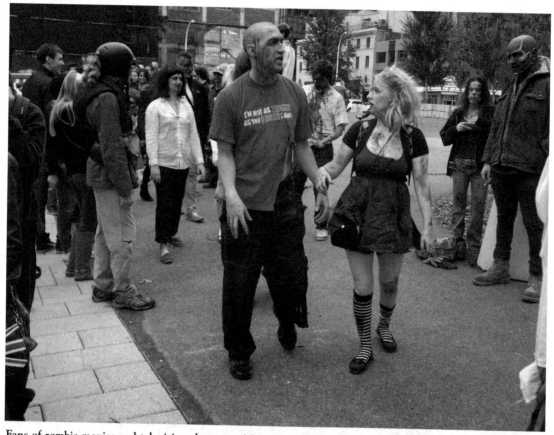

Fans of zombie movies and television shows participate in a Zombie Walk in Montréal, Canada, in 2013.

gry monsters in October 2006, when a similar event was held at the Monroeville Mall, in Monroeville, Pennsylvania—which served as the setting for George A. Romero's *Dawn of the Dead* movie of 1979. Post-2006, the figures have reached near-apocalyptic proportions, somewhat satisfyingly.

October 2009 saw more than 4,000 zombie lookalikes take over the seventh century English town of Ledbury. In the very same month, in excess of 5,000 deadheads invaded Brisbane, Australia and roughly 8,000 took control of Grand Rapids, Michigan. As impressive as such figures most certainly were, they were totally eclipsed by the fever for Zombie Walks that, in 2012, infected much of South America. In October of that year alone, somewhere between 11,000 and 13,000 dead devotees overwhelmed Santiago, the capital of Chile, and an astonishing 24,000 did likewise in the Argentinean capital of Buenos Aires. That was nothing, however, compared to the current record holder of Minneapolis/St. Paul, Minnesota, which—also in October 2012—was overrun by in excess of 30,000 faked flesh eaters. In a strange, but highly entertaining fashion, the dead really do walk. And they may soon be making their slow, ominous way to a town or city near you. But don't worry, they don't really bite.

THE ZOMBIE BOOK: THE ENCYCLOPEDIA OF THE LIVING DEAD

Zombification

It was ideas like those expressed in the "Evil Twins" entry in this book (pp. 101–102) that convinced Major General William Creasy, chief officer of the Army Chemical Corps, that LSD and other psychoactive drugs would be the weapons of the future. If CIA agents or Special Forces units spiked a city's water supply with LSD, the enemies within would offer no resistance.

Among the assignments given to Dr. Sidney Gottlieb by CIA chief Allen Dulles was to create a method of producing large scale aberrant mental states on an unsuspecting population. A substance was sought that could be used by the U.S. military when engaging an enemy that they could spray over a city and render both civilians and military opponents relatively helpless and unable to resist. The substance should be able to cause illogical thinking, or produce shock and confusion over extended periods of time, or produce physical disablement, such as paralysis of the legs or cause mental confusion. In essence, to create a population of zombies.

It would have been awkward at the time to experiment on foreign populations, so MK-ULTRA created Operation Big City in the United States. Agents modified a

Operation Big City involves experiments with hallucinogenic gases and other harmful poisons on entire U.S. cities to see if this strategy might be successful against foreign populations.

1953 Mercury so its exhaust pipe extended eighteen inches beyond its normal length. A gas concocted to cause hallucinations was then emitted through the automobile's exhaust as the agents drove the Mercury for eighty miles around New York City, making note of the effects on pedestrians.

In another test, operatives equipped with nasal filters boarded the New York subway with battery-powered emissions equipment fitted into suitcases to test the effect of LSD on people in confined areas.

An ambitious project was conducted in 1957 when operatives released a biological effects gas on the Golden Gate Bridge in San Francisco. The intent of the experiment was to blanket the entire city with the gas and then monitor how powerfully the disorienting properties of the substance would affect the population. The agents were dismayed when a sudden wind arose and blew the gas away before it could cause any harm.

It should also be noted that in an experiment to determine how susceptible an American city would be to biological attack, the U.S. Navy sprayed a cloud of bacteria from ships over San Francisco in 1950. Many residents become ill with pneumonia and other illnesses.

In 1951, the U.S. Department of Defense began open air tests over many U.S. cities, using disease-producing bacteria and viruses.

Senate hearings on Health and Scientific Research in 1977 confirmed that 239 populated areas in the United States had been contaminated with biological agents between 1949 and 1969. Some of the cities included San Francisco, Key West, Panama City, Minneapolis, and St. Louis.

Conclusion

For those who fear that, one day, a real-world zombie outbreak will actually occur, such a thing may not be entirely bad news, as strange as that must surely sound. In fact, there may be hardly any bad news whatsoever. The biggest threat posed by the fictional undead is their relentless ability to pursue their quarry. That means us, the human race, unfortunately. Whether they are of the slow walking or of the fast running kind, today's zombies are almost unstoppable in their crazed desire to feed. But how would the recently deceased really fare if, against all the odds, reanimation actually occurred and they chose to attack us?

For the possible answers—and a bit of refreshingly good news, too—we have to turn our attention to the work of one Kimberlee Sue Moran, a forensic archaeologist who knows more than a few things about the newly dead. In early 2012, Moran gave an entertaining presentation at the huge, seventy-four-acre, Laurel Hill Cemetery in Philadelphia, Pennsylvania, the subject of which was the physical nature of death and what happens to the body when life is finally over. But, to give her lecture both a high degree of spice and relevancy to today's world, Moran chose to focus on zombies to get her message across.

Rigor mortis, decomposition, and the liquefying of the corpse would, says Moran, all prevent the average zombie from launching any kind of concerted attack upon the living. In fact, the "sloshy" and "falling to bits" nature of the dead would effectively render them incapable of doing much at all—and certainly not charging or staggering around ruined cities in search of warm, human flesh to eagerly devour. She says for those who spend their time worrying that their homes may not be secure enough to keep armies of the rampaging dead firmly at bay: "If you're someone like me who's not a big fan of zombies, you can sleep easy tonight knowing that you're safe, that no zombies are going to come and get you."

As positive and as reassuring as Moran's words certainly are, there is, however, just one downside to all of this. She was strictly commenting on the literal dead

Have filmmakers like George Romero painted an accurate picture of a possible horrifying world plagued by zombies?

returning from the grave. The not quite deceased—but the highly infected living—of *28 Days Later, 28 Weeks Later, Mutants* and *Rammbock* are a very different matter indeed. With them, there is no decay, no rigor mortis, and no decomposition for the simple reason they are still alive. So, in the real world, just maybe, sleeping sound will not be quite so easy, after all. Sorry about that.

Now, our long and winding foray into the world of the zombie is at its end. The journey was one that revealed a number of significant and eye-opening points. They are points that give us a valuable insight into the macabre realm of the living dead. As we have seen, the zombie was not simply a creation of George A. Romero in 1968. Nor, even, did the phenomenon of the reanimated dead have its origins in Haitian lore and the domain of Voodoo of the relatively recent past. Quite the contrary, the zombie has been a much feared creature since the very dawn of civilization.

Whether it was the ancient Egyptians, the Chinese, the Irish, or the people of Scandinavia, they all dreaded one thing more than any other: the dead refusing to stay dead. While the names differed—for the folk of Denmark, Iceland, Sweden, and Norway, it was the Draugr, and in China it was the jiang-shi—the imagery and the actions of the dead did not. For all nations, in centuries gone, the undead were to be feared, avoided and, whenever and wherever possible, put down permanently.

This raises an important question: did literal zombies of the type that have become so popularized in today's world of entertainment once walk the Earth? Quite possibly, given the sheer scale of accounts from centuries past that have come to our attention, they really did. And, in some fashion, they have continued to do so. Take, for example, the zombified souls of Voodoo. Haitian Voodoo and the control of the living in zombified form were issues widely popularized in the 1930s and 1940s by Hollywood movie moguls. The teachings of old, however, still hold firm to this day—and particularly so in New Orleans, Louisiana, and the Caribbean, two places where the zombie-slave is accepted as being all too shockingly real.

We have also seen the terrible outcome of what happens when people *act* like zombies, rather than literally transform into them. While so called "Zombie Walks" are solely designed for the fun and entertainment for those that partake in such events, the same cannot be said for those who—by choice or circumstances—have literally fed on the living. Take the Fore tribe of Papua New Guinea as a classic example. They developed a devastating brain condition—Kuru, meaning "shiver"—after eating human brains. Or, the nightmarish situation in the United Kingdom, when, post-mid-1980s onwards, the eating of cannibalized cows led to the terrifying spread of variant

Creutzfeldt-Jacob disease (vCJD). So many people have learned, to their fatal cost, that cannibalism and the devouring of our own kind can only ever end in disaster. You, the reader, have also hopefully learned that eating one's fellow man is never a wise idea.

We have also seen how George A. Romero may very well have accurately predicted the rise of the infected. In *Night of the Living Dead*, the apocalypse is triggered by outer space contamination that is brought back to Earth on a space probe. History, and this book, has shown time and again that NASA, and other worldwide space agencies, have exhibited a great deal of concern in relation to the matter of how a deadly virus of extraterrestrial proportions might lead to our entire downfall and extermination as a species.

Then there are those strange and almost surreal conspiracy theories that have become staple parts of zombie lore today: why are agencies such as the Centers for Disease Control (CDC) and the Federal Emergency Management Agency (FEMA) speaking openly and seriously about zombies, to the extent that they have entire sections of their websites devoted to the study of such matters? Why is the Social Security Administration secretly buying up hundreds of thousands of bullets? What about the rumors of agencies of officialdom trying to create real-life equivalents of the "Rage Virus" of *28 Days Later*, and *28 Weeks Later*?

Is it just a case that officialdom has become infected by the zombie bug, in the very same fashion that the general public has? Or, is there a top secret fear—or even a terrible knowledge—that, very soon, the jiang-shi and the Draugr of old will be making appearances all across the world; appearances that will require drastic action be taken to try and quell the apocalypse? Just possibly, the answers may arrive sooner than we think or hope.

And, finally, there is the zombie of entertainment, one that, as the pages of *The Zombie Book* demonstrate, has increased in scale and visibility to a massive degree in the last decade. Even if a real zombie apocalypse does not occur, and the CDC, FEMA, and the military are not at the forefront of a mission to destroy the dead and save the living, the likelihood is that the fictional zombie will continue to thrive for many years to come. *The Walking Dead*, *Night of the Living Dead*, *28 Days Later*, *Resident Evil*, *World War Z*, and countless other television shows, movies, and books have all ensured that no matter what we do, the zombie's presence in society is as guaranteed as its need to kill and eat us.

Long "live" the zombie!

Bibliography

Abanes, Richard. *End-Time Visions*. Nashville, TN: Broadman & Holman, 1998.

"Animal Mutilation." http://vault.fbi.gov/Animal%20Mutilation. 2014.

Ardrey, Adam. *Finding Arthur: The True Origins of the Once and Future King*. New York: Overlook, 2013.

Atwater, P.M.H. *The Big Book of Near-Death Experiences: The Ultimate Guide to What Happens When We Die*. Newburyport, MA: Hampton Roads Publishing, 2007.

Austen, Jane, and Grahame-Smith, Seth. *Pride and Prejudice and Zombies*. Philadelphia, PA: Quirk Books, 2009.

Bach, Marcus. *Inside Voodoo*. New York: Signet, 1968.

Baer, Elizabeth R. *The Golem Redux: From Prague to Post-Holocaust Fiction*. Detroit, MI: Wayne State University Press, 2012.

Barker, J.C. *Scared to Death*. New York: Dell Books, 1969.

Barone, Matt. "The 25 Most Underrated Zombie Movies." http://www.complex.com/pop-culture/2012/10/25-most-underrated-zombie-movies/mutants. October 9, 2012.

Baxter, Jessica. "George A. Romero's Survival of the Dead." http://www.filmthreat.com/reviews/22284/. May 29, 2010.

"Beef Brain Curry." http://www.melroseflowers.com/mkic/indo_recipes/meat/beef_brain_curry.html. 2014.

Bekkum, Gary. "Operation Often: Satanism in the CIA." http://coverthistory.blogspot.com/2007/12/operation-often-satanism-in-cia-this.html. December 17, 2007.

Berkeley, Ziggy. "King of the Zombies (1941)." http://cinemaontherocks.com/reviews/kingofthezombies.html. October 2011.

Bernard, Rafe. *Army of the Undead*. New York: Pyramid Books, 1967.

"Bhangarh Fort: The Most 'Haunted' Place in India?" http://articles.timesofindia.indiatimes.com/2013-11-29/travel/40589314_1_ghosts-fort-area-sariska-reserve. November 29, 2013.

Bidwell, Allie. "Human Head Transplants Close to Becoming Reality: Italian Scientist." http://www.nydailynews.com/life-style/health/transplant-human-heads-italian-scientist-article-1.1388169. July 2, 2013.

Billings, Molly. "The Influenza Pandemic of 1918." http://virus.stanford.edu/uda/. June 1997, modified February 2005.

"Black Dog of Newgate, Parts 1 and 2." http://www.lostplays.org/index.php/Black_Dog_of_Newgate,_Parts_1_and_2. 2009.

"Black Sheep." http://www.imdb.com/title/tt0779982/. 2014.

"Bodyless Dog's Head Brought Back to Life: 1940's Russian Experiment." http://www.thelivingmoon.com/45jack_files/03files/Russian_Experiment_Dead_Dog.html. 2011.

Borntreger, Andrew. "Redneck Zombies." http://www.badmovies.org/movies/redneck zombies/. 2014.

Bowart, Walter. *Operation Mind Control*. London, U.K.: Fontana, 1978.

Bower, Bruce. "Human Ancestors Had Taste for Meat, Brains." https://www.science news.org/article/human-ancestors-had-taste-meat-brains. June 1, 2013.

"Bowery at Midnight." http://www.rottentomatoes.com/m/bowery_at_midnight/. 2014.

Brandon, S.G.F. *Religion in Ancient History*. New York: Charles Scribners Sons, 1969.

"A Brief History of Disembodied Dog Heads." http://blog.wfmu.org/freeform/2006/02/a_brief_history.html. July 4, 2008.

Britt, Robert Roy. "Alien Microbe Reported Found in Earth's Atmosphere." http://www.space.com/scienceastronomy/planetearth/alien_bacteria_001127.html. November 27, 2000.

Brooks, Max. *The Zombie Survival Guide: Complete Protection from the Living Dead*. New York: Broadway Books, 2003.

———. *World War Z*. New York: Three Rivers Press, 2006.

Bryant, Ben. "Man with 'Walking Corpse Syndrome' Believes He Is Dead." http://www.telegraph.co.uk/health/healthnews/10081702/Man-with-Walking-Corpse-Syndrome-believes-he-is-dead.html. May 26, 2013.

"BSE (Bovine Spongiform Encephalopathy, or Mad Cow Disease)." http://www.cdc.gov/ncidod/dvrd/bse/. 2014.

Buckland, Raymond. *Bucklands Complete Book of Witchcraft*. St. Paul, MN: Llewellyn Publications, 1986, 1997.

Budge, E.A. Wallis. *Egyptian Magic*. New York: Dover Books, 1971.

"Bulldog Jack." http://www.timeout.com/london/film/bulldog-jack. 2014.

Canon, M., and S. Hutin. *The Alchemists*. Translated by Helen R. Lane. New York: Grove Press, 1961.

"Caribbean Primate Research Center." http://cprc.rcm.upr.edu/. 2014.

Carter, John. *Sex and Rockets: The Occult World of Jack Parsons.* Venice, CA: Feral House, 1999.

"Cat Mutilations and Taigheirm." http://www.enigmaticearth.com/2013/06/cat-mutilations-and-taigheirm.html#.Us7ZzXbnaM8. June 2013.

"Celebrating Christmas with 13 Trolls." http://www.iceland.is/the-big-picture/news/celebrating-christmas-with-13-trolls/7916/. 2014.

"Centers for Disease Control and Prevention." http://www.cdc.gov/. 2014.

Christopher, Neil. "The Video Nasties Furore." http://www.hysteria-lives.co.uk/hysterialives/nasties/nastiesmain1.htm. 2014.

"Chupacabras Headquarters." http://www.cuerochupacabra.com/. 2014.

Coghlan, Andy. "Mysterious Bursts of Activity in Flatlining Brain." http://www.newscientist.com/article/dn24228-mysterious-bursts-of-activity-in-flatlining-brain.html#.Us7uKXbnaM8. September 19, 2013.

Colman, Penny. *Corpses, Coffins, and Crypts: A History of Burial.* New York: Henry Holt & Co., 1997.

Crim, Keith. *The Perennial Dictionary of World Religions.* San Francisco: Harper Collins, 1989.

"Crosse, Andrew." http://www.crosseconnections.org.uk/crosse/bios/andrew.htm. 2014.

DaRajinCajun. "Mongol Psychological Warfare Tactics." http://daragincajun.blogspot.com/2011/09/mongol-psychological-warfare-tactics.html. September 2, 2011.

Davies, Jon. *Death, Burial and the Rebirth in the Religions of Antiquity.* London and New York: Routledge, 1999.

Davis, Wade. *The Serpent and the Rainbow: A Harvard Scientist Uncovers the Startling Truth about the Secret World of Haitian Voodoo and Zombies.* New York: Simon & Schuster, 1985.

"Dawn of the Dead." http://boxofficemojo.com/movies/?id=dawnofthedead.htm. 2014.

"Dawn of the Dead." http://www.horrorlair.com/scripts/dawnofthedead.txt. 2014.

"The Dead 2: India." http://www.imdb.com/title/tt2917336/. 2013.

"Death Line 1973." http://www.britishhorrorfilms.co.uk/deathline.shtml. February 22, 2010.

"Diary of the Dead." http://www.metacritic.com/movie/diary-of-the-dead. February 15, 2008.

Dicks, Terrence. *Dr. Who and the Auton Invasion.* London: BBC Books, 2011.

Downes, Jon. "Fine Young Cannibals." http://forteanzoology.blogspot.com/2009/04/fine-young-cannibals.html. April 2, 2009.

Drake, Frank, and Dava Sobel. *Is Anyone Out There?* Concord, CA: Delta, 1994.

"Draugr the Real Zombie." http://themystified.com/index.php/topics/creatures-of-the-night/zombies/47-draugr-the-modern-zombie. 2013.

Duggan Oliver. "'Vampire' Graveyard? Heads Placed between Legs of Decapitated Skeletons Found in Poland." http://www.independent.co.uk/news/world/europe/vampire-graveyard-heads-placed-between-legs-of-decapitated-skeletons-found-in-poland-8706220.html. July 12, 2013.

Duke, Philip, S. *The AIDS-ET Connection*. Omaha, NE: Cosmos Press, 1999.

_____. "The AIDS–ET Connection Hypothesis." http://www.bibliotecapleyades.net/vida_alien/alien_aids.htm. 2014.

Ebert, Roger. "I Am Legend". http://www.rogerebert.com/reviews/i-am-legend-2007. December 13, 2007.

"Elves, Trolls, and Hidden Beings—Iceland's Love of the Supernatural." http://www.odditycentral.com/news/elves-trolls-and-hidden-beings-icelands-love-of-the-supernatural.html. May 21, 2012.

"Experiments with Mandrake Roots and Homunculus Creation." http://www.thingsthatexist.com/2013/04/experiments-with-mandrake-roots-and.html. April 9, 2013.

Faraci, Devin. "Schlock Corridor: THE LAST MAN ON EARTH (1964)." http://badassdigest.com/2012/03/23/schlock-corridor-the-last-man-on-earth-1964/. March 23, 2012.

"Federal Emergency Management Agency." *http://fema.gov*. 2014.

Ferm, Vergilius, ed. *Ancient Religions*. New York: Philosophical Library, 1950.

Finney, Jack. *The Body Snatchers*. Cutchogue, NY: Buccaneer Books, 1993.

Fischer, Martha. "Ukraine Not Down with Zombies." http://news.moviefone.com/2005/09/13/ukraine-not-down-with-zombies/. September, 13, 2005.

Flamehorse. "Top 10 Zombie Apocalypse Conspiracy Theories." http://listverse.com/2012/11/22/top-10-zombie-apocalypse-conspiracy-theories/. November 22, 2012.

Florescu, Radu. *In Search of Frankenstein*. New York: Little Brown & Co., 1975.

"Fort Detrick, Md." http://www.detrick.army.mil. 2014.

Franke-Ruta, Garance. "NASA Official Battles the Bugs of Space Travel." http://www.washingtonpost.com/wp-dyn/content/article/2010/04/19/AR2010041904604.html. April 20, 2010.

Fraser, Gerald C. "Duane L. Jones, 51, Actor and Director of Stage Work, Dies." http://www.nytimes.com/1988/07/28/obituaries/duane-l-jones-51-actor-and-director-of-stage-works-dies.html. July 28, 1988.

Freeman, Richard. *CFZ Expedition Report: Guyana 2007*. Woolsery, U.K.: CFZ Press, 2008.

Gallman, Brett. "Psychomania." http://www.oh-the-horror.com/page.php?id=564. October 25, 2009.

Garbarini, Todd. "Review: George A. Romero's 'Day of the Dead' (1985) on Blue-Ray from Scream Factory." http://www.cinemaretro.com/index.php?/archives/7669-REVIEW-GEORGE-A.-ROMEROS-DAY-OF-THE-DEAD-1985-ON-BLU-RAY-FROM-SCREAM-FACTORY.html. September 14, 2013.

Garland, Ian. "So How Does Human Flesh Taste? Just Like Veal, According to American Adventurer Who Set Out to Explore the World of Cannibals." http://www.dailymail.co.uk/news/article-2155412/Just-like-veal-Following-spate-cannibal-crimes—1920s-explorer-provides-answer-question-everyones-lips—does-human-flesh-taste-like.html. June 6, 2012.

Gentleman, Amelia, and Robin McKie. "Red Rain Could Prove That Aliens Have Landed." http://www.theguardian.com/science/2006/mar/05/spaceexploration.theobserver. March 4, 2006.

"George A. Romero. Biography." http://www.biography.com/people/george-a-romero-193499. 2014.

Gerhard, Ken. *Encounters with Flying Humanoids*. Woodbury, MN: Llewellyn Publications, 2013.

Gerhard, Ken, and Nick Redfern. *Monsters of Texas*. Woolsery, U.K.: CFZ Press, 2010.

Gibron, Bill. "'The Colony' Exploits Its B-Movie Beats." http://www.popmatters.com/post/the-colony-exploits-its-b-movie-beats/. September 20, 2013.

"Giovanni Aldini: From Animal Electricity to Human Brain Stimulation." http://www.ncbi.nlm.nih.gov/pubmed/15595271. November 2004.

"Giovanni Aldini (1862–1834)." http://corrosion-doctors.org/Biographies/Aldini Bio.htm. 2013.

"Goat Man Bridge." http://www.goatmansbridge.com/. May 14, 2014.

Goetz, William R. *Apocalypse Next*. Camp Hill, PA: Horizon Books, 1996.

"The Green Children of Woolpit." http://www.mysteriousbritain.co.uk/england/suffolk/folklore/the-green-children-of-woolpit.html. 2014.

Haining, Peter. *The Man Who Was Frankenstein*. London, U.K.: Frederick Muller, Ltd. 1979.

Hanks, Micah. "Vietnam and (High) Strangeness in Wartime." http://mysterious universe.org/2012/11/vietnam-and-high-humanoid-strangeness-in-wartime/. November 28, 2012.

Harper, Mark J. "Dead Scientists and Microbiologists." http://www.rense.com/general 62/list.htm. February 5, 2005.

Harris, Mark H. "'The Dead' Movie Review." http://horror.about.com/od/2011 theatricalreviews/fr/The-Dead-Movie-Review.htm. 2014.

Hartsiotis, Kirsty. "The Wildman of Orford." http://suffolkfolktales.wordpress.com/2013/05/20/the-wildman-of-orford-2/. May 20, 2013.

Harvey, Graham. *Indigenous Religions*. New York: Cassell, 2000.

"Herbert West—Reanimator by H.P. Lovecraft." http://www.dagonbytes.com/thelibrary/lovecraft/reanimator.htm. 2014.

Hippisley Coxe, A.D., *The Cannibals of Clovelly*. Bideford, U.K.: Bideford Community College, 1982.

"History of Halloween." http://www.halloweenhistory.org/. 2014.

Hodgson, Mark. "SOYLENT GREEN (1973)—Film vs Book." http://blackhole reviews.blogspot.com/2010/12/soylent-green-1973-film-vs-book.html. December 10, 2010.

Holley, Justin. "The Mystery of the Wendigo." http://minnesotaghosts.com/index .php/library/library/84-the-mystery-of-the-wendigo. 2012.

"Holodomor Facts and History." http://www.holodomorct.org/history.html. 2014.

"Homepage of the Dead." http://www.homepageofthedead.com/. 2014.

"Horror Express." http://www.tcm.com/this-month/article/382629%7C449588/ Horror-Express.html. 2014.

"The House of Seven Corpses (1973)." http://www.rottentomatoes.com/m/house-of-the-seven-corpses/. 2014.

"A Huge Wolf Killed, Big as a Yearling." *Dallas Morning News*, June 2, 1888.

"Hunt for Phantom-like Animal." *Dallas Morning News*, January 29, 1908.

Huxley, Francis. *The Invisibles: Voodoo Gods in Haiti.* New York: McGraw-Hill, 1966.

"I Had to Eat Piece of My Friend to Survive." http://www.dailymail.co.uk/news/ article-2217141/I-eat-piece-friend-survive-Torment-1972-Andes-plane-crash-survivor-haunted-ordeal-40-years-later.html. October 13, 2012.

"In the Flesh." http://www.bbcamerica.com/in-the-flesh/. 2014.

Ireland, Tom. "The History of Chinese Zombies." http://www.theworldofchinese.com/ 2011/07/night-of-the-hopping-mad/. July 14, 2011.

"Is a Mummy on the Loose in Texas?" http://www.americanmonsters.com/site/2011/ 01/mummy-on-the-loose-in-texas/. January 12, 2011.

Jacobs, David M. *The Threat: Revealing the Secret Alien Agenda.* New York: Simon & Schuster, 1999.

Jackowitz, Stefanie. "George A. Romero's Land of the Dead." http://www.cinema blend.com/reviews/George-A-Romero-s-Land-of-the-Dead-1022.html. 2014.

"Jack Parsons: Belover of Babalon." http://www.bibliotecapleyades.net/bb/parsons .htm. 2014.

"Jiang-Shi." http://www.mythicalcreaturesguide.com/page/Jiang+Shi. 2014.

"John Carradine." http://www.biography.com/people/john-carradine-9542565. 2014.

Jones, Marie. *2013: The End of Days or a New Beginning?* Pompton Plains, NJ: Career Press, 2008.

Jones, T. Gwynn. *Welsh Folklore and Folk-Custom.* London, U.K.: Methuen & Co., 1930.

"The Joshua Lederberg Papers." http://profiles.nlm.nih.gov/BB/. 2014.

"Judith L. O'Dea." http://www.odeacommunications.com/. 2014.

Kelleher, Colm. *Brain Trust: The Hidden Connection between Mad Cow Disease and Misdiagnosed Alzheimer's Disease.* New York: Paraview Pocket Books, 2004.

Keough, Peter. "Review: White Zombie." http://thephoenix.com/boston/movies/151582-white-zombie/. February 12, 2012.

Khan, Rear Admiral, Ali S. "Preparedness 101: Zombie Apocalypse." http://blogs.cdc.gov/publichealthmatters/2011/05/preparedness-101-zombie-apocalypse/. May 16, 2011.

Klitzman, Robert. *The Trembling Mountain: A Personal Account of Kuru, Cannibals, and Mad Cow Disease.* Cambridge, MA: Da Capo Press, 2001.

"Kolchak: The Night Stalker." http://www.darrenmcgavin.net/night_stalker1.htm. 2014.

Lansdale, Edward Geary. *In the Midst of Wars.* New York: Fordham University Press, 1991.

LaVey, Anton Szandor. *The Satanic Rituals.* New York: Avon, 1972.

Lawinski, Jennifer. "'Acoustic Kitty': How the CIA Tried to Turn a Cat into a Cyborg Spy." http://news.msn.com/science-technology/acoustic-kitty-how-the-cia-tried-to-turn-a-cat-into-a-cyborg-spy. May 11, 2013.

"Lazarus Whom 'Jesus Loved' and Raised from the Dead." http://www.lazaruscomeforth.com/bible-story-lazarus-of-bethany/. 2014.

Leadbetter, Ron. "Asclepius." http://www.pantheon.org/articles/a/asclepius.html. March 3, 1997.

Lewis, Oll. "The Big Hairy Man of Nant Gwyant." http://forteanzoology.blogspot.com/2009/05/oll-lewis-big-hairy-man-of-nant-gwynant.html. May 16, 2009.

"Lifeforce." http://www.fandango.com/lifeforce_v29280/castandcrew. 2014.

Lindsey, Brian. "Live and Let Die." http://www.eccentric-cinema.com/cult_movies/live_and_let_die.htm. 2014.

Lissner, Ivar. *Man, God and Magic.* New York: Putnam, 1961.

Lloyd, J.Y.W. *The History of the Prince, the Lord's Marcher, and the Ancient Nobility of Powys Fadog and the Ancient Lords of Arwystli, Cedewen, and Meirionydd.* London, U.K.: Whiting & Co., 1887.

"London Underground Ghosts." http://web.archive.org/web/20120425151727 http://www.ghost-story.co.uk/stories/londonundergoundghostsbritishmuseum station.html. 2008.

Lovgren, Steffan. "Far-Out Theory Ties SARS Origins to Comet." http://news.nationalgeographic.com/news/2003/06/0603_030603_sarsspace.html. June 3, 2003.

Lowe, Keith. *Tunnel Vision.* London, U.K.: MTV Books, 2001.

Luhn, Alec. "Moscow Investigates 'Pigeon Apocalypse.'" http://www.theguardian.com/environment/2013/aug/19/moscow-investigates-pigeon-apocalypse-birds. August 19, 2013.

Lynch, Jacqueline T. "The Walking Dead (1936)." http://anotheroldmovieblog.blog
spot.com/2008/10/walking-dead-1936.html. October 30, 2008.

Maire, Louis III. *Soviet and Czechoslovakian Parapsychological Research*. Lulu: 2011.

Marks, John. *The Search for the Manchurian Candidate: The CIA and Mind Control*.
New York: Times Books, 1979.

Marrs, Jim. "Hidden History: Monoatomic Gold and Human Origins." http://before
itsnews.com/alternative/2013/07/hidden-history-monoatomic-gold-and-human-
origins-jim-marrs-2-2720502.html. July 25, 2013.

Martinez, Luis. "No More Jesus Rifles." http://abcnews.go.com/Blotter/jesus-rifles/
story?id=9618791. January 21, 2010.

Masters, R.E.L., and Eduard Lea. *Perverse Crimes in History*. New York: Julian Press,
1963.

Matheson, Richard. *I Am Legend*. New York: Tor, 2007.

———. *Other Kingdoms*. New York: Tor, 2011.

McGuinness, Ross. "Could Parasite Fungus That Causes 'Zombie Ants' Lead to Real-
life The Last of Us?" http://metro.co.uk/2013/06/12/zombie-ants-fungus-the-last-
of-us-playstation-3-3836808/. June 12, 2103.

Mellor, Anne K. *Mary Shelley: Her Life, Her Fiction, Her Monsters*. New York:
Methuen, 1988.

Meyer, Marvin, and Richard Smith, eds. *Ancient Christian Magic*. San Francisco:
Harper, 1994.

Meyers, Jim. "Chemical Scare Prompted Lockdown of Dugway Army Facility in
Utah." http://www.newsmax.com/Newsfront/Dugway-lockdown-chemical-scare/
2011/01/27/id/384105. January 27, 2011.

"'Miami Zombie' Victim: Cannibal Attack Survivor Ronald Poppo in 2013."
http://www.examiner.com/article/miami-zombie-victim-cannibal-attack-survivor-
ronald-poppo-2013. 2014.

Middleton, John, ed. *Magic, Witchcraft, and Curing*. Garden City, NY: Natural History Press, 1967.

Miles, Ron. "Day of the Dead (2008 Remake). http://www.jamesaxler.com/Blog/
tabid/260/EntryId/67/Day-of-the-Dead-2008-remake.aspx. March 11, 2013.

Miller, Steve. "Isle of the Dead Is among Karloff's Weaker Films." http://boriskarloff
collection.blogspot.com/2009/08/isle-of-dead-is-among-karloffs-weaker.html.
August 13, 2009.

"MI6 Payouts Over Secret LSD Tests." http://news.bbc.co.uk/2/hi/uk_news/4745748
.stm. February 24, 2006.

"The Monkey's Paw." http://www.classicshorts.com/stories/paw.html. 2014.

Morris, Henry M., Ph.D. "The Resurrection of Christ—The Best-proved Fact in History." http://www.icr.org/ChristResurrection/. 2014.

Mullen, Leslie. "Alien Infection." http://www.astrobio.net/exclusive/570/alien-infection. August 25, 2003.

"Naegleria fowleri." http://www.cdc.gov/parasites/naegleria/general.html. 2014.

"The National CJD Research & Surveillance Unit (NCJDRSU)." http://www.cjd.ed.ac.uk/. 2014.

New York Post Staff. *Heaven's Gate: Cult Suicide in San Diego*. New York: Harper Paperbacks, 1997.

"1972: Survivors Found 10 Weeks after Plane Crash." http://news.bbc.co.uk/onthis day/hi/dates/stories/december/22/newsid_3717000/3717502.stm. December 22, 2008.

"North Head Quarantine Station, Sydney—Fact Sheet 143." http://www.naa.gov .au/collection/fact-sheets/fs143.aspx. 2013.

"Operation INFEKTION: The KGB's Attempt to Persuade the World the USA Created HIV/AIDS." http://www.abovetopsecret.com/forum/thread645871/pg. January 1, 2011.

Owen, Pamela. "Revealed, Ireland's Real-Life Zombie Scare: Eighth Century Skeletons Buried with Stones in Mouths." http://www.dailymail.co.uk/sciencetech/ article-2038565/Skeletons-buried-stones-mouths-stop-returning-zombies-discovered-Ireland.html. September 17, 2011.

"Panteon de Belen. Haunted Cemetery Legends." http://www.explore-guadalajara .com/hauntedcemetery.html. 2014.

Pearce, Nicole. "The Spirit of Wendigo." http://www.playwithdeath.com/the-spirit-of-wendigo/5894/. 2014.

"The Pet Cemetery on the Haldon Hills." http://weird.stormpages.com/petcem.htm. 2014.

"Peter Stumpp, Werewolf of Bedburg." http://www.werewolves.com/peter-stumpp-werewolf-of-bedburg/. 2014.

"Pet Sematary Movie Review." http://www.horror-movies.ca/horror_222.html. 2014.

"The Plague of the Zombies (1966)." http://www.hammerfilms.com/productions/film/ filmid/237/the-plague-of-the-zombies. 2014.

"Planet Terror (2007)." http://www.rollingstone.com/movies/lists/the-10-best-zombie-movies-20121012/planet-terror-2007-19691231. 2014.

Popcorn Candy Girl. "Revenge of the Zombies (1943)—Film Review." http://stalkn slash.blogspot.com/2009/12/revenge-of-zombies-1943-film-review.html. 2009.

Price, James, and Juredini, Paul. *Witchcraft, Sorcery, Magic, and Other Psychological Phenomena and Their Implications on Military and Paramilitary Operations in the Congo*. Washington, DC: American University, 1964.

Priestner, Andy. "Survivors." http://www.survivorstvseries.com/What_Is_Survivors.htm. November 12, 2008.

Quigley, Christine, and Christ Wuigley. *The Corpse: A History*. Jefferson, NC: McFarland, 1996.

Redfern, Nick. Interview with Timothy Green Beckley, September 21, 2010.

————. Interview with Marie Jones, March 23, 2012.

————. *Man-Monkey: In Search of the British Bigfoot*. Woolsery, U.K.: CFZ Press, 2007.

————. "The Monster of Glamis." http://newpagebooks.blogspot.com/2013/08/creature-of-month-monster-of-castle-by.html. August 29, 2013.

————. "The Prestwick Baboon." http://manbeastuk.blogspot.com/2008/10/prestwick-baboon.html. October 20, 2008.

————. *The Real Men in Black*. Pompton Plains, NJ: New Page Books, 2011.

————. *Wildman! The Monstrous and Mysterious Saga of the "British Bigfoot."* Woolsery, U.K.: CFZ Press, 2012.

"Resident Evil Fan: A New Blood." http://www.residentevilfan.com/. 2014.

"Return of the Living Dead Collection." http://www.themoviedb.org/collection/101471-return-of-the-living-dead-collection. 2014.

"Review: George A. Romero's 'The Crazies' (1973)." http://www.fearnet.com/news/review/review-george-romeros-crazies-1973. March 1, 2010.

Rich, Katey. "Zombie Strippers." http://www.cinemablend.com/reviews/Zombie-Strippers-3078.html. 2014.

"Russell Streiner Biography." http://www.rottentomatoes.com/celebrity/russ_streiner/biography.php. 2014.

Ryall, Chris, and Moss, Drew. *The Colonized: Zombies vs Aliens*. San Diego, CA: IDW Publishing, 2013.

"Sample Return Missions Scare Some Researchers." http://www.space.com/searchforlife/planet_protection_000407.html. April 9, 2000.

"San Antonio's Dancing Devil of El Camaroncito." http://blogs.sacurrent.com/streetview/san-antonios-dancing-devil-of-el-camaroncito/. October 31, 2011.

Scott, Casey. "The Incredibly Strange Creatures Who Stopped Living and Became Mixed-Up Zombies (1963)." http://www.dvddrive-in.com/reviews/i-m/incrediblly strangecreatures63.htm. March 27, 2013.

Scovell, Adam. "Review: The Witches (1966)." http://www.spookyisles.com/2013/01/review-the-witches-1966/. 2014.

Selby, Lindsay. "The Kikiyaon, Real or Imaginary?" http://forteanzoology.blogspot.com/2011/01/lindsay-selby-kikiyaon-real-or.html. January 19, 2011.

Seligmann, Kurt. *The History of Magic*. New York: Pantheon Books, 1948.

Seward, Zack. "Rutgers Instructor: During Zombie Apocalypse, You'd Be Fine." http://www.newsworks.org/index.php/local/onward/60882-rutgers-instructor-during-zombie-apocalypse-youd-be-fine. October 15, 2013.

"Shaun of the Dead." http://www.focusfeatures.com/shaun_of_the_dead. 2014.

Shaw, Eva. *Eve of Destruction: Prophecies, Theories and Preparations for the End of the World.* Chicago: Contemporary Books, 1995.

Shelley, Mary. *Frankenstein.* New York: Dover Publications, 1994.

Smith, Huston. *The World's Religions.* New York: Harper San Francisco, 1991.

"Solomon Island Giants." http://www.coasttocoastam.com/show/2004/01/14. January 14, 2004.

"Somaliland President Egal Speaks on Mysterious Bomb Blast." http://www.faqs.org/cia/docs/4/0000098714/SOMALILAND-PRESIDENT-EGAL-SPEAKS-ON-MYSTERIOUS-BOMB-BLAST.html. 2014.

Spry, Jeff. "Ancient Ireland's Cure for Zombies? Bury 'em with Mouth Rocks." http://www.blastr.com/2011/09/ancient_irelands_cure_for.php. September 20, 2011.

Stanley, John. *Creature Features Strikes Again.* 4th revised edition. Pacifica, CA: Creatures at Large Press, 1994.

Steiger, Brad. *Medicine Power: The American Indians Revival of His Spiritual Heritage and Its Relevance for Modern Man.* New York: Doubleday, 1972.

———. *Real Vampires, Night Stalkers, and Creatures from the Darkside.* Canton, MI: Visible Ink Press, 2010.

———. *The Werewolf Book: The Encyclopedia of Shape-Shifting Beings.* Farmington Hills, MI: Visible Ink Press, 1999.

Steiger, Brad, and Sherry. *Conspiracies and Secret Societies: The Complete Dossier.* Canton, MI: Visible Ink Press, 2006.

———. *The Gale Encyclopedia of the Unusual and the Unexplained.* 3 vols. Farmington Hills, MI: The Gale Group, Inc., 2003.

"Story of a Legend 'Aswang in the Philippines.'" http://www.philippine-travelers.com/story-of-a-legend-aswang-in-the-philippines/. 2013.

"Streaming Review: Rammbock: Berlin Undead." http://www.geeksofdoom.com/2013/07/24/streaming-review-rammbock-berlin-undead. July 24, 2013.

Sunshine, James. "Social Security Administration Requests 174,000 Bullets." http://www.huffingtonpost.com/2012/08/17/social-security-administration-bullets_n_1797069.html. August 20, 2012.

Susman, Gary. "This Week in Movie History: 'The Omega Man' Takes on the World." http://news.moviefone.com/2011/08/06/the-omega-man-movie-history/. August 6, 2011.

"Swift Runner." http://murderpedia.org/male.R/r/runner-swift.htm. 2014.

Tallant, Robert. *Voodoo in New Orleans.* Gretna, LA: Pelican Publishing Company, Inc., 1998.

"Texas State Research Sheds Light on Panspermia." http://www.txstate.edu/news/news_releases/news_archive/2006/02/PanspermiaResearch0022206.html. February 22, 2006.

Than, Kur. "'Zombie Virus' Possible via Rabies-Flu Hybrid?" http://news.national geographic.com/news/2010/10/1001027-rabies-influenza-zombie-virus-science/. October, 27, 2010.

Tooze, Gary W. "I Walked with a Zombie." http://www.dvdbeaver.com/film/DVD Review2/iwalkedwithazombie.htm. 2014.

"The Tragic Fate of the Donner Party, 1847." http://www.eyewitnesstohistory.com/donnerparty.htm. 1847.

The Treaty on Principles Governing the Activities of States in the Exploration and Use of Outer Space, Including the Moon and Other Celestial Bodies. http://www.state.gov/t/isn/5181.htm. 2014.

Tripzibit. "Miami 'Zombie' Attack." http://unmyst3.blogspot.com/2013/09/miami-zombie-attack.html. September 27, 2013.

Trubshaw, Bob. *Explore Phantom Black Dogs.* Avebury, U.K.: Heart of Albion Press, 2007.

"28 Days Later—The Movie." http://www.28dayslaterthemovie.co.uk/. 2014.

"28 Weeks Later—Review." http://www.ign.com/movies/28-weeks-later/theater-820981. 2014.

Ty, Eleanor. "Mary Wollstone Craft Shelley." http://people.brandeis.edu/~teuber/shelleybio.html. 2014.

Unterman, Alan. *Dictionary of Jewish Lore and Legend.* New York: Thames & Hudson, 1991.

"US Is 'Battling Satan' Says General." http://news.bbc.co.uk/2/hi/americas/3199212.stm. October 17, 2003.

"US Military Pondered Love Not War." http://news.bbc.co.uk/2/hi/4174519.stm. January 15, 2005.

VanDerBeek, David Lory. "National Scout Jamboree Zombie Virus Attack." http://beforeitsnews.com/politics/2013/08/national-scout-jamboree-zombie-virus-attack-nevada-governor-2014-david-lory-vanderbeek-2540888.html. August 9, 2013.

Viegas, Jennifer. "The Cat Who Couldn't Spy: A CIA Fail." http://news.discovery.com/animals/pets/cat-spies-fail-130510.htm. May 10, 2013.

Vomitron. "Zombie Honeymoon." http://www.cultreviews.com/reviews/zombie-honeymoon/. June 1, 2009.

"The Walking Dead." http://www.amctv.com/shows/the-walking-dead. 2014.

"The Walking Dead: Draugr and Aptrgangr in Old Norse Literature." http://www.vikinganswerlady.com/ghosts.shtml. 2014.

Walling, William. *Mary Shelley.* New York: Twayne Books, 1972.

Walton, Allan. "Karl Hardman: He Lives on in Death." http://www.post-gazette.com/ae/how-awful-about-allan/2007/09/27/Karl-Hardman-He-lives-on-in-death.print. September 27, 2007.

Watson, Julie. "Marines, Police Prep for Mock Zombie Invasion." http://cnsnews.com/news/article/marines-police-prep-mock-zombie-invasion. October 27, 2012.

Wellington, David. *Monster Island: A Zombie Novel*. Philadelphia, PA: Running Press, 2006.

———. *Monster Nation: A Zombie Novel*. Philadelphia, PA. Running Press, 2006.

———. *Monster Planet: A Zombie Novel*. Philadelphia, PA: Running Press, 2007.

"The Wild Man of the Navidad." http://www.wildmanofthenavidad.com/_movie/about.html. 2014.

Wilson, Andrew, ed. *World Scripture: A Comparative Anthology of Sacred Texts*. New York: Paragon House, 1995.

Wood, Dr. Robert M. *Alien Viruses: Crashed UFOs, MJ-12 & Biowarfare*. Richard Dolan Press. 2013.

"World War Z." http://www.worldwarzmovie.com/. 2014.

Zachner, R.C. *Encyclopedia of the World's Religions*. New York: Barnes & Noble, 1997.

"Zombie History: The Draugr." http://www.herebezombies.com/zombies/zombie-history-the-draugr/. December 7, 2011.

Zombie Hunter Sam. "Zombie Bite in New Orleans?" http://www.undeadreport.com/2009/05/zombie-bite-in-new-orleans/. May 5, 2009.

"Zombie Lake (1981)." http://www.allthingszombie.com/movies/zombielake.php. 2014.

"Zombieland." http://www.sonypictures.com/movies/zombieland/. 2014.

"Zombiewalk.com." http://www.zombiewalk.com/. 2014.

INDEX

Note: (ill.) indicates photos and illustrations.

THE ZOMBIE BOOK: THE ENCYCLOPEDIA OF THE LIVING DEAD

ALSO FROM VISIBLE INK PRESS

Please visit us at visibleinkpress.com.